TAP!

APR 2 5 1996

TAP!

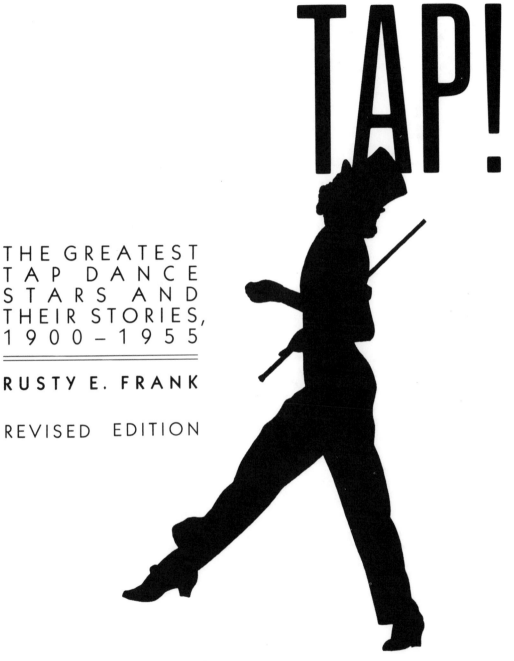

THE GREATEST TAP DANCE STARS AND THEIR STORIES, 1900–1955

RUSTY E. FRANK

REVISED EDITION

DA CAPO PRESS
NEW YORK

This Da Capo Press paperback edition of *TAP!* is a republication of the first edition published in New York in 1990, with textual emendations, updates, and a new chapter on Toy and Wing. It is published by arrangement with the author.

Published by Da Capo Press, Inc.
A Subsidiary of Plenum Publishing Corporation
233 Spring Street, New York, N.Y. 10013

Library of Congress Cataloging in Publication Data

Frank, Rusty E.
  Tap!: the greatest tap dance stars and their stories, 1900–1955 / Rusty E. Frank.—Rev. ed.
      p.   cm.
  Includes bibliographical references (p.   ) and index.
  Filmography: p.
  Discography: p.
  ISBN 0-306-80635-5
  1. Dancers—United States—Biography. 2. Tap dancing—History. I. Title.
GV1785.A1F69 1994
792.8′028′922—dc20
[B]   94-45756
                                                 CIP

BOOK DESIGN BY JAYE ZIMET

For my tap dance teacher
Louis DaPron, 1913–1987

For all the hoofers who, through their artistry and lifelong devotion, made tap dancing a national treasure

For anyone who has ever been ignited by the syncopated sounds of a tap dancer's feet

F O R E W O R D

GREGORY HINES

When I was thinking about how I wanted to begin this foreword, I tried to remember the earliest moment of my life where I either began to understand rhythm, or had it explained to me, or felt it—that first recognition of what rhythm is. And I remember that in 1957, when I was eleven years old, my brother Maurice and I, we were called The Hines Kids, were going to perform at the Will Rogers Memorial Hospital. It was an AGVA show, American Guild of Variety Artists. And there were a lot of people going down there. I forget exactly where it was, but I know we had to take an overnight train which was so exciting to me. A train is *filled* with rhythm! Among the other artists who were on the show was Bunny Briggs. Bunny Briggs knew us and we knew him. He had seen us, and we had gone to see him many times at the Apollo. I just admired him. Bunny stood apart from the tap dancers I saw in the way he dressed, in the way he danced, in the way he moved.

We were on the train, and we ate dinner and then it was time for us to go to bed. My brother and I got in our bunks, and Bunny came into our berth. He sat down and he began to talk to us—about great tap dancers and great acts like Pops and Louis, The Chocolateers, Buck and Bubbles, and Bill Robinson, who he knew when he was a kid. And he started talking about The Nicholas Brothers,

The Hines Kids, Maurice and Gregory, 1955

and The Berry Brothers, and The Step Brothers, and about the kinds of tap dancers they were, and their approach to *rhythm*. And over the next three hours, he talked about rhythm, and he talked about the application of it. And he would stand up and demonstrate steps to us. It's still so very vivid in my mind.

After that, I would go see tap dancers, and I began to understand what they were doing. I didn't need anyone to explain it to me anymore, I wasn't missing anything. All of a sudden I began to understand the beginning, the middle, and the end of pieces that tap dancers were doing. I began to understand to the point that I could start to *steal* steps! I would hear certain combinations, and I would just keep singin' them over and over in my head till I got some place I could do it. For me, this was an important breakthrough.

I think that it was a very fortunate time for me to be born and to see what I saw. Because my heroes were the ones that I saw on the screen, and on the TV, and live in person. I'd see Gene Kelly in a movie. I'd see Bunny Briggs live. I'd see Gene Nelson on the TV. I'd see Baby Lawrence at the Apollo. I'd get to meet those guys. All these great dancers—I began to understand what they were doing. And it had a profound effect on me as a dancer. I felt I was beginning to understand expression.

I remember once I read where Muhammad Ali, at the height of his career, would psych other fighters out, because he would say to them, "You know, you're not just fightin' me. When you fight me, you're fightin' Joe Louis, Sugar Ray Robinson, Jack Johnson, and all the great champions that came before me." Sometimes that's how I feel—when I tap dance for people, they're not just seeing me, they're seeing me *and* they're seeing Bunny Briggs—Harold and Fayard Nicholas—Gene Kelly—Sandman Sims—

Baby Lawrence—Steve Condos—and, of course, Henry LeTang, my teacher.

This book is a formidable accomplishment. One of the things it will do is bring tap dancers together in a way that no book has done before—because each tap dancer's experience is really the same experience. Everybody can feel it! Something happens—they see somebody, they have a moment, they take lessons—and they all of a sudden decide, "That's it. That's my thing. I'm gonna do that! I'm gonna *be* a tap dancer."

February 5, 1990
Venice, California

AUTHOR'S NOTE AND ACKNOWLEDGMENTS

In July of 1987, I read in the newspaper that Louis DaPron had died at the age of seventy-four. Louis was not only one of the tap greats; he also happened to be my teacher and my inspiration.

Louis was from a dancing family and got his start as a small child performing in vaudeville. He was twenty-two years old when he was discovered at Hollywood's Club Trocadero and signed by Paramount Pictures. He went on to dance and choreograph for film and television working alongside many legendary artists, including Donald O'Connor, Ruby Keeler, and Ann Miller. From the 1920s through the 1980s, Louis DaPron was one of the best choreographers, the best teachers, and the best dancers on the tap dance scene. He lived in the midst of tap's most celebrated and remarkable years, but when he died he took with him his stories and his recollections. They are lost forever.

Louis's was not the only obituary I've read. Many legendary tap dancers have died in recent years. And in just about every case, the story was the same: These artists' lives went undocumented, their stories untold. Before the last generations of tap's legendary stars and their histories disappeared into oblivion, something had to be done. Hence—*TAP!, The Greatest Tap Dance Stars and Their Stories, 1900–1955.*

In 1988, I began a trek around the United States, going from San Francisco to New York, from New Orleans to Chicago, and to dozens of cities in between. I met and interviewed thirty dancers, and their stories are here in *TAP!*. They were headliners as well as kids in the chorus, and they represent every aspect of tap dancing during the first half of the twentieth century: dancers who performed in vaudeville, in musical shows, overseas, in the army, on the radio, in clubs, in movies, in burlesque, in carnivals, in white shows, and in black shows. These are artists who developed and performed different styles of tap dancing including eccentric, classical, flash, legomania, rhythm, and Buck and Wing. Together these individuals encapsulate the tradition of tap dance in America.

TAP! is not meant to be a history of tap, rather it is the *story* of tap—an everlasting tribute to those people who made tap dancing their passion and profession.

It is with the deepest love and gratitude that I thank all those involved in the creation of *TAP!*

First and foremost I thank those individuals I saw

Louis DaPron dances for servicemen during World War II at the Hollywood Canteen, 1940s.

and interviewed in the course of preparing this book: Maceo Anderson, Cholly Atkins, Peg Leg Bates, Gene Bell, Warren Berry, Peg E. Brant, Bunny Briggs, Eddie Brown, Ralph Brown, Brenda Bufalino, Louis Simms Carpenter, Honi Coles, Steve Condos, Cookie Cook, Ralph Cooper, Willie Covan, Skip Cunningham, Paul Draper, Vilma Ebsen, Carita Harbert, Sybil Jason, Stanley Kahn, Ruby Keeler, Fred Kelly, Gene Kelly, Jeni LeGon, Flash McDonald, Ann Miller, George Murphy, Frances Nealy, Gene Nelson, Fayard Nicholas, Harold Nicholas, Donald O'Connor, Hermes Pan, Pete Peterson, Leonard Reed, LaVaughn Robinson, Peggy Ryan, Glenn Shipley, Jimmy Slyde, Price Spencer, Shirley Temple, Paul Wing, Tony Wing, and Jane Withers.

Their lives are an inspiration to all who cross their paths, and I thank most especially these individuals for letting me delve into their personal collections of photographs, and for sharing countless hours of their time to unfold before me their unique legacies. They are not only stars of tap dance's history, they are also the stars in my eyes. In one year I found my way to dancers who had been some of the greatest tap dancers of the twentieth century. And not only did I find them, I became friends with them. I even danced with them, I spent *hours* dancing with them: Fayard Nicholas showed me how to Pull the Trenches; Leonard Reed showed me the Shim Sham Shimmy; Frances Nealy put down her tap mat and showed me how to trade eights, and Gene Nelson worked with me for nearly three months while I was doing research in Los Angeles. These people have enriched my life forever.

Special thanks to one man who is not in the book, Fred Astaire. Until I recently found my way to the artists in *TAP!*, he was an inestimable source of inspiration.

The appendices were of special importance to me, and without dedicated record, film, and sheet music collectors, and film historians, I never could have even considered including these sections. Invaluable in compiling the three appendices were Eric Bernhoft, Mark Cantor, Honi Coles, Michael Feinstein, Michael Fitzgerald, Bob Grimes, Mark Jones, Fred Kelly, Miles Kreuger, Tom Lehrer, Robert Merchant, Peter Mintun, Gene Nelson, James Parten, Leonard Reed, Robert Reed, Roger Robles, Joe Savage, Ernie Smith, and Dave Wells, and to the cable television channels American Movie Classics (AMC) and Turner Network Television (TNT) for their outstanding reclamation, restoration, and programming of rare vintage movie musicals. Special thanks to Glenn Shipley for permission to use his tap terminology, as found in *The Complete Tap Dictionary*, for the glossary.

Chris Belliou, outstanding French tap dancer, was instrumental in getting me started on *Tap!* by connecting me with my first group of interviewees.

Thanks from the heart to all those who lent support and assistance on so many different tasks and quests for information: Cassandra Barbour, Joel Blum, Robert Bryan, Maxine Cass, Linda Christensen, Rachel

Cohen, Sue DaPron, Arthur Dong, Audrey Flint, Dottie Friedrich, Hal Glatzer, Laurie Gordon, Peggy Gordon, J. Greg Gormick, Samm Grey, Edward Guthmann, Steve Hanson, James Haskins, Alex Hassan, Gary Hirsh, Sari Horwitz, Robert Huweiler, Dan Kalb, Debbie Kassel, Wayne Knight, Joey Liebman, Desmond Marsh, Rob McKay, Patti Meagher, Ron Mencz, Leroy Meyers, Joe Mitchell, Norman Mitgang, Gerald Nachman, Vladimir Naroditsky, George T. Nierenberg, Todd Norton, Micheál O'Connor, Alan Olson, Mel Owen, Bruce Patriquin, Stuart Pollak, Rodney Price, Charles Pruzansky, Lynn Rabin, Barbara Reed, Deborah Reed, Jean Reese, David Rinehart, Elana Rosen, Sara Sambach, Sasha, Bill Schultz, Ida Shreiber, Bryan Smith, Ernie Smith, Bree Soland, Stephan, Louis Trujillo, Mark Viera, Dianne Walker, Allan Winter, Tanya Wodinsky, Steve Zee, Hebrew Free Loan, Studio J, and a unique thanks to Karen Lane, Geoff Lucas, and Mark Biggs for rescuing me from my San Francisco Marina apartment after the 1989 7.1 earthquake. (To Mother Nature—thanks for crashing everything in my house *around* the computer and not on it!) I thank with great love all my friends who had the tremendous patience to keep from disowning me during the past two years when I could never do anything with them because I was "working on the book." And a very special thanks to Jim Bernstein, Mark Cantor, Teri Davis Greenberg, Bob Grimes, Mark Jones, Dianna Marguleas, Melanie Mayer, Cyra McFadden, Peter Mintun, Pattie O'Connell, Robert Reed, Bryan Torfeh, and Weslia Whitfield for all their loving guidance, nurturing, wisdom, and enthusiastic support. To all of the above I am forever indebted for your knowledge, support, and heartfelt encouragement.

To my proofreaders—Barbara Frank, Fritz Golden, Bob Grimes, Frederick Hodges, Mark Jones, Peter Mintun, Pattie O'Connell, and Richard Raucci—I give thanks from the bottom of my heart. Rarely does one get the gift of such devoted readers with the added specialty of such expertise in the era 1900 –1955. They were, and continue to be, absolute jewels.

The following libraries were especially helpful: the Schomberg Library in Harlem, the Academy Library in Los Angeles, and the Lincoln Center Dance Library in New York. Marshall and Jean Stearns's masterpiece *Jazz Dance* was valuable beyond estimation.

To Mike Williams, my transcriber—who prior to receiving over one hundred hours of taped interviews, knew nothing about tap dancing—I humbly bow. He was absolutely a dream to work with.

Boon Woon, from Fotorama in Hollywood, California, was invaluable for his terrific work in handling and duplicating all the photographs in this work.

Simply beyond thanks is Gregory Hines for his continual support of *Tap!*, and especially for his paramount efforts to bring tap dancing through to the twenty-first century.

To my agent, Jane Dystel, I extend gratitude for believing in *Tap!* and having faith in this first-time author.

I thank with genuine fondness and appreciation my first editors at William Morrow, Jim Donahue and Jennifer Williams. They made it quite clear from the start that *Tap!* was indeed something special, and were a continuous source of support and friendship.

To my second editor, Margaret Talcott, I am most deeply grateful. Her genuine elatedness about the project, and her own superb talent, brought *Tap!* to fruition. She was an absolute joy in every way.

I thank my final editor, Connie Roosevelt, and her assistant, Jon Howard, for coming in at *TAP!*'s final stages and ensuring that it went from galleys to the bookstore shelves.

I especially thank Jim Landis, publisher of William Morrow, for his enthusiasm, Jaye Zimet and Teresa Bonner for their beautiful design work—and everyone else at Morrow.

I lovingly embrace my family with profound gratitude. Their support throughout my lifetime gave me the character to go ahead with such a project. So it is with love that I thank my brother and sister-in-law David and Davida, my brother and sister-in-law Paul and Leora, and my mother and father, Barbara and Harrison. Not only did my parents take me to my first Fred Astaire movie and endure countless Sunday afternoons of Shirley Temple and Bill Rob-

Louis DaPron in a 1930s glamour portrait. This photograph was taken when he was first discovered at Hollywood's Trocardero Club. He would soon go under contract at Paramount, where he became one of the industry's top tap choreographers.

inson movies, but they also paid for and schlepped me to years of tap dancing lessons. They were also responsible for introducing me to my dance teacher, the late Louis DaPron.

To Louis DaPron, then, the final note of thanks. He was my inspiration not only as a dancer and teacher, but in the idea of *Tap!* I would have liked for him to see this, because knowing him, he would have gotten a big kick out of it.

—Rusty E. Frank, M.N.A.
SAN FRANCISCO
JANUARY 26, 1990

AUTHOR'S NOTE AND ACKNOWLEDGMENTS

Revised Edition

When I began work on my book in 1987, I limited its scope to the first half of the twentieth century; I truly did not know what the future of tap was going to be, nor whether there was indeed going to be a future. Now, only eight short years since I began the book, I realize that what was supposedly a "dead" art form is far from dead.

Tap has been evolving for well over a hundred years, and there is absolutely no reason for it to stop now. There are leaders, innovators, geniuses, teachers, and masters. There is enough inspiration right now to last another century. As long as there is someone who gets ignited by the sound of rhythmic syncopation and the accompanying sight of connected dance—tap is here to stay. Alive and well . . . and kicking!

There were many people who helped in gathering information and lending invaluable support for this second edition. First to my new publisher, Da Capo Press, deepest thanks. Specifically, I thank my editor, Yuval Taylor, who championed this reprint.

To Dorothy Toy and Paul Wing,[1] thank you both so much for your time and wonderful memories.

Your stories add a unique and compelling chapter to tap's history.

To my constant friends/proofreaders I owe a depth of gratitude: Emelda "Jean-Jean" Brown, Robert Fitch, Micki and the late Steve Granger, Tom Lehrer, Theresa Medbury, Peter Mintun, Pattie O'Connell, Brent Spiner, and Lou Wills, Jr. To those encyclopedic storehouses of vaudevillian information—Milton Berle, Leonard Maltin, and Leonard Reed—thank you for only being a phone call away and ever-willing to share with me even the most obscure piece of trivia found in no document, but alive in your memories. To one of the greatest old-movie buffs of all time, Hugh M. Hefner, thank you for sharing your love of movie musicals by viewing the rarest of these on a regular basis at your home; not only have these showings been a fabulous source of research for me, they have also provided a unique opportunity to watch these jewels with a small group of very enthusiastic kindred spirits.

To the National Endowment for the Arts for awarding seed funding for *TAP! The Tempo of*

America, the documentary version of this book, thank you for supporting the on-going documentation of this great American art form. And to Arthur Dong, who has been working with me for five years on the film as director, co-producer and co-writer—you are a brilliant talent. To Mark Cantor, who has opened up his archive of tap dance clips night after night for our viewing ecstasy—you are an absolute treasure.

There is a saying, "A dream is often lonely. But provided you are prepared to prevail, it is invincible." I often think that no one knows this better than an author. Therefore, my very special and personal thanks to Robert J. Scheerer who believes in everything I do; it's a lot less lonely because of you.

Finally, to everyone who has ever laced up a pair of tap shoes (in dreams or reality), this is for you. Enjoy. Enjoy.

Rusty E. Frank, M.N.A.
Los Angeles
August 16, 1994

[1]The Toy and Wing chapter replaces Steve Condos' chapter from the first edition. Steve's chapter was removed upon special request from his widow, Lorraine Condos.

CONTENTS

Foreword   *Gregory Hines*   7
Author's Note and Acknowledgments   9

PART 1:   1900 – 1929

1— FROM PICKANINNY TO THE PALACE   23
   WILLIE COVAN   25
       We were stoppin' shows wherever we went.
       Couldn't tear us off the stage!
       They had never seen nuthin' like us.
       We got to be so big, we were just about the
       biggest thing around!

2— FIRST TAP DANCING STAR OF THE SILVER SCREEN 30
   RUBY KEELER   32
       I'd say I was a hoofer.
       A real Buck and Wing dancer.

3— THE HOOFERS CLUB   37
   LEONARD REED   39
       They used to say there wasn't such a thing
       as not having a tap dancer in your show!

4— KING OF THE ONE-LEGGED DANCERS   46
   PEG LEG BATES   48
       I was very ambitious when I was dancing.
       I wanted to be so good,
       I wanted to surpass the two-leg dancers!
       And in a lot of cases I did.

5— 1920s REHEARSAL HALLS   52
GEORGE MURPHY   53

Got into show business by accident
and enjoyed the trip.

P A R T   2 :   1 9 3 0 – 1 9 3 9

6— THE COTTON CLUB:
THE NICHOLAS BROTHERS   64
FAYARD NICHOLAS   66

Everyone was ravin' over us at the Cotton Club.
They saw these new little guys
and they were amazed.

7— FRED ASTAIRE'S CHOREOGRAPHER   75
HERMES PAN   77

Boy, we thought the same way.
His rhythms were almost identical with mine.

8— BILL ROBINSON'S "DARLIN'"   86
SHIRLEY TEMPLE   88

It was hard work and concentration,
and it was no time to be a baby.

9— JUST A HOOFER   94
RALPH BROWN   96

You keep trying.
You keep trying.
You keep trying.
And finally it comes to you—
the trick of tap dancing!

10—"THE CHINESE FRED ASTAIRE AND
GINGER ROGERS": TOY AND WING
PAUL WING   103
DOROTHY TOY   107

We just lived tap dancing.
Didn't know what time of day it was.

11—DANCING INTO SOCIETY   111
BUNNY BRIGGS   112

Some people ask me about my sound.
I've been blessed in so many ways,
because I danced in the streets,
I danced in hallways,
I danced in hot-dog stands,
and I danced for society.

12—"THE SEPIA CINDERELLA GIRL"   118
JENI LeGON   120

I did their step . . . and
they just stood back and said, "Man,
look at that little ol' skinny girl dance!"

13—LAST OF THE STREET TAP DANCERS   128
LaVAUGHN ROBINSON   129

To be on Broad and South,
you had to have your shoes on tight!
'Cause that was the corner!

14—SPONTANEOUS COMBUSTION
ON THE DANCE FLOOR:
BUDDY AND VILMA EBSEN   134
VILMA EBSEN   136

We would dance, and it was called
"the hottest cool dancing in town."

15—FROM VAUDEVILLE TO PICTURES   144
DONALD O'CONNOR   146

I knew that the harder I worked,
the more laughs and more applause I got.
No one had to teach me that. I could hear it.

16—THE TAP DANCER'S DILEMMA:
THE BERRY BROTHERS   153
WARREN BERRY   156

I was so tired of hearing that music . . .
I would stand in the wings before going onstage,
and just grit my teeth every time.

17—HOLLYWOOD'S TAPPIN'-EST CHILD STAR   162
JANE WITHERS   163

We were making my pictures
in twenty-one to twenty-four days!
That's it. That's why I was known as
"One-Take Withers."

CONTENTS

18—EXTRA-SPECIAL ADDED ATTRACTION:
GENE AND FRED KELLY   169
FRED KELLY   171

> *Well, Cab Calloway played the thing,*
> *and Gene and I danced the thing,*
> *and as soon as it was over,*
> *they all stood up and clapped and cheered.*
> *That was really something.*
> *The guys we were nuts about were applauding us!*

19—DANCING WITH THE GREAT
BILL "BOJANGLES" ROBINSON   180
EDDIE BROWN   183

> *Bill was a very fine man. He wanted everybody*
> *to recognize him as a big star. Which he was.*
> *You don't call him Bill Robinson. You call him*
> *Mr. Bill Robinson.*

P A R T 3 : 1 9 4 0 – 1 9 5 5

20—WWII'S *THIS IS THE ARMY*   190
GENE NELSON   191

> *The GI audiences were the greatest. . . .*
> *They were so glad to be there watching*
> *something that brought them closer to home.*
> *Our show was a jewel in the night.*

21—THE JIVIN' JACKS AND JILLS   202
PEGGY RYAN   203

> *You only have two feet and four taps*
> *to make magic.*

22—EIGHT FEET OF RHYTHM:
THE FOUR STEP BROTHERS   211
MACEO ANDERSON   212

> *You may be nervous when you go*
> *on the stage, you anxious to get out there.*
> *But when you get out there, man,*
> *like you in heaven.*

23—DANCING AT THE APOLLO   217
FLASH McDONALD   219

> *Whenever we finished our dance,*
> *that applause in your ear,*
> *you wouldn't believe it.*
> *Oh, that's what would win you over.*
> *That's the sweetest thing in the world.*

24—THE "STORY" OF TAP   223
PRINCE SPENCER   224

> *They called me "On-Too-Long,"*
> *because I would go on the stage*
> *and never know when to leave!*
> *I was stagestruck.*

25—TAPPING INTO THE CLASSICS   231
PAUL DRAPER   232

> *I was a very serious type of dancer.*
> *I didn't sell the steps to the audience.*
> *I was anxious to do the dance, not to sell it.*
> *I wanted to be a part of the art.*

26—DANCE DIRECTORS WHO DO NOT DANCE   241
ANN MILLER   243

> *When [performers] came under contract at [MGM],*
> *they were asked if they sang and danced.*
> *And if they didn't, they didn't get hired!*

27—NIGHTCLUB CHORUS GIRL   250
FRANCES NEALY   252

> *I always could tap dance.*
> *I loved tap dancing.*
> *And they always had tap dancers in the shows.*

28—DANCING WITH THE BIG BANDS   257
JIMMY SLYDE   259

> *And what I can say is, it's been a wonderful*
> *way of life.*

29—THE "CLASS ACT":
   COLES AND ATKINS   262
   CHOLLY ATKINS   264

     There were just so many Class Acts,
     I can't remember most of them.
     Because back in the late twenties
     and early thirties . . . it was class all the way.

30—ON THE ROAD TO BEBOP   271
   BRENDA BUFALINO   273

     When you read the Charlie Parker charts,
     they're very complicated rhythmically,
     but, in fact, nowhere near what we do still.
     It's pretty sophisticated, what a tap dancer
     can do.

Glossary   279

Appendix A   283
Tap Dancers and Tap Acts, 1900–1955

Appendix B   297
Filmography—Tap Dancers on Film, 1900–1955

Appendix C   320
Discography—Tap Dancers on Record, 1900–1955

References: Books, Films/Videos   326

Photo Acknowledgments   332

Index   333

1900
1929

Americans love tap dancing. During the first three decades of the twentieth century, it was the high style and the staple of show business. Everybody wanted to see it, everybody wanted to hear it, and everybody wanted to do it. Jazz rhythms of syncopated feet poured forth from nightclubs, street corners, radios, theaters, and movie screens. Tap was simply the most popular dance entertainment the country had ever known.

Tap dancing is an American art form. It was born in the 1800s, from the meeting and meshing of the wide spectrum of ethnic percussive dance styles brought to the United States during that time, predominantly African, English, Irish, and Scottish. In the years to come, the great music revolutions of ragtime, jazz, swing, bebop, and avant-garde all played a tremendous role in the evolution of tap dancing. And there was another element to tap—its spirit, which was drawn from America itself, from the tempo, the excitement of the Machine Age. Tap mirrored the rest of the country—both were revving up at a terrific pace. The clickety-clack of electric streetcars, the crash and pound of the subway, the riveting cry of buildings going up and coming down—all these modernistic sounds were echoed in the rhythms pouring out of thousands of hoofers' feet.

The turn of the century was a thrilling time in America. New inventions were changing the way of life: automobiles, aeroplanes, flickers, and radio brought the country and the world closer together. But this age of innocence was quickly shattered by the events of World War I. And when "the uncertainties of 1919 were over," F. Scott Fitzgerald wrote, America entered the "greatest, gaudiest spree in history."

By the mid-1920s, the postwar recession had ended. Everyone was spending avidly and the economy was spiraling upward at a record clip. America's wild and flaming youth wore daring clothes and attended late-night parties; sensual jazz and scandalous dances were the last word. They imitated the stars in Hollywood movies and on the big theatrical stages. This was the Jazz Age, and jazz took the country by storm. There was "jazz style," "jazz poetry," and "jazz dance," better known as tap.

At the turn of the century tap dancing had already been in existence for over fifty years. But it was not until the turn of the century that tap dancing really took off and became an established American art form. Then the entertainment world was opening up to include the whole country, and entertainment magnified the public's taste in humor, sentimentality, spectacle, music, and dance. It was a transition period from the innocent past into a more sophisticated future—all set to a syncopated beat. By

1916, Broadway had over three dozen marquees ablaze with show titles, only three of which were serious dramas. The rest were comedies, farces, revues, and musicals. Americans were simply music and dance crazed. Tap dancers were major stars in minstrel shows, burlesque, carnivals, vaudeville, theater, radio, speakeasies, revues, nightclubs, and by 1928, talking motion pictures. Names like Bill Robinson, Fred and Adele Astaire, The Four Covans, Jack Donahue, and Will Mahony were part and parcel of every prominent show.

Styles were being introduced and developed in tap dancing that rocketed it up to new heights. There was flash, legomania, eccentric, class, soft shoe, and for each style there was a stylist to propel the artistry even further. These individuals were fundamental to tap dancing's evolution, for they were still innovating, creating, and perfecting styles that have since become common vocabulary. The Shim Sham Shimmy, Pulling the Trenches, and a veritable list of steps were still on the cutting boards during these years. Tap rhythms were changing right along with the jazz phenomenon compelling the nation. Close rhythm, jazz tap, rhythm tap were all names for the rhythmic style that was yet in its infancy.

In those first decades of the twentieth century, taps rang throughout the country in every possible musical venue. In truth, the tap acts rarely sat still during those decades: they traveled all across the United States to large and small towns; they made their way to anyone anywhere seeking entertainment. Hoofers brought their artistry to such exotic places as Russia, Japan, Cuba, Australia, and the world was thrilled to see them—and *hear* them.

FROM PICKANINNY TO THE PALACE

WILLIE COVAN

We were stoppin' shows wherever we went. Couldn't tear us off the stage! They had never seen nuthin' like us. We got to be so big, we were just about the biggest thing around!

The Wild West conjures up many images, the last of which is tap dancers. But at the turn of the century, tap dancers were there "hitting the boards," not to an Eastern ragtime beat, rather to the hipping and hollering of irrepressible, rascally cowboys. Many of the tap dancers who ventured west to play the dance halls and saloons were boys under the age of twelve. These kids had more adventure packed in their young lives than the average person could ever hope to see in an entire lifetime. Primarily from the South and the East Coast, these children were all black. They fulfilled a specific purpose in show business during that time: They could sing, they could dance, they could tell jokes, they could look cute up onstage, and most important, with their youthful talent, they could lift up a sagging show and supply the much-needed punch. The official theatrical term for these children was pickaninny, "pick" for short. Many young tap dancers entered the business and spent their early years as picks.

Willie Covan started out as a "pickaninny" in the 1900s, and rose to the heights of show business when he played the Palace Theatre, pinnacle of all vaudeville. Covan's sparkle and self-confidence reflects those successful days, circa 1920.

A pick was between the ages of six and twelve. Usually there was a group of them in a show, perhaps four to eight children in all. In essence, they were a ragamuffin chorus for a single woman singer. Headliners such as Sophie Tucker, Eva Tanguay, Blossom Seeley, and Nora Bayes each carried a troupe of picks. The kids may have started as ragamuffins, but they ended up being just as classy as the rest of the entertainers, often adorned in tuxedo jackets, short pants, black silk stockings, and black opera hats. And it was said that picks never flopped, that indeed they were insurance for a "sock" finish. Sarah Venable and Her Picks, Nora Bayes and Her Picks, and Cosie Smith and Her Six Pickaninnies were just a handful of the acts popular at the turn of the century.

For a black youngster, working as a pick was sometimes the easiest way to land a job in white vaudeville. A child who had never before worked professionally might very well find himself suddenly being sent right to the top, working the Keith circuit or the Orpheum circuit. It was a way to work vaudeville without working T.O.B.A.—the black vaudeville circuit—thereby staying out of the South (a highly desirable situation for black entertainers, considering the prejudiced times). The children found themselves working with sensational stars and spent years watching and learning from these seasoned professionals. All the kids had to be able to do was sing and dance—remarkably. And at the turn of the century, there were plenty of kids who fit the bill. One such youngster was Willie Covan. He started as a pick and rose right up the echelons of American entertainment.

Willie Covan's life is a chronicle and testimony of tap dancing at the beginning of the twentieth century. He was born on March 4, 1897 in Atlanta, Georgia. Shortly thereafter, his family moved to Chicago. By 1902, when Willie was five years old, he was already tapping to the rhythms of the city. When he was six years old, he began what would be a six-year career as a pick tap dancing in minstrel shows, which enabled him to observe firsthand the country and its citizens—from "city slickers" to wild cowboys. Willie Covan's pick days were over by the time he reached twelve, and it was then that he entered his second career in show business.

He got his first big break winning an amateur tap contest around 1910, and went on to work with dance legends "Slow Kid" Thompson, then Leonard Ruffin as Covan and Ruffin. In 1917, he formed the legendary tap dancing quartet The Four Covans. They were an instant sensation not only in the United States, but around the globe as well. In 1922, The Four Covans appeared in the historic all-black Broadway musical show, Miller and Lyles's sensation

Shuffle Along. In the 1930s, when movie musicals became the rage, Willie Covan moved to Hollywood where he began working with screen stars including Shirley Temple, Mae West, Mickey Rooney, and Ann Miller. It was at Eleanor Powell's personal insistence that Willie Covan became the head dance instructor at MGM Studios.

Willie Covan perfected tap techniques that are still praised and practiced today, and is credited with creating many classic tap dance steps, including the Rhythm Waltz Clog and the Around the World—with no hands. He brought style and graceful body movement to the art of tap dance, an innovation that was emulated by generations of dancers, on both stage and screen. From pickaninny to stylist, Willie Covan was a true innovator and an integral member of tap's history.

WILLIE COVAN— I came up in Chicago. When I was just a little kid, five years old, I used to get up real early and sit on the curb. From about five-thirty to six A.M., the city was absolutely stone silent except for one thing. The streetcars. I used to sit on that curb and listen to those streetcars—*tchuk, tchuk, tchuk, tchuket, tchuk, tchuk*—that clickety sound, that's where I first started hearin' it. That rhythm. That's when I first started dancin'. I took it right from the streetcars. You see, I was just in love with dancin'. And I was in love with rhythm. I never took a lesson in my life. Never. I never learned rhythm, neither. I mean, I was never taught it. I taught myself from that streetcar in Chicago.

I started dancin' in minstrel shows when I was six years old, and just kept on dancin'. Around 1908, there was this lady singer Cosie Smith. She was Canadian-Indian. She asked my mother if I could go on tour with her to the West Coast—San Francisco, Los Angeles, Seattle, Portland, and the likes. My mother let me go with the show, and my brother Dewey, too. The name of her show was *Cosie Smith and Her Six Pickaninnies.* And us six kids tap danced like crazy in her show. I was nine years old and ready for the big time!

We played a town in Montana called Roundup. It was a real cowboy town. Those fellows in their chaps with their guns, bringin' in horses—this was the real West. They had never seen coloreds before. But, the cowboys didn't care nuthin' about no prejudice. They loved the dancin'! They'd encouraged us, "Yeah, come on, dance!" So after the show, a white boy who lived in Roundup comes backstage. He was a youngster, must have been about seventeen years old. He seen us, and he loved us! Brought us peanuts and Cracker Jacks backstage. Say, he was crazy about us! So he asked us, "What are you doin' after the show?" We were just gonna go home, so we said, "Nuthin', why?" He said, "You wanna make some money?" We say, "Yeah!" He said, "Well, I can take you to a place where you can make some money." He had one of them old Fords, and we all piled in.

Now, the theater was right in town. But this place must have been seven miles out of town. We were drivin' out there, and he said, "You see them lights out there? That's where we're goin'." It was, well, I guess you would call it a saloon. They was gamblin' in there, carryin' on, shootin' craps. A real Western saloon. We went in there and went up to the bartender. He said, "What do you do?" We said, "We sing and we dance." So we sang "Sweet Adeline." And then all the cowboys gathered in a circle around us and we danced. We tap danced like crazy. And they started throwin' money. We danced and we danced, and we picked up that money and stuffed it in our pockets! We kept dancin'. They kept throwin' money! Some of those old cowboys got so excited and were havin' so much fun that they just picked up their guns and started shootin' around our feet! But we weren't afraid. We just kept dancin' and singin' and pickin' up that money. Our pockets were bulging with coins. We were flyin'! We were a hit!

When we couldn't pick up any more money, we went outside to count all those coins. That white boy asked us if we made any money. We said, "Oh, yeah! We made a lot of money. Our pockets are full of pennies. We probably made five or ten dollars—each!" Which was a lot of money in those days. So, he said, "Take it out of your pockets and count it." I think he was excited as we were! We began taking the coins out. And you know what? It wasn't no pennies they was throwin' at us. It was gold! Gold coins! We each had pockets full of gold coins! It turned out there was a gold rush on there. But we didn't know that, we was just kids. And now we was rich! We made eleven hundred dollars!

When I was growin' up, there was lots of minstrel shows, and when I was about ten or eleven, the biggest one was called *Old Kentucky*. Except for the picks, it was all white people in the show, whites playin' coloreds. Coloreds wasn't allowed in shows with whites. So the whites would black up with cork. (And when coloreds was onstage, they had to black up so no one would know they was colored!) The last night of the show, they had a dancin' contest. They advertised all over town for both whites and colored. You didn't have too many colored, a lot of white boys, but we were good dancers. Now I must tell you, in those days, even though I was in the minstrel shows and not supposed to be workin' because I was colored, I never thought of color. I honestly didn't think of no prejudice. White or colored. It didn't matter to me. No, all I thought about was dancin!

So, anyway, this contest began. Each kid was given a number. I was number eight. They had an orchestra, but you didn't want the orchestra to play too much. Stop time, that's what you wanted. Because in those days, they didn't go by the audience response. Rhythm and timing was everything. They had eight dancers under the stage just to hear how much rhythm you had! Yeah, under that stage—listenin'. Those were the execution judges. Then there was the time judges, they sat in the wings. And the style judges sat in the orchestra pit. There was judges everywhere except in the audience! Well, the emcee called out, "Number one!" The first boy went out there and did a Time Step. It was good. And then the emcee called out, "Number two!" And that boy went out and did a Time Step. As a matter of fact, they all did the Time Step. "Number seven!" He came out there and started to do a Time Step. And I stood in the wings and watched. Then it happened, "Number eight!" I was shakin' so much, I thought to myself, "You done lost already shakin' like this!" "Number eight!" I came out. But I didn't do a Time Step. I went straight into a Buck and Wing. Yes, I started right in with the Wings. And they sounded good. There was rhythm in the way I did them. And what happened? Did I win? Did

The Four Covans in 1933, (top to bottom) John "Jack" Jackson, Carita Harbert, Willie Covan, and Florence Covan

The Four Covans stop the show with Class and Flash. In costumes typical of many tap acts of the era, Carita Harbert, Dewey Covan, Willie Covan, and Florence Covan, circa 1932.

I win! All the way from here to New York! I had a pocketful of money from winnin' that contest. And all my family was there. They come backstage and pick me up, put me on their shoulders and carried me that way all the way home. And we lived on the outside of Chicago! I had *arrived*. Everybody in Chicago was sayin', "That little Covan boy, he is something else!" And I was! From that moment on I was a star.

There were many dance competitions that I was involved in where the competition was stiff, and boy, you had to create and come up with something really hot, something different. In one competition, I remember ruinin' a brand-new hundred-dollar suit just to win that thing. 'Cause when it came up to be my turn and do my steps, I went out there and did my routine and finished with an Around The World—with no hands. I did it alright, but ripped my suit to shreds. And it was worth it, ain't never been nobody that did this step with no hands before!

Well, by around 1917, I started The Four Covans. Two boys and two girls, and we were sensational. In those days you couldn't play in a white house. Only whites played in a white theater. You could play in a colored theater. We played plenty of those. Yeah, you bet we played that T.O.B.A. See, in those days, not even a handful of colored acts broke into white vaudeville—Bill Robinson, Williams and Walker, that's just about it. But you know this for sure, The Four Covans made it! Not only did we make it, we headlined white vaudeville! That was something else altogether. Nobody did that! But, there it was as big as life, our name on the marquee, The Four Dancing Covans. We was the star of every show we was on. We were terrific! We stopped all shows. They was crazy

about us. Our act was eight minutes. Eight minutes of sensational dancin'. We were no phonies. That's what it was. We could dance!

And then, too, I had an act with another outstanding dancer, Leonard Ruffin. He was one soft shoe dancer, let me tell you. Our act was subtitled "Every Move a Picture." We played around in vaudeville for quite some time, and then in 1923, we played the Palace. If you played the Palace, everyone in the world called you a star. Then coloreds couldn't play the Palace. You couldn't go in there, let alone play it. But we were in there with all the biggest white headliners. All headliners. And we were headliners, too! We were stoppin' shows wherever we went. Couldn't tear us off the stage! They had never seen nuthin' like us. We were a sensation. We got to be *so* big, we were just about the biggest thing around!

So when we played the Palace, we stopped that show. I mean we stopped that show! Nobody could follow us. They got booed right off the stage. You see, we were rehearsin' for the show at the Palace Theatre, and Eubie Blake was workin' on a new song for this same show. And I was listenin' to him pick out the song on the piano while we were workin' on our routine, and I went over to him and asked him to play that again the way he had just played it. You see, he was pickin' out the song, pick pick pick with his fingers, each note at one time. Now what that song was, was "Sweet Georgia Brown." So Eubie says to us, he says, "Hey man, why don't you use this song as the closing song in your act, and introduce this in the show tonight?" So we changed our routine to fit this song, and thought we was crazy. Because we hadn't played the Palace before, and here we were goin' to change the last number in our act! Well, you know what happened, we went out on that stage and did this number—"stop time."

People had never seen a song fit the rhythms

of a dance so perfectly before. "Sweet Georgia Brown" became an instant hit because of us. They went out of the theater singin' this song! We just stopped that show. It was madness! Encore after encore. We just kept runnin' out there takin' more bows. No one could follow us. So the manager tried to rearrange the bill. But no matter what he did, we still stopped that show. For three days, during all those shows (and remember this was vaudeville, something like five a day), he rearranged that bill. But we still stopped the show. The audience just wouldn't stop. So after three days, they solved the problem. They fired us! But we were such a sensation, the Hippodrome picked us up. The same thing happened there. So after three days at the Hippodrome, we were fired there, too. You see, they could have really solved the problem by havin' us go on next to last, and we could go on bowin' forever. But that was the most prestigious spot on the bill, and those were different times. There was no way they was gonna have no colored act top the bill at the Palace. However, one thing they couldn't control, prejudice or no prejudice, Covan and Ruffin from bein' a hit. We were a sensation wherever we went!

After his years with The Four Covans in vaudeville, on Broadway, and around the world, Willie Covan went to Hollywood, and upon Eleanor Powell's personal insistence became resident choreographer and dance instructor at MGM Studios. Performing in "Willie Covan's Dance Studio Annual Revue," Willie Covan demonstrates some of the fine steps he picked up and invented through his sixty years in show business, circa 1950.

So you see, all my life, tap dancin', that's what I know! Yeah, I love it. I never come away from it and come back to it like some. Never did that. I been in it all my life. I was just *in love* with tap dancin'.

What is it about tap dancin' that people love so much? It's beautiful.

June 9, 1988
Los Angeles, California
(Died May 7, 1989)

2

FIRST TAP DANCING STAR OF THE SILVER SCREEN

RUBY KEELER

I'd say I was a hoofer.
A real Buck and Wing dancer.

Get the beat of people's feet
Walkin' up and down the street,
    and do the New York.
Get the sound, the crash and
    pound,
Of the subway underground,
    and do the New York.
You'll find there's something old and
    something new in it
Something hot and something blue in it
Seven million people doin' it
What a rhythm!
Get the feel, of stone and steel
Add a little sex appeal,
    and do the New York.*

The Roaring Twenties, a decade of wild excitement, carefree abandon, and frenzied joy. Just like a modern symphony, this era had its own score—the new rhythm of the twentieth century set to hot jazz music. The glamorous images this time conjures up: young couples frantically

*"Do the New York"

dancing the Charleston; fast, shiny automobiles; flappers with bobbed hair; gangsters, gats. And New York had it all, including Prohibition.

Despite all Prohibition attempts to restrict the flow of alcohol, bootleg hootch flowed like rivers in nightclubs, or as they were then called, speakeasies. All could be had by knocking on the passage window of a side-street speakeasy door and telling the man behind it that "Joe sent me." Once inside, nightclub revelers saw the twenties unfold before them: chorus girls, underworld characters, bathtub gin, jazz bands, and Manhattan's most vivacious entertainment. High brows and low brows, society dames and politicians, flappers and sheiks all jammed in like sardines to take part in the hysteria of the Jazz Age.

One of the entertainers they went to see was a sweet, nondescript hoofer who had the twenties right in her lap—Ruby Keeler. This thirteen-year-old girl, with all the unself-conscious charm of a puppy dog, first took New York, then Hollywood, by storm, and by 1933, was destined to become America's premier tap dancing star.

Ruby Keeler was born in Halifax, Nova Scotia, on August 25, 1910. Three years later, her family packed up for New York City. She began dancing at an early age, and by the time she was thirteen, she was in the chorus of a George M. Cohan show, *The Rise of Rosie O'Reilly* (1923). From Broadway she moved into the reigning nightclubs of the 1920s, including "incendiary-blond" Texas Guinan's infamous speakeasy, the El Fey Club, and the glamorous and sophisticated Silver Slipper. She was not much of a singer or tap dancer, but her engaging charm and fresh innocence were enormously appealing and more than compensated for any want in musical ability. In 1923, she moved back onto the Broadway stage in such shows as *Bye, Bye, Bonnie* (1927) and *The Sidewalks of New York* (1927).

In 1928, Ruby Keeler went to Los Angeles to make a Fox short about dancing and to appear in theater

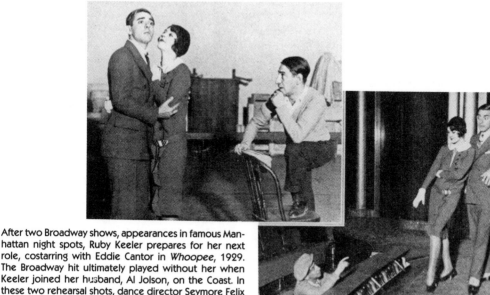

After two Broadway shows, appearances in famous Manhattan night spots, Ruby Keeler prepares for her next role, costarring with Eddie Cantor in *Whoopee*, 1929. The Broadway hit ultimately played without her when Keeler joined her husband, Al Jolson, on the Coast. In these two rehearsal shots, dance director Seymore Felix looks on.

prologues. When her train pulled into Union Station, she was spotted by Al Jolson, who was there to meet fellow passenger Fanny Brice. He asked to be introduced to Miss Keeler, whom he had seen onstage in New York City. A whirlwind courtship ensued, with Jolson following his new sweetheart back to New York. On September 21, 1928, Ruby Keeler became the third Mrs. Al Jolson. She was eighteen, he was forty-two. He was the "World's Greatest Entertainer," she a demure buck and wing dancer. They moved from Broadway to Hollywood, where Jolson had become involved with Warner Bros. studio after his smash hit, the most successful early talking motion picture, *The Jazz Singer* (1927).

Ruby Keeler was not anxious to be a movie star, unlike so many of her coworkers. She was happy to live a quiet home life. But everlasting fame was thrust upon her with the role of Peggy Sawyer, the ingenue in the upcoming "All Talking, All Singing, All Dancing" musical comedy/drama *42nd Street* (1933). Ruby Keeler played the role with all the sweetness that she herself possessed, and when she tapped in the great finale number to the title song, she won all America. With the release of *42nd Street*, Ruby Keeler became the first tap dancing star of motion pictures.

Despite her tremendous popularity, Ruby Keeler was the first to admit she was not as talented a performer as so many of her contemporaries, including Ginger Rogers and Eleanor Powell. And to set the record straight, she was not primarily a tap dancer: Ruby Keeler was a Buck dancer, and quite an accomplished one at that. The shoes, as well as the style, were quite different from tap: Buck dancers' soles were wooden, and the concern was more with the rhythm than the look; they danced primarily in one place onstage, and always on the balls of their feet, confining dance movement to below the waist. Screen tap dancers of the same time period were then developing an all-encompassing dance style, incorporating ballet and jazz movements. These tap dancers displayed a more nimble quality, using upper-body movement with finesse and to a much greater extent than the Buck dancers. In retrospect, this earlier tap style of Buck dancing may appear "klutzy," yet it was a legitimate and popular percussive dance form of the day.

Throughout the 1930s, Ruby Keeler continued to star in a series of successful Warner Bros. musical films, dancing with some of the finest tap dancers under contract with the studio. Her films included *Gold Diggers of 1933, Dames* (1934), *Footlight Parade* (1933, tap partner, James Cagney), *Flirtation Walk* (1934), *Go Into Your Dance* (1935, costarring with her husband, Al Jolson), *Colleen* (1936, tap partner, Paul Draper), and *Ready, Willing and Able* (1937, tap partner, Lee Dixon). It was also during her contract with Warner Bros. that she first met and worked with the legendary Busby Berkeley, the kaleidoscope mind of choreography. And though she was not really a tap dancer, and not the most accomplished actress or singer, nonetheless, Ruby Keeler will always be remembered with great warmth and affection as the first tap dancing star of the silver screen.

R U B Y   K E E L E R — I got started tap dancing at school. I'm Catholic and went to a parochial school on the East Side of New York. At school we had one period a week with a lovely lady who was a dancer. She came to our school and taught us all sorts of dances like the Irish Jig, the Highland Fling, and the Sailor's Hornpipe. The Irish Jig was actually the first tap dancing I did.

Our dancing teacher thought I had a little talent I guess, because she spoke to my mother about me taking dancing lessons. And my mother, God bless her soul, would have done it in a minute,

SHE'S A LATIN FROM MANHATTAN

This wonderful sheet music cover from *Go Into Your Dance* (Warner Bros., 1935) shows a smartly dressed Ruby Keeler ready to go into her dance. Ruby Keeler had a prolific career in Hollywood, beginning with the sensational triumph of *42nd Street* (Warner Bros., 1932), yet this was her only screen appearance with husband Al Jolson.

but there were six children and we didn't have very much money, least of all to send *me* to dancing school. But she asked Mama if she'd be willing to bring me in on Saturdays to a class lesson. And Mama said yes. I was about ten or twelve at the time.

A girl who was in dancing school with me told me about an audition for chorus girls. We were thirteen, but we looked sixteen. Now, I had never been in a theater, let alone backstage. So I went with her. I saw all these gals sitting there, and I watched what they did. It was a George M. Cohan show—*The Rise of Rosie O'Reilly* [1923]. Doesn't that sound like George M. Cohan!

Julian Mitchell was the dance director for the show, and when I came backstage with my friend, he was auditioning a lot of girls. I looked around and noticed that the apron of the stage was wooden, but that the rest of the stage was cov-

ered up. I thought, "When it gets to me, I'm going to dance up on the apron so he can hear my taps." That's a typical tap dancer, eh!

When he came to me, I said, "May I dance up there?" I didn't get an answer, so I did anyway. While I was dancing I heard him ask, "Who said you could dance up here?" I said, "Well, I asked you." And to make a long story short, I got the job. I got forty-five dollars a week! That really helped my family.

After working awhile, I found out that I could have danced at home, because Julian Mitchell was deaf! He couldn't hear. I could have auditioned out in the alley!

After *The Rise of Rosie O'Reilly*, I started working in nightclubs. You see, in those days word always got around town to the big producers about good tap dancers. There was a gentleman by the name of N.T.G.—Nils T. Granlund. All the girls called him Granny. He placed the girls in nightclubs. Someone had told him about me, and Granny took me over to Texas Guinan's the El Fey Club. I got a job in there, and you know, I had my fourteenth, fifteenth, and sixteenth birthdays there!

During this time the Gerry Society got after me. There was a law that kids in New York could not work until they were sixteen, regardless of the work they did. Somehow, they found out about

Dancing with Paul Draper in *Colleen* (Warner Bros., 1935), Ruby Keeler takes a gigantic step up from Buck and Wing dancer to Classical tapper. Draper's style of intricate and musical footwork, combined with smooth and fluid body-work, had a tremendous influence on Keeler, and she never looked more gracefully polished than in their number "You Gotta Know How to Dance."

Ruby Keeler's most difficult number by far is this dance with Lee Dixon in *Ready Willing and Able* (Warner Bros., 1937). They actually tap on the gigantic typewriter, carefully judging the jumps from key to key. Lee Dixon, Warner Bros.' most outstanding stock hoofer, incorporates his keen sense of Rhythm Tap into this amazing routine.

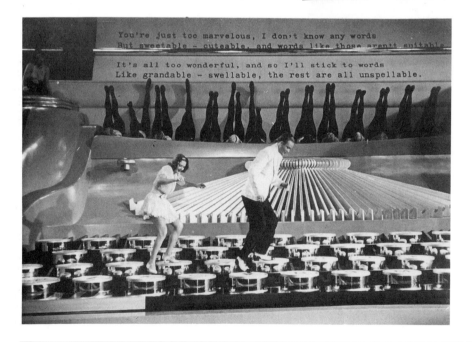

You're just too marvelous, I don't know any words
But sweetable - cuteable, and words like those aren't suitable

It's all too wonderful, and so I'll stick to words
Like grandable - swellable, the rest are all unspellable.

me, and of course I had been lying a lot about my age! Anyway, if you worked before you were sixteen years old, you had to go to what they called continuation school. Well, I didn't think much of that. But I didn't have anything to prove that I was sixteen. My birth certificate had been destroyed in an explosion during World War I in Halifax. I thought, well, to keep them off my back I'll go to school for a week to see what it's like. So I took morning session, because I worked at the club until about six A.M. I went to class at eight A.M. The first day, I learned how to stuff dates. Now, you know *that's* going to help me a lot in my life! And then you had to eat them. Well, that was the end of continuation school!

I was just a chorus girl in the Cohan show, but I was a specialty dancer at the club—I always had my very own spot on the show. It was like this: Texas Guinan would always introduce me. (She was responsible and famous for the expression, "Give this little girl a great big hand!") I had a chorus of about six to eight girls behind me, and we would come out and do little audience participation numbers. For example, I might be dressed as a mailman, and they'd be dressed in little skirts. They'd all tap dance out to the tables and hand out letters while I sang the song, "I've got a letter for you . . ." Then I'd do a tap solo. That kind of thing.

I loved working at the clubs. I say *clubs* because you see, I doubled really. I also worked at the Silver Slipper. So, from the Guinan club I'd walk over to the Slipper and do a show there. The girls all did that so you'd get two salaries,

In a scene with Al Jolson from *Go Into Your Dance* (Warner Bros., 1935), Ruby Keeler holds a classic pair of wooden-soled "Buck Shoes" under her arm.

you know. And it was great fun!

My first film was *42nd Street* [1933]. I had just come out from New York to join my husband, Al Jolson, who was working on a series of motion pictures in Hollywood. When I first started work on *42nd Street*, I was awed by everything. 'Cause I was a real movie fan. I used to go to the movies all the time. And there I was with all these movie people and actors. I was scared to death! Since it was my first picture, they didn't invite me to see rushes. So I used to follow Buz [Busby Berkeley] around and ask, "How was it? How was it? Was it all right?" And he would answer, "Oh great, great, Ruby. You're doing fine!"

In *42nd Street*, I did my own choreography. In pictures, there was always a dance director; but he took care of the big numbers. I always did my own routines—it was always my dancing. Of course when I was with a partner, like Lee Dixon

or Paul Draper, we would work it out together.

I'd say I was a hoofer. A real Buck and Wing dancer. I never wore taps. Never. I wore wooden soles like Bill Robinson. Not many people had them. If you watch *42nd Street*, you'll see I'm wearing them. I look like I have club feet! I used to call them my "Buck Shoes."

When I think about it, my father, Lord rest his soul, was the one who sparked my love for dancing. When I was a little girl, we lived in a neighbor-hood where there were social functions, parties with sawdust on the floor. Everyone attended—even the kids. A band would play, and Papa would always waltz with me. He was a big man. We would waltz and waltz. And I was so proud. He would turn me around, say to the right, and then we would waltz a little more. He would lean over and whisper to me, "reverse," which meant that he was going to spin me around the other way. And one day when Papa and I danced, he didn't have to say "reverse"—I just followed him. I was so happy, you'd think I'd won the championship of the world! That was when I first realized what it was to dance.

September 9, 1988
Rancho Mirage, California
(Died February 28, 1993)

THE HOOFERS CLUB

3

LEONARD REED

They used to say there wasn't such a thing as not having a tap dancer in your show!

In the 1920s, American entertainment was at its peak. And one of the most prolific venues for entertainers during this time was vaudeville. There was the Keith Circuit, the Orpheum Circuit, the Gus Sun Time Circuit, and there was T.O.B.A. Not many people remember T.O.B.A. today, that is, except the kind of entertainers who played it. "*Kind*" here doesn't mean singers, or dancers, or comedians—it was the *kind* meaning race. T.O.B.A. was for blacks—black entertainers in black theaters. That was the state of affairs in America in the 1920s.

T.O.B.A., the Theater Owners Booking Association, was first conceived of in the middle 1910s, when comedian Sherman Dudley began leasing and buying theaters. This chain of theaters continued to expand until the 1920s, penetrating much of the South, the Southwest and many Northern cities. It functioned as a vaudeville circuit for blacks and went through some of the most racist regions in the United States. T.O.B.A. was also known as "Toby," politely as "Tough on Black Artists," and, more honestly, as "Tough on Black Asses." Entertainers could perform in towns and be greeted with genuine appreciation for their art, yet they had to enter through

Leonard Reed has the air of a polished performer, from shiny top hat to silver-tipped cane, 1930s.

service and delivery doors of even the hotels that booked them. Although guaranteed work, the entertainers were naturally paid on a scale lower than their counterparts on the white circuits.

T.O.B.A., or "Toby Time" shows, were typical revues of the day, tabloid-style musical comedy productions. They usually ran three a night and each lasted about forty-five minutes. A T.O.B.A. company consisted of about thirty-five top black entertainers, and the show included comedy skits, chorus numbers, solo specialties, and, of course, plenty of tap dancing. Many of the best tap acts of the twentieth century cut their teeth on this circuit, including Bill Robinson, Eddie Rector, and The Berry Brothers.

When black entertainers were finally permitted to appear in white vaudeville, they were restricted by the "two colored" rule—that blacks could only perform in pairs. It was the legendary tap dancer Bill Robinson who finally broke that barrier as the first black entertainer to appear as a single in white vaudeville. By 1918, to the utter delight of thousands, he was performing his inimitable stair dance at the undisputed crown jewel of American vaudeville theaters, New York's Palace Theatre on West Forty-seventh Street and Broadway. Despite this, Bill Robinson was one of only three black acts to be invited to play the Palace during World War I, the others being Bert Williams, and the team Greenlee and Drayton. The modus operandi was vaudeville for whites and T.O.B.A. for blacks.

But in the 1920s, the phenomenon of "passing" could blur the distinctions between black and white: If individuals of mixed racial heritage could "pass" for white, they could work for all the big-time white vaudeville circuits of the day without "detection." However, if their racial background was disclosed, they were literally chased off the scene.

One such entertainer who passed during the 1920s was Leonard Reed, credited with inventing the celebrated tap dance the Shim Sham Shimmy. Half white, one quarter Choctaw Cherokee, and one quarter black, Leonard Reed—handsome and fair with startling blue eyes—was able to go back and forth between the then-segregated worlds of entertainment from 1922 to 1933. In 1922, he began his professional career as a dancer, first performing the dance craze the Charleston. In 1925, when the Tap Charleston hit the scene, he began frequenting Harlem's fabled Hoofers Club, honing in on his new occupation as a tap dancer. The Hoofers Club was *the* informal gathering place of the country's best black tap dancers, and it was there that they would "jam" the day and night away "stealing" steps from one another. It was a competitive atmosphere, and a dancer had to be quick on his feet to successfully walk away with new material.

In the early 1930s, Reed teamed up with Willie Bryant and played white vaudeville, including the dream spot of all vaudevillians, the Palace Theatre. In 1934, Leonard Reed began a second career as producer with an all-black musical revue called *Rhythm Bound*. He continued producing throughout the 1930s, at such prestigious night spots as the Cotton Club and the Apollo Theatre. Throughout his career, Leonard Reed was responsible for nurturing young talent, as well as inspiring new talent through his own artistry.

L E O N A R D   R E E D — I was born in 1907, in a southern city called Nowata, Oklahoma. Well, when I say I was born in Nowata, I really shouldn't lie. It wasn't Nowata, it was Lightning Creek. Now, Lightning Creek was *nothing*—it was woods and a couple of houses, you know. And it was eleven, twelve miles from Nowata. That's where I ended up in school.

My mother died when I was two years old. I never saw my father. I came from an interracial marriage. My father was white, my mother was one half Choctaw Cherokee and one half black. Being half and half you can be in trouble. The black people don't realize it, nor the white people. It didn't bother me, though, in the early years of my career, because I never looked upon it as a prejudice.

I was in about fourth or fifth grade when I went to Kansas City. I was living with my guardians, who weren't blood relatives. One of my guardians, a man named Taylor, was very mean. He had beat me so hard I had welts. So I ran away from home, from them, even though I was still in school. No matter how many times I ran away from home, I'd go back to school. And that's where Taylor would find me. He'd come to the school, you see, because I would never duck school.

Anyway, when I was about twelve years old, I got into a very bad situation. Some of us kids were caught drinking, and we were arrested. When we went to court, everybody's parents was there except mine. All the other kids were released in the custody of their parents, pending another hearing. One of the kids told the principal of the high school that I was in jail. So he came down. Now, court was every Monday, and he came down on a Thursday to see me. He asked me a lot of questions, and I told him the truth about the whole thing. When I went to court the next Monday, they were ready to send me to Boonville, the reformatory. Four years was what I was goin' to get, you know. The previous Monday in court, they'd called, "Lemille Jackson." When he walked up they said, "Four years in Boonville." The girls, "Two years in Chillicothi." But all the kids were suspended and were taken home by their parents, you see. But I had nobody to speak for me, so when I got to court the next Monday, I *knew* I was going to Boonville. I just *knew* I was going to Boonville. But when they called all the names for everybody to go to court, they didn't call my name! The kids who were there were lined up and taken across the street. I couldn't figure out what was happenin' with me. That afternoon they came and got me and took me into the judge's chambers, and I showed him the scars on my back. The principal said he would take me into his home. His name was H. L. Cook. I credit it to him the fact that I did have that amount of education.

In around 1922, when I was fifteen years old, the Charleston came out. And on the schoolyard

---

In the early 1920s, the Charleston swept the country. Then, in 1925, came the Tap Charleston. Leonard Reed, one of its finest exponents, won every contest he entered. Standard Theatre, Philadelphia, 1927.

everyone was doin' the little clap [keeping time], you know, and doin' the Charleston. No music, no nothing. So, *I* did the Charleston. I learned by watching. I was watching everyone.

As an extra job, I sold peanuts, popcorn, candy, and Cracker Jacks at the local theater, the Lincoln Theatre. They had shows every week. And every week a dancer would come. Every show had a dancer, or two dancers, maybe three. Anyway, I couldn't sell candy during the show, so I would stay backstage and watch all the dancers. "Show me that. Show me a step," I'd ask them.

There were Charleston contests at all the local theaters. So I entered a Charleston contest and won. I was so excited. Then I started going to *all* of the Charleston contests in Kansas City. During this time, there was a weekly contest at the Orpheum Theatre. It was for "whites only." I won the contest, but I was snitched on by one of my friends, my school friends. I was standin' there after the contest. I saw the manager and I could tell something was up. So I grabbed the prize money and ran. The manager started yelling, "Catch that nigger, catch that nigger!" When somebody said, "Where?" I didn't even think about it, I was so nervous. So, I chimed in with, "Catch that nigger!" The theater was letting out, and everybody was coming out the side entrance. I just ran through that shuttle, right through that alleyway. And when I was running, yelling, "Catch that nigger," they all started runnin' along with me tryin' to help!

My first job during the summer was at a carnival with another fella. They called him Jack Johnson—he was kind of dark. And they called me Jim Jeffries. Now those were famous heavyweight fighters of the day. They gave us big boxing gloves, and we'd box each other and they'd throw money in the ring and we'd try to pick up the money with the boxing gloves on! Our job was to go out on the ballyhoo and do the Charleston to draw the people into the tent for the wrestlers.

Let me explain. All the shows were done in a tent. Outside of the tent they put up a platform. The platform was about eleven feet long and about twelve feet wide. Now the platform wasn't the bally, what you *did* was called the bally. All the girls in the show would come out on the bally and shake their little shimmies and do their thing. The Shimmy was in then. And the Black Bottom. They'd do the Black Bottom. And when my turn came, I did the Charleston with tambourines, no music, just hittin' the tambourines. And everybody in the tent would run out and go on the bally. And that was my first job—with S. B. Williams.

They called the black shows in a carnival the Jig Top. I later became the barker for it because of my light complexion, and because I stood out. I stood in a box and called everyone around. I'd been given a speech: "Ladies and gentlemen, gather up closer. I've got a colossal collection of cannibalistic curiosities on the inside. I tell you what I'm gonna do, pay one quarter of a dollar, twenty-five cents ..." That's what they told me to say, "Cannibalistic curiosities on the inside." Now doesn't that say something about attitudes toward black people in those days!

I came back to Kansas City after my first year of experiences with carnivals to finish my high school year. H. L. Cook, who was my father then, had made arrangements for me to go to school where he had gone to school, at Cornell University. After I finished school that year, I went up to Cornell to see whether or not I was gonna like things. During the time I was there, I met some friends. At a local Charleston contest one of them said, "You always tellin' us about how good you are. Let's see you go down *there* to the contest and win." I said, "If they got one, I'll win it!"

All the time, I'd not seen any black people at all. All I'd been around was white people, you know, except for at the carnival. When I went in

that contest, they thought I was white. Anyway, I won! This was Ithaca, New York. I was asked to join the show. From Dayton, Ohio, I left the show and I hoboed back to Kansas. I hopped a freight in Dayton and went to Chicago, and outta Chicago, got right back to Kansas, *right* to the Lincoln Theatre to see the show there, where I'd started selling popcorn and candy! I'd done all this within a year.

There was a fella there by the name of Travis Tucker, who had a show called *Hits and Bits of 1922*. Yeah, little bits, lasted ten, twelve minutes. I got in it, and it was the first *regular* show for me. I worked with Travis Tucker down through the middle of August. We did week stands and split-week stands: We played one town three days and one town four days. We did three shows a day. Now remember, up until this time from 1922, I am strictly Charleston! That's what my role was, to be a Charleston dancer. That's all I could do, I couldn't do *anything* else!

Hits and Bits was an all-black revue. I'd already gone back and forth. I would be with a white show, then I'd go back to a black show. I never got to any strategic city where anybody recognized me or knew what I was or what I wasn't. In addition to the white vaudeville circuits, I was playin' the T.O.B.A.. I played T.O.B.A. more than once, you know. Every time you'd look up, you'd see *me*. But I always had a different act: Pen and Ink, Leonard and Willie, Cutout and Leonard, Leonard and Crackaloo, Sadie Montgomery and Leonard....

Well, Travis Tucker was really the instigator of my being in show business and responsible for my knowing and doing what I have done. He said to me, "I'm gonna sit you in this wing. I want you to watch *every* performer on that stage. Watch everything that they do. I want you to *learn* everything that they're doing, including the soubrette." One day she got sick, and he said, "You got to do her part today." And I remember the thing. She sang in front of the girls, who then came onstage and did a dance. Then she did the dance along with them. Now, *I* had to do that. I did the Charleston in front of the girls to the tune of, "I'm Looking at the World Through Rose-Colored Glasses." I sang this song, then I did my dance. Now that was quite a thrill! That was in the opener, and it was really a bang with me doin' the Charleston. That's when I learned about pacing. Travis Tucker always said, "Put the best things up front. And the rest of it will take care of itself."

Travis Tucker was a boozer, but not to the point where he was an alcoholic. He drank a lot, and when he muffed his lines, you knew he was drunk. Anyway, one day I'm standin' in the wings stage right watching the entrance of the other comic who would come from stage left. Travis, who normally joined this guy from where I was standin', just gave me a shove and said, "You're on. Do me." I turned around and looked at him—I was petrified. He said, "Do me." Well, I knew the bit. So I did it! Every time he didn't feel like it, I would do the bit. And I learned. But I still hadn't learned a single tap dance step!

The lobby of the theater ran uphill a little. Not much of a hill, but just graduated, you know. There was a fella in the show, Teddy Right, who was a terrific tap dancer. The first step I ever learned in my life other than the Charleston was from him. Going up the hill, Teddy showed me how to do that famous step Pulling the Trenches. And then I learned the Time Step from him.

Even by 1925, I knew very little tap, maybe one or two Time Steps. So when I got into New York, I started frequently going to the Hoofers Club. It was down in the basement, two or three doors up from the Lafayette Theatre at Seventh Avenue between One hundred and thirty-first and One hundred and thirty-second Streets. When you walked down the stairs of the Hoofers Club, there was a lunch counter directly in front of you. They sold hot dogs and such. Over to the left, like you come downstairs and make a U-turn, there were two card tables where people were always playing poker and blackjack. If you turned left and went directly left, like going "uptown," it was called. (You know like the front of the building was crosstown. The right-hand part of the building going in was downtown, and the left-hand was uptown.) So when you got in the building if you turned uptown, you would see two pool tables and a billiard table. If you went straight east, crosstown, you would go into a little room. The room was no bigger than thirty by twenty feet. It had a piano in the corner and a good floor.

All the dancers around town came in. You could hear dancing the minute you got in the building. There was always dancin' going on, known dancers and unknown dancers. Bubbles would come occasionally. Bill Robinson came in occasionally. Bill spent most of the time upstairs in the poolroom. All the dancers would hang out, and they would trade ideas. That was affectionately called "stealin' steps." Everybody did it. That's how you learned. You would do something, and you'd say to the other dancers, "You tryin' to steal it? Allright, do it!" "Let me see you do this!" And they'd try it. Of course, when they did it, it was slightly different. But that's how it was. Everybody was always showin' steps and trying to steal steps. It was an amazing time.

I was in a show called *Sundown Revue* at the

as he held on to that piano, he could *really* Wing. He invented all sorts of things, and we would do them.

Before long, Willie Bryant and I were dancing together as a team—a tap act Reed and Bryant —Brains as well as Feet. You know, by this time I was really tapping. Oh yes. We opened with a tap, then we did a Soft Shoe. We did all this in eight minutes. Eight minutes was a long time! In vaudeville they only wanted you to do *six*.

We played all through the vaudeville circuit, and we played independent houses, too. One thing I have to my credit is having played the Palace Theatre in New York. That was the pinnacle of all vaudeville. All the acts dreamed of playing the Palace. That's when you knew you had really made it!

For a while, Willie and I were with The Whitman Sisters troupe. They were by far the greatest incubator of dancing talent for black shows on or off T.O.B.A, and they traveled all over the United States with their own show. Willie and I were doin' what they call Shim Sham. But we would do it in a very goofy way, and we called it "Goofus." And everybody else called it Goofus, too. There was a little boy named Billy who was dancin' with Pops Whitman, but when he left the show, he went to New York and formed a group called Three Little Words. This is where the confusion came. Instead of him going in doing a dance and callin' it Goofus, he named it the Shim Sham Shimmy. Now the reason Billy called it the *shimmy* was that he added the shakin' of the

Lafayette Theatre in 1927, and everybody from the show was going down to the Hoofers Club. *Sundown Revue* had three or four dancers who had an act called The Midnight Steppers. We were all going downstairs, and someone would say, "Hey, you goin' to the Hoofers Club? Yeah? Come on!" So we would go there between shows. We were originating, or doing, or trying to learn new steps. That's where I *learned* to dance.

What really started me tap dancin' was a guy down in the Hoofers Club by the name of "Piano." I don't know his real name, and I don't know if anybody ever did, but we called him Piano. He would hold on to the piano and do the most fabulous Wings you've ever seen. But if he turned the piano loose, he couldn't do nothin'. As long

Leonard Reed during the days of vaudeville "three-a-day." Reed and Bryant both wear this dapper suit for the afternoon show, a beautifully tailored tuxedo for the dinner show, and the classic top hat, white tie, and tails for the evening show, circa 1932.

After being blacklisted from white show business, Leonard Reed took up producing. His first show—*Rhythm Bound*—was put on at the Harlem Opera House and was filled with hot music and spectacular show dancing. Leonard Reed, front and center, holding baton, 1934.

shoulders to it. But we didn't do the shakin'—it was a fun thing with us, you know. But, it really doesn't matter.

There was a little boy named Frankie Owens who was Willie's and my valet when we were with white shows. Frankie could out-dance both Willie and myself. He could sit in the chair dancin' better than anybody I'd ever seen. He was the first one I'd seen do that—and remember, this was 1929, 1930, 1931. I'll tell you a very funny story. Willie Bryant and I were playin' Birmingham, Alabama. Willie would curse at Frankie at the drop of a hat. "Come here, you little black son of a bitch. Come here and pick up my things! Hey you little black so-and-so!" He'd done it all along, and Frankie had taken it, you know.

But when we got to Birmingham, Frankie said, "Mr. Bryant, Mr. Reed, I'm gonna tell you something. This is my hometown. This is where I was born. Now, I'm gettin' sick and tired of you callin' me all these names. And I want to tell you, if you call me any more names, I'm gonna tell 'em you're a *nigger*! And I'm gonna get ya hurt! And another thing. I don't want you to introduce me as your valet who's gonna do your encore. I want you to introduce me as an extra attraction to your act."

Well, Willie don't open his mouth, and neither did I! He had us over a barrel. You should have heard Willie's introduction for Frank at the next show! "Well, we have a *gentleman* with us who can really dance. We discovered this young boy in Tulsa, Oklahoma, and we thought we'd take him to New York with us." At other times he'd said, "Now we have our valet who works for us, and we wanna show you how he can dance— come on, boy! Show 'em how you can dance!" Well, we had to be white, and he had to be black, you know.

When I was with Willie, everything was white. Until they found out that we were colored who could go white and be around the girls. They didn't like that. See, we had a two-week layoff, and we made a mistake. We went into the black houses to keep on working during the layoff, and somebody told 'em who we were. I don't know whether it was a mistake. I don't regret it. I never thought about whether it was strange going back and forth. I think about it now! I think about the danger, and all the things we did. But after that I never did work white again. That was 1933.

In 1934, I became a producer. Basically, my dancing career went from 1922 to 1933. I had always wanted to do a Broadway show. And in 1934, I got an offer to do my own show. It was called *Rhythm Bound*. I had about forty great singers and great dancers in the show. It was booked into the Harlem Opera House, one of the great black theaters up in Harlem. We did four numbers in the show: an opener, a soft shoe number, a soldier number, and then the finale. All tap.

They used to say there wasn't such a thing as not having a tap dancer in your show! 'Cause in my day, no matter where you went you would run into tap dancers. *Everything* had tap!

June 8, 1988
Hollywood, California

KING OF THE
ONE-LEGGED
DANCERS

PEG LEG BATES

I was very ambitious when I was
dancing. I wanted to be so good, I
wanted to *surpass* the two-leg
dancers! And in a lot of cases I did.

4

Throughout tap's heyday, legions of syncopated
steppers lit the stages of American entertainment. Each of these tap acts had a specific
style of putting the dance across: flash, novelty,
eccentric, legomania, soft shoe, buck and wing,
class. An act became known for one of these specific styles of tap dancing, and the dancers took the
art soaring to new heights. It was not that the individuals were unable to do other types of tap
dancing. It was just that they excelled specifically
in one area, and the audiences loved them for it.
The Four Step Brothers perfected acrobatic flash,
The Nicholas Brothers, classical tap, Coles and Atkins, class and soft shoe, The Ebsens, comedy and
eccentric. Indeed, their names were synonymous
with their style: Bill Robinson's name alone paints a
picture of a derby-hatted, nattily-dressed dancer
tapping his way up and down a staircase; Fred
Astaire, a vision of gentlemanly grace suited in top
hat, white tie, and tails wittily tapping out some
clever romantic melody; Ann Miller, a dazzling array
of riveting taps and turns.

But there is one tap dancer who defies this concept of singularity. He did everything including ac-

robatic turns, graceful Soft Shoes, Buck and Wings, and powerful rhythm tap dances. And if that alone weren't enough, this man did it all on one leg—and a peg. Peg Leg Bates—the undisputed king of the one-legged dancers.

Peg Leg Bates began tap dancing as a child. By the time he was fifteen years old, he was firmly entrenched in a professional career as a tap dancer. He worked his way up from minstrel shows to carnivals, from the black vaudeville circuit T.O.B.A. to the white vaudeville circuits. In 1929, he joined *Lew Leslie's Blackbirds* in Paris, France. In this all-black revue were some of the most outstanding black entertainers of the day. Peg Leg Bates returned to the United States and, throughout the 1930s, played the top Harlem nightclubs, including the Cotton Club and Connie's Inn. In the late thirties, he was the opening act for the *Ed Sullivan Revue* and traveled

the Keith and Loews circuits, appearing in the reigning vaudeville theaters. During the 1950s, Peg Leg Bates appeared on Ed Sullivan's television show more times than any other tap dancer—a total of twenty-one appearances.

Part of Peg Leg Bates's success was the sound he created, especially when doing a rhythm dance. The end of his peg was half rubber and half leather; on the inside of the peg leg was leather, on the outside of the peg leg was rubber. When he was tapping, he worked inside on the leather for the sound. When he was doing novelty steps, for example, balancing on the peg, then he worked outside to keep from slipping. With his right leg, he used a tap shoe, with regular metal taps. But it was the peg that really brought in a strong rhythm sound.

Like all others of his era, Peg Leg Bates actively "stole" steps. This was just the business. Tap dancers emulated each others' steps; that is, as much as they could, and then refashioned the steps to become their own. Whereas two-legged dancers had four taps with which to design their steps (a tap on the ball of each foot and a tap on the heel of each foot), Peg had only three contacts for the floor (a ball tap, a heel tap, and the peg). Every step he saw, he had to reinvent for this specification. And because his had a very deep and resonant tone, he was capable of producing intense rhythms that quite surpassed those created by many of the ace rhythm tap dancers of his time. In addition to his top-rate ability as a rhythm tap dancer, Peg Leg Bates was thoroughly accomplished in acrobatics, flash, legomania, and novelty repertoire, all of which he incorporated widely into his dancing. That Peg Leg Bates remains the leader in the category of one-legged tap dancers is a sentiment unchallenged by any of his peers. In fact, he figures in among the finest tap dancers ever to have lived.

PEG LEG BATES — I could not truthfully explain to you why or how I really started into dancing. I've been tap dancing since I was five years old, before I even knew that I was tap dancing. I used to tap dance barefoot, making noise with no shoes on at all! Not having any music, we would just clap our hands, and that's where the rhythm came from at that particular time.

See, I was born in a little town in South Carolina by the name of Fountain Inn. My father deserted my mother when I was three years old, and after that my mother had a pretty tough time taking care of me and her mother. We were sharecroppers raising cotton, corn, and vegetables. We were poor, very poor. Had to reach up to touch bottom.

When I was twelve years old, I started working in a cottonseed gin. This is 1918, during World War 1, when men was in service and women and children was working jobs of this caliber. This cottonseed gin was where they took cotton to a gin mill (not gin that you drink!), and they separated the seeds to be made into linseed oil and the cotton to be used for other purposes. There was an auger conveyer, which was like a giant corkscrew, that took the seeds from one building to another where they could be separated. One night around three o'clock in the morning, a light went out in the back. I'd only been working there for three days, and I went in the back to see why the light was out. Not knowing where I was going nor what I was doing, I stepped in the open conveyer. It started chewing my leg up. There was one other person in the building, and when he heard my screams, he ran over and stopped the machinery. The doctors looked at my leg, but

it was so badly mangled, the next day they amputated it about eight inches below the knee. That it was amputated below the knee was important, because if I didn't have the knee, I couldn't be on the peg leg.

After losing the leg, for some unknown reason, I still wanted to dance. At first, I was walking around on crutches, and I started making musical rhythm with them. Then my uncle made me a peg leg. I removed the crutches and started walking and dancing on the peg leg. I just wanted to dance. It was just something that I liked, and something that I wanted to do. And at school, the more active I was on the peg leg, the more compliments I got from my school chums. That was an encouraging factor. I went into sports, swimming, horseback riding, riding a bicycle, playing baseball—anything that anybody else did. See, I did not realize the importance of losing a leg. I thought it was just like stubbing my toe and knocking off a toenail that was going to grow back. Being a kid, and a dumb kid at that, I didn't realize the importance of losing my leg. And I guess that was helpful.

I never took a dancing lesson in my life. If I saw a two-leg dancer doing a step, I would copy that step. But I would do it with one leg, which made it look like an entirely different step than what the two-leg dancer was doing. And I loved novelty things. I loved to be up in the air! I loved a lot of legomania. I was very ambitious when I was dancing. And the reason for these different styles—the acrobatics, the rhythm, the legomania—was I wanted to be so good, I wanted to *surpass* the two-leg dancers! And in a lot of cases I did.

Well, I was around fifteen, and people started complimenting my tap dancing. I went into amateur shows, and I won every first prize! It was definitely encouraging. I liked it, I liked to hear the applause. Then I went into minstrel shows.

From minstrel shows I went to carnivals. And from carnivals to the T.O.B.A. I was with T.O.B.A. from 1922 until 1926. I came to New York through the roof of the T.O.B.A. During those years, the T.O.B.A. brought you to the large cities. T.O.B.A. was not only in the South. T.O.B.A. was Cleveland. T.O.B.A. was Pittsburgh. T.O.B.A was Philadelphia. T.O.B.A. was black theaters that played nothing but black performers. That's what the T.O.B.A. was. And it was through them that brought me to the Lafayette Theatre in New York, one of the most important black theaters in Harlem. While there, I was seen by Lew Leslie, who at that particular time was the producer of *Blackbirds of 1928*, and that started me on my career as a professional tap dancer. I went to Europe in 1929 with *Blackbirds*, where we played the Moulin Rouge for eleven months.

In those days, there were *dancers*. There were dancers, I'm talking about, that laid down some iron! And laid down some rhythm! There was a guy—he died before he really became known—Teddy Hale. And there was the team Buck and Bubbles, I knew them very well. Derby Wilson, Bill Bailey—he was Pearl Bailey's brother. And Baby Lawrence! Another guy that could lay down more rhythm, you couldn't believe it—Chuck Green. Those were all tap dancers that laid down iron. This was not novelty, not legomania. You saw it. It sounded good. It looked good. And made you feel good! That's what I'm talking about. There were some dancers that I knew that was dancers! Eddie Rector was something else. Now, I am referring to stylists. I'm talking about guys that had their own style. You didn't have to see them. Listening to the rhythm you knew exactly who that was. It's just like a singer that is a stylist. When you hear that voice, you don't have to see the person. You hear it. Tap dancers got their own language, just like singers got their own language. And the girl tap dancers! The best tap dancer among females that I've heard was Eleanor Powell. She could dance! I'll give you another one that could dance—taps, twist, turns—Ann Miller. Yes, there were some dancers out there! I'll tell you another guy, white guy, Steve Condos of The Condos Brothers. He can dance! Can lay down some iron. And this is the beauty of tap dancing that I have always found. I guess this is one of

Maurice of Chicago captures a dapper Peg Leg Bates while the dancer is on tour with *Connie's Inn—Hot Chocolate*. Connie's Inn along with the Cotton Club were two of Harlem's leading night spots in 1932.

the nice things about race relations in show business. If a white boy can dance, a black boy gives him credit: "Hey, that guy can dance! He can lay down some iron!" And anytime you hear a good tap dancer saying that about a white boy, that means that boy can dance!

Well, after *Blackbirds* closed, we left Paris and I went into vaudeville and nightclubs in the East. In vaudeville, I played the Keith and Loews Circuits and an independent circuit called Fanchon and Marco. I worked my way up to the top independent theaters like the Paramount, the Roxy, the Capitol, the Strand. And I played the great uptown Harlem clubs—Connie's Inn, the Cotton Club, Club Zanzibar.

It was during the 1930s that I first met up with Ed Sullivan. At that time he was a newspaper man, and he used to emcee the Harvest Moon Ballroom. They had amateur contests there, and he would take the winners on the Loews Circuit. At that particular time, I was booked from the William Morris office. He wanted a strong act to open his show, but he couldn't find anybody to really open the show, to get it off. So he got hold of the William Morris office. He had some friends in there, and asked them about an opening act. William Morris office said, "I got just the man for you. Got a man that, matter of fact, he is an opening act. Peg Leg Bates, a one-leg dancer." Ed hired me, saw to it that my salary was raised, and used to divulge his entire column to me! We played the Keith Circuit, the Loews Circuit.

Through the use of his peg, Peg Leg Bates introduced a strong Rhythm element to his dancing. Here he performs in a Loews Unit at the Roxy Theatre, 1935.

This was all around 1937, 1938.

In 1938, I went to Australia and played the Tivoli Circuit, their big-time vaudeville circuit. Unlike American vaudeville circuits, which only kept an act in a theater for one week or a split week, the Australians would keep a vaudeville show in one theater for five weeks at a time! I was in Australia for ten weeks, five weeks in Melbourne, and five weeks in Sydney. The Australians had no color barrier and were very fond of blacks. They showed strong appreciation for my talent, and I was always invited to their homes and to parties. Remember that was 1938, and I was the only black on the Tivoli. As a matter of fact, most all of my career I worked with white performers. Very few black revues I've been in. Mostly white. Even in vaudeville. And back then there were not

Peg Leg Bates dancing in the Los Angeles production of *Ken Murray's Blackouts*, 1948. Virtually airborne, Bates proves he not only challenged the two-legged dancers, he often surpassed them.

an awful lot of black people on the circuit. Most of it was white. It was just a situation that existed.

But, I am fortunate that I was able to do something with one leg and got the recognition from it. It was not a sympathetic thing. I was actually tap dancing! Actually laying down some iron. I'm thankful that I was blessed to be one of the main people in the tap dancing field, and in my category, the leader of dancing on the peg. There's no one to come near me. And I say that cocky. Because it's the truth. I don't know why, but nobody ever caught up with me. And there's been a lot that tried. I guess it was just 'cause I was just that good.

I rehearsed a lot. I'd get by myself and I would see how it sounded to *me*, not how it sounded to someone else, but how it would sound to *me*. I had to be satisfied with it myself. It had to be pure—it had to be foolproof. I was an ad-libber, but I had to have some set things. I had some novelty steps that I knew was going to get applause, and I would ad lib around that. If I saw that something was not working, then I threw in a couple of my steps that I knew was going to get applause.

I'm into rhythm. Well, I'm into rhythm and I'm into novelty. I'm into doing things that it looks almost impossible to do. I guess that's the best way that I can describe it. I loved the compliments. I loved the applause. And it all came through tap dancing . . . I think that's the best way that I can describe it.

Tap dancing was my life. Tap dancing is my life. Tap dancing will be my life the longest day I live.

November 13, 1988
Kerhonskon, New York

5

1920s REHEARSAL HALLS

GEORGE MURPHY

Got into show business by
accident and enjoyed the trip.

They had to practice somewhere, all those tap dancers. And they did—on rooftops, in basements, on street corners, in soda shops, and on empty stages. Any spot big enough to lay down a Shuffle became victim to a tap dancer's metal. But the best places of all to work on new material and really go crazy with it were the rehearsal halls. There were good wooden floors, a piano in the corner, and other dancers around to lend a few pointers. Tap dancers spent endless hours in these halls working on new routines to "simply slay 'em" and adding new steps to their repertoires that would "knock 'em in the aisles."

Michael's, Phil Waiman's, Johnny Nit's, Erving Plummer's—all of the rehearsal halls had atmosphere and all were different. Rental for one of these rooms in the 1920s would not cost over fifty cents an hour. A piano player accompanist cost a dollar an hour. A dancer could actually work for five hours for $7.50. If an act was not quite rolling in lucre at the time, they could skip the pianist and bring in a wind-up Victrola, or a radio. A lot of people just hummed.

Then there were the large rehearsal halls, where

all their melodies blended into one mad symphony.

George Murphy frequented rehearsal halls during the 1920s. It must have done him some good, because by the early 1930s, he was appearing in Broadway musicals, including *Roberta* (1933), and *Anything Goes* (Road show, 1935); and by the mid-1930s through the early forties he was a leading man in Hollywood musical films including *Little Miss Broadway* (1938), *Broadway Melody of 1940*, and *For Me and My Gal* (1942).

He started out as part of the dance team Johnson and Murphy and performed in nightclubs throughout New York during show business' vibrant years of the 1920s. In 1926, he appeared in London in his first musical show, *Good News*. In 1931, he was cast personally by George Gershwin in the Pulitzer Prize–winning show *Of Thee I Sing*, in which he played the role of Sam Jenkins. By 1934, this debonair performer had moved from stage musicals to appear in musical motion pictures, initially cast as a singer. One and a half years later, he was finally cast as a dancer, and dance he did—with some of the most delightful tap dancers to appear on the American screen: Fred Astaire, Eleanor Powell, Gene Kelly, and Shirley Temple. George Murphy danced with a light-hearted charm and appeal, graced with a controlled elegance that combined the movements of both tap and ballet.

lots of tap dancers practiced at one time, learned —and stole—from each other. If they wanted to work specifically on a new step they had seen, there were roving instructors who knew it all.

Then there were the "snake pits." These were large halls, forty feet wide by sixty feet long. They were separated and rented out as little alcoves. Anybody could use those alcoves—it was not restricted to dancers. But there was no shutting off from anything else. The cacophony of sounds that started out as the music that the act used for an accompaniment, ended up as so many varied sounds floating wildly overhead. There were snake charmers, magicians, jugglers, acrobatic acts, hoofers, ballet dancers. They all had their own little space, and

GEORGE MURPHY — I didn't enter show business, really. I just slipped in the side door. I was born in New Haven, Connecticut in 1902, and my father was a professional athletic

coach and trainer. So I grew up as an athlete. My dad died when I was eleven, and my mother died two years later. When I was twelve years old, I started to work in drug stores, places like that. I worked at everything.

Then I met a girl that I thought a great deal of, Juliet Johnson. She wanted to be a dancer. So I said, "Why don't we be a dance team?" because she had a job to go to in Florida with a show. She said, "If you get us a job as a dance team before the show goes, we'll be a dance team." I went around and watched other dancers and tried to copy them. Then we put together three dances. I made arrangements with a Chinese chop suey restaurant up on Ninety-third and Broadway [in New York], where he'd let us come and practice in the evening after dinner.

We got jobs dancing in nightclubs. The name of our team was Johnson and Murphy. We danced at the Montmartre in New York, which was the best nightclub in New York for about fifteen years. We also danced at the Central Park Casino for three years. We did a straight tap number. We used to use a waltz tune: Irving Berlin's "Always."

And everytime we took it out and changed it, we had to put it back. People would say, "What's that? We like that other song better." So we got to be good friends with Irving Berlin.

It was great dancing in the nightclubs, because you had the audience right up close and you knew right away whether you were getting over or not! And I learned one thing: Never go on later than twelve midnight—because that would give the audience time to go to the theaters, come back and have one drink, maybe two. If they've had the third drink, forget it. They don't want to be entertained. They want to entertain *you*. You get to be a human engineer. You have to understand your people. Of course, the Central Park Casino was great, because the same people would come back regularly. But then you'd go broke, because your dancing partner had to be dressed

George Murphy was already a tap dancing star on Broadway by the time he came to Hollywood in 1934. But it took nearly two years before the studios let him dance on film.

better than anybody in the room. By the time you paid for the costumes, you were lucky to break even!

In those days, fellows used to meet in doorways—you know, where there was a light—and they'd swap steps. This was around 1925, and you never knew who you were going to meet. You could pick up a lot of dancing there. Oh, and then there was a very important place called Michael's. Michael's was a dance hall. For a dollar you could stay as long as you wanted, and they would give you a locker and towel so you could take a shower afterwards. Anybody that wanted to be a dancer would go up there. It was a good place to work out. They had mirrors all around the hall, practice barres. And there was a fellow that would walk around, and you could ask him and he'd show you a step, or he would give you a little advice. That was Jimmy Cagney! He was kind of an instructor. He and his wife had a vaudeville act. Then, of course, when he came to Hollywood he was great.

Every Sunday night, we used to go up to the Cotton Club. A fellow named Danny Healy, another dancer from Boston, put on this show up there with Duke Ellington. It couldn't have been nicer. They had six black dancers. They called them The Six Birds of Rhythm, and I used to get up and dance with them at night. I'd be introduced and just get up and ad-lib with them. This was all during the twenties. Cab Calloway was a skinny little kid then.

During that time, I used to go and watch Jack Donahue. Jack was a big, tall, skinny Irish fellow from Boston. And he was a sensational dancer. He was a great star on Broadway with Marilyn Miller in the Ziegfeld shows. And he was a good friend of Johnny Boyle. Johnny Boyle was a great dancer from the waist down, from the waist up—nothing. Then there was a third fellow called Harlan Dixon. The three of those fellows put to-gether entertainment shows for the club members at the Lambs Club, an actors' club in New York. They did a tap routine to "Rhapsody in Blue," just the way Paul Whiteman's orchestra had scored and recorded it. One of the most sensational things I ever watched.

In 1926, Juliet and I went to London in the show called *Good News*. We were hired to do the "Varsity Drag." They didn't like the leading man, so they fired him and made me the leading man. Then, while we were in London, we danced at the Kit Kat Club, at the Café de Paris, and then finally at a place called the Mayfair Hotel. Mayfair was the best job, because they had an American orchestra. The American orchestras were, in those days, much better than the English orchestras. They had more rhythm.

I came back from that, and then the young fellow in a show called *Hold Everything* [1928] got married, so I got the job as leading man. Then I got a job in *Shoot the Works* [1931]. And then *Of Thee I Sing* [1931]. That was a great show—the best musical, I think, ever. It won the Pulitzer Prize. During all this time, we were able to make a living dancing. But just barely. The Crash affected show business, but it didn't hurt *Of Thee I Sing*. We didn't have an empty seat for eighty-six weeks. And the top price at the box office was five dollars and fifty cents. It's interesting how I got in the show. I was taken in a taxi by Louis Shurr, the famous agent, uptown to George Gershwin's apartment. There were about six people in the apartment, and I didn't know why I was there. I went out on the roof and played with his dog. Finally, they called me back in, and everybody had gone. Gershwin was there, and he said, "Do you sing?" And I said, "A little bit, not too

George Murphy and Eleanor Powell in a beautiful rare rehearsal shot taken during *Broadway Melody of 1938* (MGM)

much." And he said, "What do you sing?" And I said, "Well . . ." and picked out a song that he had written and sang about eight bars. He says, "That's OK. That's fine." He picked up the phone and he called another man and said, "OK, Sam, he's fine with me." So Louis Shurr says, "Come on." I said, "Where?" He says, "Never mind. Get in the cab." So we went down to the Music Box Theatre into Sam Harris's office and that's where I got the job in *Of Thee I Sing*. Sam said, "There's two parts. One part pays two hundred and fifty dollars a week. The other part pays a hundred and seventy-five. I'll put them together and pay you four hundred dollars." And I said, "OK, you got a deal." He said, "You want a contract?" I said, "Not unless you do." He said, "I'd rather just shake hands. That's the way I do business." He was a great man, Sam Harris.

The first picture I did in Hollywood was *Kid Millions* [1934]. I did a song with Ann Sothern. I wasn't allowed to dance in Hollywood for about a year and a half. I had been a dancer, but nobody would give me a job to dance. But when I did, I danced with the greatest. I did two pictures with Eleanor Powell, three with Judy Garland, one with Shirley Temple, one with Kelly, one with Astaire. You can imagine my nerve; first number I did with Eleanor Powell I said, "All your numbers look alike. Let's make them all look different." So she said, "Great." What was I doing? I did turns like a hockey player. You can imagine me trying to teach her how to do hockey turns!

Of course, Fred Astaire was the best dancer of all. He could do anything better than anybody else. I used to watch Fred every chance I'd get. Fred was a perfectionist. He would rehearse until the day after tomorrow. In the *Broadway Melody of 1940*, he said, "Let's rehearse some more." And I said, "Well Fred, you know, I think I'm rehearsed out, and I'm going to save my energy for when the cameras are running. And if they're looking at me instead of you, you ought to give back half of the money and two thirds of the billing!" I had met Fred many years earlier, in 1926, when I was in London for *Good News*. Fred and his sister Adele were over there in *Funny Face*. We lived in the same apartment house, and we used to get together every night after work. Adele was a character, a great comedienne. She wasn't as serious as Fred. She was just the same way as she was on the stage;

Shirley Temple and George Murphy dance to "We Should Be Together" from *Little Miss Broadway* (20th Century-Fox, 1938).

George Murphy visits Fred Astaire in costume on the RKO lot during Astaire's filming of *Swing Time* (RKO, 1936). Four years later the two hoofers worked together in *Broadway Melody of 1940* (MGM).

Three hoofers dressed to the hilt in *Broadway Melody of 1938* (MGM), Buddy Ebsen, Eleanor Powell, and George Murphy

1940

she couldn't be nicer, and a lot of fun.

Shirley Temple was great. She picked up things faster than anybody. Knew everybody's part in the script. Her mother used to read the script to her, and she'd memorize the whole thing. As soon as the shot was over, her mother would take her off to a little bungalow. None of that stage mother adulation nonsense that happens. And so she was a great little gal. When we worked together on *Little Miss Broadway* [1938], I said to her, "Shirley, you know, a lot of the dances that you do look like the one you just did. Let's make them look different. Let's have you dance like a grown-up." And I said, "We'll get a table, and you dance on the table, and I'll put my arms around you." Well, she thought that was sensational. And we did that in "We Should Be Together." And then there was the song that had the lyric "I'll build a Broadway for you . . ." So I said, "We'll build it." And we made Times Square, a little set in a courtroom, to look like Times Square. Oh, Shirley was great to work with.

When I was in pictures, I was asked what I eventually wanted to do. I said, "I'd like to be a producer and I'd take charge of all the musical numbers. And I'll take ten percent of what I could save the studio as my salary." I was told that I was crazy, because I would own the studio in two years! But, it was true. As a matter of fact, once I walked in on the set, and I had a diagram that I showed to this director, Roy Del Ruth. He said, "Let Murphy shoot the number." I think he was being sarcastic. But I said, "OK, I will." So I did, and we got it done in no time. And years later, Eddie Mannix, who was number-two man at the studio, said, "Murphy will sometimes argue with you about the script and the lines, but don't pay too much attention to him because he's generally right." I used to get in trouble with the writers. The writers were dealing with a spoken word; the spoken word was one thing, the written word is another thing.

In the 1940s, I was part of a royal command performance in London. I was kind of the leader of the group. There was Ann Sothern, Errol Flynn, two or three others. In any event, I was the first one on the stage. And I looked down as I came down the stairs; they had carpeted the stage! I said, "Your Majesty. I've had some success as a Soft Shoe dancer. But they've carpeted the stage. So with your Majesty's permission, you will see the softest Soft Shoe dance that's ever been done." And they had the big BBC orchestra, forty men in the pit. I doubt they could hear any taps. But I could have danced all night.

===

You know, I've only missed two years of this century. What a life I've had. It's been a beauty. Got into show business by accident and enjoyed the trip.

September 19, 1988
Cashiers, North Carolina
(Died May 3, 1992)

(*Left*) Eleanor Powell and George Murphy from *Broadway Melody of 1940* (MGM). The brilliant teaming of Fred Astaire with these two elegant artists resulted in some of the most enchanting tap work seen in film.

1930
–1939

The 1930s saw the country fall headlong into the Great Depression. One third of the nation's people lived in abject poverty. On many city street corners apple sellers attempted to earn a few meager pennies to survive another day. And on other corners, some were doing a bit better—tap dancers. Because, despite the economic collapse, the country still had rhythm, and some of its greatest pedal exponents came off the streets and went into the dance studios, onto the stage, and on the silver screen.

Anyone who spent time at the movies during the thirties might never have guessed that the nation was down and out. Most screen productions were filled with a rich array of glamour, drama, music, and, of course, dance. Throughout the 1930s, Hollywood's brand of Heaven on Earth provided eighty-five million people a week with an escape from their lives. In the celluloid paradise fashioned by Hollywood, some of the purest bits of delight were the musicals. Movie stars like Fred Astaire and Ginger Rogers, Bill Robinson, Shirley Temple, and Eleanor Powell brought an indulgence of entertainment, evening-gown elegance, and happy endings to their vast audiences.

Though vaudeville was beginning to run its course by the 1930s, lavish shows still accompanied the silver screen spectaculars, and provided eager audiences with a tremendous variety of music, comedy, and dance. In addition to vaudeville, tap dancers could work in a large variety of live venues—in nightclubs and with swing bands.

Tap dancing during the 1930s was running full speed ahead.

THE COTTON CLUB

THE NICHOLAS BROTHERS

Everyone was ravin' over us at the Cotton Club. They saw these new little guys, and they were amazed.

Harlem in the 1920s and 1930s was the most prosperous black community in the United States. This uptown district of Manhattan was also an area bursting with hope, gaiety, and the new phenomenon called jazz. Every Friday night Lenox Avenue transformed into the Easter Parade. Gorgeous women in elegant gowns, jewels, and furs, with marcel waves in their hair, strolled arm in arm with handsome men dressed to the hilt in the snappiest of tuxedos, white silk scarves, high hats, canes, patent leather shoes, and patent leather hair. The fashionable set drove up and down the streets in their magnificent shiny cars, cars that were more works of art than mere machinery. The sleek of Art Deco and speed of jazz set the scene for the era. The innate rhythm of the city was the heartbeat of Harlem. And from 1923 to 1936, the Cotton Club was the hottest night spot there, the one place that epitomized the frenzy of the day. If you were white, it was *the* place to go. If you were black, it was *the* show to be *in*.

The Cotton Club was located on the corner of 142nd Street and Lenox Avenue, right in the midst of Harlem. The doors first opened in 1923, and the place was an instant success. The formula was simple: A riotous revue of the top black dancers, singers, comics, and jazz orchestras; whites only permitted to see the show; blacks only in the show. It worked. Whites from downtown arrived nightly by the thousands to see the bands of Duke Ellington, Cab Calloway, Jimmie Lunceford. They went to listen to such famous singers as Ethel Waters, Lena Horne, the Dandridge Sisters, June Richmond. They came for tap dancers such as The Four Step Brothers, Bill Robinson, The Berry Brothers, Tip, Tap and Toe. The Cotton Club presented, in the vernacular of the day, a "socko" show.

The Cotton Club was owned and operated by gangsters in the midst of Prohibition. The elite of New York society were ushered into the club night after night, risking arrest so they might witness firsthand the "New Negro" music-and-dance scene. The Cotton Club shows were filled with exoticism, a wild explosion of creativity that could only be

experienced in Harlem. The show had such a dazzling magnitude of talent, that leading Broadway and movie stars packed the club every night.

It is easy to say that the entire show consisted of show-stopping acts. But there was one act in the Cotton Club that literally stopped the show every night—just a couple of little boys known as The Nicholas Brothers. And, could these kids dance! What set The Nicholas Brothers apart from other child acts of the day was that they danced, not with the awkward charm of innocent children, but with the grace, agility, and sophistication of the top adult tap acts. The Nicholas Brothers met the challenge of the Jazz Age and thoroughly enchanted and thrilled audiences with their charismatic dancing.

Fayard and Harold continued stopping the show at the Cotton Club from 1932 through 1935, and from 1936 (when the Cotton Club moved downtown to Broadway and Forty-eighth in the heart of the Great White Way) until 1939, when the club closed its doors for good. Throughout the thirties, the Cotton Club was The Nicholas Brothers' home base between appearances in Hollywood movies, Broadway and London shows, vaudeville, and coast-to-coast national radio.

Unlike most black dancers, The Nicholas Brothers were invited to appear extensively in film, dancing in more than fifty movies, including *Pie, Pie Blackbird* (1932), *Kid Millions* (1934), *The All-Colored Vaudeville Show* (1935), *The Big Broadcast of 1936* (1935), *Down Argentine Way* (1940), *Tin Pan Alley* (1940), *Sun Valley Serenade* (1941), and *The Pirate* (1948). The epitome of their work has been preserved forever in the 1943 20th Century-Fox movie *Stormy Weather*. In this film Fayard and Harold were an explosion of dance. They incorporated their fast-

The Nicholas Brothers uptown at the Cotton Club. By the time this shot was taken, Fayard (left) and Harold (right) had been working professionally for five years (New York City), 1935.

paced tap with unbelievable leaps—flying over one another in full split (as opposed to a "jive" split that most of the tap dancers of the day were performing) down a series of huge white stairs, jumping rhythmically back up the stairs, then sliding in the splits down two separate ramps, and ending this breathtaking routine with an exuberant bow and run-off exit. To see this number is to understand their style, the excitement they generated through their dance, and, most important, their individual contribution to the legacy of tap dance.

FAYARD NICHOLAS — My father and mother were the leaders of their own band, Nicholas' Collegians. It was a vaudeville pit band, and my mother played piano and my father played drums. They traveled all over the country and ended up in Philadelphia. Now, the story goes that my parents sat me in the audience during their shows. No, they didn't sit me in the audience, I sat *myself* in the audience!

I would come from school every day and listen to them as they played, and I would watch the performers onstage. These were some of the great acts of the 1920s: Louis Armstrong, Buck and Bubbles, Adelaide Hall, Leonard Reed and Willie Bryant. Oh, many, many different celebrities. The first dancers I remember seeing at the Standard Theatre in Philadelphia were Reed and Bryant. They were the first great influence on me as a dancer. Willie Covan had an act called The Four Covans. The first time I saw Willie Covan and The Four Covans, they were in a film called *On With the Show* with Ethel Waters [1929]. They impressed me so much the way they danced. The four of them looked so good up there on that screen. At that time I still don't think I heard about Fred Astaire. I had heard about Bill Robinson.

When I finally saw Bill Robinson, he was doin' a benefit at a theater in Philadelphia called the Lincoln Theatre. They had many, many entertainers who were performin' at this benefit. They introduced Bill Robinson. He came out on the stage. And he started talkin' about how he didn't feel well, because he had four teeth extracted. And he was angry about what was goin' on backstage. So, he started talkin' about the people backstage. He finally got into his dance. And do you know, he did not impress me at all! I guess it was because he didn't feel well. Everybody talkin' about the great Bill Robinson. He didn't move me. He didn't move me at all.

Then, in 1930, I saw *Dixiana* this motion picture that he was in. The orchestra was playin', and all of the sudden he went into his dance. They had a long shot of him, and he was way up on the top of a flight of stairs. Those steps looked like they was a mile long! And he came down and tapped on each one of those steps. All the way down. As he got down, he did his little break. And then he smiled. That wonderful smile. Now, that's the Bill Robinson I been hearin' about! That's the Bill Robinson! When I saw him in that motion picture, that did it for me, that's when I fell in love with him.

I was just taken by the whole of show business right when I was a little boy. I loved all the music and loved the entertainers onstage. I used to say,

"My, they're having fun up there! I would like to be doing something like that." There was a guy—his name was Jack Wiggins—and he had a famous step that he invented called the Tango Twist. He did a split—goin' down and comin' up. So, I tried that. I did it the first time, and it worked out all right. I was a limber little guy! Do you know, I was doing splits before I became a professional. I used to just walk down the street and jump over a fireplug or something into a split!

So, just by watchin' other entertainers, I taught myself how to perform. Then I taught my sister Dorothy and then my brother Harold. We got a little act together, and we called ourselves The Nicholas Kids. But, my sister, she couldn't keep the late hours—nine P.M., she'd had it! So, we told her, "Go on, finish school. Let us do the work."

From the start, my father was a great influence on me. He said to me one day while I was dancing, "Son, that's fine. You do it very well. But don't do what the other people do. Do your own thing." And he said, "Here's another thing—don't look down at your feet when you're dancin'. Look out at the audience, because they are the ones that you're entertainin'. Smile. And enjoy it. Have fun." And my father said, "There's another thing I like that you do." "What is that, Dad?" I asked. "I like the way you use your hands. That adds a lot to your dancing." I said, "Well, OK, Dad!"

I started dancin' in the late twenties. But us kids started professionally in 1930, when I was about eleven years old. That was when we were in Philadelphia, and we performed at the Standard Theatre where my parents worked. I think my little brother was seven. We were real young—little kids when we started. But we danced like men! We played all the other theaters in Philadelphia: the Warner Brothers Theatre, the Lincoln Theatre, the Pearl Theatre.

It was at the Pearl Theatre that Schiffman, the manager of Harlem's big-time black theater, the Lafayette, came over to see us. Schiffman was hearin' so much about The Nicholas Kids. Everybody was talkin' about us—in Baltimore, Philadelphia, Washington, D.C. He heard about these Nicholas brothers who were stopping the show everywhere they would go. Nobody could follow them. That was the talk *all over* New York.

The Nicholas Brothers take New York by storm, 1935.

"Who the hell are these Nicholas brothers? I got to go see them!" He came backstage after he saw the show and knocked on the door of our dressing room. My father greeted him. "I've heard so much about your sons. They're famous in New York before they get there! I'd like to put them in my theater in New York."

Now, during this time, everyone still called us The Nicholas Kids. Like when we played in Philadelphia it was The Nicholas Kids. When we played in Baltimore, Maryland, The Nicholas Kids. But when we arrived in New York City, The Nicholas Brothers!

We opened in the Cotton Club in 1932. Mind you, this was just a short time being in show business. Most of the time you had to be in it for *years* and *years* before you became stars, but we were little stars in 1932! Everyone was ravin' over us at the Cotton Club. All the Broadway stars would come to the Cotton Club. Movie stars would come to the Cotton Club. They saw these new little guys, The Nicholas Brothers, and they were amazed. We always closed the show, we closed the show everywhere. Nobody could follow us. Stopped the show every night! Yeah, they called us The Show Stoppers. In those days everybody had some kind of name: Bill Robinson was "The World's Greatest Tap Dancer"; The Nicholas Brothers were "The Show Stoppers!"

At the time, there were strict child labor laws in New York. But at the Cotton Club? There was *no* child labor law! Those laws didn't affect us at all, because the gangsters owned the Cotton Club, and they were runnin' it! We were dancin' until five o'clock in the morning. It's so funny, because it was all over the newspapers that we were working there. Everybody read it. We weren't allowed to work at the Paramount or any other legitimate theater in town. But the Cotton Club, we could work there. I guess the gangsters were payin' the policemen, so nothing was said. It was just never brought up!

Dan Healy was the producer of the Cotton Club show. After the show, he would come out on the stage as the master of ceremonies and introduce all the celebrities who were in the audience at the Cotton Club: Tallulah Bankhead, George Raft, Charlie Chaplin, Gloria Swanson, Harold Lloyd, The Marx Brothers, Al Jolson. All these wonderful entertainers of those beautiful years.

I told my manager, "Gee I'd love to meet these people," 'cause I had seen them in movies. He said, "Go on out there." So, after the show we would go over to their tables and sit with them, talk with them and have our little orange juice. Every night we would do that. I guess you would call us the pioneers. No other black entertainers did that—go out and sit with the audience. The other people in the show would peek through the curtain to see how we were doin'. See, we could go out there, but they couldn't. When I start thinkin' about it, it was because we were kids.

Black people couldn't come to see the show. And it was in Harlem! Couldn't come to see their own people. Isn't that crazy! The only people who could come there were people like Bill Robinson, Ethel Waters, Jack Johnson, Joe Louis . . . but when they were there, they didn't even sit ringside, they sat *way* over in the corner. They were in there, but they weren't seated where everyone else was seated!

There was a number that my brother did at the Cotton Club, an impression of Cab Calloway. Cab, he loved the way my brother did it. Now, when Cab sang "Minnie the Moocher," they had a microphone that came from the ceiling. It would come down and Cab could sing and dance about

This fabulous Art Deco-style sheet music cover does not quite get the Nicholas Brothers' name right, 1935.

started, my brother and I would be onstage. The radio announcer would say, "And now ladies and gentlemen, here's the taps of The Nicholas Brothers. The show is still on. The Nicholas Brothers will do their act, and then you will hear the finale, and then Cab Calloway will do his regular broadcast." That happened *every* night.

We played the Cotton Club two years before going to Hollywood to do *Kid Millions* [1934] with Eddie Cantor. Seymour Felix was the dance director on the picture. He did all the chorus scenes, but he didn't show us anything. Not one step. So you see, we were our own choreographers. We didn't get screen credit—but *we* did it. We were too young to know about credits then!

It was wonderful working with Eddie Cantor. We had fun with him, Ethel Merman, Ann Sothern, and George Murphy. And Lucy Ball. She was just in the chorus, but she was the same way then as she is now. That was in 1934! Same exactly. With all that personality and everything. One day during the filming of *Kid Millions*, we were sittin' outside between takes and she came over to us. She had a little dog. We were sittin' down on the grass, so she sat down on the grass with us. My brother said, "Oooh, what a nice little dog!" She said, "You like it?" He said, "Yes." She said, "It's yours." And she gave him that dog. But, listen to this, *I* had to take care of the dog!

After *Kid Millions*, we went back to the Cotton Club. That was always our home during the 1930s.

freely. But my brother couldn't reach it. He was so little! So, Cab had the waiters or the busboys bring out a table and put it right there on the stage. And he'd lift my little brother onto this table so he could sing into this microphone! Harold sang *"Hi-dee hi-dee hi-dee-ho,"* just like Cab. And Cab would beam. Everyone sang along with him. Even Cab was singin'! "Hi-dee hi-dee hi-dee-ho." And naturally, I would sing it, too. And the band. And the people in the audience. It stopped the show every night. Word got around that my brother was doin' this impression of Calloway, and we couldn't get off the stage until that happened.

The Cotton Club was our first big engagement. I remember Cab Calloway did a radio show there every night. Right from the Cotton Club it was broadcast all over the country. When the program

Every six months the Cotton Club introduced a new show, and all the entertainment columnists came up to the club to review the show. Walter Winchell, Louis Sobol, and Ed Sullivan were the big critics then, and they didn't miss an opening. So naturally, we got to know them. During those years Ed Sullivan had a daily column in the New York *Daily News*. He wrote about show business, radio, night clubs, movies, scandals! He used to write about us in his column all the time. During one of the Cotton Club openings in 1935, I told him we were going to Hollywood to be in *The Big Broadcast of 1936*. He said, "When you get to Hollywood, I want you to stop by and see a good friend of mine—Fred Astaire." Well, I was thrilled! I thought Astaire was terrific. I had seen all of his movies. Then Ed Sullivan said, "And I'll write a note of introduction for you to Fred, and you can take it with you." The minute we got to Hollywood, we called Astaire's secretary and we told her that we would like very much to meet him, and we told her about Sullivan's note. We could hear some talking on the other end of the wire, and then she came back and said, "How about today?" Astaire was right there with the secretary!

Astaire was in the midst of dubbing his taps for *Top Hat* over at RKO. We arranged it with the secretary that we would meet him in the dubbing studio. So we went there and watched him. After he was finished, he came up and greeted us. We shook hands with him and asked if he would come outside with us and do a little Time Step. Mother had her movie camera and filmed us pretending we were directing him and showing him some steps! I told him how good I thought he looked with Ginger Rogers. He just said, "Uh huh."

No comments, nothing, just "uh huh." She wasn't the greatest tap dancer in the world, not like some of the other ladies he danced with, but she was box office with him. You know what Katharine Hepburn said—"Ginger gave Fred sex appeal, and he gave her class."

The first time we ever had our picture taken with Astaire was years later, and I remember Astaire said, "At last I'm with *the brothers*!" We did a little dance pose for the shot, and then he said to the newspaper photographer, "I want a copy of that one!" You might have called it a real mutual admiration society.

Well, after *The Big Broadcast of 1936*, we returned to New York. In 1936, we performed on Broadway in *The Ziegfeld Follies* and after that headed over to Europe for the first time to appear in *Lew Leslie's Blackbirds of 1936* in London's Gaiety Theatre. We loved being in London. Can you imagine, we saw three kings! Then we came back to this country to the Cotton Club. And then *Babes in Arms* [stage show, 1937]. We had roles in *Babes in Arms*. Our choreographer was George Balanchine. It had a wonderful score composed by Richard Rodgers and Larry Hart, with songs like "The Lady is a Tramp," "Where or When," "My Funny Valentine," "Johnny One Note." All hit songs. All beautiful songs. But the song they had *us* sing and dance to was *never* a hit—it was called "All Dark People Is Light on Their Feet" [All Dark People]! On opening night, my mother said, "Don't sing 'All dark people *is* light on their feet,' sing, 'All dark people *are* light on their feet'!" So, we did that opening night. After the show the stage manager told us, "Hey, that's not the right way! Say '*is*' light on their feet, not '*are*' light on their feet." "Well," I said, "that's the way I talk!"

When we worked for George Balanchine in *Babes in Arms*, we were also doubling at the Cotton Club. During rehearsal Balanchine watched us as we performed. When we did certain things,

Harold Nicholas, a very young tap dancing Bob Hope, and Fayard Nicholas in a number from *Ziegfeld Follies of 1936* (New York City).

In 1936, Lew Leslie once again took his *Blackbirds* over to London, this time accompanied by the sensational Nicholas Brothers.

Harold (left) and Fayard (right) Nicholas as featured in *The Great American Broadcast* (20th Century-Fox), 1941

like when my brother would slide through my legs in a full split, he'd say, "Hey, I like that!" He fixed it so that eight girls were standing like that and my brother slid right through their legs! He would think of these things, see? Without even showin' us, he would say, "Now, this is what I would like to see." It worked out well. That's how he made up the routine, just talkin' to us. Not showin' us anything.

Our type of dancing we called "classical tap." I'll try to explain that. When we tapped, we added a little ballet to it, plus a little eccentric, a little flash, and we used our hands a great deal. With style and grace we used the whole body from our heads down to our toes. And that's why we called our type of dancing classical tap. That's what it is—the lacing together of tap, balletic leaps and turns, and dazzling acrobatics. You put it all together and it's The Nicholas Brothers! It's not a "white style" and it's not a "black style." When you look at The Nicholas Brothers, you're looking at classical tap.

There were so many different styles of tap dancing during our time: Buck and Wing, rhythm, comic, flash, legomania, improvisation. . . . All the dancers had their own style. And all the dancers were great. But I wouldn't call any one of these great dancers the "world's greatest tap dancer." And I'll tell you why. Because *each* one of them had their own style. And I wouldn't compare any of them. And when I see any of these dancers, I'm looking at *them* entertainin' *me*. At *that* moment *that* dancer is the world's greatest tap dancer!

Like Bill "Bojangles" Robinson. Well, Bill Robinson had his particular style where he'd dance on his toes most of the time. He'd come down on his heels, but most of the time he's on his toes. He could do the simplest little step that you ever saw and get a big hand. Someone else did that, nothin' would happen. But he had this personality. I loved to watch him when he was dancin'. A little step and he'd go, *ta ta ta ta*—which was *so* simple, but the way he did it, it made it important up on that stage. And people would just go, "Wow! What a dancer!" He never missed a tap. He was so clear. And as you may know he wore wooden soles on his toes and on the heel. It's a funny thing, when he first met us, he fell in love with us right away. We were very young at that time. And we said to him, "Let's do something together." We called him "Uncle Bo," and we were his "nephews." He taught us one of his soft shoe numbers. Whenever we played a benefit with him, say, at the Madison Square Garden in New York, he'd call us up on the stage and we'd do this Soft Shoe with him. He got us some of those shoes with the wooden soles and the wooden heels. We tried to dance in them, but we couldn't make it—we were so used to the metal taps. But long as we were dancin' with him, it was all right, because it was a nice type of soft shoe that we did with him.

John Bubbles was another tap dancer who was crazy about us. Remember the team Buck and Bubbles? Well, some of the time they would do the Cotton Club shows with us. And they would take the Cotton Club show from uptown and bring it downtown to the Capitol Theatre on Broadway in New York City. They'd bring the *whole* revue. Bubbles would sing and dance, Buck played the piano, and they did comedy. They were a real variety team. Afterward, I would go to their dressing room and tell them how much I enjoyed their

act, 'cause not only were they great singers and dancers, they were great *entertainers*. When I first saw Bubbles dance, I was so amazed, because his was a new type of tap dancin'. Most dancers only danced on their toes. He brought this heel beat into tap dancin'—rhythm and syncopation! It was really something. Bubbles had this style, and even dancers like Fred Astaire were greatly influenced by him. What you used to see Fred Astaire do in the movies, Bubbles had done long before. When Fred Astaire would strut, the style he had when he would walk, or twirl his cane, or kind of tip his hat—he got a lot of that from John Bubbles.

Now, Ray Bolger had a style completely all his own, 'cause he was tappin' and clownin' at the same time! There's a thing that he did—the split. He would go down and go down and he go all the way down, and then he couldn't get up. He would push and push. He would get up so far, and then *whop*, he'd drop back down again. And he would say, "Oh my goodness." So he tried again, and he'd be laughin'—oh he was laughin' and all of the sudden he would drop back down again! He'd push and push, and he'd finally get up. Then he would dance around again! Oh you should've seen the way he did that. He was a master of incorporating tap and comedy. But he could be serious and dance with a lady, just like Fred Astaire did, and really do a good job. But, when people think of him, they always think of him doin' comedy.

The electric energy of the Nicholas Brothers is clearly in evidence as Fayard flies above brother Harold in their trademark move—the split. Paris, France, 1947.

The Berry Brothers were the greatest of the flash dancers. They danced with canes, and that was an art in itself. There was Ananias, James, and Warren. Ananias was the oldest one of the three and really the stylist of that team, because he did a Strut that was so polished. He was magnificent. Let me explain a Strut: You have your cane, and you're dressed in a full-dress suit with a high hat. And you would walk. You ever see a chicken strut when he walks? Something like that. You kick one leg up, and then you kick the other one up. And then you slide back. And then you do a spin, and you stop right there. And then maybe you do a little split. And then for your exit, you have your cane under your arm, and you tip your head back, and take your hat up like that and kind of wave it, and go off.

Hal Leroy had the rubber legs! He tapped with his legs flyin' all over the place. It was so fantastic to watch him. I'd say, "How can he have his legs goin' like that and still tap?" And, man, could he tap. In between all that legomania stuff was some fantastic rhythm. He was one of the few white tap dancers to become a member of the Hoofers Club! As a matter of fact, Bill Robinson was the one who brought him up to Harlem to join!

One tap dancer who came along after all the other great dancers were established was Teddy Hale. He had all that rhythm and syncopation in his feet. But do you know, I never saw him do the same show twice, even if he was appearin' at the Apollo Theatre in New York and was doin' let's say five shows a day. I remember one time sittin' in the theater and being so amazed seein' this man as he was goin' through his act. I stayed for the next show, and he did a different dance altogether! He was an improvisation dancer. Like a drummer. I watched him for *five* shows; each show was different. And to the same music! He was makin' up the dance as he was goin' along! At the time he was doing that most other dancers were doing set choreography, set routines that were written to music. But Teddy Hale could play anything! You could just beat on the table, and he'd dance, just do anything—and always look good!

So you see, all the dancers had their own style. And all the dancers were great. So you see why I say, when I'm watchin' a particular dancer, *that's* the world's greatest dancer.

When I first saw myself on that big screen, I said to my mother and father and my sister and brother, "Wow, I didn't know I looked that good!" See, 'cause I had always been performin' and people were always lookin' at me. It was a thrill. I mean, I was a movie buff from day one. And then suddenly there we were, *we* were in motion pictures. We had became a part of all that like the other stars: The Nicholas Brothers!

June 4, 1988
Woodland Hills, California

FRED ASTAIRE'S CHOREOGRAPHER

HERMES PAN

Boy, we thought the same way.
His rhythms were almost identical
with mine.

Anyone who has ever seen Fred Astaire dance knows firsthand what a unique style of elegance, charm, and grace he brought to movies. But, Astaire did much more than just bring this artistry to films. When he came to Hollywood in 1933, he revolutionized the movie musical forever.

With the popularity of talking motion pictures in the late 1920s, there was a mad rush in Hollywood to produce musical photoplays. Initially, movie musicals were filmed directly from stage productions from the theater audience's perspective. With straight-on shots from a single camera angle, cameramen mixed, without restraint, "cutaways." A cutaway from the dancer might focus on someone else watching the dance, another shot to the dancer's feet, to the dancer's face, back to the person watching, back to the dancer's feet, off to the chorus, and finally, with dizzying finality, back to the dancer. Consequently, dances were never filmed in their entirety.

As the movie musical progressed from the late twenties to the early thirties, so did the ingenuity of those individuals behind the camera. New musical stories were created and filmed. Top dance directors and dancing stars were lured off the stages of Broadway and onto the soundstages of Hollywood. Creative geniuses such as Busby Berkeley

Hermes Pan not only set the dances for numerous pictures, he often found himself appearing in cameo dance spots. In this publicity shot from *Moon Over Miami* (20th Century-Fox), he takes Betty Grable for a delightful whirl, 1941.

delivered musical extravaganzas filmed with a variety of new and exciting camera angles. Oftentimes, these sequences involved no dancing whatsoever, rather, the dynamic movement of great numbers of dancers through a series of fascinating geometric formations. *Footlight Parade* (1933), *42nd Street* (1933), *Gold Diggers of 1933* (1933), and *Dames* (1934) were just a few examples of films packed with Berkeley's classic work.

Fred Astaire was in the midst of a successful Broadway career as a musical comedy star when he decided to go out to Hollywood and try his luck in movies. He had started dancing professionally at the age of six along with his older sister Adele, and they enjoyed a terrific success. When Adele retired from the stage in the early 1930s, Fred continued performing without his sister, and it was during this time that the movie musical was rapidly picking up steam. In 1933, Fred was called out to Hollywood to appear in the MGM picture *Dancing Lady*, in which he partnered a very young Joan Crawford. In his second picture, *Flying Down to Rio* (1933), Astaire was joined by Hermes Pan to create the dance numbers, and it was during the filming of this picture that they carried the movie musical a gigantic leap forward.

Hermes Pan was born in Memphis, Tennessee on December 10, 1910. In 1933, Pan got through the doors of RKO pictures, and was assigned as dance-director assistant to Dave Gould. Like Berkeley, Gould was a mover of dancers, and like Berkeley, was not a dancer himself. Pan's first task was to assist Fred Astaire in *Flying Down to Rio*. They met—and when they danced they found their styles matched exactly, and that their respective geniuses simply sparked one another's. It was not surprising that their styles were such a perfect match. During the 1920s, both dancers had been greatly influenced by black rhythm dancers: Pan learned tap dancing from a black youngster, and Astaire absorbed and added to his style from the likes of the great John Bubbles. They brought this style to film and embellished it with total body movement. This was a first. Previously the movie-going public had primarily seen the style of Buck and Wing tap dancing in films.

From their very first film together, Astaire and Pan insisted on full-frame shots involving absolutely no cutaways. They maintained that dance must be filmed in its entirety, and this was true genius. For the first time in motion picture history, the audiences were fully experiencing dances—the movement, the rhythm, and the style of the artists. Using this format, Hermes Pan and Fred Astaire created some of the best-loved tap dances ever to hit the screen.

Pan continued to work with Astaire throughout the Astaire-Rogers series. In 1938, Pan won an Academy Award for his work on *A Damsel in Distress*. When the RKO Astaire-Rogers liaison came to an end in 1939 after nine pictures (the trio were teamed

FRED ASTAIRE'S CHOREOGRAPHER

together once more in MGM's 1949 film *The Barkleys of Broadway*), Pan went on to choreograph for countless other dancers, and appeared on the screen himself, dancing with such stars as Betty Grable and Rita Hayworth.

H E R M E S   P A N — I always liked to dance when I was a kid. I particularly liked black rhythms. There was a black boy older than I was who worked for the family. He used to teach me all kinds of tap steps, so my rhythms became strictly black. The style of Buck and Wing dancing was always foreign to me, because I used my whole foot—my heel and toe and flat foot. In fact, I never thought of myself as a tap dancer; I thought of myself as a rhythm dancer.

When I was in my early teens, my father died. My mother, my sister, and I went to New York, and as things sometimes happen, we suddenly found that we were broke. There I was, about thirteen years old and living in a strange new city, so I got a job as an errand boy. Finally, when I was about sixteen, I got my first job in the "entertainment" field—in a speakeasy dancing the Charleston, the Black Bottom and playing the ukulele. A terrible place for a kid, an after-hours joint called Boeuf sur le Toit. Gangsters used to hang out there with their molls. It was a high-class place, but it wasn't a place for a sixteen-year-old boy! I didn't even go to work until ten or eleven in the evening, and didn't finish until about four in the morning. I worked there during Prohibition, and every time the police raided it, I was hidden. That I was a minor working in there was a much more serious offense than the fact that the liquor law was being broken!

Then somebody told me they were having a call for dancers for *My Maryland*, a vaudeville show. I answered the call. But it was for singers. So I started to leave, but my friend said, "Why don't you just try out—sing a scale." So I said, "All right. Nothing to lose." I got in line, did a few notes, and they said, "fine." I just happened to fit in with the voice range. So my first job on stage was as a singer!

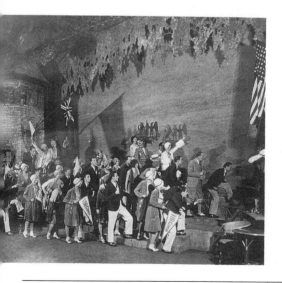

Top Speed was Hermes Pan's first Broadway role in a dancing chorus and Ginger Rogers's Broadway debut. They met again in Hollywood several years later, he as dance director, she as partner and costar with Fred Astaire (Pan, fourth from right), 1928.

After *My Maryland*, I got a job with the Marx Brothers in *Animal Crackers* [stage show, 1928]. I was still singing then, but I was dying to be a dancer. During those different shows, I learned by watching dancers. Between shows I would practice the dancing I had seen and just taught myself tap, rhythm, and all kinds of dancing. Then I got in *Top Speed* [1929], where I finally got to dance, even though it was just in the chorus. Incidentally, this was Ginger Rogers's first show.

I have to admit, I had trouble dancing in the chorus, because I never wanted to do the set routine. In fact, I got kicked out of that last show because I was changing some of the steps. The stage manager obviously wanted me to do just what was set. When I did it "my way," that didn't go too well with the production. I guess it was the choreographer coming out in me!

When I got kicked out of the show, my family moved to California. I went to all the casting calls, sometimes Busby Berkeley's, but he seemed to have his pets—"You, you, you, and you. All right, the rest of you go home." It was a pretty rough period. In 1930, I finally got a job in a Tab Show called *Cushman's Garden of Glorious Girls*. This production was a series of one-night-stand shows that played small towns, and I got a job putting

A publicity gag photo has Fred Astaire and Hermes Pan working out a little simple choreography for *Roberta* (RKO, 1934).

FRED ASTAIRE'S CHOREOGRAPHER

on the dances. That show closed in 1933, and I came back to California.

Somebody told me that Dave Gould was looking for an assistant for a movie he was doing called *Flying Down to Rio* [1933] over at RKO Pictures. You know, in those days, dance instructors hardly ever danced. Berkeley couldn't dance. They were mostly cameramen who staged top shots of girls in formation, or on top of pianos, or playing violins. Anything but dancing. *Flying Down to Rio* was Fred Astaire's second picture and his first with Ginger Rogers.

I got the job with Dave Gould as his assistant the same day he interviewed me. He said, "Well, Fred Astaire's up on Stage A. Why don't you go up and see if you can be of some help to him." I was terrified! After all, Astaire was an internationally famous dancer. So, I went in *very* timidly, introduced myself and said, "I just thought maybe I could be of some help to you." And he said, "Well, I'm working on a routine, but it's not finished. Would you like to see it?" I said "I'd love to." He called the pianist over and went through this half-routine. Then he said, "Well, I'm stuck here. I need a break at this point." Right on the spot I happened to think of one. It was a simple one, but he said, "I like that. Do it again." And he used it! Later I said to myself, "If the great Astaire can use one of my steps, maybe I'm not so bad after all!"

From then on, whenever Astaire was going into a picture at RKO, he would always say, "Where's Pan?" You see, when I'd first met him he said, "What's your name?" I answered, "My name's Pan." And so he'd always ask, "Where's Pan? Where's Pan?" He'd never ask for Dave, the dance director, because Dave Gould couldn't do anything anyway!

We got along [snaps fingers] like that! Boy, we thought the same way. His rhythms were almost identical with mine. It's a very weird thing, because we would automatically do the same steps. Slap, bang, turn—you know. We just seemed to think alike. So after two pictures as an assistant, they gave me a contract as dance director for all the rest of the Fred Astaire and Ginger Rogers films at RKO.

Now, before *Flying Down to Rio*, no one had ever seen a dance number on the screen from beginning to end. You might see somebody dancing, but then the camera would cut down to the feet, then to the face smiling, and then to a table at somebody applauding. But you never saw a whole dance routine. When we were working on the first number, "The Carioca," I said right away, "This number should be shot without a cut. I mean no cutting away from it or cutting to the feet." We discussed it with the director and the cameramen, and we said, "Now we want head to foot, a tight full figure all the way through. And if you have to cut in the middle, just change angles so it's still full figure." We didn't want the audience to be conscious of cutting away.

When the picture was previewed in Pomona, California, something happened that had never happened before at a movie. After "The Carioca," the house came down. People applauded like crazy! The producers said, "My gosh, what is this?" They knew they had something very hot. And from then on it was Astaire and Rogers. In doing that straight-on shot, Astaire and I completely revolutionized the way dance was presented on film.

Fred and I would spend hours, weeks, and oftentimes months, working on new material, new ideas for steps, movement, and stories for our dances. There really was a creative spark between us. Yes, we were quite the team. However, there

A sultry dance number, "Once Too Often," featuring Betty Grable and Hermes Pan from *Pin-Up Girl* (20th Century-Fox, 1944)

Hermes Pan dances with a very young Lucille Ball in between shots of *Roberta* (RKO, 1935).

Hermes Pan and the beautiful Rita Hayworth (who had come from a theatrical dancing family), in "On the Gay White Way" from *My Gal Sal* (20th Century-Fox, 1942)

Hermes Pan with Carmen Miranda in *That Night in Rio* (20th Century-Fox, 1941)

The RKO geniuses going over the musical score for *Shall We Dance* (RKO, 1936). (Standing left to right) Hermes Pan, Mark Sandrich, Ira Gershwin, and Nathaniel Shilkret; (seated left to right) Fred Astaire, Ginger Rogers, and George Gershwin.

was more to this team than just Astaire and Pan —someone who was perhaps just as instrumental in the shaping of these dances as either of us— a gentleman by the name of Hal Borne. Hal was always our rehearsal pianist. He could take a thing, play certain breaks and rhythms that would inspire steps. For example, Astaire and I wanted to do a waltz in swing time. And so we told this to Jerome Kern, who was doing the music for our upcoming picture *Swing Time* [1936]. Kern brought in his music, but it was just almost impossible. Nothing that we had thought—you know. So, Hal took the music and sort of did it himself. *He* practically wrote the "Waltz in Swing Time" rather than Kern. He had made it what we wanted, made it—you know, a real *jazz* waltz.

We just seemed to lead charmed lives as far as music went. Besides the creative genius of Hal Borne, Astaire and I worked with the biggest composers of the day, such as George Gershwin, Irving Berlin, Jerome Kern, and Cole Porter. When I was assigned to *Shall We Dance* [1937], I had the sheet music for the score, but I hadn't heard it yet. So, I went on the rehearsal stage, and there was this man at the piano. I said, "Hello, I'm the dance director for this picture" (That was before Agnes de Mille. You know she started "choreography." Until Agnes de Mille staged the dances for *Oklahoma*, we were always called "dance directors." She changed this by using the term

"choreographer," which is correct. And from then on it was "choreography by . . ."). I said, "Would you mind playing this? I've got to start rehearsing it tomorrow." He said, "Well certainly." He started to go. I said, "Gee, that's like a march—can you play a little slower?" He said, "Oh sure." But it got worse. I said, "Well, that's like a funeral march!" He tried it different ways, but nothing worked for me. You know something? I said, "Gershwin or no Gershwin, I think this stinks!" After trying it a few more times, I finally said, "Well, excuse me, but there's a meeting I have to go to. I'll see you later." After I'd been in the meeting for about five minutes, the rehearsal pianist came in. *Everybody* stood up and said, "Mr. Gershwin!" Oh, I—I practically went through the floor, you know. Finally, after everybody had gone, I said, "Mr. Gershwin, as you know, I'm embarrassed and very sorry I said what I did." And he said, "You know something? You might be right!" That's how nice he was. George Gershwin was just a very modest person. He would go along with anything you

FRED ASTAIRE'S CHOREOGRAPHER

suggested. "Oh sure, do that," he would say. "How about this?" He was very, very modest and agreeable. You would never think that he was the genius that he was.

Astaire and I would rehearse our numbers on one of the blank stages with the movie set stacked up against the corner. At first we had a big ceiling-to-floor portable mirror. We liked to work out in front of it to see how we looked in the mirror as we did the dance. But we'd get so used to looking at ourselves, which is dangerous because we wanted to be able to do the routine completely naturally without being stuck on that mirror! So, during the last week or so before shooting, we covered it so we couldn't watch ourselves dance.

Usually, I'd work with Fred first, before Ginger came in. In fact, a lot of times, Fred would leave to do other things and I would teach Ginger the routine. This meant that I had to learn the dances both ways—the man's and the woman's part! And most people don't know this, but I used to dub Ginger's taps during the recording sessions. So, most of the time, those are actually my taps you hear when you watch the Astaire-Rogers films. See, when it came time to dub the taps, she was often working on another picture or something. But actually, her taps weren't quite clear—she did a few "air" Shuffles, if you know what I mean.

Speaking of taps, we rarely used taps on our shoes. Even in a lot of Astaire's solos, he didn't use taps. We danced on a hardwood floor. We experimented with different woods and things to see what kind of sound we could get. I remember one time we had water under the wood to give our taps a dull sound, so they wouldn't be too clicky or too high. Astaire and I worked hard to get our sound just the way we wanted it.

Through those RKO days, I worked a lot with Fred on his solos. He was such a hard worker and such a perfectionist, too. But he was so much fun to work with. There were never any fights or fusses,

but he was adamant, you know, when he wanted something. If somebody—say a director or a producer—wanted to change something, he could be *very* adamant and insist, "No, this is the way it's going to be." He was the same way about the movie scripts. Astaire would never say anything or use any language that he didn't feel was gentlemanly. I remember once there was a line which read, "my feet hurt." That's it, just "my feet hurt." Astaire looked at that script and said, "I won't say it! I would never say it!" He was so

Hermes Pan's only appearance on film with Fred Astaire, in the "Me and the Ghost Upstairs" number from *Second Chorus* (Paramount, 1941). Unfortunately, the dance number was cut before the picture's release.

Ginger Rogers and Fred Astaire take a break on the sound stage for *The Story of Vernon and Irene Castle* (RKO, 1939) to celebrate Hermes Pan's birthday. This film culminated an extraordinarily successful nine-picture deal at RKO. (The trio made one more picture together, *The Barkleys of Broadway* at MGM in 1949.)

upset, he even hit the script, "My feet hurt? Never!" And he never did say it.

During rehearsals for a picture, we'd usually come in at about ten in the morning. We'd work till twelve-thirty or one o'clock, take an hour break, and then work until five o'clock or so. Astaire would come in Sundays and work dance material for a couple hours. I'd come in, too. He said that he didn't like to get cold, wanted to keep the dance in his mind. He just didn't want to lay off a weekend and then go back into the number. He was a perfectionist. But I suppose I was, too. Had to be, working with him.

Sometimes when we started working on a new number we would have no idea what we were going to do, and we'd just noodle around, make up steps, ad-lib, and something would hit. Or, sometimes we'd have a definite idea of what we were going to do. If we got one good step or something, we'd always say, "Well, we got one good deed done!" Fred was such a worrier that he used to call me after work a lot and ask, "Did we get a good deed today?" I'd reassure him, "Oh sure, remember we did this . . . we did that . . ."—and then, just maybe, he'd feel a little bit better. His sister Adele used to call him "Moaning Minnie," and boy was it true! Astaire was just never satisfied with his dancing. He would do the same steps over and over again to get it just right. I remember Eleanor Powell describing her experience working with Astaire on their big dance number for *Broadway Melody of 1940*. Each time after finishing a run-through of the routine they had worked out, one would say to the other, "Let's do it one more time." Well, being that they were both perfectionists, they did it "one more time" and "one more time" until this

"one more time" had the definite possibility of becoming infinity! Even during the shooting of the number, Fred said to Eleanor after each take, "Just one more time, Ellie."—and she was just as pleased as he was to do it again. Finally, the director said, "This is it kids! It's fine. It's great. No more takes, 'cause if you keep doing it 'one more time,' we'll never get out of here!" And the guy was absolutely right. Astaire was a one-hundred-percent perfectionist. If there was anything about him that you could pinpoint, that was it. But, you know, the fact that he was a perfectionist is the reason he looks so good up there on that screen. Fred worked on his dances with such intensity that he actually had the uncanny skill to make it look easy. With the kind of intricate work he was doing, both rhythmically and physically, you can't imagine what an amazing phenomenon that was!

There was one more thing that I loved about Fred, and that was his sense of humor—*very* dry. After *Follow the Fleet* [1936], he gave me one of his old rehearsal shoes along with a note:

"To Pan,

in memory of those thousands of rotten hours in rotten rehearsal halls."

August 31, 1989
Beverly Hills, California
(Died September 19, 1990)

BILL
ROBINSON'S
"DARLIN'"

SHIRLEY TEMPLE

It was hard work and concentration,
and it was no time to be a baby.

8

Among tap's greatest stars, one little girl, a curly-topped bundle of joy, captured the hearts of Americans young and old. Something about the way this tiny tot tap danced simply made the rest of the world want to do it too. When Fred Astaire or Eleanor Powell tapped, it was the work of magnificent stars. But little Shirley Temple was just a kid. If she could do it, certainly any average Tommy and Suzie could, too. And so it happened that every time one of her films was released, tap enrollment skyrocketed across the country in dance schools.

Shirley Jane Temple was born in Santa Monica, California on April 23, 1928. When barely three years old, she became a student at the Ethel Meglin Dance Studio and simultaneously a Famous Meglin Kiddie. Even in 1931, The Meglin Kiddies were regarded throughout Hollywood as superbly talented tap dancers. They were hired in hoards of tiny, tapping, patent leather feet, for such movies as *Shipmates Forever* [1935]. Shirley Temple had not been with Mrs. Meglin long before she was discovered for a new series of one-reel comedies called *Baby Burlesks*. At the age of four, Shirley began earning ten dollars a day, an excellent wage in the Depression—especially for a dancer who had not even started grade school!

In 1934, Shirley Temple astounded the film industry with her performance in the Fox film *Stand*

On Account-a I Love You

Words by
BUD GREEN

Music by
SAM H. STEP

BABY TAKE A BOW
SHIRLEY TEMPLE
JAMES DUNN
CLAIRE TREVOR

MOVIETONE

up and Cheer. She only had a bit role in the movie, however, when she sang and tap danced, the entire world smiled. Her fame was simply colossal. Her trademarks were dimples, bright eyes, and curly-top golden hair, and in the coming years she would have a musical film named after each of them.

Shirley Temple's movies were magic at the box office, too. When she first hit it big, the Motion Picture Herald listed her as number eight of the top-ten moneymaking stars for 1934. One year later, in 1935, she skyrocketed in popularity to become the number-one box-office star. She held that position through 1936, 1937, and 1938. The competition was tough, but Shirley Temple stayed right up there ranking above Clark Gable, Astaire and Rogers, Joan Crawford, Dick Powell, Claudette Colbert, Gary Cooper, James Cagney, William Powell, Myrna Loy, Robert Taylor, Mickey Rooney, Bing Crosby, and

Spencer Tracy. Exhibitors proclaimed her box-office salvation. Shirley Temple's unaffected personality and her extraordinary ability charmed audiences and critics alike. She was able to put herself across on screen without any hint of affected cuteness, while at the same time she was able to portray a wide range of adult emotional reactions. There was simply something magical about this child who cheered the soul of America during the Depression.

From 1934 to 1940, Shirley Temple made twenty-four films; of those films, fifteen included musical sequences in which she tap danced. When not performing alone, she was accompanied by first-rate veteran tap talent and vaudevillians. In 1934, she starred with James Dunn (Stand Up and Cheer and again in Baby Take a Bow). In 1935, she was first paired with Bill "Bojangles" Robinson (The Little Colonel). This combination proved to be so utterly winning that they were featured together in three more films (The Littlest Rebel 1935, Rebecca of Sunnybrook Farm 1938, and Just Around the Corner 1938). Not only did Shirley Temple and Bill Robinson become great friends, but they were the first interracial pair in films. In 1936, she danced with Buddy Ebsen (Captain January), and Alice Faye and Jack Haley (The Poor Little Rich Girl). In 1938, she danced with George Murphy (Little Miss Broadway), in 1939 with Arthur Treacher (The Little Princess), and in 1940 with Charlotte Greenwood and Jack Oakie (Young People). Shirley Temple tap danced up and down stairs, jumping rope, picking berries, in the rain, on a roof, in a courtroom, on the radio, in China, in New York, and on the farm. It did not seem to matter where or when—Shirley Temple tap dancing delighted and inspired the masses like no other.

S H I R L E Y   T E M P L E — When I was making musicals, I didn't think of myself as a tap dancing actress or an actress or a singer—didn't really think about putting myself in any particular category. I enjoyed everything I was doing. And at the time, I didn't have any idea of how much my tap dancing in those films impacted the rest of the kids in the United States. No—not at all! But Gene Kelly told me that every time a movie of mine came out, the enrollment at his dance studio just about quadrupled.

I worked with a lot of the great male tap dancers of the 1930s, including Bill Robinson, George Murphy, and Buddy Ebsen. All the men I danced with had different styles. Yes—George Murphy and Buddy Ebsen were more expansive in their moves. Bill Robinson was close to the floor—not doing broad jumps, or so forth. His was a closer range—you didn't have a great distance to move around when you worked with Bill.

The resident tap teachers at Fox Studios were Nick Castle and Geneva Sawyer, and they would help out. During a picture they were usually around, and if Bill or George or Buddy were doing something else like working on scenes, I could also work with Nick and Geneva. Nick was the primary teacher. Oh, he was super, too. He was very intense, he didn't like anyone to take any time off! But he was a very, very good teacher.

But I didn't really have any dancing teachers, per se, at the time I was working on these films. My dancing "teachers" were just the ones I was working with at the time—Bill, or Buddy, or George. When I worked with them on a film, each worked out their own dances, and then I learned them. Sometimes we'd have only a few days and sometimes we'd have a couple of weeks. It would depend on the schedule. With Buddy Ebsen, from the movie *Captain January* [1936]—"At the Codfish Ball"—we did that whole dance in one take. They had several cameras on the dance, so they were getting side shots and close-ups and long shots. But it was all done in one long segment. Then we did a couple of spot takes for close-up

Shirley Temple in *Stand Up and Cheer* (Fox, 1934). She inspired more tap pupils than any single dancer before or after her.

Shirley Temple and Buddy Ebsen, whom she remembers as being "very tall," dancing to "At the Codfish Ball" in *Captain January* (Fox, 1935).

By 1935, Shirley Temple was the nation's number-one box-office star. She held on to that position in 1936, 1937, and 1938, topping Clark Gable, Fred Astaire and Ginger Rogers, Joan Crawford, and many others along the way.

parts of the dance. But basically, the number was done all in one big long take. And we both felt very proud that we got through it, you know. I've always loved that number. When I think back about what it was like to work with Buddy, what I remember is that he was very tall! That's a child's perspective, right? I remember during the dance, Buddy actually picked me up to dance, because I was so tiny; He picked me up, and we danced cheek to cheek.

None of the dancers I worked with were patronizing to me, or treated me like a child—not at all. I'd say that they all treated me as an equal. I would include George Murphy and Buddy Ebsen and the others in that category. It was hard work and concentration, and it was no time to be a baby. But Bill Robinson was the one who treated me most as an equal. Bill Robinson and I became very close personal friends throughout our lives, and I have always had great love for him. He still is important in my heart. What was it about him that made him so important in my life? He just became a really good friend.

It was [Buddy] de Sylva who introduced Bill Robinson, waiting outside our cottage with his wife, Fannie. The first thing I noted was the way his arms and legs moved with a silky, muscular grace. He was square-jawed and shiny-cheeked, his great round eyes showing whites all around. I was instantly attracted. Mr. Robinson will show

you how to do the dances, was the way de Sylva put it.

Following introductory chitchat, we all started across the lot. Robinson walked a step ahead of us, but when he noticed me hurrying to catch up, he shortened his stride to accommodate mine. I kept reaching up for his hand, but he hadn't looked down, and seemed unaware. Fannie called his attention to what I was doing, so he stopped short, bent low over me, his eyes wide and rows of brilliant teeth showing in a wide smile. When he took my hand in his, it felt large and cool.

For a few moments we continued walking in silence. "Can I call you Uncle Billy?" I asked.

"Why, sure you can," he replied. After a few steps he again stopped.

"Mr. Robinson doesn't fit anyway." He grinned broadly. "But then I get to call you darlin'."

It was a deal.

Here Shirley Temple dances with a lifelong friend and "the world's greatest tap dancer," Bill Robinson, for the first time in *The Little Colonel* (Fox, 1935).

Shirley Temple and Bill "Bojangles" Robinson in the finale number "Toy Trumpet" from *Rebecca of Sunnybrook Farm* (20th Century-Fox, 1938). Their partnership and rapport were so winning, they were featured in four movie musicals.

From then on whenever we walked together it was hand in hand, and I was always his "darlin'."

At first we practiced in the regular mirrored rehearsal hall. Then we found it more convenient to use a contraption that when folded looked like a wooden box, but when unfolded, became three steps, up one side and down the other. At any spare moment, anywhere, we could practice.

"We'll have a hand-squeeze system," he proposed. "When I give you three quick squeezes, means we're coming to a hard part. One long squeeze, really good, darlin'! No squeeze at all? Well, let's do it again."

Before long his system of signals became superfluous. "Now we just let those hands hang loose," he instructed. "Limp wrists, loose in the shoulders. There, that's it! Copacetic! Now let's get your feet attached to your ears."

It was the same message as from Mrs. Meglin [Meglin Kiddies], but with a superlative teacher, imperturbable and kind, but demanding. Although bubbling with energy, his physical motions were so controlled and fluid, they came out looking relaxed. He made it look easy, but was not one to pick his way gingerly. I must be guided solely by muscular memory. I must visualize my own sounds, not think about them. It must all be reflexive and unthinking, the sound of my taps telling me how I am doing, setting the pace and controlling the sequence. Every one of my taps had to ring crisp and clear in the best cadence. Otherwise I had to do it over.

Just Around the Corner (20th Century-Fox, 1938) is Shirley Temple's and Bill Robinson's last picture together.

That sort of repetitive rehearsal lay behind our familiar staircase dance in the southern plantation mansion in *The Little Colonel*. We made an unusual couple. A raggedy urchin with tousled curls paired with a regal black man in striped vest and brass buttons and patent-leather shoes. Every sound matched, every gesture, the scuffle, the staccato tap, a sharp-toed kick to the stile, a triple-time race up and down the staircase, tapping as we went. The smile on my face was not acting; I was ecstatic.

Fondest memories of dancing with Uncle Billy come not only from our camera takes but from rehearsals, up and down that portable stile, or in any convenient corner. Practicing until each

move became unthinking was a joy. Learning, an exhilaration. In devising some nuance of movement or sound to make the dance only ours lay the ultimate satisfaction. Once we had reached the point of "roll 'em," each of our routines had been perfected, ready for only a final moment of elation in a long sequence totally devoid of drudgery.

But making movies is not all rehearse-and-perform. We sat around a lot, talking about boxing, for instance, and diamonds. Uncle Billy enthused about Joe Louis, then only a promising fighter from Detroit, and demonstrated uppercuts and vicious hooks while I watched transfixed.

"A dancer just like us," he said, bouncing around on tiptoe and jabbing out at an unseen opponent. "One day he'll beat Max Baer. He's world champion. But then, so am I," and he went on to describe how in Olympic Games tryouts he had won a 100-yard sprint in fourteen seconds, but running backwards.

Directors always reminded Uncle Billy to remove his ring before shooting. It was a brilliant diamond, and time and again we crouched like two mystics over his hand while he flicked his finger to catch the light and spun talks of African mines and bejeweled crowns. To him, diamonds were endowed with powers unrelated to monetary value. Perhaps that is why he gave me a gold-plated chief's badge for my police force. In the center was mounted his talisman, a small diamond.

Everyone I danced with was wonderful to work with. Buddy and George were certainly two of the finest ones. But Bill Robinson was my favorite. He was the easiest teacher I had, because we could do it by holding hands.

I think we all loved tap dancing, or we wouldn't have been doing it. We all loved what we were doing. And it was easy for me to learn from such good teachers. When you work with fine professionals, I guess it rubs off on you.

June 28, 1989
Woodside, California

9

JUST A HOOFER

RALPH BROWN

You keep trying.
You keep trying.
You keep trying.
And finally it comes to you—
the trick of tap dancing!

In the 1920s, tap dancers were a dime a dozen. Every show had a tap dancer, and so did every club, and every revue. There were great tap dancers in every town in America. But no matter how good a tap dancer became, there was one place where all but the best would just fall to the bottom of the heap: New York.

Manhattan—that was the real cutting ground for tap dancers. And the hottest spot in town to take a tap challenge was right up in Harlem at the Hoofers Club. Tap dancers would come from around the country to test their metal against the all-time greats like John Bubbles and Bill Robinson. More often than not, these out-of-towners were in for a rude awakening. They might be headliners in their hometowns, but holding their ground up in Harlem was another matter altogether.

So these young hopefuls dug their steel-plated heels into the Hoofers Club, sometimes for years at a time, watching and learning from those who could really "lay down some iron." There, the artful knowledge of "stealing steps" was perfected. Dancers would watch each other with a keen, gleaning eye, ready to grab any and all appealing steps. And if a dancer was good enough to figure out a tap step, it was for the taking. There was just no such thing as copyrighting a tap step.

Rarely, though, did a dancer steal a step and repeat it exactly. During those highly competitive

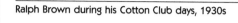
Ralph Brown during his Cotton Club days, 1930s

tests. Quickly sweeping up every award, he realized it was time to move on to New York to see where he really stood.

When Ralph Brown arrived in the city of seven million, it was 1931, and like countless tap dancers before him, he discovered he was a good dancer, but nowhere near the caliber of those residing in Harlem. For the next two years, he haunted the Hoofers Club, stealing as much as he could from the tap greats who passed through. As a matter of fact, it took him two years to catch up with the Harlem tap talent in order to land his first decent professional engagement, a job touring with The Mills Brothers.

And then in 1934, he got into the world-famous Cotton Club as a single. It was a tap dancer's dream, and quite a climb for the young hoofer from Indianapolis. Cab Calloway and his orchestra were starring there, and the show was made up of the very top black entertainers. There were singers, comedians, and, of course, plenty of tap dancers. There were novelty tap acts, eccentric, rhythm, and now the hot tap of Ralph Brown. The Cotton Club was the beginning of Ralph Brown's association with Cab Calloway's orchestra. He toured all over the United States with Calloway, and always managed to keep the program just that much "hotter" with his sure-fire tap routines.

In the years ahead, Ralph Brown danced with many more of the great bands: Charlie Parker, Dizzy Gillespie, Les Hyte, Claude Hopkins, Cootie Williams, Jimmie Lunceford, Duke Ellington, and Count Basie. The first to admit that he was not as great a dancer as a Bill Robinson or a John Bubbles, Ralph Brown represented the thousands of wonderful tap dancers who made a living at it from the 1920s to the 1950s. He was just a hoofer. And he worked.

days for tap dancers, each act had its own original style. When the stolen material was incorporated into a dancer's repertoire, it always seemed to take on a new personality—that dancer's style. A step might be changed, a rhythm, a gesture altered, and that stolen step became something unique.

That was the atmosphere Ralph Brown came up in. He was born in Indianapolis in 1914. Inspired by tap dancers performing in his hometown, he began tap dancing and entering local amateur con-

RALPH BROWN — Tap dancing was fantastic when I started. A show wasn't complete without a dancer. In the 1920s, we had shows coming to town every week in Indianapolis. And every show had a dance act that closed the bill!

I actually started tap dancing from a love of watching these dancers, fellows like Eddie Rector. He was a great tap dancer, created a dance called the Bambalina. He came to Indianapolis, and when I saw him, I just never forgot it. Then when I got an opportunity to see Bill Robinson —that did it, I just wanted to dance!

Leonard Reed was in my hometown, and he was a *real* professional dancer and producer. He had the knowledge of show business and helped me a whole lot with my beginning. Helped me when I needed help. After a time, I got good enough to start entering local amateur contests. In my hometown, the master of ceremonies would come out onstage and introduce the person who was going to perform, the amateur, who then came out and did their thing. If they were good enough, the audience would let them finish it up. But if the amateur wasn't good, they had a hook just offstage big enough to put around a human being. They make some noise, bells ring or something goes to distract the amateur, and they put that hook around him and pull him right on offstage! That's the way they did it. But if you were good, you made it through your act. Then they would introduce the next event. After it's all over, those that made it through their act came out onstage and lined up. The master of ceremonies put his hand over each amateur, one at a time, and let the audience applaud for them. The ones that got the largest applause, they were the winner. I'd win every time. They liked me that well.

It was 1931 when I first came to New York. But when I got there, my dancing wasn't qualified enough to perform onstage at the Lafayette Theatre, one of Harlem's most popular theaters. See, New York had lots of dancers. I was great in Indianapolis, but just another tap dancer in New York! However, the Hoofers Club was right next door to the Lafayette Theatre. The great dancers in New York went down there, including John Bubbles, Derby Wilson, Eddie Rector. I stayed down in that Hoofers Club *day* and *night* to watch

A hoofer who "just wanted to dance " does just that—Ralph Brown, 1940s.

create your own steps and develop more and more. You can take whatever you stole, because you never learned the complete step anyway! You learned how to do part of it, so you take that part and put something else with it. Then you made your own step. A lot of steps are the same, like the Shim Sham Shimmy is done one way, and everybody does it the same way. Only some do it better than others, they add a little something to it to make it different. But it's like if a group of dancers got onstage at one time, everybody knows the national anthem of tap, it's the same thing, "Do the Shim." Then of course, there's a dance called the B.S. Chorus. It's four steps that everyone knows that danced over a period of time. You know, "Everybody, let's do the B.S. and the Shim Sham." And that's two thirty-two bar choruses. You do the thing, and then everybody just exits shimming off after that.

You see, you can't copyright a dance step. If you could learn it, you could do it. Of course, you don't do it in the presence of the creator of the step. Like Bill Robinson was the only one that had a style and had a variety of steps that you didn't do in his presence. You'd do it behind his back, when he wasn't around!

Bill Robinson was the greatest, because he could do more with his feet an inch off the floor, just high enough for him to come down. Bill Robinson was strictly a tap dancer. Best tap dancer in the world. Why, he could do more with his feet than any dancer I'ver ever heard. He did little things where it was close rhythm. But taps, lots of taps.

the other dancers and learn—and steal. Because everybody steals—you know what I mean—to perfect their dancing. Once in a while you might get someone to show you how to do a step, but not many that would take you by the hand and carry you through it. You would just have to steal it. That's the way it went. And that's how I became a dancer.

Through the years you learn, and it's like the key to a door. You keep trying, you keep trying, you keep trying. And finally it comes to you—the trick of tap dancing! That's like, you finally get the key, and you can get in. Then you learn to

He could do a step that would make you say, "What did he do back there!" It drives you crazy!

Once I was playing up in Boston with a show, and Bill Robinson was up there with his show at the same time. We did our show, see, eleven in the morning, and his time was about the same. But one day something had gone wrong, where his show went on late and our cast knew (we were keeping wise up to whatever was happening), and we were able to get finished and get over to the theater to catch the last part of his show. I ran over there five times to watch him dance—five performances. This man gave me a *headache*! Now, this is the truth. I was watching him and I said, "Where is he getting it at? Where is it coming from!" Because you don't see his feet go but so high off the wood from the stage—but he did so many things. And I say, "How can he do it!" He gave me that headache, I'm telling you, because I was straining so to try to understand it. It's hard to understand what you don't know, and especially when you haven't seen it before. Bill Robinson was, as I say, the greatest tap dancer I've seen. And I've seen some nice dancers. I've seen some good dancers. But nobody danced like Bill Robinson.

In 1934, Herman Stark, who was the manager of the Cotton Club, came up to the Harlem Opera House to see me dance. He was looking for a tap dancer, and he had heard about me. He came back to talk to me and asked if I had a manager. At the time, I didn't have a manager. And he says, "How would you like me to manage you?" I thought, "The man *owns* the Cotton Club! He could send me out on the road with Cab Cal-loway and Duke Ellington. Continuous work." I didn't need to think about it too long! I said, "Of course, I want you to manage me!" So that's the way that went down, and that's how I went in the Cotton Club. Cab Calloway had his orchestra there, and Lena Horne was in there too—just a chorus girl at the time. She was just getting her singing career on the way in 1934.

Well, it was a big show in 1934 at the Cotton Club. A featured singer opened the show, and then the ensemble, twelve beautiful girls, danced. After the dance was finished, then I came on. I was a single dancer. My music would strike up and I was in! I used "Yankee Rose." It was a very bright tune. See, the shows got to start off with a *bang*! My music was fast. It had fire to it! Then after I danced, they had a comedy act, and after that, a featured singer, then they may have a novelty dance act that followed the singer that followed me. Then a comedy song-and-dance person. Then it was a band number. It went down like variety. They tried to mix it up to the point where it was very interesting. And they always saved the heavyweights, such as Ethel Waters, The Nicholas Brothers, and Cab Calloway, to balance off the last half of the show.

Cab Calloway was a big thing, and he closed the show with band numbers and his singing. He was doing "Minnie the Moocher," "Saint James' Infirmary." Cab was young and frantic, and the people loved him. During his heyday, he was the most sensational performer onstage. Cab was a stylist. He would throw his whole body and soul into it. He was the first one I ever did see do that style of entertaining. His dancing wasn't as accurate as the average dancer—he never wore taps—he just did more or less eccentric dancing—where he'd spin around, just make the dance fit whatever number he was doing. The audience loved him, the man was *sensational*! He was the greatest thing that hit the stage during

1934, and right on through.

Cab had been good before then, you see, because he was well established in 1934. The Cotton Club got him out of the Savoy Ballroom. He used to come up to the Savoy and just get up on the stage and perform in front of the band. People knew that Cab was going to be at the Savoy, and they would come from downtown—white people I'm talking about—come from downtown and flock in there to see Cab. Finally, the Savoy Ballroom signed him to a contract.

The Cotton Club was just around the corner—Savoy was at Hundred-fortieth Street, and the Cotton Club was Hundred-forty-second on Lenox Avenue. The Cotton Club was run by gangsters and racketeers. Owney Madden owned the Cotton Club, and he was a big mob man. He had Herman Stark run the club for him, and Madden had his henchmen there to back Stark. Anyway, at the Cotton Club they were all wondering why everybody was coming uptown and stopping at the Savoy. So they went over to see what was happening, and it turned out that Cab was everything everyone had been talking about. And they said, "We would like to buy Cab's contract." However, the Savoy didn't want to sell the contract, 'cause it would kill their business. The owner of the Savoy said, "Man, I'm in business. I want Cab here. I don't want to sell his contract." So they said, "We'll give you a thousand dollars for his contract." He said, "A thousand dollars wouldn't

A jumpin' jive jubilee. Ralph Brown on tour with Cab Calloway's rip-roaring entertainment revue that also includes veteran hoofers Cholly and Dotty, 1940s.

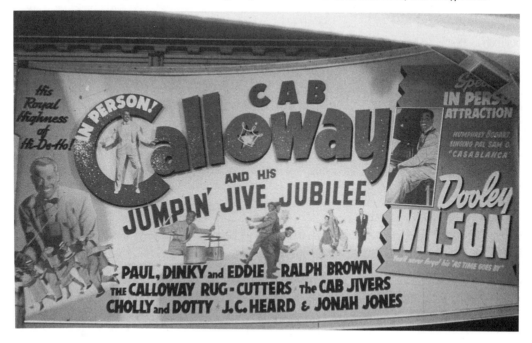

touch him," because that man made that in a night with Cab. However, when this all occurred, they said, "Well when we come back it's going to be *less!*" They went back to the Cotton Club, talked it over, and set up what they wanted to do. They went back to the Savoy and said they wanted to see Cab's contract. The owner of the Savoy brought out the contract and showed it to them. Why, they took that contract and tore it right up, and said, "Come on Cab!" They just took Cab from him, two blocks up the street and put Cab in the Cotton Club. And he was in the Cotton Club ever since!

Later on, I joined Cab for his tour that carried us all the way to the West Coast, to Los Angeles. My first trip out there. I must say they had a reception for him that you don't find *every* day in the theatrical walk of life. When we got off the pullman sleeper into Los Angeles, they had a carpet of rosebuds go out from the sleeper to the limousines that were waiting for him. We had motorcycle escorts to take us to the Club Alabam on Central Avenue, then back down to City Hall to meet the mayor. They had banners across the street. They gave Cab a beautiful reception. He was following Benny Goodman in the Paramount. This was back before Benny Goodman's band had been East, and he had yet to be crowned "The King of Swing."

In Calloway's tour I did two dances in my performance. I did a rhythm dance to the "New Low-Down," which was a three-chorus dance. Then a four-bar intro to the "Yankee Rose" number that I did in the Cotton Club. See, because it was such a fast-moving show, they wanted my dance up there to follow the opening. That ran about six choruses! Oh, it was a hell of a long dance. I was moving, I was dancing! But I was *young* and I had *lots* of energy.

I was a very eccentric tap dancer, because my tempos were very bright. When I did my rhythm dancing, it was faster than the average rhythm dance. You see, rhythm dancing, at the time that I learned it, used a lot of heel business, because John Bubbles had created the Cramp Roll. But I didn't use too much of that. I used Triplets instead of Cramp Rolls. I used a Triplet and got off the toe, I didn't get it from the heel. I also got around and did a lot of movements, spins and stuff, all that sort of thing—which was somewhat eccentric, different, because the average tap dancer just stood up straight and danced. I did not do a whole lot of kicks or nothing like that. I traveled a lot up and down the stage. For my climax, I used to spin and go to the half split, and that was it. You got to bring your climax in, you see. You say to yourself, "Enough—build up toward the finish and get off with a bang—if you can!"

And that's the way it was. During those years, show business was fantastic! Because you see, nobody was making a whole lot of money, other than the big names. But it was a thing where you were meeting so many people. It was such a thrill to be on a bill where you got a chance to perform four and five times a day. It was very educational and enlightening, because you learned so much. You might say, "I want to do this, I want to do that," and you try this, you try that. You tried everything and you had a place to do it and you could perform. And like I say, going to different towns. A week here and a week there. We weren't doing no stopping, like stay in one place a long time—we were traveling and going to different cities, different audiences. It was very exciting.

My first show was a big show out of New York. I went to Cleveland, from New York to Cleveland with The Mills Brothers, and they were drawing people for blocks. People were standing at the box office waiting to buy a ticket to get in. And then after this performance was over and the people would leave, there's another line waiting to go in. The shows didn't run but about forty-five to fifty-five minutes. They had a short newsreel and then the performers were back on stage *again!* You had maybe a half hour, forty minutes, in between each show. And that ran from the time we began at eleven in the morning until eleven at night!

But I was young. It was fantastic. Learning—just interested—and loved show business. And that was the greatest part about it.

November 15, 1988
Manhattan, New York
(Died November 19, 1990)

10

"THE CHINESE FRED ASTAIRE AND GINGER ROGERS"

TOY AND WING

We just lived tap dancing.
Didn't know what time of day it was.

Asian Americans are not readily associated with popular entertainers of the first half of the twentieth century. In fact, they were right among the entertainers travelling the circuits as singers, acrobats, and dancers. Their presence was felt in vaudeville, nightclubs, movies, and musical shows. These individuals brought their own creativity to the forefront of the American entertainment scene—and their story is a fascinating one.

By the 1940s, a series of successful "Chinese" nightclubs such as the China Doll in New York and Forbidden City in San Francisco had begun to crop up. Similar to the Cotton Club, which featured all-black revues playing to white trade, these clubs featured all-Asian revues playing to white audiences. Many Asian American entertainers learned their craft in these clubs, and after this early apprenticeship formed their own acts to go out on the road in "Oriental" revues on the "Chop Suey Circuit."

Like their black counterparts, Asian American entertainers faced great prejudice in their attempts to have careers in the show business world. The general public had a difficult time believing that Asian Americans could sing and

Toy and Wing—"An Oriental Terp Duo," 1937

robes stuck hard and fast. In motion pictures, Asian Americans were relegated to typed roles such as valets, maids, hatchet men, and vamps—rarely appearing as main characters in the story. The prejudice felt and experienced by the Asian American entertainers was equaled by the prejudice some felt from within their own community, a community which traditionally looked down on the "white devil's" world of shameless entertainment. Those who were able to overcome both of these prejudices were remarkable people filled with drive, strength, courage, and inspiration—not to mention talent.

Two such determined individuals were Paul Wing and Dorothy Toy. Their backgrounds were diverse: He, a Chinese-American, took tap dancing "lessons" by watching vaudeville and film tap dancers; she, a Japanese-American, had formal tap training. Toy and Wing's participation among the big-time tap dancers illustrates that tap is a uniquely American dance reflecting the country's multi-ethnic roots. Tap, one of the few art forms consistently crossing social, economic, gender, and racial barriers, was found in Harlem's Cotton Club, Hollywood's Cocoanut Grove, and in San Francisco Chinatown's Forbidden City Nightclub.

dance in the popular mode; the image of the old-fashioned Chinese with the queues and

PAUL WING — I was born October the fourteenth, 1912, in Palo Alto, California. Born and raised there. I come from a family of nine, five sisters and three brothers, I'm being the oldest. My father, he was in the restaurant business. He also owned a laundry, and he owned some

land. He's one of the first Chinese pioneers in Palo Alto, so to speak. My father came to America around 1898. My mother was born and raised in San Francisco; she went to Cal.

I started dancing selling newspapers on a street corner when I was around eleven years old. I see this little colored boy kitty-corner from me, and he's doing a little Charleston, doing a little Jig, and he selling a lotta papers! I figure, "Hey, that's good idea. Oh, I'm gonna do that."

In those days, every Friday night in your local theaters they had Charleston contests. Fifteen dollars was the first prize. Naturally I had all my schoolmates come see me and applaud. I won the first prize, and I treat 'em all to milkshakes with the fifteen dollars. You can imagine how many I invited! And that started in me the urge to dance. You hear the music, you see the atmosphere, you get the feel—unknowingly that it's getting to you.

After I got interested in dancing, I always looked for tap dancers on a bill before I'd go see the show. When I lived in Palo Alto, I used to hitch-hike to San Francisco to the Orpheum Theatre, or the Golden Gate Theatre, or the Pantages Theatre on Market Street when they had vaudeville and stage shows. Used to pay twenty-five cents to get in and stay two or three shows, 'cause it's continuous. I would hide under the seat so I can stay for the midnight performance!

My mother wasn't too happy about my dancing because I practice on the kitchen linoleum floor and made a lotta noise. My father didn't approve of it at all. He wanted me to go to Stanford to become a doctor or lawyer. One day he sees me dancing with a chair as a partner. And he says to my mother, "You know our number one son? Something wrong somewhere!" But I couldn't concentrate in school, even when I was a senior in high school. The teacher calls out my name, "Paul, what are dreaming of?" I says, "I'm dreaming of being a dancer."

I graduate from Palo Alto High School in 1932, summer. Next week I left. Told nobody. Hitch-

hiked to Los Angeles. Had a few suitcases. My tap dancing shoes. I ran away from home to be in show business. I didn't know what I was goin' into, didn't know where to get the booking. I was in a Chinese restaurant and there was this Chinese waiter singing Irish songs! He's waiting on tables to make a dollar to eat to wait for a chance in motion pictures or theaters. Through him I found out they're looking for Oriental talent at the Grauman's Chinese Theatre for the *Rain* [1932] prologue.

I went to the audition. I danced. I had a Chinese costume which I wore, and underneath I had Chinese blouse and pants. Sid Grauman sitting there. He said to me, "I like your costume. I like your dancing. How much do you like a week?" It didn't dawn upon me that he's hiring me 'cause I'm so new in the business. I said, "'Bout a hundred dollars." I didn't know. Twenty-five dollars would be sufficient! "I will give you one hundred-twenty-five dollars. That is if you

Paul Wing—"The Chinese Fred Astaire," circa 1940

"THE CHINESE FRED ASTAIRE AND GINGER ROGERS

wear the same costume!" I said, "Oh, there's a catch to it!" And I laughed. They laughed too. I got the booking. Played six months. Got a write-up in *Variety.* I danced tap-Legomania to American music dubbed in Chinese background. Leroy Prinze was the dance director for this prologue.

After six months, the show closes. Now I'm out of a job. I go back to my agency, Lou Dorn. He send me out on these one-nighters called Saturday Night, Friday Night in theaters that have movie, then four acts of vaudeville. You only get four or five dollars. I didn't care. Just the idea of working before a theater audience! One theater there called the Regent Theatre near the Cherry Blossom Café. I walk in there to eat my dinner between shows and Dorothy Takahashi and Helen were there, and the mother was in the back helping cooking with the father. That's how we met. Dorothy, Helen, and I put an act to-

gether and we played the Orpheum Theatre and the Paramount as "The Three Mahjongs—Kicking the Gong Around" in the Fanchon and Marco "Ideas." In those days there's a song called "Minnie the Moocher": "I took her down to Chinatown, kicking that gong around." In other words, went down to Chinatown and had fun.

Dorothy and I, we team up. Go to Chicago. "Toy and Wing"—we had to go like that because Japanese weren't as popular as the Chinese in those days. Everything was Chinese. All the culture was Chinese. I cut Dorothy's name to T-O-Y. It's short and it's easy to remember and easy to see on a marquee. I figure all that. Wing is not my last name. Jew is my last name. But I use Wing. "Takahashi and Jew"? Ha, ha, no way! They started called us "The Chinese Fred Astaire and Ginger Rogers" back East, in the newspaper. One newspaper write-up says, "They dance like Astaire and Rogers. They stop the show. Outstanding." We were called an "Oriental Terp Duo" and "Youthful Chinese Dance Stylists."

We really worked. Perspire. Rehearse. Rehearse anywhere—hotel lobby floor, wherever we could. We couldn't afford a rehearsal hall, we go to the hotel basement. You forget to eat! But you rehearse. Lotta time we have sprained ankle, still go on. Can hardly walk, still go on. Four shows a day. Ah, yeah. We played one theater and it was snowing outside. The dressing room outside the alley! You gotta shovel coal to keep warm. Dorothy's in her gown. I'm in my full dress tails. Just like Fred Astaire. Only Fred Astaire isn't shoveling coal!

We were doing vaudeville '35, '36, '37, '38 and we played the circuits: RKO, Fanchon and Marco, Bert Levey Circuit, Publix. All the big theaters: We played the Paramount, New York. The Roxy, New York. We played Hippodrome, Baltimore. The Loews Warfield. The Golden Gate, San Francisco. We played the RKO Palace in Cleveland. Shea's Theatre in Buffalo. The RKO Theatre in Cincinnati. Chicago Theatre, State and Lake Theatre, and Oriental Theatre in Chicago. Seattle, Orpheum Theatre. Portland Orpheum. Los Angeles Orpheum. San Diego Orpheum. The Tower Theatre in Kansas. These theaters all accommodated 2,500 to 3,000 at least. The Paramount—3,000. Roxy Theatre—5,000. Chicago Theatre—3,500. I remember all these. State and Lake—2,500. It's pretty good!

We opened at the London Palladium number fourteenth on the bill. That's next-to closing on a fifteen-act bill. To be next-to-closing, you gotta be some kinda an act, boy! Now, we didn't get a rehearsal on stage, we just talk over music. Fifteen acts—I mean, you're lucky to get a talkover! Come out. Good thing we didn't know—the stage slants! [raked stage] Try to do some turns on a slant. Go ahead! Go right down towards the audience. Hard to get the balance. But we managed. I do a spin into a split, I fly in front. Well, we manage. We have to.

The London Palladium is like a palace. The seats are on tiers. Fabulous. Everything was drapery. Backstage you have valets. They dress you. Bring you tea. The audiences were great! If you're playing the London Palladium they know you're good. Okay, we come out in our Chinese robes, very grandioso music. Take her robe. She takes mine. Boom! Right into the Soft Shoe. Big

applause. Then we come out with the Jitterbug. We kill 'em. Then the toe number and the splits for a finish. Stopped the show! Just like that. Can't beat it. Hard to follow. And then they finish with the tumblers. What else? Somebody come out and talk or sing? Forget it!

Palladium we do a matinee, go over to the Berkeley Hotel do one show there. Doubling. Another $1000. Two thousand dollars a week, for a dance team! That's success!

During the war, Dorothy was doin' The Toy Sisters' act and I was in Europe doing the "march song." I was in the army infantry. Five-man tank in E.T.O.—Europe, Belgium, France, and Germany. Dancer doin' all that. All the mud work. Sleep in fox holes. Once in awhile, on a weekend pass, I go to the theater of that town and do a show. After V.E. Day, they asked me if I'd like to be in Special Services. "Just ship me back to the States!"

Toy and Wing on the vaudeville circuit, circa 1941

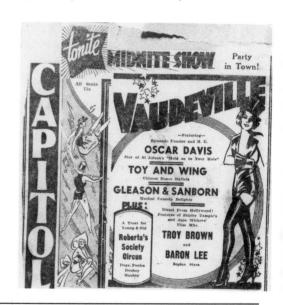

"THE CHINESE FRED ASTAIRE AND GINGER ROGERS

Dorothy and I went right into the Paramount Theatre, New York. Because Bob Whiteman, the manager, says, "Right after you get outta the army, I'll book you." Two years later, booked back into the Paramount. Ella Logan, Ben Blue, Tony Pastor and His Orchestra, and Toy and Wing up on the marquee—New York! Times Square!

The Chinese love us, 'cause we're the originals. The old-fashioned Chinese, some of 'em say, "You're a disgrace." That's the old days. But we were the first, Dorothy and I. Toy and Wing at the Chez Paree in Chicago as one of the foremost dance teams? Who ever heard of that from an Oriental race?

Toy and Wing didn't encounter much bigotry when we were travelling around. They see us perform, then they're very gracious. If they didn't see our act, we're just another Oriental to them. They call you a "chink," you forget it. Walk by. Why do you want to cause any animosity or any difficulty? You get beat up or you beat them up, and you're in trouble. "I got to do my shows. The hell with you!"

We just lived tap dancing. Didn't know what time of day it was sometimes. The other entertainers respected us because we're good. We *were* good. Who would be booked in the London Palladium? The Nicholas Brothers? Yes. But who else? Toy and Wing!

October 9, 1992
San Francisco, California

D O R O T H Y   T O Y —I was born Dorothy Takahashi on May 28th, many years ago in San Francisco. My family was from Yokohama and Wakayama, Japan. My mother was only about fifteen or sixteen when they came over here. I was raised in Los Angeles more or less with my sister, Helen. My brother had moved back to Japan.

My parents, it used to be they owned a restaurant. When I was a little girl, about seven years old, I used to dance around in the front of the restaurant. There was a vaudeville theater right across the street from my parents' restaurant and I used to watch all the vaudeville acts including my future partner, Paul Wing. The manager of the theater saw me in my parents' restaurant dancing around, and he said to my mother that I should take dancing lessons. You have to remember that in those days Asian people did not take dancing lessons. But then one day he sent a teacher over, and he again said to my mother that I should take dancing lessons. My mother said, "We can't afford it." The teacher said, "What I'll do is exchange meals for her dancing lessons." And that's how I started.

It was Ransdell Dance School at the Conservatory of Music near Westlake Park in Los Angeles. I practically lived there; after school I used to go there all the time. Of course, my mother's relatives shook their heads and said, "Oh, that's very bad. You shouldn't do that." But my mother was very young and she was much more modern than our relatives, so she just continued to let me take dancing lessons.

One day, there was a call for tap dancers for a movie *Happiness Ahead* [First National, 1934]. We went to the studio, my sister and I. Paul Wing was there too. The producer was

Mervyn LeRoy. He picked us three and two other Asian girls; one was Korean and one was Japanese. I believe it was Busby Berkeley that put the number on for us for this little sequence in a Chinese nightclub. After we did that movie, Paul said to my sister and me, "Why don't we get a show together?" That's how we first got together.

My partner, Paul Wing, knew more about different dancers than I did, and he said that Willie Covan was a very big name with a studio somewhere on Central Avenue in Los Angeles. He said, "Let's call him and ask him if he won't help us and teach us." And that's what he did. I think we took lessons from him for about three years. As kids we would go down there every day to learn tap dancing from Willie Covan. 'Cause what we were doing before was just ordinary dancing school type of tap. He taught us all the real intricate things.

In 1936, I was finally a little older and we set out for "big time." We got a contract to go to Salt Lake City, Omaha, and a couple of other cities on the way to Chicago. We didn't have a contract in Chicago; we just thought we'll "hit" the big city. But we found out after we got to Chicago that we were five years behind times with our tap dancing! We were stuck. So we said, "We have to practice some more. We have to better ourselves." We used to practice our tap on the landing of the hallway going up to the apartment, and my sister would cry 'cause she couldn't get the steps. And so we said, "Why don't you just go out as a single singer, and Paul and I will be the tap dancers." And we decided to do that.

We had to find someone to teach us the up-to-date tap dancing. We were at the Croyden Hotel in Chicago. Staying there was a fella named Steve Condos. We asked him to help us, and he taught us all the modern close-to-the-floor work that they were doing at that time. We really worked hard to learn that type of dancing. We were in Chicago about two years or so working little places at night, because we had to make a living. Practicing and taking lessons from Steve. At that time we were considered a novelty, because there weren't any other dancers that were Asian. Because of this, all these entertainers kind of took care of us.

We gradually made our way working and working, and finally we got to New York where we signed with William Morris. And they sent us way out of town to keep us going until they thought we would be ready for Broadway. In

Dorothy Toy, circa 1937

"THE CHINESE FRED ASTAIRE AND GINGER ROGERS

1938, while on the road, we received a wire from our agent Freddie Elswit, and it says, "You open at the Strand, New York." My partner looked at it and thought we were getting a repeat booking at the Strand Theatre—York, Pennsylvania, another one-nighter. But, I said, "Look at it again. It says the New York Strand! Broadway ! We've made it!" And . . . we *stopped* the show completely! Leo Reisman's band played one whole chorus of "My Reverie," and the people did not stop clapping for us. The band had to stop and bring us out to take another bow. From then on it was fine.

In 1939, we followed the Nicholas Brothers into the London Palladium! The last three days of our run the blackouts began. I think that was the time when Hitler went into Poland. Anyway, you can't see a thing. The cab driver that took us to the theater couldn't see where he was going. It was very frightening. But we had to go, because the theater did not close. We had very few people in the audience, but for the morale of the people we went on.

Sunday, my partner and I were in church with our gas masks we had been given. All of a sudden, there was a siren going over. We didn't know what it was. We just sat there. Pretty soon we looked around, and little by little, quietly, the people were leaving. Very quietly. Then we saw the priest and the altar boys leaving. I said to my partner, "I think we better go, too! Let's follow the priest!" We didn't know where to go, so we followed them to the shelters and stayed there until we heard the all-clear signal.

Before and after London, we were playing mostly big-time vaudeville and with name bands. Oh, the bands were the greatest! We opened the shows for them, because we had a sort of an act that got the people going. They had such good bands. Seventeen pieces, you know. We had one rehearsal and that's it. Oh, they cut the music fast. Yeah, you can dance to that. We were with Artie Shaw at the Fox Theatre in Detroit. We played Atlantic City on the Pier with Benny Goodman. We were at the Paramount with Tony Pastor, Leo Reisman at the Strand. Carmen Cavallaro at the Hotel Chase in St. Louis. Abe Lyman at the Strand. Lionel Hampton in Hartford, Connecticut. We toured with Martha Raye, and even Chico Marx and his band in 1940. We had to leave him in San Diego, because we couldn't stay after the war started.

In 1940, we got this contract in Rio de Janiero. We were on the same ship with Peg Leg Bates. We had such a *wonderful* time! Swimming with him, ballroom dancing at night with him. We later worked with him at the Roxy Theatre. I remember watching him dance. I never saw a man that worked so hard. He would come off exhausted. He did everything with that peg leg. He was wonderful.

Paul Wing and Dorothy Toy stop the show at the Strand Theatre in New York, January 29, 1939. Dancing in front of the Leo Reisman Orchestra.

In 1941, we were working at the Beachcomber in New York, a nightclub owned by Monte Proser. We went to work one day and saw the papers—it was Pearl Harbor. Ed Sullivan got hold of it that one of us was Japanese and put an article in his column. But he said Paul is Japanese. Danton Walker wrote the same thing. We told Monte Proser that "we think it's best that we don't stay on." He said, "It doesn't matter." But we didn't want any problems because of the articles. We headed off and played all the little towns, staying away from New York for a time.

We eventually made our way back to New York, and Paul got his greetings from Uncle Sam right when we had a four-week engagement at the Paramount. The day after we finished he had to go in. I went back to California. My sister was there too. During World War II, my parents were forced to go to a [Japanese internment] camp in Topaz, Utah. They did not want us to have to go there, too. So my sister and I managed to get to Chicago and did an act together during the war. It was The Toy Sisters. I did the dancing and she sang. We went to New York and had a choreographer, Joseph Adolphous, put our number together. He was a very fine choreographer. It took us months and months to learn this act. We had a hard time. I remember the Thanksgiving dinner—we shared it together because we didn't have any money!

Then the war ended. Paul came out of the service and we went back dancing together. What was it that set our act apart? Well, we did very good dancing. And we had personality. We sold. Because we loved what we were doing, and it took us so many years to get there. Remember, we started very young, and it was a hard struggle climbing that ladder. So when we

Toy and Wing hit the big time - New York, 1939

did dance—it didn't matter if it was a small place or a big place—we danced the same way. We loved it. And we blended together. We were like one person dancing together. That was the main thing.

During all those years of our act it's just like you don't have to eat. Like somebody gave you a *million* dollars! The applause was *all* you worked for. When you get that kind of applause, you just walk out of there floating. You did a good job. The most important thing is they liked you. It's just, "How did we go over? Did they like us?" We loved dancing. I guess it comes across to the people what you feel inside.

October 8, 1992
Oakland, California

11

DANCING INTO SOCIETY

BUNNY BRIGGS

Some people ask me about my sound. I've been blessed in so many ways, because I danced in the streets, I danced in hallways, I danced in hot-dog stands, and I danced for society.

The late 1920s and early 1930s may have been difficult times for most Americans, but for "society" folk, glamour and high living reached its peak. The Astor, Vanderbilt, and Wanamaker families symbolized the very essence of chic sophistication. Though America always had its upper crust, there was something that set this assemblage of millionaires apart—the regal glamour and jazzy opulence of Art Deco. The "high society" were the epitome of Art Deco living. They lived in palatial mansions, drove luxurious automobiles, dressed opulently, ate delectable fare, and had all this accompanied by the rhythms of the Jazz Age. But *their* jazz music had a "society sound." It was sophisticated, smooth, and mellifluous.

The gentle tones of this jazz affected one little guy from Harlem and reverberated through the sounds of his taps. Bunny Briggs had great big eyes, which were constantly gazing joyfully out at the world. Because to him, the world seemed always to be affording a delightful array of wonder. He was born in New York City on February 26, 1922. He entered show business, like thousands of other youngsters of his time, dancing on the streets of Harlem. While still a little boy, Bunny Briggs was discovered by Luckey Roberts (C. Luckeyth Roberts), the black society orchestra leader. Bunny spent the next few years of his life dancing with Luckey Roberts and his Society Entertainers in the homes of America's wealthiest. If every tap dancer has an innate rhythm and sound, Bunny's was a perfect fit for the people he was entertaining. His style was sumptuously soft, delicate, and filled with a knowing humor. The taps he plied reflected the twinkle in his eye.

By the time Bunny Briggs was in his teens, swing music had entered the scene (or as a popular song of the day stated, "Swing is here to sway, you can't deny it . . ."), and he found himself tap dancing with many of the top bands. One night he might be with Earl Hines, the next Count Basie, another with Charlie Barnet. It was easy for Bunny Briggs to migrate from band to band, because his tap was based on improvisation, so no matter the style of music, he matched it with musical wit and brilliance. His dances possessed a rhythmically hypnotic quality that thoroughly entranced viewers. And whatever the beat, Bunny Briggs brought the influence of his early childhood with him—a captivatingly light and breezy style that became his trademark.

BUNNY BRIGGS — Well, I just started dancing! It was born in me. My mother told me when she was carrying me that she would still go to dances. And I'm a staunch believer in, "If you're goin' to have a child, whatever you're around, that child becomes." Anyway, she told me when I was born, when I finally faced the world, my legs were kickin'. When they hold you up and all of that, they let me loose, and I just started dancin'. Just started right out dancin'. And been dancin' ever since.

When I was about three or four, I would go to the Lincoln Theatre in Harlem to see my Aunt Gladys, because she was a chorus girl. I used to love watchin' shows. They would always put me in a different atmosphere, because I lived in Harlem. Not that we were livin' in squalor. But when I would see a show, it would just take me out of Harlem altogether. I would see all these beautiful girls onstage dancing with big hats on top of their beautiful heads, doing their production numbers, and they'd have a fellow to sing while they dancin'. It was just seventh heaven as far as I was concerned. It would just take me to another world. And I think this is what made me want to be in show business. Because at that time, I didn't think they were human beings! I didn't think they had to eat, or nothing like that! Because they looked so *good*. In the 1920s, you couldn't come on the stage with your hair lookin' all straggly and wearin' all funny-looking clothes. It was just not allowed. You had to look your very best, because the people that were coming to see you, they're tryin' to escape. They don't want to see what they can see in the street. They want to see some glamour. And these people *were* glamorous.

When I was coming up, Bill Robinson was the top tap dancer in the world. And one particular day, he was on the bill at the Lincoln Theatre. I saw this man walk out on the stage with a derby on and neatly dressed—which I was surprised to see, because at that time, mostly all the dancers were in uniforms—bellhop uniforms, or what have you. But he was dressed like a gentleman that's walkin' down Fifth Avenue! He started dancin', and I just sat there in awe. At that time, I *knew*

Captured by the camera of James Kriegsmann is Bunny Briggs's gentle style of tap in which he so excelled, 1930s.

Atkins, and I'd see a step and say, "Hey, that's not bad!" I wouldn't do it like that. I'd add or do something, but nothin' like they did, you know. So it just adds on. Because there's only about five or six steps in the whole thing. It's the way you present it. It's the *way* you execute your steps.

See, I liked to dance. That's the first thing. I just loved it! And my family, we were not well off, but we were not poor. I was born on Lenox Avenue and One hundred thirty-eighth Street, a swingin' area, I'll tell you that. I think I was about four or five years old, no older than that, and *Amos and Andy* was very popular, and the people in Harlem used to gather around a record shop to listen to the show, because there were not too many radios. I guess some people had them, but the majority of them didn't—so they would gather around this record shop to listen. At that time, it was only fifteen minutes. Well, right after *Amos and Andy* would finish, the owner of the record shop would put on a record, and I would come out and do what they called at that time the Charleston, the Shimmy—things like that. Then they started throwin' money. And the money was comin'—quarters, half dollars. . . . They gave it all to me, and I'd run right up and give it to my mother. I think the first time the money amounted to about fifteen dollars. Fifteen dollars in those days was just the end! Everything was cheap, so fifteen dollars you could live off it for weeks.

Around 1927, when I was five years old, some

what I was going to do. After the show, I saw my mother and said to her, "Mamma, I want to be a tap dancer." And I started doin' something for her. I started doin' his routine, because it was a very simple routine really—puttin' your hands on your hips and smiling and things like that. And she laughed and said, "OK, honey."

Well, that would be how I learned to tap dance—watchin' other dancers. They called it "stealin' steps." But I've never stole any steps. I've looked at a step and said, "Well, I can do it this way." So I would see Bill Robinson, or Coles and

man by the name of Porkchops saw me dance there in front of the record shop. He asked me where I lived, and I said, "I live right upstairs." He came up and asked my mother if he could take me around the dance halls. And he said, "I'll split the money with you, whatever you make." So he started takin' me around to the Renaissance Casino and other clubs and ballrooms around New York City. All I did at that time would be the Charleston and the Mess Around. The cute things, you know. People would just fall in love with me, because I was a little kid! So whatever I did was all right. They just—"Aw, look at there!"—you know, that kind of thing. I didn't have to do anything to be accepted—just dance or roll my eyes, and the people would just go crazy!

Later, Porkchops added two more kids to the act, Junie Miller and Paul White. Our name was Porkchops, Navy, Rice, and Beans. The places that Porkchops took us to were ballrooms. It was during the 1920s, that you could just go on into a club and say you'd like to dance. "OK, go ahead." You know, it was one of those kind of things. We'd work there between halves. And we'd run out, the three of us, and Porkchops would come out behind us. And we all danced to the "Bugle Call Blues." And they'd throw money. That went on for quite some time. Quite some time. About five or six years.

In the early 1930s, Porkchops took us to a party for the very rich. Now, how we got in there, I don't know. Luckey Roberts had the orchestra

there. He was called Luckey Roberts and his Society Entertainers, because the only people he entertained were the—in those days we called them the Four Hundreds. The Vincent Astors, the John Wanamakers, the Vanderbilts. For those kind of people. Nobody knew Luckey Roberts in Harlem! He never worked for nobody in Harlem. He didn't work the Lincoln Theatre or the Lafayette. He just worked for the *very, very* rich! So, we were in there, and we danced. Then they wanted to give us something to eat from the kitchen. My mother told me never accept no food from anybody. So when they asked me, I said, "No, thank you." The other two ate, and Porkchops ate. And I sat there. Later, Luckey told my mother that he just kept lookin' at me, you know, because I sat on the side, a little kid with great big eyes. And

Bunny Briggs during his days with Luckey Roberts and His Society Entertainers, 1920s

DANCING INTO SOCIETY

he asked my mother if I could go with him. That's how I started workin' for the Astors, the Vanderbilts, and people like that—workin' for this society.

Well, here we go again. Another world! Another world! The homes—I'd never seen nothin' like this. Butlers, maids, and things like this. What's goin' on here? You know, you take a kid up there and then bring him back to Harlem. For a minute I'm here, and next minute I'm back in this nonsense. So, I start thinkin' to myself, "What is this? Why haven't we got this?" Everything was running through my mind.

They had me to sit down at the table with them one day. There was all the beautiful china. This great big smoked salmon and champagne. And they wouldn't eat all of it! And being young, well, I spoke right up and said, "You not goin' to eat all of that!" Never knowing that you're not supposed to do that. I was too young to know! So it came from the heart, and it just broke up everybody at the table. The next thing I know, I came home I had *everything* that you would want—caviar, just name it. I had it. And that went on for years. Luckey kept me with him for years.

Luckey Roberts was a pianist. He's the one that wrote "Moonlight Cocktail." I would say that he was in the same framework as a Scott Joplin. He wrote a lot of things, but they didn't come out till years later, and he died very bitter. Well anyway, he would play at all the society affairs. They'd call for him because he had that society sound. I was the only entertainer there. He would have me do a little dance.

Some people ask me about my sound. And I've been blessed in so many ways, because I danced in the streets, I danced in hallways, I danced in hot-dog stands, and I danced for society. When I would work for the society people, they would have a good time, but soft. You wouldn't hear no hollering goin' on. Yet, they'd have a beautiful time. When I would dance, they would sit on the floor right around me. Therefore, I had to dance soft. I couldn't bang or go on in that kind of thing. I would dance very soft.

I was always an improvisation dancer. I never danced to the same tune more than two or three times. My style is carefree. It's carefree and hard, but I try to make it look easy. Because what I found out as long as I've been in show business was that your audience goes along with you. But

if you look strained and scufflin' going on, well, they scufflin' there with you. If you look like it's calm and nice, it usually goes over. Not all the time, but most of the time it goes over. An act that split, make the jumps and all, makes you on edge and you're glad when they're finished because you're scared they're going to hurt themselves, and that kind of thing. I like to see a performer that's smooth, where the music is nice so you can relax.

I remember one incident workin' with Luckey. The Astors were having what they called a pageant, and Mrs. Astor wanted me to be her page boy. They dressed me up with what the sultans wear—they put a turban on my head, gold shoes, a parrot in my hand. Oh, it was just magical. They even sent a chauffeur for me. In my neighborhood a chauffeur—*please*! And everybody from my building came out there to see me. They felt so happy.

After the pageant was over, this lady called me over and sat me on her knee. All she did was make funny faces. Well, I fell out! I just laughed —*ha ha ha . . . ha ha ha . . .* Then she turned to me and said, "If there's anything in the world that you would love to have, what would it be?" Junie Miller, my partner, had a bicycle. But he wouldn't let me ride it. I don't know why, but he said, "No." All the other kids rode this bike but me. So right away it hit me in the head, and I said, "I'd like to have a bicycle." She said, "You'll have it tomorrow." Well, that lady turned out to be Fanny Brice!

The bike arrived from John Wanamaker's in New York. And it had *everything* on it! It had horns. It had lights. It was a gorgeous bike. Junie just had a bike, I mean it was—it was just a little poor-lookin' bike. But I had the back lights on it and little things you can see when it's dark. It had this thing where you do like that, and it goes "ring, ring, ring!" I came out on that bike, and all the kids gravitated to me right away. They forgot about Junie. And then he came to me and said, "Can I have a ride?" I said, "Sure," you know, hey! Later on, when I was at reasoning age, I said, "That was

Fanny Brice that gave me that bicycle!" Yes, I had a real enchanted childhood.

The greatest compliment that was ever paid to me was at a place that nobody knows nothin' about, but I was working at a place called the Moulin Rouge on Staten Island. I have a tendency to sometimes go off. But I'm a Pisces, and that happens with Pisces people. Sometimes they go off. This particular night I was dancing, and when I finished dancing, I noticed this girl and fellow sittin' there. So I turned to them and said, "Why don't you put your arm around the lady? Enjoy yourself. You're sittin' there . . . it's either your wife or girlfriend or something. You're sittin' there with your hands folded." I said, "Put your arm around her!" So I started to dance to "I'll Be Loving You, Always." Now, just straight away the band looked at me like I was crazy, which I am at times! I said,

"Dim the lights." Next thing you know—and I don't think they've ever done this for a tap dancer anywhere—all the men in there that were with ladies put their arms around them. I said, "This is the first and last time I'll ask for this. I don't want no applause. Just stay like that." And I danced. I think I did two choruses of what they call a Soft Shoe. And the next thing, when the band finished, I just walked off. I just walked off and left them there with their arms around the girls. They were kissin' and huggin'. And that to me was the greatest compliment I've ever had. It was just beautiful.

December 10, 1988
Las Vegas, Nevada

12

"THE SEPIA CINDERELLA GIRL"

JENI LeGON

I did their step . . . and they just stood back and said, "Man, look at that little ol' skinny girl dance!"

uring tap dance's heyday, every show, every nightclub, every theater, and every revue had a bevy of beautiful chorines. These extraordinarily talented hoofers could just about, if not, out-tap any of the featured acts around. Thousands and thousands of girls tied the bows on their pretty little patent leather Mary Janes, stepped into chorus lines, and in complete synchronization, tapped out the rhythms of the age. Every chorus line had a soubrette, a young girl who was featured in front of the line. And there were a few sister tap acts like The Edward Sisters, though not many compared to the brother acts that proliferated throughout these years. There were brother-and-sister tap acts like Vilma and Buddy Ebsen. There were boy-and-girl tap acts like Cholly and Dotty. There were two-boys-and-a-girl tap acts like Miller Brothers and Lois. But the rarest act of all was the girl solo.

From 1900 to 1955, there were few of them. Women tappers had the talent, but they were rarely promoted as solo acts. Ruby Keeler, Eleanor Powell, Vera-Ellen, Eleanore Whitney, Dixie Dunbar, Shirley Temple, Ann Miller, and Peggy Ryan were in films. On stage and in clubs the real headliners were Alice Whitman, Eleanor Powell, Cora LaRedd, Grace McDonald, Juanita Pitts, Ann Pennington, Marilyn Miller, and Marie Bryant. And that was basically it.

There was one more among the girl tappers who

was their star dancer and was billed as "The Queen of Taps." According to all who saw her, she was. Alice married dancer Aaron Palmer, and in 1919, they had a son nicknamed "Pops," who became one of the first great acrobatic tap dancers. In the early 1930s, he was teamed up with Louis Williams and they formed the outstanding tap team Pops and Louis.

The Whitman sisters' show was variety. They featured singers, dancers, comedians, a chorus line, and a jazz band. The size of the company was anywhere between twenty to thirty performers. It was considered the fastest-paced show on the road, and was undeniably the royalty of black vaudeville. For up-and-coming entertainers, it was also the highest-paying act on the T.O.B.A. The Whitman sisters knew talent when they saw it and gave hundreds of dancers their first big break. They were also responsible for featuring dancers as just that—dancers (as opposed to singer-dancers, comedians-dancers). Much of the finest tap dance talent around came up with The Whitman Sisters, including Jeni LeGon.

Jeni LeGon went on to a career as a solo tap act that can be matched by few. She appeared in films, on stage, abroad, and was greeted with success in all venues. She was quite unlike the other female tap dancers of her time, because she wore pants rather than sweet skirts, and she included the rigorous flash work of splits, flips, and Toe Stands that were usually the copyright material of the male ranks in the tap world. Needless to say, the color barriers of the day prevented her from breaking into films in a big way, though she got closer than any other female black dancing star of her time.

did buck the trend and become a great solo tap star—Jeni LeGon. She also had the recognition of being the only black woman teamed to tap dance with Bill Robinson in film. Before she made her way to Hollywood, Jeni got her training tap dancing in chorus lines, and with the famous Whitman Sisters Troupe—Mabel, Essie, Alberta, and Alice. In 1904, they organized their first company called The Whitman Sisters' New Orleans Troubadours. Mabel began managing the group, and was at that time acknowledged as the only black woman managing her own company and booking them continuously in the leading Southern houses. Around 1910, The Whitman Sisters act was developed as a regular road show. They were an impressive show business family: May handled the bookings; Essie designed and made the costumes; Alberta (who had cut her hair short, dressed as a man in the act, became one of the best male impersonators) composed their shows' music and was the troupe's financial secretary. Alice

JENI LeGON — My real love for the theater came actually from my family. On Sundays, my sister used to take me to the Chicago Theatre, where they had musical and stage shows. One Christmas, I'll never forget, there was this fabulous, fabulous show, and there were little girls dressed up as poinsettias who pranced around to the song "Hallelujah." I just stood up out of my seat and shouted, "I'm going to do that! I want to be up there! I want to do that!" I was about seven, and that's when the bug really hit me.

I was born in Chicago August 14, 1916 and raised near South Side. All the neighborhood children used to play theater on the front of our houses. We used the steps for the theater and the sidewalks for the stage. For music we had a little string band with the kazoos and the bass and somebody playing the boxes and stuff for drums, and things like that. We used to sing and dance; we really learned to perform on the sidewalks down in front [of] our houses. We had little gangs, acting gangs, you know, and we used to have kids audition for us. If they were good, we would keep them in our neighborhood gang— if not we'd send them down to others! We felt we were the best on the block, you know, the best in the area.

My brother also was a singer and an exhibition ballroom dancer. When I was about ten, I used to do some things with him on exhibition for ballroom. All of the neighborhood movie houses used to have Christmas shows, and then when I was about thirteen, my brother went on an audition for one and got the job. He came back and told me that they were having an audition for a chorus line. I went down and auditioned

and was accepted, because I was a fairly good dancer. But I hadn't started to develop at all, and all the other girls had nice little figures with little bumpies and stuff like that. We went backstage and tried the costumes on, and here I still had my little boyish figure, with no bubs and no hips or nothin'. We all came out and posed, and my costume just hung off of me. It was ridiculous. The director said, "Oh, my God. What am I going to do with you!" I, with my big mouth, said, "I don't dance in dresses in things like this, I dance . . . in pants. I sing and dance in pants." I really didn't do it, I just had a big mouth and said I did. But he said, "Oh, well that's wonderful." He said, "Then you don't have to dance in the line. You can be the soubrette." So I had to dash madly home and make up a costume. Fortunately, I knew that Santa was bringing one of my cousins a brand-new suit for Christmas, and his old black suit that he used to wear for his Sunday best was being demoted. I had my mom call my aunt and ask if we could borrow his pants. My brothers were waiters, and a friend of my sister cut down one of the white jackets and made me a little Eton jacket. That's how I got into the pants, and I danced in the pants from then on.

When I was about fourteen, Count Basie had his first introduction to the big time. In Chicago there was a circuit of theaters called the Balaban and Katz, and they had theaters all over the city in different areas. The Chicago Theatre was their flagship theater. The Uptown was way out on the North Side. They had one out on the South Side called the Tivoli. And then they had one on the West Side, and I think it was called the West End or West Side, or something like that. Later on, they built the Regal in the black neighborhood, on the South Side. For this particular engagement, Count Basie was being showcased, and they put together a sixteen-girl chorus line which I got in. I was on the left end of the second line, and I used to cut up a bit. Josephine Baker was my idol, and that's what she had done. She had been an end girl in the line—that was a choice position in those days. We played the Uptown. Usually a show only stayed one week, but they kept us two weeks because it was such a heck of a good show!

After working in the Basie line, someone suggested that I audition for the chorus with The Whitman Sisters. I was fourteen and a half, I guess, going into fifteen. I went to the rehearsal hall at the Regal Theatre to audition for the job, and four guys—I'm almost certain it was The Four Step Brothers—were rehearsing in another studio. I was early for my appointment, and this other studio

was open. They were practicing, and I went in and asked if I could sit and watch. And they said, of course. You see, I learned to tap dance by watching other dancers. I used to go to the theaters, especially when Duke, Cab, Fletcher Henderson, or one of the bands came in with a dance act. I would go and watch the movies and then watch the stage show. Then when the movies were on the second time, I would go out in the lobby of the theater and practice what I had seen the guys do on stage. I did this all day long until it was time to go home. That's how I used to learn a lot of steps and add to it and, you know, detract what I could do and what I couldn't do. I had seen The Four Step Brothers before, and had learned their routine! So, here I was, early for the audition, and I sat down and watched as they were putting some new steps in their routine and changing some stuff about. They got to this one particular step of theirs that I had loved. I had already learned this step, perfected it, and had added something different to it on the end. So, automatically, when they got to it and they were saying, "We ought to do so and so and so . . ." I said, "Look, could you do this?" And they said, "What!" And I said, "Well look, let—let me show you what I mean." I did their step and then did whatever this little ending that I had put on—and they just stood back and said, "Man, look at that little ol' skinny girl dance!" And they just hugged and kissed me and said, "Wow, girl, you can sure lay it down!" When it came time for my audition, they went down the hall with me and

Jeni LeGon's trademark—a nifty suit with long pants, 1935

told the director of the show, "Man, you don't have to audition this girl, just put her on your payroll, because she can really do it!"

With the good word of The Four Step Brothers, I was asked to join The Whitman Sisters. They were something in themselves. The Whitman Sisters featured the younger sister, who was named Alice Whitman, and actually of the tap dancers, she was the best there was. She was tops. She was better than Ann Miller and Eleanor Powell and me and anybody else you wanted to put her to. Oh, she was just an excellent dancer. I mean she did it all. She could do all the ballet-style stuff like Eleanor. And then she could hoof! But she never went out on her own, you know, she stayed with the sisters. I think they came from Atlanta, if I'm not mistaken. They were four sisters who had been a vocal group earlier and sang in the churches and stuff like that. And they just branched out and started having their own complete revue that they traveled the South and played only to black theaters. They carried about an eight-piece band, two comedians usually, a chorus line of eight girls featuring Alice. And in the group was their other sister, whose name was Alberta, and they used to call "Bert." She dressed in the pants like I used to do and imitated a boy, and she and Alice did things together. There was another sister, who was a beautiful Mae West type. In fact, Mae must have seen her work, because she copied her exactly. The older sister was the manager of the group, and her name was Sister May.

When you joined The Whitman Sisters, you went with them, you worked with them, and you just learned—that was all. You just learned to perform. They developed lots and lots of our black people who are stars of then and now. Willie Bryant and Leonard Reed were two. Oh, I could go on and on, you know. It was during the year that I was with them they got Louis from New Orleans and put him with Pops Whitman, and they became a real popular team. They were as popular as The Nicholas Brothers were at their time, during that same era, you see, and even later than that. They were Pops and Louis and they did the same kind of stuff that The Berry Brothers and the other teams like that did.

I was in the line. The Whitman sisters had fixed the line so we had all the colors that our race is known for. All the pretty shading—from the darkest darkest, to the palest of pale. Each one of us was a distinct-looking kid. It was a rainbow of beautiful girls. Three of us girls did the Snake Hips, imitating "Snake Hips" Tucker, with the shimmery blouses and all that sort of business. We wore orange blouses with the big sleeves, green satin pants, and a sash around our waists. And of course, when you'd shake, you know, with being in this satin stuff, it would just shake—but we had nice little bums at that time, so we would just shake and it would look very good! We used to stop the show a lot of times. I was with The Whitman Sisters for about six months, and it was a wonderful experience. You really learned show business.

After The Whitman Sisters, my foster sister and I put together a little act and worked nightclubs in Chicago. We worked as a boy-and-girl team; I wore the pants and danced as a boy, and she was the girl. We were invited to go to California for a show, but when we got out there, there wasn't anything for us! So we all had to scuffle and carry on, you know, to make ends meet and to survive. We heard about an audition that was being held by Earl Dancer, Ethel Waters's former manager. He was producing a show for the heads of Fox Studios—Winfield Sheenan and Will Rogers. I got a part in it as a single and so did my

ONE—TWO—THREE—FOUR! PRETTY LEGS GO PRETTIER

Advertising campaign for Jeni LeGon, 1935

about ten minutes, and that's when I first got discovered. See, I danced like The Nicholas Brothers. I did flips, double spins, Knee Drops, Toe Stands, and all that sort of business. All the things that the boys did, I did. It was rare for a girl doing that sort of stuff. That's why I used to stop the show, because I could hoof and do the flash.

RKO Pictures had just signed Bill Robinson for the movie *Hooray for Love* [1935], and it was suggested that I dance with him. This was just completely amazing to me. I had never thought of being in the movies—being a movie star had never entered my mind. I just wanted to sing and dance. I just wanted to be onstage. That was my ultimate game, and I had accomplished that. So when the movie opportunity came along, it was something entirely different. Then when I was put on with Bill, who at that time was considered the greatest tap dancer in the world—well, I mean, it was just mind-boggling! You couldn't believe it, me, a little snot that had just come out of the woods in a sense and hadn't been dancing that long. But, you know, it was just a wonderful opportunity. And suddenly, I found myself in a dressing room that was in the same building with Fred Astaire and Ginger Rogers, and they were rehearsing and we were rehearsing right on the same lot. Off times we'd stop by one another's rehearsals and do a little bit of exchanging of steps and yakkity yakkin' and stuff like that. It was fantastic.

But of course, in those times it was a "black-and-white world." You didn't associate too much

sister. The show was at the Wilshire Ebell Theatre in Los Angeles. Every Sunday night they used to showcase new talent. All of the casting directors from the studios used to come, and that's when they saw me. I stopped the show that night for

Jeni LeGon and Bill Robinson, the dancing sensation of R. K. O.'s "Hooray for Love," are pictured here stepping high, wide and handsome. The big flicker will be released soon. Ann Southern and Jean Raymond are the featured stars.

1935

socially with any of the stars. You saw them at the studio, you know, nice—but they didn't invite. The only ones that ever invited us home for a visit was Al Jolson and Ruby Keeler. Al Jolson was a friend of Earl's—they had scuffled together when he was working with Ethel. They had a rapport that was very good. A couple of others later on that I met who were nice, but I mean it was just the times and that was the things that happened.

Anyway, there I was working with the great Bill Robinson. He was the perfectionist, definitely, and would rehearse for hours and hours and hours. And he was an excellent teacher. He was patient. But he wanted your undivided attention when he was showing you something, because he didn't care about doing it two or three different times. He just wanted it to be good—which it happened to turn out to be.

I had never been to a preview before, and I didn't know what to expect. After *Hooray for Love* was shown, we went out in the lobby, and the people just descended on me like it was no tomorrow!—asking for my autograph and congratulating me, and all that sort of business. As I've said before, at that time, we lived in this black-and-white world, definitely. But here were all these people of the opposite race hugging and kissing me, and man, I thought they had lost their minds! I thought, "What in the world is all this about?" It was just glorious that all those people would stop me and talk to me that way. It was just heavenly.

Fats Waller was in *Hooray for Love*, too, and we became very close friends. Fats. He's my dreamboat. He's my love. I got to work with him on four shows after *Hooray for Love*. He was very, very supportive. If you couldn't do something quite like you wanted to, well, he would offer up a suggestion, and usually it was right. He had me come to his home and rehearse things before we'd go onstage, because I was still in awful fast company. I needed a lot of bolstering, because I was out there by myself and it was difficult. He taught me some songs and how to deliver them. He was just that kind of person. He was just wonderful, and we were friends until he died.

We became a very tight package, as far as working together was concerned. Our act consisted of what we would call a *challenge*. I'd do steps, and he'd say, "Look at that little girl go, she really thinks she's something. I bet she couldn't do this." And he'd play something on the piano, a rhythm pattern—and I would imitate it with my feet. Then I'd say, "I bet he can't do this," and I'd do one, and he'd answer on the piano. We would do that back and forth maybe for a chorus. He would crack some of his famous one-liners—"All that meat and no potatoes," his asides, I guess you could call them. Then finally he and the whole band would play for me. Then I'd challenge him to come and dance with me. And he'd get up, and we would do a couple of jive steps and exit together. And when we'd get to the wings, we would do that nonsense of "You go first,"—"No, you go first," and we'd change positions and keep walking around each other, and finally I would exit, and he would grab the curtain and shake his bum! We would tear up the place!

After making *Hooray for Love*, I went to Europe for the first time. There was a show going on in New York called *At Home Abroad*, and it starred Bea Lillie and Ethel Waters. The other person in it was Eleanor Powell. But MGM signed Eleanor Powell out of that show to be groomed and everything, see. C. B. Cochran, who was considered the Ziegfeld of London, bought the rights to *At Home Abroad*. I was brought over to do both the songs that Ethel had sung and also the dances that Eleanor Powell had done! That's where I met the Nicholases again. I had first met The Nicholas Brothers on my way to London stopping in New York. They were working with Cab at the Cotton Club up in Harlem. And then we met in London. They were over there in *Lew Leslie's Blackbirds of 1936*, and we did lots of things together. They came to my birthday party that year, and what a party that was. The Nicholases were there with their mom and sister, and some of the stars from the show that I was in, and some

of the stars from their show. Paul Robeson was there, too. He was a good friend of Josephine Baker. I had read about her and heard about her all my life. As I said, she was my idol. Through Paul and Earl, I finally met her—over the phone. Oh, I just carried on like a fool!

It was wonderful living over in London then. I got the star treatment. I had lots of publicity, and people recognized me on the street. The reviews were stupendous. From *News of the World*: "Plenty of zest. Cochran is a genius. Jeni LeGon and company have never known a liverish moment. Mr. Cochran's wizardry at its best. Some things may be overlooked in inventory of so bountiful a cornucopia, but not Miss Jeni LeGon. The temptation

---

Hollywood's "Sepia Cinderella Girl," Jeni LeGon, was signed by MGM Studios, but the contract was bought out after MGM decided they *already* had a tap dancer —Eleanor Powell, 1936.

to hail her as the new Florence Mills [the first *Blackbirds* star] . . . she has a distinctive charm of her own. A great show . . . Never before have a riot of color and glamour and talent been seen upon any one stage." *Empire News:* "Jeni LeGon is one of the brightest spirits that ever stepped on the stage. It seems that little Jeni LeGon is overshadowing all other entertainers . . . Jeni LeGon, the sepia Cinderella girl who set London agog

Jay Jackson's cartoon sums up the vivacious tap dancer Jeni LeGon just prior to her first sailing to Europe for a role in *At Home Abroad* (London, 1936).

with her clever dancing and cute antics to the musical production of "Charlie" B. Cochran, follows on the current success of the Adelphi Theatre."

Back in New York, I think it was John Bubbles that first brought me down to the Hoofers Club. The Hoofers Club was down underneath the Lafayette, and it was where all the hoofers used to go and dance. It was just dance. That's all. It was just a room with an old beat-up piano, and there was always somebody who could play stop time. Basically, it was just the piano and a wonderful dance floor. And you'd come in and do your stuff—if you got in and didn't do a good performance, you didn't get invited back again! But you knew if you were doing well, because they'd say, "OK, man!" "Good, good." Then you'd know if you weren't doing well, because there was no grunts, you know, that admiration—"Dance!" "Do it!" "Lay it down!"—or whatever the hell it was. If you didn't get any of those, well then you tucked your tail and went out! You practiced another two or three months and you'd come back. Then maybe you laid down something that the guys thought, "Oh yeah, not bad, not bad, man. You can come on in," you know. Then you had entree. I was one of the only girls that was ever invited to come in and dance. But the guys didn't mind, because I could do it! I was a *real* hoofer!

There were many women that could "do it." Alice Whitman was the best. She was a better dancer than I'd ever be. And there was a set of sisters, The Edward Sisters, they were very, very good. Pearl Bailey was a tap dancer before she was anything else. And, of course, there was Eleanor Powell, Ann Miller, Peggy Ryan, Dixie Dunbar. But all in all, there just weren't too many girl tap acts around. I don't know why. You had to tap to be in the chorus line, and there were excellent girl tap dancers all over the place. I just don't know why there weren't many soloists. Most of them danced in the chorus or did soubrette out in front of the chorus. But not too many of them went in for doing solo.

Oh, there was another girl who was an excellent dancer—Marie Bryant. She could do just about everything, and she was very, very good. She was mostly a soubrette. She worked in Duke Ellington's show *Jump For Joy* [1941] with a boy named Paul White, who was an excellent dancer, too. That was a funny incident. One night Paul and Marie did a number in the show—I think they did the musical number called "Jump For Joy." It was set in a drive-in for waitresses and waiters, and they did this jitterbug number. During that period, girls wore these long falls. Well, she had on one of these falls, and one night she didn't pin it on quite as tight as it should have been. She and Paul were doing this Jitterbug, and he slung her front, and this wig just took off like a bird! *Vroom!* Duke was leadin' the band and playin', and he just bent his head to one side, let it pass over him and kept directing. Never missed a beat. The kids never stopped. And the band never stopped. They just kept on. The damn thing fell out in the first row! It was a riot, oh God, it was funny. I love comedy and stuff, and I just screamed and fell out on the floor laughing. I was so embarrassed, I crawled up the aisle on my hands and knees right out of the theater. The kids got a standing ovation, because they never stopped dancing. They just kept on going!

Well, from the very start, when I really found out that tap was my thing, then that's all I ever did was just dance and improve and get to the point where I was a good salesman and pretty good craftsman. I *absorbed* it. Every time I'd see something that I liked, I would take it and tear it to pieces and make it my own. And I made my living at it. It's simply the love of my life.

Tap is how I got started, why I got started, and it's how I intend to end! They'll put me in the coffin with a "wing," and they're going to have to make a funny kind of coffin, because when I leave I'll be doing the Time Step!

August 17, 1989
Vancouver, B.C. Canada

13

LAST OF THE STREET TAP DANCERS

LaVAUGHN ROBINSON

To be on Broad and South, you had to have your shoes on tight! 'Cause that was *the* corner!

Some of the greatest tap dancers of all time never had a formal dance lesson. Many danced for years without ever owning a pair of tap dance shoes. Though these kids never had formal training, they studied with some of the finest teachers around and became the top artists in the field. Their training was right off the street from other dancers.

Dancing on street corners was an integral part of many a dancer's schooling, and it was not, by any means, casual. There a dancer had to demonstrate bona fide skill to "survive." If a dancer could not "cut it," there was just no staying on that particular corner. Corners were ranked, and a dancer's goal was to move up to the top corner. It was not easy. There was a tremendous amount of competition.

One of the last of the street tap dancers was LaVaughn Robinson. He came right out of the heart of it all—Philadelphia, perhaps the most competitive town for tap dancers. Throughout his childhood, LaVaughn Robinson watched dancers like The Condos Brothers. He began the long trek up through the streets, venturing from one corner to the next, until finally reaching the top. His experience encompassed the entire breadth of tap on the streets, first with a "tramp band," then on the corners, then as a busker in bars, then dancing out a living with some of the big bands.

LaVaughn Robinson grew up around the best of the tap artists. He danced with them on the streets, he saw them in the theaters, he saw them in the clubs. And through it all he developed his own unique style of tap, a rapid-fire close rhythm technique that sent energy flying off the floor and ignited anyone lucky enough to be present.

LAVAUGHN ROBINSON — I was born in 1927 and grew up in Philadelphia. When I was seven years old, my mother taught me a Time Step. My mother was a terrific tap dancer! She never did it professionally, but she was an excellent dancer. You know, a lot of tap dancers come out of Philadelphia. A *lot* of tap dancers! Philadelphia breeded tap dancers and prize fighters. It was just that everybody in Philadelphia *could* do it. You understand me? People didn't learn in no [tap] schools then. See, you learned right out on the street.

I had seven brothers, countin' me, and seven sisters. My mother was pretty shrewd. You know why I say that? Because she taught me the Time Step and made me study it. But the reason why she did that, she had a method to that: It kept me outta the kitchen and kept me from, you know, stayin' around her all the time. Because my mother was a great cook. And she used to make all these different puddin's and cobblers. I would always be the one that would lick the pan and bother her. I was a pest. The rest of the boys and girls had their chores. I was the one that she chose to teach this to, so I would have something to do so I wouldn't get on her nerves. I'll put it that way, 'cause I think I got on her nerves a lot!

I learned how to tap by watchin' other tap dancers. I got affiliated with a lot of other young guys that were street players, you know. And we had one of them "tramp bands." A tramp band is when you have a washboard with thimbles on your fingers, and a tub with the cat guts on it, and you play it like a bass. You put cigarette wrapping paper in the kazoo and play it. And you tap dance on the street, you see. That's how I started. To me it was a fun thing. The police used to run us off the corners, 'cause we used to block up all the traffic.

So we would go down to John Wanamaker's, which is one of the big department stores. And we all used to buy little shoeshine boxes that they had, little shoeshine boxes with straps on them, and wear 'em around our neck. We would play music, and then a couple of us would get up and dance. Then—all of us were dancers. I mean, tryin' to learn to dance. We made up little routines. You know. And we'd watch other dancers, and we would steal from them. Like we'd take maybe two or three bars from them, and we'd put it all together. The next day we'd hook it up together. And then we'd say, "We're gonna do this, this time." You know, stuff like that. When we get down in the main district and start to playin', we had one guy that used to watch out for the police. When the police used to come, he'd let us know, and then we'd put our shoeshine boxes down and start shinin' shoes!

LaVaughn Robinson (right) learned tap by working his way up the street corners in 1930s Philadelphia. Pictured here during a series of club dates, 1950s

When I got older, I started watchin' other tap dancers that came to Philadelphia. 'Cause Philadelphia was like a mecca for tap dancers. See, Steve's [Condos] father had a restaurant at Eleventh and South called the Standard Restaurant. A lot of the tap dancers would mingle in that area 'cause the Standard Theatre was there, see. The Standard Restaurant was right across the street. The Nicholas Brothers come out of one of them little streets, Nordane and Sixteenth Street. And their father used to play, I think it was the drums or the piano, in one of the pit bands in the theaters, you know.

Steve and his brother, anytime they would come to a theater in the movies, we'd always be in there. And The Nicholas Brothers. Yeah. By the time I start learnin' tap, they was already in movies. Anytime they would come to a movie in one of them pictures, we would all be at the movies. When The Nicholas Brothers got through dancing in the movies, the people just lookin' at the movies stood up and clapped. I mean not in the movies, but the people in the theater that was watchin' the movie. When The Nicholas Brothers got through, the people in the theater got up and clapped. Now they watchin' this on a screen! You understand what I mean? With nobody but The Nicholas Brothers did that happen. Nobody but The Nicholas Brothers.

The Nicholas Brothers, see they came outta Philadelphia, too. But they didn't hang on them corners. Yeah—well see—they were fortunate. 'Cause

I know a friend of mine who went to school with them, and he went to school one morning and the teacher kept callin' Harold's name out, "Harold Nicholas." You know how they name out in the roll call? Never got no answer for a whole week. And never got no answer. That Saturday he went round the corner to the movies, and there they were on the screen. The teacher said, "Harold Nicholas," never get an answer. 'Cause they didn't know that they were out makin' that picture. And he went to the movies and looked up, and there they come out on the screen!

When I was seven years old, I was going to the movies. But, if it wasn't The Condos Brothers or The Nicholas Brothers ... I guess I was a little prejudiced. I'm tellin' you, The Condos Brothers —see they was something else. 'Cause when they would come into town in one of them pictures, everybody in the community would go to see that picture. And when The Nicholas Brothers was in them pictures, EVERYBODY would go see them. It was the style. See, they were rhythm-enthusiast tap dancers. They was like percussionists, you know, percussionists.

In the 1930s, you could walk from one end of South Street to the other and see a different style of tap dancing just about on every corner. You'd see a lot of tap dancers that were great Wing dancers. And then you had tap dancers who did a lot of rhythm dancing. You had flash tap dancers—you understand what I'm sayin'? But you saw all this on the street. This was not in the theater or nothing like that, you know. This is just like what you would see on the streets. And that's how I learned how to tap, because I used to hang out on them corners and watch all the tap dancers.

Yeah, it got so with me that I could look at a tap dancer and tell what part of the country he was from, because certain styles of tap went with where he was from. If a dancer came in from the West Coast, he was doin' that Western rhythm. There was really a big difference between East

Coast dancers and West Coast dancers, oh, yeah!

We had a spot where the dancers jammed, in a little street called Kater Street. And in Kater Street it was at night that the streetlight would shine down, and it was like a spotlight. They would meet there at certain times. You ever see The [Four] Step Brothers? They used to do a thing like clap their hands as they're dancin'. That come off the street. Everybody on the street did that— keep time with their hands and feet while the other guy was tap dancin'. The Step Brothers did it as part of their act when they were doin' it. But the guys that were dancin' on the street did it automatically, 'cause this is what they did. See, they didn't have no instruments or nuthin .

Some of the greatest tap dancers I've seen came off the street. And for me to be able to survive on the street was a gas. Because a lot of times when you came around, if you couldn't hold your own, then you couldn't stay out there. See, they had certain corners that all tap dancers couldn't come on unless you was—you understand what I'm sayin'? One of the main corners was Broad and South. You had to be of certain caliber to be on that corner. Now, you could be down on Fifteenth Street, Fifteenth and South or Thirteenth and South, going down farther. But to be on Broad and South, you had to have your shoes on tight! 'Cause that was *the* corner!

Tap dancing had become very competitive. It was like gunfighters. When a dancer would come in town, there was always somebody there ready

Many of the twentieth century's best tap dancers came right off the street corners, developing their skills in the highly competitive challenges, 1930s.

to challenge him. If you couldn't hold your own, they make you wish you hadn't come on that corner. The easiest corner in town would be like from the beginning, like Twenty-fifth and South or down Second and South comin' back. It wasn't uptown or downtown, it was just a section in the city; if you could hang, if you could dance on the corner of Broad and South, then you was in.

You know that stamp of approval. But, now you go down around Twentieth and South, Twenty-first and South, it was like mediocre. You want to get away from there, because you feel as though you wasn't learnin' nuthin'. So you want to move down. That's the way it was.

Twenty-fifth, that was like the startin' point. And

This spruced-up film version of street dancing features The High Hatters: Bernard Bradley, Clarence "Frenchy" Landry, and Eudell Johnson. From the Universal short *Dancing on a Dime* (1939).

then you worked your way up. See, and Broad Street was like the fourteen-hundred block—that's where all the tap dancers were morning, noon, and night. And not just men—women. You had some good women tap dancers when I came up. I was thirteen the first time I tried Broad and South. But see, I had a lot of buddies, and a lot of guys liked me 'cause they said I had a lot of nerve. So they'd take me and say, "You might as well come on and lay down on this corner for a while." And that's what I did. That's how I learned how to tap. And it was fun!

When we got a little older, we came off the street and start buskin' into different clubs. Buskin' is when you go into a club and dance and you pass the hat around. That was a higher echelon than dancin' on the streets. A lot of the bars at that time in Philadelphia had two pieces, like a piano and a drummer, or either piano, bass, and drums. You had a lot of dancers that were buskin' in these clubs and had to pick your time. Then you had to get in with the musicians, you know, 'cause we'd give them half of the money that we made. So they'd be glad to see us come. They would tell you when would be the best time to come.

They had a theater in Philadelphia called the Earle Theatre. And when the big bands came, they always had a tap dancer or a tap team. It got so that anytime a band came, whatever band it was, I knew what tap dancer was gonna be at the Earle at that particular time, you know, that week they came through. Like if Charlie Barnet came, Charlie Barnet had Bunny Briggs. If Duke Ellington came, Duke Ellington had either Baby Lawrence or one of the others. Now Cab Calloway always brought Honi Coles. See? And if I saw a big band that came in like Louis Jordan, he would always have Teddy Hale. You understand. Basie always had Baby Lawrence. And Lionel Hampton always brought Reds and Curly with him—that was a dance team. This was in the late forties. I used to go to the Earle every Monday, because I knew the tap dancer that I wanted to see, that I wanted to watch and try to steal something from.

===

I think I am one of the last of the street dancers. During the time that we were doin' it, we were the last of the street performers. One of the best things I really got out of it was the knack of learnin' to dance. And it was fun. I enjoyed it.

June 14, 1988
Boston, Massachusetts

14

SPONTANEOUS COMBUSTION ON THE DANCE FLOOR

BUDDY AND VILMA EBSEN

We would dance and it was called "the hottest cool dancing in town."

The graceful and sleek tap movie stars—Astaire, Robinson, Powell—were not the only dancers in demand in the 1930s. There was another world of tap dancers out there hoofing away through the Depression. Twisting and entwining their arms and legs, they danced a comedy style called legomania. Full of humor and delightful eccentricities, this dance form was extremely intricate and difficult to perform.

Legomania, eccentric tap, comedic tap were all names for tap dancing that was funny in movement. While the theater and vaudeville stages were swarming with hoofers, rhythm tappers, flash tappers, and Soft Shoe dancers, few among the legions could really put comedy tap across. Edmond Kean, the British Victorian actor, put it right when on his deathbed he said, "Dying is easy. Try comedy!" In reaching back through tap's history, two men immediately pop to mind among "legomaniacs": Ray Bolger and Hal Leroy.

Ray Bolger is perhaps the best known in the comedy tap department because of his immortalization as the Scarecrow in *The Wizard of Oz* (1939). Though he does not tap dance, per se, in that film, his

Vilma and Buddy Ebsen—"five-a-day" in vaudeville, 1930

legomania style comes across clearly in his delightful "If I Only Had a Brain" number.

Hal Leroy was one of the kings of legomania. He could do the simplest tap step and make it impossible to "steal," because of his fantastic leg movements. But Hal Leroy was also a sensational rhythm tapper, and was one of the few white tap dancers to become a member of Harlem's Hoofers Club. Hal Leroy's combination of rhythm tap and legomania has yet to be surpassed.

There were also The Ebsens. Buddy and Vilma Ebsen—"spontaneous combustion" on the dance floor. The Ebsens were one of the longest running brother-and-sister tap acts to light the American stage, performing together from 1930 to 1942. Buddy's style was all arms and legs; Vilma's was graceful comedic wit. Together they formed one of tap's happiest teams, appearing in such memorable shows as *Whoopee* (1930) and *Ziegfeld Follies* (1933). They also appeared together along with Eleanor Powell in the motion picture musical *Broadway Melody of 1936* (1935). Reflecting their style, they often dressed in casual cotton knits, and they performed with a refreshingly breezy and comedic style that endeared them to audiences for over a decade.

V I L M A   E B S E N — Buddy and I were born in Belleville, Illinois. I was born in 1911, and Buddy is three years older. We moved to Florida early on. Dad was a Danish ballet master, so we learned to dance the way the young European children learned—folk dances, story dances. These dances were based on rhythm, coordination, balance, and imagination. Therefore, we almost always worked some kind of a theme into our tap dancing, something that was interesting to the audience and always interesting to us, because of the exchange. Instead of just getting out there doing step after step and hoofing, we had a play exchange—you know, playing one against the other. They called us young, wholesome hoofers,

Sheet music cover for "Broadway Rhythm" from *Broadway Melody of 1936* (MGM, 1935). The entire cast (Buddy Ebsen, Eleanor Powell, June Knight, and Nick Long, Jr.) is here except for Vilma, whose body is actually in the picture—Frances Langford's head is superimposed over hers!

back of how amusing that must have been. Although the people bought it.

Sometimes Daddy would take us to North Carolina, and we'd camp all summer. One day, we were about nine and twelve, this big car drove up. A fellow got out, and he said, "I understand that there are a couple of kids here that dance." And my dad said, "Well, I have a son and daughter." The man said, "I happen to be social director of the Grove Park Inn in Asheville, and I'd like very much to see them dance. Perhaps I could put them on my tea dance program." Well, we danced for him all summer. It was Arthur Murray!

but actually we hoofed about as much as Astaire.

Before 1928, there was a funny little company that would come through Orlando. Buddy would go back in the alley backstage and see them tap dancing. So he stayed and watched a few little things. Then he showed me the steps. He'd go back again and pick up some more. The name of the group was The Honey Bunch Company, an itinerant acting company—but then a lot of the actors could dance. So Buddy would go back there to study some more steps, and finally someone said, "Kid, you want to learn these?" And some old guy would show him, and then he'd come back and teach me.

Somehow or other we got booked throughout Florida. We had an act that he put together where I was the dancing teacher and he came in like a country bumpkin and wanted to learn to dance. Then I taught him, and then we danced. I think

Buddy had three years of premed and I was entering my freshman year at Rollins College, and the big Crash hit Florida. So Buddy borrowed fifty dollars from my sister Norma and went to New York. He wrote from New York, "Could I have Vilma up for my birthday?" That was April second, 1929. I went to New York, and we ended up dancing together for the next twelve years.

At the start, I set out to go to some dancing school, and as luck would have it, I found Jack Donahue. He was such a big star in those days. This man had such a joyful teaching technique. And the exquisite contrabody! But basically, Buddy and I learned to tap dance by doing what everybody did: finding somebody who couldn't help but tap dance—finding somebody like this wonderful boy that Buddy met named Chisey Malone. Chisey could never dance the same thing twice.

So when he was dancing with us, I'd say, "Don't forget that." Or Buddy would say to me, "Don't forget that move." Because Chisey would never do it again. He was a street kid who could dance tap out of this world. Just incredible, the most beautiful stylist. We lived in a brownstone front on Riverside Drive, and the three of us would go down into the cellar to practice tap dancing looking like white kids, and we'd come up looking like black kids, because we'd be covered with soot from head to foot.

Finally, Buddy got a job in the musical show *Whoopee* [in 1930]. When *Whoopee* was getting ready to leave town, Buddy said, "I can't leave you in New York by yourself. We're going to have to get you into *Whoopee* for the road." So I auditioned. They had a line-up of girls, and when it came to my turn, I did the Time Step. They said, "Thank you, now step over there." They came around again, and I did the Time Step again, again, and then again. Finally, I walked forward and said, "I've auditioned for you four times. You must have, by now, made up your mind whether I'm going to be chosen or not. Otherwise, if you're laughing at me, I'd like to go." And they said, "Oh, no. You're hired. But, what we really want to know is, are you by any chance related to that big guy over there?" Because we danced the Time Step just exactly alike!

We both got in *Whoopee*, so now every day we could rehearse on stage. But when we were in Chicago, somebody complained that we were using the work lights to rehearse. So they told us we couldn't do it because they had a long run in Chicago. I guess the word got around, and about two nights later there was a big sign on the bulletin board: IF ANY YOUNGSTERS ARE AMBITIOUS

After *Whoopee* closed, we went back to Florida just to breathe, you know—to be kids again. We had a wonderful time. I got a call to go into another club in Atlantic City. I went, and Buddy came along. But this time it was the reverse. He didn't have a job. As a matter of fact, it created a headline that said, EVERYBODY THINKS THERE'S GOLD IN ONE OF THEM THAR EBSENS. You know, because one day they wanted me for a Broadway show, then they wanted Buddy. Anyway, I kept asking this lady, couldn't Buddy and I dance together? But she'd always say no. I'd do my little solo and every night ask. It was always the same answer

Hirschfeld's caricature aptly captures The Ebsens' style during their appearance in *Flying Colors* at the Imperial Theatre in New York City, 1932.

Original pen and ink drawing of Buddy and Vilma Ebsen in *Flying Colors* copyright © by Al Hirschfeld. Drawing reproduced by special arrangement with Hirschfeld's exclusive representative, The Margo Feiden Galleries, New York.

This breathtakingly beautiful portrait of Buddy and Vilma shows another side to the comic eccentric team of The Ebsens, 1934.

put us on stage and we danced, sort of as a guest shot. This was in the early 1930s. There was such a great excitement in those days. And Winchell wrote us up in his column every week. He just couldn't have been nicer to us.

You know where we opened? Our first thing as a team? The Palace. That's where most of the people thought they'd die in, you know. But that was where we opened. I never thought it was that great until years later when somebody said, "Do you realize what you guys did? You opened where most people hope that one day that's where they'd be!"

Our act was called The Ebsens, or Vilma and Buddy Ebsen. Well, we'd go from town to town. On one marquee it said The Ebsteins. On another marquee it said The Ebsons. On another marquee it said The Ebsins. And on another marquee it said Buddy Ebsen and Sister Vilma. Well, we went to the next town and again it said Buddy Ebsen and Sister Vilma. So I said to Buddy in a very soft voice, "If that is not replaced with Vilma and Buddy Ebsen, or The Ebsens, you will be very interested to know that I'm doing the whole act in a nun's habit. If I'm going to be Sister Vilma, I'll be 'Sister Vilma!' " So that was changed fast. He knew that I had a sense of humor.

Buddy was adorable. Just adorable. Just as sweet—well, for instance, supposing I took a cab somewhere by myself, and I happened to look out the back window—there he's writing the license of the cab in a little book. He was so caring.

—"no." One night, I guess she was in a very soft mood, probably a little tipsy—and I said to her, "Couldn't my brother just dance with me after I'm through?" She said, "Oh, OK honey, go ahead." Well, it so happened that Walter Winchell was in the audience that night. He did two paragraphs on us in his column, and by eleven A.M. that next day, we had thirty-two offers. We'd never look for work again!

Walter Winchell would take us up to Harlem to the Cotton Club to see the dancers. Wonderful dancing, wonderful singing, wonderful movement. I mean, that was expressing the way the music should have been expressed. Then when there was a break during an intermission, they'd

But I did everything he wanted, so—you see, I was trained in a Danish and Norwegian family that the boy was always right. It wasn't done in a mean way. If Buddy said something, I said "Sure." I never said anything to Buddy but "sure" my whole

life! We were so close. As a matter of fact, when we split, when Buddy decided to stay on the Coast, and I went back and did a show with Chuck Walters, I was as close to a wreck as you can be. And my doctor explained that it was because we were like one. Now we were split, and I had lost my identity.

Once Buddy and I did a benefit show with Ziegfeld, Marilyn Miller, Jack Donahue, the whole cast of the Ziegfeld show [*Smiles*, 1930] including Adele and Fred Astaire. Leo Reisman was the orchestra leader. The floor was terribly slippery. And we slipped and slid all over, and our routine was awful. After it was over, we sat in a corner very glum because we knew we hadn't danced our best. And the next thing you know, there stood Astaire, and he said, "I know he played

Buddy and Vilma appear in their first motion picture, *Broadway Melody of 1936* (MGM, 1935), costarring with the great lady of tap, Eleanor Powell. The film's rooftop song and dance "Sing Before Breakfast" is one of the silver screen's most delightful romps.

too fast. I know the floor was too slippery. Don't you let it worry you. You kids are going to be great." He was that kind of guy. He just wanted to let us know that he knew what we were up against. Did you know they used to call us the "Baby Astaires" during the 1930s? We were a brother and sister act too, and we came along a decade after Adele and Fred.

There's one thing that you have to know about these show people. Their hearts were so open, and they were so kind to you and so good. Let me give an example. We had always stopped the show. But it was very difficult to go from, say, a small theater to a large theater which seats thousands. This happened to us once. We were used to condensing—we didn't want to knock people over with our power. So we made our movements subtle. Now, we went on this big stage, and those subtle movements didn't read. We did our first show and it was a bomb. The manager said, "Look, we're overtime anyway, so we don't need you." Buddy and I were feeling quite sad, so we went to a little coffee shop. We sat there and had something to eat. The next show was over, and some of the performers came in, and they saw us sitting there. We couldn't get ourselves to go home. We just stayed there. And then the next show came, and some of the performers saw us sitting glumly at our little table. Then just before the last show, about six of them came over to us, and they said, "Look, you're going on for the last show. We've all cut our act so there's room for you." And they said, "We want you to go on, and the manager says OK." So we get in our costumes, and our music comes on, and those performers are in the wings flapping jackets and hitting their hands and yelling at us to dance it up. And we stopped the show. From then on, it was easy again. Because we now had broken that barrier of the big, big, big space. See what I mean? They couldn't have been nicer.

Buddy and I had a wonderful Soft Shoe dance for nightclubs. It was arranged so that I'd be sitting with friends here, and he'd be sitting with friends there. They'd announce us, and Buddy would get up and dance over to where I would be finishing, and I'd say, "OK, I have to go, and I'll see you in a little while." Buddy would go [taps and sings], and I'd go [taps and sings], then we'd go [taps and sings]. Now by the time we did this for, I think, sixteen counts and then sixteen counts of more skips, I have seen everybody in the audience. I knew everybody who was there and what they were wearing. I'd made contact with them all. And then we'd go into this very charming Soft Shoe. You know, with no effort. A walk, a walk, a step, swing. A walk, a walk, a step, swing. Now we dance. Waltz time.

When dancing, we were alter egos you might say. And we were one. We danced with that same wonderful relationship we shared as brother and sister. I wouldn't say we were such great dancers. The total thing that we gave out was a relationship. When we danced, we were grateful to the audience, and we wanted to do it for them. For example, one of my friends was in the audience in Miami. She went backstage to see me, and the doorman said, "Just a minute and I'll let her know that you're here." She said, "Oh you don't have to, because she smiled at me the whole time she was dancing." See what I mean? Has to be like that. It's a one on one. It's a one on one with a great joy.

Yet, what we danced, I don't know. Paul Draper put it very well. He was in an act with us, and he watched us night after night. I loved Paul Draper's dancing. He was a power technician. A Horowitz of the tap. Finally, one day he was standing

Vilma and Buddy Ebsen on the MGM lot in costume for
Broadway Melody of 1936 (MGM, 1935)

in the wings, and he said, "You goddamned Ebsens, you can't dance, and you always stop the
show!" It was very sweet dancing, you know. One
of the fine, fine columnists in New York said, "The
Ebsens don't dance, it's spontaneous combustion." It had a lot of wholesome energy. No gimmicks. Nothing trite in our dancing. Because we
danced like nobody else.

I remember our understudies in the *Ziegfeld
Follies* [1934 edition] kept after me and after me:
"What if you get sick, we got to know your dance."
So I said, "OK. Meet me in the theater at such-
and-such a time." I worked with them for about
two hours. As they were leaving they said, "Oh
wonderful. Now we know your dance." I said,
"Well, you know my part." And they said, "What
is Buddy doing?" I said, "I haven't the slightest
idea!" Which was true. We always worked coun-
terpoint.

Buddy would get a lot of ideas, and he was
very good about music. We would go into a
rehearsal hall. They were never vented or air con-
ditioned, and boy, would we sweat. There were
these pools of water. And as people came in
afterwards, they'd look and say, "Were the Ebsens
here?" During rehearsals we just sang our songs,
didn't have any recordings or a pianist. Buddy
would get an idea, and then we would toy around
with it. We were very fortunate, because a lot of
our arrangements were done by Glenn Miller, and
they were great. He used to put a lot of brass in
them. As a matter of fact, in one arrangement the

brass was meant to be very high. But in some towns they wouldn't play it. And Buddy said to me, "Will you go give them your brass-section smile!"

Well, we would dance and it was called the "hottest cool dancing in town." The audience was just with us. And it was so much fun. Our dancing was like light quicksilver. It was a gossamer thing.

We never could have been called hoofers in our lives. We used tap, but were not like those wonderful hoofers; they're like drummers. Incredible what comes out. It's great. But us, we were more movers. More dancers. You want me to describe our style of tap dancing? Well, let me describe what got us thrown out of an agent's office in Chicago. We were in this office, and the agent asked, "What kind of dancing do you do?" And Buddy said, "Well—well, we do a kind of a . . . a sort of a . . . kind of a . . . sort of . . ." And we're out the door and the agent said, "When you figure out what you do, let me know!"

Well, what can I tell you. We used our early ability to move, our love for rhythm. Buddy had a more eccentric feel, the way he danced. My movements were more graceful. And we had twelve straight harmonious years of dancing. We never fussed. It was just the most amazing thing—people couldn't get over us. When we finished a dance, maybe I didn't dance as well as I should, or maybe I'd stepped in a hole in the stage or something. Instead of yelling at me or my yelling at him, we'd get offstage and he'd say, "Where do you want to go to eat?"

September 1, 1988
Pacific Palisades, California

15

FROM VAUDEVILLE TO PICTURES

DONALD O'CONNOR

I knew that the harder I worked, the more laughs and more applause I got. No one had to teach me that. I could hear it.

Vaudeville was an American institution, and upon its thousands of stages appeared every conceivable kind of act: trained seals, burnt-cork comics, barbershop quartets, jugglers, acrobats, magicians, female impersonators, xylophonists, monologists, dog-and-pony acts, harmonica players, unicyclists, and, of course, tap dancers. Vaudeville in America began with America's birth. It grew with America. And for decades, it was America's favorite entertainment. The first vaudeville show was presented by theatrical innovator Tony Pastor on October 24, 1881, at Tony Pastor's New Fourteenth Street Theatre. By 1913 alone, there were 2,973 regularly booked vaudeville theaters. The "circuits," as they were called, could keep an act busy for seasons at a time in their chains of vaudeville houses: the Keith Circuit, the Loews Circuit, the Orpheum Circuit, the Gus Sun Time, the T.O.B.A., the Pantages. By the late teens, there were more than five thousand vaudeville theaters in the country. Every city had several theaters and most small towns had at least one. There were so many theaters on the vaudeville circuits that if an act had fourteen good minutes, they could work six years

Intermission. The sixth act was the largest on the bill, perhaps a musical act featuring as many as fifteen beautiful girls, lavish costumes, and elaborate sets. The seventh act, "next-to-closing," was the top spot on the bill and lasted up to forty minutes. It was the star spot. So important was this position on the bill, that it was every vaudevillian's dream to play next-to-closing on the Orpheum Circuit—and there were the tap acts that did. The eighth and final act on the bill was another dumb act, oftentimes an animal act such as a trained seal or an Arabian stallion—needless to say, the animal act was put on last in order to clean the stage between shows. The entire vaudeville show lasted about an hour and forty-five minutes, and when it was over, a twelve-minute newsreel was shown, primarily to clear the house for the next show.

When silent pictures entered the scene, theater owners began showing "shorts" along with their vaudeville shows, which they then cut down to five acts. However, the films were considered *secondary* in importance to the live show; the variety vaudeville show was still what drew the crowd. These silent pictures were just a novelty item. Indeed, the showing of these one and two reelers offered an excellent opportunity to clear the house of adoring fans who would normally stay a second and third time to watch their beloved vaudeville performers. By 1926, however, the tide was turning and there were only a dozen theaters in America that offered nothing but big-time vaudeville. As the years rolled along, the chasm between vaudeville's and pictures' popularity closed. And by the 1930s,

without changing a word or playing the same theater twice. By 1925, B. F. Keith and E. F. Albee together owned a circuit involving some three hundred fifty theaters employing twenty thousand performers. With salaries ranging from a hundred and fifty to fifteen hundred dollars a week, vaudeville was a magnet for entertainers, and talent was lured to a life on the American stage from New York City to the fledgling Los Angeles, from the Rio Grande to Saskatchewan.

A big-time vaudeville bill consisted of eight acts. The position on the bill was very important to the performers—the better the spot, the higher the salary, and the better chance for high-paying bookings. The first spot on the bill was always a dumb act, an act that had no talking or singing, such as an acrobatic act. This gave the theater ushers a chance to seat noisy latecomers. The second act might be a song and dance act, and the third act a ten- to twelve-minute sketch, or one-act play—anything from heavy drama to slapstick comedy. The fourth and fifth spots might be headliners (big-time vaudeville might have as many as three headliners on one bill).

the situation had reversed completely: The vaudeville show was now secondary to the picture. But movies had come a long way from those early one- and two-reelers. They were now full-length, full-fledged talking motion pictures. Radio was another major contributing factor to the demise of vaudeville. The public simply refused to pay for a live show when they could flip a switch in the comfort of their own home and listen to their favorite acts. Vaudeville lingered on in various forms for another twenty years, but never again would it achieve the massive fame and popularity that it did from the turn of the century to the 1920s. Despite vaudeville's decline, many acts continued to make a living touring the circuits.

There was one family that was the very essence of vaudeville—The O'Connor Family—The Royal Family of Vaudeville. They started out as a circus family and made their way up the entertainment ladder to vaudeville. The father was an Irish dancer-comedian and one of Ringling Brothers' greatest acrobats; the mother was a circus tightrope walker and bareback rider. And the seventh child of this wildly talented mom and pop was named Donald O'Connor. The O'Connor family's act included remnants of its circus days—balancing acts, barrel jumping, as well as the familiar vaudeville varieties

such as singing and dancing. Donald O'Connor's specialty in his family act was a knock-'em-dead tap dance.

With vaudeville on the wane, Donald had the good fortune to be discovered by Hollywood, and, starting in 1938, he made scores of popular films there. He appeared in fourteen films with The Jivin' Jacks and Jills during the 1940s. After World War II, he made as many as twenty films a year, including the *Francis the Mule* series. Donald turned Universal Studios around into a highly profitable film company.

In 1952, he reached the zenith of his career when he was teamed up with Gene Kelly to costar in the film classic *Singin' in the Rain*. Donald O'Connor's brilliant comic dance to "Make 'Em Laugh," which he staged himself, remains the most hilarious routine ever recorded on film.

Donald O'Connor's musical films include *Mr. Big* (1943), *Top Man* (1943), *Bowery to Broadway* (1944), *The Milkman* (1950), *Call Me Madam* (1953), and *There's No Business Like Show Business* (1954). He played to generations of fans—in vaudeville, in films, in musical shows—and his comic style of tap dance was a style that he embellished with grace, solid talent, and an honesty that shows through in all his work. He claims he learned comedy because he could not tap dance well. Though this may have motivated his comedy tap, he certainly was well-trained by the top comics of the century throughout his years on the road in American vaudeville.

DONALD O'CONNOR — I came from a circus family. By the time I was born in 1925, they had graduated into vaudeville. I started onstage when I was three *days* old. See, after I was born, my mother played the piano in the act before going back to the heavy dancing and that kind of stuff. And I was on the piano bench with her. And I've been on the stage ever since. My first dancing, as far as I understand, was

when I was thirteen months old. I was paid twenty-five dollars a week to dance to the Black Bottom. I couldn't actually dance, but they held me up by the back of my skirt, and I moved my feet like crazy!

The name of the act was The O'Connor Family. The original act consisted of my mother, my father, my sister, my two brothers, and myself. When I was born, there was singing, dancing, comedy, acrobatics, and barrel jumping in the act. Sometimes they'd still use the flagpoles, where my father put the pole on his shoulder and my brothers would do tricks on the top of a little stand there.

My sister and I were hit by an automobile when I was thirteen months old and she was six. She was killed. Then my father dropped dead on stage thirteen weeks later. There was a guy that my mother brought in to play my father for a while. But that didn't work out. Eventually, the act was built up again to include my mother, my two brothers, and my sister-in-law. She was known as

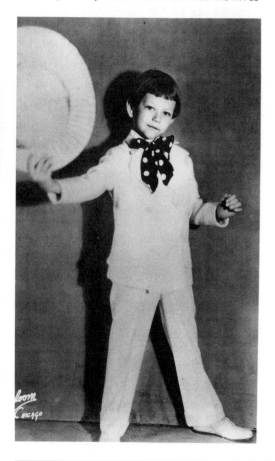

one of The Three Ra Ra Girls, and she was a hell of a dancer, real great. She married my oldest brother, Jack. They had a baby daughter, Patsy, and she went in the act. So that brought us back to six again. We did comedy, singing, dancing, and acrobatics. The dancing was primarily tap dancing.

I don't remember who taught me my first routines. I was just too young; I never paid any attention, I guess. Because it was second nature for me to pick up something and do the act. I do remember though, getting together with other dancers in drug stores or on street corners and learning new dancing routines.

I started out by doing the Black Bottom. Then the family did the Shim Sham. And then we did a very pretty dance to "Bye Bye Blues." And then I did a Buck and Wing, which I did until I was twelve years of age, when I went in the movies for the first time. In my Buck and Wing, I did my Time Step, a Triple Wing, back slides and then forward slides off. This was on one full chorus. That's basically what I did. Eight bars each: eight bars of my Time Step, eight bars of my Wings, eight bars of my back slide, eight bars on my forward slide. That was it. That was what people did in those days—set routines. Like we would repeat the Maxies. You know, and do it back and forth to get some mileage out of it. And then, of course, it builds up applause too, when you're working live with an audience. If you keep doing the Time Step long enough, people applaud! But when Fred Astaire came along, it was the most

Little Donald O'Connor was a seasoned professional by the time this photo was taken, Chicago, 1934.

incredible thing that ever happened! He never repeated anything. If he got something going good for him in a step, he would go for four bars of it. Maybe six. But that's the unique thing about his dancing. That's why no one has ever measured up to his style, really.

During my family's vaudeville days, we played all the circuits: Gus Sun Time, the Loews . . . we worked a couple of units with Fanchon and Marco. Burt Levy had some theaters. We'd pick up the West Coast and then pick up another one for down South, another one for up North—one through Canada, and work Montreal, Toronto, Winnipeg, and Vancouver. And then we'd come down from the north, from Vancouver to Seattle to Portland to Salem, Oregon, San Francisco, Bakersfield, Fresno—they all had full weeks. And they had gorgeous theaters. Big, big, big, beautiful vaudeville houses. Fresno, Bakersfield, Sacramento. They had a gorgeous theater over on Manchester Avenue here in Los Angeles. And the Detroit Theatre in Detroit, the Fox Theatre in Saint Louis, or in Atlanta, any of those. They were absolute palaces.

During these vaudeville days, our whole family traveled together. In the early days we'd hire our own railroad car. Then we would travel with other people on the train. And then we had a big Reo Speedwagon. We traveled with a big drop, the tumbling mats, barrels, tap shoes, all the costumes, scenery, everything. We'd all get in the car, and my brother Jack was the last one to get in.

Donald O'Connor makes a successful bid in pictures as teenage comic-heart throb in *Patrick the Great* (Universal, 1945).

He'd get in through the window. Because we used to rope all this stuff in, you know, so it wouldn't fall off. And one day around the noon hour, the Reo caught fire. There was just a little smoke coming out of it. But somebody yelled, "Fire!" and before you knew it, people were coming out of office buildings with fire extinguishers and axes, and they literally beat our act to death!

When I was tap dancing in the thirties, in the vaudeville circuits, there usually weren't lots of other tap dancers on the same bill. See, they wouldn't put a lot of like acts together. They'd have one family act. That's why I never worked with Judy Garland—it was The Gumm Sisters then. They would rarely ever put two family acts to-

Donald O'Connor's and Peggy Ryan's first A-picture leading roles; they play the children of veteran vaudevillian and hoofer Jack Oakie, 1944.

gether. Same thing with dancers. They might put a dancer who was eccentric, or legomania, on with tap dancers because of the completely different styles. Bill Robinson, let's say. I knew Bill very well. He was a wonderful guy and great to me as a kid. When I was fourteen, my family would work a lot at the Apollo Theatre on One hundred twenty-fifth Street in New York. I met Bill up there a couple of times, and we'd go around to different night clubs. White guys, well, they weren't permitted in. With Bill I got in all the time. Everybody got to know me, and they nicknamed me King. They started calling, "Where's the King, where's the King." And after a while I was known as the "King of Harlem"!

During my vaudeville days, I saw such a variety of acts—well, that's what it was all about. Sometimes people don't even believe me when I describe an act! For example, there was a girl dancer who used to tap dance on toe shoes. And then she invented ball bearings in her toe shoes to turn faster! Gloria Gilbert was her name. She was always known for spinning fast, but then she had invented this thing so she could spin even faster. She used to tap dance in regular pointe shoes with taps, then she changed her toe shoes, get into the ball bearings. It was crazy!

In those days, all the performers wanted to do everything but what they were doing. Acrobats always wanted to be comedians. And they had the least sense of humor of anybody!

Back in those days it seemed every act tap danced. A talking act usually didn't have a real strong ending. None of the jokes at the end were that good to go off. So they always wound up by dancing off. Mostly all the one-man or two-man acts, or your man-and-woman acts, would finish off by doing a dance. Everybody had to double in brass. If you went out and were just a singer, that didn't mean too much. Or just a dancer, that didn't mean too much. But if you could sing, dance, tell jokes, and what have you, that would mean you were really outstanding. And so everybody tried to be a triple threat. And most of your talking people, most of your acts, would wind up by doing some kind of a tap step to get off.

The first time I was discovered for movies was in 1938, at the Ambassador Hotel in downtown

Donald O'Connor as Cosmo Brown, pictured with Gene Kelly in "Fit as a Fiddle," from *Singin' in the Rain* (MGM, 1952). Donald O'Connor reached the peak of comic excellence in "Make 'Em Laugh," incorporating dance moves and comic bits recalled from the wide variety of acts he watched during his family's early years on the vaudeville stages.

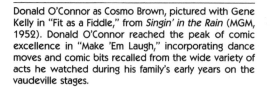

Donald O'Connor, 1940s

Los Angeles. We were doing a benefit for the Motion Picture Relief Fund. We did our act, and there was a man who worked for Paramount Studios. He saw me, got in touch with us, and I went over and got the part for *Sing You Sinners* [1938] that was starring Bing Crosby. That started my first official career in pictures. In 1939, I went back on the road to work with the family. My brother Billy died during this time, and I stayed with the act until the early part of 1942. Some talent scout saw me and sent us the money for me to go out and make a picture called *What's Cookin'?* [1942] with Gloria Jean, Peggy Ryan, and The Jivin' Jacks and Jills. And that led to my second career in pictures.

Now, in the old days of vaudeville, you never changed your routine. I learned just two or three dance routines, and I never learned anything else. That's all we ever did. People wanted to see the same thing. Many times in the old days if you'd changed material or routines, the audience wouldn't like it. Because they were used to the old stuff, and that's what they paid to see. So, when I went to Universal, and I was working with all these great dancers like Dottie Babb, Bobby Scheerer, Roland Dupree, Peggy Ryan, and trying to learn these things from Universal's choreographer Louis DaPron, I couldn't learn them. And it became so embarrassing for me, because these kids could pick up a routine in five minutes.

So they were pushing me farther and farther in the back when I was making all those pictures, because I couldn't learn the routines. I looked lousy up there with all those other kids. But there was something about me. I had charisma, and the studio wanted to keep pushing me in the front. There's Louis, and everybody, pushing me in the back. And I was becoming a bigger star all the time. They got to a point they were shooting so fast, they didn't have time for me to take all day and learn the dance routine! So when I

was a big star, they sent me to Johnny Boyle to teach me how to dance! I was with him for two weeks, and he gave me a letter to give to the studio. And in the letter it said that I was unteachable. I drove him crazy. And *he* drove *me* crazy!

When I started dancing in movies, my style changed quite a bit. The hoofers would dance with their arms stiff, because they were trying to hit all those riffs—which were very, very hard. And they were working on fast stages, slippery stages, with taps on. And you had to do it on one spot. In the movies, we could move all over the stage and not slip, because we weren't filming with taps on. But it wasn't until I worked with Gene Kelly and Bob Alton that I started to dance as, what I called, a total dancer. Alton was a painter with choreography. The man was incredible. He didn't know how to hoof. I'd have to put in all my own taps and stuff. So it wasn't until I started working with Bob Alton and Gene Kelly that I started dancing from the waist up, using my arms, my hands, and synchronization in that way.

When I first met Gene Kelly, he was telling me about *Singin' in the Rain* [1952]. Explaining to me about our characters, how we were supposed to be together, that we grew up together, we danced together—our hands in the same position, we look the same place, leap to the same heights. All of this. Oh, everything sounded wonderful. And as I was driving home, I thought, "Oh my God, which way does he turn?" I only turned to the left. That's why I drove Louis crazy, and everybody else. So the next day when I saw Kelly, I was just about to ask him which way he turned, and he asked me. He said, "Which way do *you* turn?" I said, "To the left." And he said, "*Thank God. So do I!*"

======

I guess I was never impressed with myself as a performer. That's just something that I learned when I was a child. Like breathing and eating. It's just something I did. I was never impressed with myself being different than any other kid. Although I never knew what other kids were like, because I was always with adults. Children used to frighten me. Really. I always thought they were strange creatures. Little creatures running around without any talent.

That I was out there working with the act, doing hand-balancing and singing and dancing and all of that stuff, it was just something that I went out and did. I loved those years on the road. I loved fooling around in front of the audience. I worked very hard. I knew that the harder I worked, the more laughs and more applause I got. No one had to teach me *that*. I could hear it. And that was my thing. That's what I was there for. And I really *lived* to do just that.

September 2, 1988
Sherman Oaks, California

16

THE TAP
DANCER'S
DILEMMA

THE BERRY BROTHERS

I was so tired of hearing that music . . .
I would stand in the wings before
going onstage, and just grit my teeth
every time.

I f "Repetition is the mother of learning," what
happens when a tap act does the same routine
for thirty years? Each move of a routine, each
subtlety, gets worked through to perfection. The
routine becomes exquisitely polished, and the
act becomes one of the top talents in the country.
In sum—excellence.

Although dancing the same act over and over
might have been good for the dance act, it was not
always good for the dancers. While some could
take the monotony, some could not and did not.

The formula of repetition was a sound one for
routine work. By doing a dance over and over, the
dancer became intimately acquainted with all the
dance's intricacies. And so did the audience. During
the days of the vaudeville circuits, this repetition
was mandatory. Audiences demanded the same
routine which they had seen on the act's last tour
through town. The routine was the audience's fa-
miliarity and connection to the act. If an act finally
could not take doing the same old steps anymore
and tried to change their act, they might find themselves faced with no bookings. And therein was the
"tap dancer's dilemma." Quite a paradox. Their agent

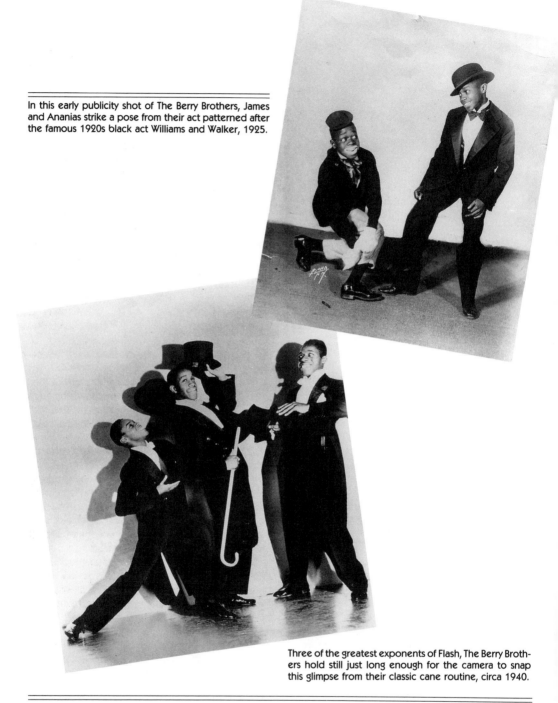

In this early publicity shot of The Berry Brothers, James and Ananias strike a pose from their act patterned after the famous 1920s black act Williams and Walker, 1925.

Three of the greatest exponents of Flash, The Berry Brothers hold still just long enough for the camera to snap this glimpse from their classic cane routine, circa 1940.

THE TAP DANCER'S DILEMMA

simply would not be able to book this new material. So the act would have to hold on to their tried-and-true routine.

It was quite a predicament: An act works for years and years to perfect material, and by the time they perfect it, they're tired and don't want to do it anymore. However, this situation was not at all funny to one of tap's most durable trios—The Berry Brothers, especially the group's youngest member, Warren Berry. The Berry Brothers began in the early 1920s with Ananias and James touring the church circuit. Their act was molded after the famous black team of the day Williams and Walker, and thus the boys were dubbed The Miniature Williams and Walker. By the mid·1920s, the Berry family had migrated to Hollywood, and James danced at parties given by some of the reigning silent film stars, including Mary Pickford and Clara Bow, and appeared in *Our Gang Comedies*. By the late 1920s, The Berry Brothers had hit the big time. In 1929, James and Ananias opened as a duo with Duke Ellington in Harlem's Cotton Club, and for the next four and a half years, the famous night spot remained their home base. In between engagements at the Cotton Club, they were featured in such prestigious productions as the highly acclaimed and popular all-black revue, *Lew Leslie's Blackbirds of 1929*, playing in London. On December 27, 1932, the brothers opened *the* Art Deco movie palace of New York—Radio City Music Hall.

Ananias was the oldest, born circa 1912. James was next, born circa 1914. Eight years later came Warren, in 1922. Unlike his brothers, Warren did not grow up in the act. When Warren was not traveling with the family, he attended public school and happily studied piano, acrobatics, and tap, and generally luxuriated in the contentment of family, friends, and home. However, his childhood serenity was over in 1934 when Ananias left the act to marry another popular entertainer, Valaida Snow, at which time Warren was drafted into the act. James taught him The Berry Brothers' act, move for move, exactly what Ananias and James had done before him. Monotony's first grip on Warren Berry.

Ananias's marriage did not last, however, and a year or so later, he talked James and Warren into joining him in Hollywood. The Berry Brothers—now Ananias, James, and Warren—enjoyed tremendous success in their newly formed trio and appeared extensively throughout the United States on stage, in clubs, and in film, and they also worked throughout Europe. They possessed three distinct personalities and styles: James was the comedian and singer; Ananias was the king of the Strut; and Warren was the solid dancer/acrobat. Together, they combined their talents to form one of the most exciting flash acts known. But theirs was not merely a flash act. Their mixture of the Cakewalk Strut and the acrobatics of the flash acts was a winning and lasting formula. The act was only four and a half minutes, extremely short for a tap act at that time. It consisted of two parts—the Strut, and the cane number—and can be seen in its entirety in the film *Lady Be Good* (1941). They also appeared on film in *Panama Hattie* (1942), *Boarding House Blues* (1948), and *You're My Everything* (Ananias and Warren only, 1949). Every moment of their act was strictly timed, every step in syncopation. The secret of the act was tempo, precision, and dynamics. The Berry Brothers were masters of the "freeze and melt," the sparkling contrasts between posed immobility and sudden flashing action.

The act stayed together, and stayed the same, until Ananias's untimely death at the age of thirty-nine. Warren Berry suffered a hip injury, and ironically, was happily released from the chains of monotony the act had meant to him over the years. By 1951, the act dissolved.

Though Warren Berry faced the dancer's dilemma of the nonchanging routine, his thirty years in show business were not pure torment. The adventure of being in show business was still mostly fun and dreams. The Berry Brothers were stars, and among the tap stars, they shone brilliantly.

W A R R E N B E R R Y — I was going to school, on my way to getting a decent education. As a matter of fact, studying piano. And what happened was that Nyas [Ananias] got married to Valaida Snow and left the act. She was very famous at that time, a tremendously talented lady. She had been to China and traveled extensively throughout Europe, spoke a couple of languages, and played every instrument in the band. I'm certain she was older than my brother, and my mother had a fit when she heard that Nyas was marrying her. She called her a few nice choice names, for those days. So, he went off and married her, and I was sort of drafted into his spot. This was around 1933, '34, somewhere around then, and James basically taught me the act. I was the only one of the brothers who had actually studied dance. They learned by performing—I had had the opportunity of studying acrobatics and tap dance. As a matter of fact, I studied with one of the finest tap dance teachers in New York—Derby Wilson. Old Derby! He was an excellent dancer.

Nyas came back. He was out in Los Angeles during the time when he decided that he wanted to rejoin the group, because he was having trouble with his wife. James didn't want to, because we were in New York and had just started doing fairly well as a duo, working primarily in clubs, vaudeville theaters, you know, the old circuit. And James was really very put out when the old man [their father] told him that Nyas wanted us to come out. See, Nyas had sent for the old man first, and from there, it was his way of sort of getting back into the thing. His plan worked, and James and I came out to California. That was somewhere in '35, '36 type thing. We got together and from there on in, the act resumed—and we

started playing at bigger places and went to Europe a couple of times.

Somewhere in '36, '37, all three of us were in the downtown Cotton Club. On the show were Cab Calloway, The Nicholas Brothers, The Six Cotton Club Boys, and I think Bill was on that show, too—Bill Robinson. W.C. Handy [1873–1958, acknowledged "Father of the Blues"] was on the show, and he did a little reminiscent bit of his

The Berry Brothers, circa 1936

era playing "Saint Louis Blues." He was an old man at that time, on the way out, about ready for the final curtain. On the bill was also a guy called Dynamite Hooker—he was terrific. He opened that show up like crazy. Oh, yes, of course—The Dandridge Sisters. And I think that was just about it.

Well, that was one tap dancing show. Boy, was it ever! But the audience didn't tire of all that dancing. Apparently not! They were still there when we showed up, and we were the last on the bill. For me, it was the most fun I've ever had in show business, because Harold and Fayard [Nicholas] and The Dandridge Sisters were all my equal, age-wise. I loved that show because we had so much fun together. We were at the club for about six months. Practically every night in between shows we would go across the street where there was one of those little pinball-machine places, and we would go down there and play Ping-Pong. It was absolutely wonderful. We used to beat just about everybody that would come down there. There would be guys who were like pool sharks, only they were Ping-Pong sharks. So they would come down, and if Harold didn't beat them, I would beat them, and if I didn't beat them, Fayard would beat them! No money exchanging, no betting and none of that stuff. It was strictly really kid stuff, and it was just a great moment in my life.

Because both The Nicholas Brothers and The Berry Brothers were on the same show, everyone was always trying to have a competition thing going. Who was going to do this and who was going to do that. And there were always people who loved The Nicholas Brothers or people who liked us, you know—it was that sort of thing. But for us, what was really the paramount issue was the fact that we were the last act on a bill of two and a half hours of tremendous tap dancing! Nyas went to the owner, Herman Stark, and said, "Say,

what are you guys trying to do? You're putting us down at the very end of the show after all this dancing and what not!" When Nyas reported back to us, he told us that they said, "Aw, you guys don't need to worry. Look, The Berry Brothers will be able to make it." So that's the way that went down. Nyas said to us, "Well, now we got to do something here," he says, "because we're closing this two-and-a-half-hour show with nothing but dancing up front, and everybody's doing everything," so he says, "We've got to put a finish to the act." Sunshine Sammy was there and said, "Why don't you guys jump off the upstairs stage?" They had an upstairs platform where the show girls used to stand and do little things up top over the band. And so Nyas came to us and said, "Well, why don't we? You want to try jumping off of that thing and see if it will work?"—to James, because they were the ones that had to do it, not me. James said, "OK, I'll go up there and try it." So he went up and he just flew off —shew, boom! Nyas looked at him and said, "How did it feel?" James said, "Yeah, feels OK. We can do it." It was ten or twelve feet all on its own! But they had to jump up and out over the Cab Calloway Orchestra. And the idea of them jumping that height and landing in a split was quite something at that time.

Now, the whole thing about this act, incidentally, was the fact—between Nyas and Jimmy— that they hated to rehearse. They just hated to rehearse. So with this thing being the way it was, none of them went up to try it out before doing it. After James did it, he said, "OK, well, it can be done. It's capable of being done." With that, Nyas and James said, "Now this is what we're going to do. . . ." I said, "Well when you guys are

Ananias Berry, "King of the Strut," circa 1930

jumping off the thing, I'll be right in the center of the floor, and when you converge upon me"—because it was a thing that they would be jumping at an angle and we'd meet right in the center—"and at the point where you hit the floor, I'll do a Flip-Flop-Twist into a split." A "Flip-Flop-Twist," that's where you flip back, land on your hands, twist while you are on your hands, and then land in the split. And that was what I did. At exactly the time they hit the floor, I did the Flip-Flop-Twist. We all three landed facing the audience—they were sliding down to where I was, because their momentum carried them to a slide (just jumping up and down would have killed them). So they would slide, and as they slid down to where I was (I had just completed my Flip-Flop-Twist), we would be up—the three of us—and then do a hand spring, split, up—and bow right on the beat. It was terrific. At that point, the people went crazy. That was the closing of that two-and-a-half-hour dance session. It gave us a little handle! We used to stop the finale on that. Three or four times they would have to stop the finale for us to come back and take a bow. People talked about it for a long time.

During the thirties, we were making pretty good money. Great money, actually! During the terrible time of Depression, we were living the height of luxury compared to the average Joe. Especially being colored (not "black" yet!). At that point, we had a home up on Sugar Hill, in New York,

which was supposed to be a big spot to live in those days. And we had a shack out here in L.A. Chauffeur. Sixteen-cylinder Cadillac. Valet. Cook. Maid. Ananias had a purple Mercedes-Benz. That was when he married Valaida Snow. It wasn't exactly purple, it was another color like purple. And he made quite a sensation driving around in that thing!

Like many people on stage, I was a movie buff. My thing was going to the movies. When we were appearing at the Cotton Club, I would wake up eight o'clock in the morning to start my movie rounds. During those days, they had all these shows on Broadway, you know, movie houses, vaude-

THE TAP DANCER'S DILEMMA

ville. They had the Capitol, Roxy, Radio City, Paramount, Strand, the Palace Theatre, the Criterion. I remember those well, because I would map out my plan for the day, you see: "At ten I'll be over at Paramount, and then twelve I'll be over at the Roxy, and then three-thirty I'll be over at Radio City," and like that. I would just take a whole day of going to the movies! And then I would go over to the Cotton Club for work. We were doing three shows a night then; I think it was around nine, twelve, and two.

Warren and Ananias Berry are joined by Dan Dailey in the exciting "new" routine "Chattanooga Choo-Choo" featured in *You're My Everything* (20th Century-Fox, 1949).

Everybody in the world says The Berry Brothers didn't tap dance. We never wore tap shoes. We tapped—but without taps on the shoes. That was the difference. Tap dancers would be more or less people that used taps, which we didn't do. People are confused by the fact that they're watching us twirl the cane, they don't realize that what we're doing is also dancing. Doing the cane thing, at the same time, one is not aware of the dancing that goes along with it.

We always had a lovely description of our act—exotic Soft Shoe dancing, acrobatic Soft

Shoe dancing. Flashy, yes. But not really in the flash range. I wouldn't say it was a "flash act." There were other acts that would come out in a real *bam bam* and hit 'em, you know, it was real flash. Everybody was going and moving and—well, that is my interpretation of flash. The problem is, we could tap. Nyas used to do a great amount of tapping. I would tap every now and then, but I never thought of myself as a tap dancer. I was capable of tapping. One note is that I couldn't keep time. And it was years, because I had no sense of timing. Nyas would say—"What is this, a white boy we got here!" At any rate, I couldn't keep time, and it was a long, long time before I really got the feeling of time. Which was very interesting, of course, as I naturally grew up into it, it was no trick. But at the very beginning I didn't have "time." I had an off-time, more in the Fred Astaire vein type of thing. I think that is the reason why I like Fred Astaire so much, because he was doing things that I could understand.

During all the time that The Berry Brothers were together, we had the same numbers: "Papa De Da Da," which we used to call affectionately "Bugle Blues." You probably never heard of it—we were the only ones that used it, I think. We used that song until we ran into Teddy Hill. Not Hale, the tap dancer— *Hill*, the band leader. We were on our way to Europe, and as fate would have it, somehow the music was lost or misplaced, and we didn't have our regular music. So what happened was, Teddy said, "Well look, I've got a piece here that would probably fit the act." It turned out to be his arrangement to "Between the Devil and the Deep Blue Sea." This was a

terrific arrangement, and from that day on we used it. We used that son of a gun until we did the picture *Lady Be Good* [1941]. This was our cane number, and we did in the movie exactly what we did in our act. As a matter of fact, that number was exactly the same—oh, thirty years this thing went on it seemed. Uh-huh. That's why it was so good. Yeah.

Well, I *hated* it. Um-hmm, I did. I grew to hate it. Because it never changed. It *never* changed. And my whole idea of life is that one has to change. There has to be a progress somewhere. It has to go someplace else. I threatened to leave the act two or three times because they wouldn't change. But that's another story. It got resolved, but it got resolved the hard way. Nyas died, and my hip went. When my hip went, it was not a catastrophe. You see, it was like a way out, in a sense. I was so tired of hearing that music going on the stage. I would stand in the wings before going onstage, and just grit my teeth every time. That's right. Absolutely. Every time I would hear the music I'd go, "Oh, Lord! Do I have to do this?" But they wanted to keep it the same. Not just Nyas and James—the producers, the agents, and the public. You see, that was the problem. The audiences were wonderful. They all reacted great, and they wanted to see our same number. I had a run-in with the agent because I said, "Look, I want to change the act." And he said, "We can't book you if you change the act."

James was a very talented person. As a comedian, he had a great magnetic thing about him that shone right on through. That was the reason why he was in *Our Gang Comedies*. That thing was there even then. Nyas was a great dancer, nice-looking guy, and capable of doing more in dancing. Nyas excelled in his ability to do the Strut. He was considered exceptional at this. And there were very few that could. That was the reason why he was unique in this particular dance.

He brought it out, his ability to kick above his head with ease and pointed toes, all that sort of thing. The Strut was always attached to elegance, it was a dance like a proud peacock. Strutters held their shoulders erect, their head up. And style. It was an exceptional thing for him to do, for most people just didn't do it, you see. Now, to utilize our talents more fully would have been absolutely terrific. It was a change and would have opened the scope of what we could do. I felt that we could put this together and make an act that could go into the future. Which is exactly what would have happened, you see.

My feeling about tap dancing is—"dancing is dancing." I never would say, "He's a good tap dancer," in that particular sense. He's a good *dancer*, whatever his speciality is. But the tap dancing—it's great, you know. I think it could be incorporated in many ways, even with ballet. I like the idea. Which of course, is something I had in mind for years and years and years, but tap dancers don't like ballet dancers. And ballet dancers hate tap dancers. So never the twain shall meet! But I think there's a certain amount of freedom that one gets from tap dancing, and I think that is what makes it such an enjoyable thing to watch and to do. And moving. My feeling is that there's movement going on there. There is the exhilaration of hearing the beat and coming out on time and making the sounds click at the right point. All this has a great deal to do with it. Most tap dancers, I think—even people who are learning it—have a certain sense of freedom about it, because there's a structure without a structure attached to tap dancing. They feel, "I can do anything as long as I'm tapping." That's the reason why it brings so much joy to them, you see. It's a great art.

My feeling was I learned, I did the best I could . . . and I wanted more progress.

October 1, 1989
Los Angeles, California

17

HOLLYWOOD'S TAPPIN'-EST CHILD STAR

JANE WITHERS

We were making my pictures in twenty-one to twenty-four days! That's it. That's why I was known as "One-Take Withers."

During the Great Depression, one of America's greatest escapes was going to the movies. The silver screen swept people momentarily away from their difficult lives. They were transported to another place and time. Glittering musicals with lush sets, glorious fashions, and glamorous characters entertained millions of people mesmerized by the magic of the screen. And some of the most popular musical films of all had talented tap dancing child stars. The first child that comes to mind is, of course, Shirley Temple. However, Shirley was not the only one making musicals.

Jane Withers made her big break in films playing opposite Shirley Temple in the 1934 film *Bright Eyes*. In this movie, Withers played a brat. Being mean to Shirley Temple was the nastiest thing anyone could do—and the child became an overnight sensation. After that film, she was one of Fox's biggest draws, though she never made an A movie again at that studio. She was dubbed the "Queen of the B's," and "One-Take Withers," and she tap danced in more films than any other child star.

Jane Withers was born on April 12, 1926, and

entered show business at the age of two in her hometown, Atlanta, Georgia. She landed her first regular spot on *Aunt Sally's Kiddie Club* radio program. The following year, three-year-old Jane landed her own radio show, singing and doing imitations of W. C. Fields, Greta Garbo, ZaSu Pitts, and Maurice Chevalier. Encouraged by the tot's tremendous talent, the Withers family packed up and moved to Hollywood in 1932, where Jane began a successful career in movies. She spent her first two years in Hollywood doing over one hundred extra and bit parts in movies, animal and sound effects for cartoons, and impersonation coaching for Will Rogers. After her role in *Bright Eyes*, she won a contract at Fox in 1934, and from then until 1947 she made musical films for the studio. Hers were all B movies—in other words, low-budget films that were hurriedly made. Still, by 1939, she was ranked sixth at the box office, and her movies were among the studio's most dependable money-makers, sometimes earning better profits than Shirley Temple's films.

Like so many of her tap dance contemporaries, she was a movie fanatic. She went to movies, while she made them; she wrote fan letters, while receiving tons of them herself. And she had the enchanted experience of getting to meet so many of the movie stars she loved—among them, Eleanor Powell and Bill Robinson. The spunky and cheerful little girl whom she portrayed in so many of her movies, was also her character in real life. She loved everybody and everything she did—and it showed.

JANE WITHERS — Long before I was born, when my mother was fourteen, she made up her mind she was going to get married, but she had to have an understanding husband because she wanted one child that would be very successful in show business. She chose show business because she thought it would be a very interesting life. And she used to literally study the marquees before I was born and say, "Withers is the last name. She will have to have a short first name to look right on the marquees." And so she chose Jane, Jane Withers.

I started at two, working on the radio. I sang and danced and did impersonations. I was "Dixie's Dainty Dew Drop." Isn't that a hoot? By the time I was five, I'd gone, really, about as far as I could go, because I was known all over the South and just had tons and tons of fans. And everybody said, "She's so talented, you must take her to Hollywood." My mom and dad made the decision that we would go out there and try it for six months to see if I could get anywhere in pictures. So when I was five and a half years old, on March the tenth, 1932, we arrived in Hollywood armed with seventeen scrapbooks all filled with wonderful write-ups of what I had done and accomplished so far at the age of five and a half. And of course, nobody could have cared less. It took us over six months to get even inside of a studio gate!

I finally started doing extra-work. I did over a hundred films doing extra-work before I ever got my big part opposite Shirley Temple in *Bright Eyes* [1934]. It had been very discouraging to me, because every interview I'd go on, they would never give me a chance to show what I could do. They'd stand us up in a line and treat us like a herd of cattle. They come down the line and ask, "What are your credits?" And I'd say, "How much time do you have?" Because I had so many credits. But they would never give me a chance to show what I could do. Finally I thought, "Every

interview I go on, all little girls are so gorgeous, they all have blond curls and frilly dresses, and I'm such a 'plain Jane.' " But I thought, "I believe in what I can do, and I know that if I just can get that opportunity, I could prove to the world that I do have some kind of talent. And some day they've got to need an opposite."

Well, one day I was working on a radio show with some other kids that were also breaking into the business—Judy Garland (who was then one of The Gumm Sisters), Mickey Rooney (who then was doing the *Mickey McGuire Comedies*), Edith Fellows, and Sydney Miller. One of the mothers came in with a publication that told about interviews and auditions, and she said "Oh, listen to this—they're looking for a little girl to play opposite Shirley Temple in a film called *Bright Eyes* at Fox." I was in the middle of rehearsing my number with Sydney Miller, and I said, "Excuse me please, Mrs. Grundy, would you repeat that —what you just said?" After hearing it again, I said "Mama, you get me to that studio as fast as you can because, boy howdy, if there ever was an opposite to Shirley Temple, it's me!"

She took me over to Fox Studios, and again, it was the same old interview where they stand you like a herd of cattle, never giving you a chance to prove anything. When they got to me they asked, "How old are you?" I replied, "How old do you have to be for this particular part?" They looked at me and said, "You're rather precocious." "I don't know what that means," I said,

"but I've got talent, and all I need is a chance to prove it. Isn't David Butler directing this film? He gave me my first job in this town, and if you would just allow me five minutes of his time, I think I can show him that this is the role that was made for me." I kept at them all the way, and I guess I was persuasive enough, because they called Mr. Butler and said, "She said to tell you it's that little Southern girl you gave her first job to here in town." He said, "Lord, I've been looking all over this town for her. You send her over here as fast as you can."

I got that role opposite Shirley. We started work on the film in the beginning of '34, Shirley was six and I was seven. I knew right from the start that she was enormously special. I had been a big fan of hers anyway and was just thrilled to pieces to get to work with her. I thought without a doubt she's the most adorable child in the entire world. In this movie I played the meanest, you'd want to kill her, you know! It was an incredible role. But it was very difficult for me to do some of the things. Especially when I had to tear her doll apart. Oh, I nearly died inside. It was really, literally, one of the hardest things I ever had to do in my life, because I collected dolls. I took such care of everything, even the most infinitesimal little thing. And if anybody was kind enough to share something with me or give me a gift, it just meant the world to me! And to have to go in and tear up a doll was just devastating to me. So I had the prop man promise me he would save all the pieces so I could save the doll and sew it back together. Which he did, bless his heart. And, of course, the doll went right into my collection, which would eventually grow to over fourteen thousand dolls.

Bright Eyes was such an overwhelming success that I was signed at Fox, and that same year I started my second big picture, *Ginger*. When I arrived on the set, there were two big, huge baskets filled with roses. One was pink roses and one was red roses. I said, "Oh, there must be some mistake. These are gorgeous. They must be for Shirley Temple, and she's on a different soundstage." They said, "No Jane, these are for you." They were waiting to take a picture of my expression when I opened the cards. Well, one was from Will Rogers . . . you see, a while back, I had been hired by the studio to teach him impressions of Bing Crosby and Rudy Vallee for one of his pictures. We became real bosom buddies. So he sent me this gorgeous big basket of pink roses. And the other card with all the red roses said, "Dear little friend, I know you're going to knock them cold. God bless you, and I can hardly wait to see you as 'Ginger.' Love, from your fan, President Franklin Delano Roosevelt." I still cry every time I think about it. It was such a switch for *me* to be the little girl who counted!

My friendship with Franklin Delano Roosevelt went back when I was still living in Atlanta, Georgia, working on my own radio show. That was when I was doing impersonations. He was run-

ning for the presidency of the United States, and I did an impersonation of him. Well, some newsreel caught it, and somehow he saw it. He said, "I want to know who that little girl is who did that incredible impersonation of me." When they found me, he wrote me the most wonderful letter which read, "You are one of the most talented young ladies I have ever seen, and you've really caught me right on the nose. Here's a button to wear, which I hope you will wear, from me for good luck for my running for the Presidency of the United States." And he said, "I hope you'll always keep in touch." And we did. He was a big fan of mine, Franklin Delano Roosevelt. There was a very extraordinary group of men that he would have to dinner, and he'd say "Now gentlemen, I have a real treat for you. After dinner, for

Jane Withers won a contract at Fox Studios and tap danced her way through a series of B pictures, earning her nicknames "One-Take Withers" and "Queen of the B's." In *This Is the Life* (Fox, 1935), the nine-year-old talent takes a well-deserved bow.

your dessert, we're going in and view a film of my favorite star, little Jane Withers." And in 1939, he had Eleanor bring me, in person, (he would not send it through the mail) his teddy bear. He knew I collected them, and he wanted me to have his.

In the movie *Ginger*, I didn't get a chance to sing or dance, but they realized very fast that I could do both extremely well, and I was crazy to dance. So I kept after them, and the next film that I did *This is the Life* [1935] I had three big, big musical numbers with dancing girls behind

Jane Withers in blackface for *Can This Be Dixie?* (Fox, 1936)

me and everything—oh, it was wonderful. I had great costumes, including a white satin tuxedo.

Musicals were always my most favorite thing in the world. I was such a movie fan as a child, and I actually had a clipping service for all my favorite stars! I absolutely adored Ginger Rogers and always wished I could dance like she did. I loved Donald O'Connor, The Nicholas Brothers, Gene Nelson, and, of course, I adored Bill Robinson. Absolutely adored him! He'd always come up to me at the studio, and every time, he'd do a little step and I would mimic his step. Then I'd give him another one. And he'd say, "Oh, I'd give anything in the world if I could get to dance with you in a picture." I said, "Mr. Robinson, that's never going to happen. You make A pictures and I make B's, and I guess you belong to Shirley Temple." But he said, "Well we could always dream, can't we." I said, "Yes, sir. That's what life is made of."

On a lot of my pictures I got to work with one of Hollywood's greatest choreographers and tap dancers—Nick Castle. I was just so thrilled with his dancing and his style and his steps. They were outstanding. Every time I finished one picture, I just could hardly wait to do another musical number with Nick. And he was just an absolute doll. I remember the first time we worked together, he asked the director when shooting started. When they said, "in two days," he just about fell over. He said, "It's impossible for this child to learn the material that quickly." I said, "Oh, no. Please Mr. Castle, wait a minute. You just show me the routine and what you think would be right for me." He said, "Well, we'll have to work it out, but two days, you can't—it's—that's impossible." I said, "Mr. Castle, I've been doing the impossible since I was born!" He said, "I just don't see how it's possible in two days." But we did it. We did it in a day. And he couldn't believe it.

Nick Castle had never worked with a kid be-

In this lariat number, Jane Withers aptly demonstrates why dance director Nick Castle dubbed her the "miracle kid." Working under the hectic time schedules of B pictures (the studio cranked out pictures every twenty-four days), Jane Withers learned her dance material—plus gimmicks—in a matter of days.

Jane Withers, *Rascals* (20th Century-Fox, 1938)

fore, and I worked with him from 1935 to 1943. He was easy going, he was fun, and he had a wonderful sense of humor. And he always called me his "miracle kid." He said, "This kid can do the impossible." And he said to me, "You're the biggest challenge of anybody I work with, because you always want something new. You really make me draw from way down within to give you something new and something special." Which I thought was very sweet. But he really meant it, because all I was making were B pictures (as a matter of fact, I was called "The Queen of the B's"!), and in those B pictures, I only had about two days to work on these tap numbers. If that. That's the truth. That is God's truth. And of course, in addition to the film work, I'd have to have three hours of school and an hour for lunch. So we'd really only have four hours a day to work. That's it.

Most of the time, Nick Castle and I never knew what the set was going to be like. That was so maddening. We could choreograph a number and then when we got to the studio where the set was built, we'd have to change the whole routine. I'd say, "Good gravy Nick, we can't do that spin and that double whammy." There might be a set with some obstacle that would totally destroy what we'd created. And of course, he would be thinking of camera angles, too. He was marvelous in that way. So we'd have to rearrange it right then and there. Consequently, a lot of it was ad-libbed. Had to. Because there never was enough time to work on it. That really bothered me as a child. Because I loved things to be right, or not at all. But we were making my pictures in

twenty-one to twenty-four days! That's it. That's why I was known as "One-Take Withers."

I finally insisted that we have a rehearsal hall at home so that at night I could practice with the proper kind of floor and the mirror and so on. Twentieth didn't know about it, but Nick Castle came over to the house at night, if it was a number that I felt was extremely challenging. The only thing I really wished for was more time to be able to rehearse, because there were so many times that I felt, "Gosh, this could be so much better if I could have just had more time to practice." And that was—that was the only thing that was really disappointing to me. It hurt when I didn't think I was doing my very best. Nick said, "Kid" —he always called me 'kid'—he said, "Kid, don't worry about it. You are very special in what you do and it's your own inimitable way." I said, "But this is not my way, Nick. I can do it better than this and I know it, and I like to do my best." A couple of times I really burst into tears because I was just so frustrated that I didn't have more time. That was about the only thing that really ever got to me. And I'd say, "Well, I guess I just have to accept the way it is and do the best I can and keep going. Some day, maybe, I'll have more time!"

I just *loved* tap dancing. It made me happy. Besides having it in your toes, your feet, your legs, and your bones, you've got to be born with tap dancing in your *soul*. It really is wonderful, and I just *love* it.

February 9, 1989
Los Angeles, California

18

EXTRA-SPECIAL ADDED ATTRACTION

GENE AND FRED KELLY

Well, Cab Calloway played the thing, and Gene and I danced the thing, and as soon as it was over, they all stood up and clapped and cheered. That was really something. The guys we were nuts about were applauding us!

The impact of Hollywood 1930s movie musicals was so phenomenal that any dance school worth its mettle offered classes in tap dance instruction. The Gene Kelly Studio of Dance was no exception. Located in Pittsburgh, Pennsylvania, it was one of the most popular tap studios in its area. With the young and handsome Gene Kelly as the main instructor, boys and girls alike packed tap classes year after year.

Decades before his successful screen career, Gene Kelly was just one of five little Kellys. In descending order, they were Joan, James, Gene, Louise, and Fred—a dancing family from the start. Patterned after the popular vaudeville act The Seven Little Foys, The Five Kellys were often seen during the 1920s dancing on the stages in major Pittsburgh theaters. But, it was little Gene, Louise, and Fred who really had the passion for dance. In the early 1930s, when the opportunity came to take over a local dancing school, they hopped to it. Their father did the books, their mother ran the studio, and the three children became the principal instructors. The dance school was such a success that soon after, they opened another studio in Johnstown, Pennsylvania. The Kellys taught classes in musical comedy, ballet, acrobatic, and, of course, tap.

With the school well underway, Gene and Fred joined forces and became The Kelly Brothers, performing whenever they got the opportunity. In the late 1930s, Gene traveled to New York and began a successful career on the Broadway stage, while brother Fred and sister Louise taught in the studio. Gene appeared in *Leave It to Me* (1938), *One for the Money* (1939), and *The Time of Your Life* (1939). When Gene was offered the lead role in *Pal Joey* (1940), Fred successfully took his place in *The Time of Your Life*, during which time the show won both the Critics Circle Award and the Pulitzer Prize (the first time ever any show won both these prestigious awards). Fred Kelly received two awards in 1940 for his role as Harry the Hoofer—"Most Outstanding Dancer on Broadway," awarded to him by Antoinette Perry, and another for "Most Valued New Player," awarded to him by Charlie Chaplin.

In November 1941, Gene went to Hollywood to begin one of the greatest musical movie careers, and Fred joined the *This Is the Army* (1942) unit as a principal dancer and choreographer for the Irving Berlin show. After the war, Gene remained in Hollywood dancing, acting, and directing major motion pictures, and Fred choreographed, danced, or directed seven Broadway shows and continued teaching in New York City. Their paths crossed professionally once again in the 1954 MGM film *Deep in My Heart*, where their dancing partnership was recorded for posterity in a nifty vaudeville-style tap dance, "I Love to Go Swimmin' With Wimmen."

Fred continued to have an extraordinarily active career; he directed *The Ice Capades*, produced lavish dancing stage shows at the Roxy, and directed and choreographed over a thousand hours of network television. The Roseland Ballroom hangs his shoes on their Wall of Fame for introducing the Big Apple and the Mambo, and inventing the Cha-Cha.

From The Five Kellys, to The Kelly Brothers, to the personas of Gene Kelly and Fred Kelly, the brothers engaged in a delightful relationship rare to performing arts siblings. Whether working together or separately, the Kelly boys knew how to enjoy their art. And throughout the decades, their enjoyment cascaded off stages, off movie screens, and out of the dance studio to delight millions of people throughout the world.

During the 1920s, uniforms were all the vogue for tap acts: Dancers were quickly transformed into bellhops, waiters, and policemen. Here the three Kelly boys, James, Gene, and Fred (age four), line up for a shot from their act at the Nixon Theatre in Pittsburgh, 1920.

FRED KELLY — All five of us were born and raised in Pittsburgh. From top to bottom, Joan, James, Eugene, Louise, Fred. And we all sang and danced right from the start. See, we came from a very musical family. Dad met my mother backstage in a show that she was in. And around the turn of the century, my dad was the top salesman for Columbia Phonograph. As a matter of fact, he made the largest single sale in music that ever happened. He went out to the Midwest and sold the first phonograph ever in the state to the governors of Missouri, Nebraska, and Kansas. And what he did was, he had all the phonographs shipped to arrive on the same weekend. My dad sold a hundred trains loaded with phonographs and records. In other words, entire trainloads with each train consisting of one hundred boxcars! These were the first phonographs ever to be on the other side of the Mississippi. It was the arts coming to the Wild West. Got written up on the front page with big, two-inch banner headlines. And I never believed my dad. I always thought it was the blarney. But there it was, one hundred trains, with one hundred boxcars. All filled with phonographs and records! Front-page pictures!

So my folks got us all playing musical instruments. We had to learn piano, and then we were allowed another instrument. I was lazy, so I picked drums, because I liked rhythm. And, of course, we all went to dancing school. Gene never wanted to be a dancer. This was not his ambition in life. He wanted to be a ball player, he wanted to be a priest, he wanted to be a lawyer. But he was a natural dancer. And he also had a great singing voice. He was a tenor, and it embarrassed him

This "platinum portrait" of Fred Kelly was taken at the time of his award-winning appearance in *The Time of Your Life* (1941) on Broadway.

no end. He was so glad when his voice changed, because then he didn't have to sing "When Irish Eyes Are Smiling." Anyway, we three little boys would leave home for dancing class dressed up beautifully, and we'd come home in rags. Dancers were thought of as sissies, and the neighborhood guys would lay in wait for us. Jim was very tough and he'd fight, or Gene would start the fight and Jim would finish it. Jim was our protector. But it was sort of our daily routine. Fighting, that was the style in Pittsburgh in those days. I talked to Stevie [Condos] years later, and he said the same thing happened to him and his brother in Philadelphia!

When The Seven Little Foys were held up by bad weather, Joan, James, Gene, Louise, and Fred formed The Five Kellys and tap danced into their spot at the Nixon Theatre. From then on, no Pittsburgh show went on "without a Kelly," 1921.

Aside from being a fighting town—more prize fighters came out of Pittsburgh—Fritzie Zivic, Billy Conn, et al.—Pittsburgh was a real show business town. The Kelly kids were surrounded by it. We had two stock companies and two legitimate theaters, three vaudeville theaters, and then three production houses. In the city of Pittsburgh alone there were twelve first-string theaters. So around 1921, we started a little act and called ourselves The Five Kellys. We worked in every benefit show, every church and hospital show in the city. Our act was fashioned around The Seven Little Foys. I was the baby (born in 1916, and Gene was born in 1912), and we sang the song "K-E-L-L-. . ." and the only thing I had to sing was *Y*. I remember the orchestra cracked up, laughing even at rehearsals. They just stopped playing their instruments because my little voice screamed out. My big sister had the *K*, my brother James had the *E*, Gene had *L*, my other sister had the other *L*, and then I came in with the *Y* whenever I felt like it. I wasn't at all with the music, I just took a great big breath and yelled *Y*!

That same year that we did the Kelly show, we got a big break. The Foys were supposed to come in for the end of the season. But they were held up in some kind of a rainstorm, or held over, or something. It was just impossible to get them to Pittsburgh. The manager of the theater had seen our act in a dance school "Kirmiss" [recital] at the

Nixon Theatre, and so he put us in. After that, we became very popular in shows in Pittsburgh. And when we all weren't available, they would have two of us or three of us. Every show in Pittsburgh had to have a Kelly on it. And boy, did I love it. I ate it up.

During those early years, we all studied at different dancing schools. Then this hip guy from Chicago came in and opened a New York–style dance studio in the Aldine Theatre building in downtown Pittsburgh. He was a pretty clever guy. He literally raided the other schools' pupils and brought in the best New York dancing teachers, and he had all the students pay for class a year in advance. And then the second month he took off! He bolted with the money!

My mother had business savvy for a woman in those days that was sensational. She reached into her pocketbook and paid the teachers' salaries. My mother personally guaranteed the teachers' salaries for this and the following year, and she guaranteed the parents that The Five Kellys would be taking dancing lessons there. So my mother

EXTRA-SPECIAL ADDED ATTRACTION

took over the studio. But it needed a name. My eldest sister and brother were not greatly interested in dancing at that time. So the studio was named the Gene Kelly Studio. Gene became the known teacher. He was just a senior in high school and I was in eighth grade, but we had the studio going. This was around 1928, and there was no general Depression yet. Everything was going well. People wanted to take dancing. When the arts do well, it means the country's doing well. Then when they want to take particular forms of dancing, like tap, it means we're in a buoyant period.

Gene actually set up the idea of eight graded basic routines, and Louise wrote them all down on paper. And my job was to take any of the kids who had missed a lesson and teach them the new material. I think we were the only dance studio in the world that did this. I was twelve,

Sixteen-year-old Fred Kelly partners Betty Conrad, 1932.

too young to "waste time with girls," but old enough to remember all the dance routines! And I knew every dance routine in the studio including the Soft Shoes and Waltz Clogs, sandwiched between the eight graded routines.

In the early 1930s, it was a very serious business taking a tap class. The teacher was *King*. He came in with a long pointer or a yardstick, and he would rap on the ballet barre. There was always a row of long mirrors, usually purchased from closed barber shops, because beards and moustaches were going out of style, and men were getting

Juvenile On Jamboree

Fred Kelly

. . . tap dancer featured in the WWSW musical comedy, "Will Ya Listen?", produced by Howdy Nemitz and Dutch Haid, playing now in Pittsburgh suburbs and vicinity. On April 27th, the revue in enlarged form moves into Syria Mosque for a three day stand, under the auspices of the American Legion of Allegheny County. Kelly is also a star on the Sunday afternoon "JAMBO-REE," featuring outstanding talent of the station, and heard tomorrow afternoon from

3 to 4 P. M. Over

WWSW

NRA

Pittsburgh's Fastest Growing Radio Broadcasting Station

Even radio featured tap dancers. The Nicholas Brothers' taps were heard weekly on Cab Calloway's broadcast from the Cotton Club during the 1930s, but even before that a very young Fred Kelly was spotlighted on WWSW's *Jamboree*, 1929.

shorter, quicker haircuts. We were in that kind of an era. High collars were out, soft collars were in. Anyway, the teacher was the absolute *King*. When you were teaching, you were not interrupted. A class was one hour, and you danced. You didn't sit down.

Most of the dance studios had a uniform. When Ruby Keeler did the movie *42nd Street* [1933], that was it—that set the boys' and girls' uniforms that were worn in our studio. The top of the girls' uniform was unbelievable. It was a blouse, usually satin, with a big collar that was very flattering, and the long sleeves were bloused and they buttoned. There were no zippers, there was no Velcro. And these girls had to button all these blouses and then tie them, not to mention tying the big bows on their tap shoes. Then they wore velvet trunks with three little pearl buttons on each side. In our studio the mothers used to embroider a "*K*" on the blouse—"*K*" for Kelly.

The boys would wear their own street clothes trousers. Gene wanted to have a masculine image, so we never wore tights or short pants on the boys. Not even in ballet in the early days. They wore polo shirts. We did not have a uniform, per se, for the boys, just this casual style. But when we got into the show, we would have costume numbers, and the boys would be dressed as policemen, cowboys, firemen, mailmen, that kind of thing. Oh, we came up with some great ideas.

In the twenties, the girls' shoes were awful-looking. Clog shoes with thick wooden soles. Most of the parents had had dancing lessons sometime in their lives, so they would have their kids start dancing when they were able to fit in their folks' shoes. By now, the Depression was on. That was actually when our school came into full bloom. Metal taps were worn in our school, and my dad would order a gross at a time.

There was only one kind of metal tap in those early days. The man who invented them was Ha-

Jump Rope tap, suitcase tap, and, of course, roller skate tap. Fred Kelly stops gliding along for just a moment for this snap taken in Kansas City, 1935. Fred Astaire and Gene Kelly both used this daring gimmick in their respective films *Shall We Dance* (RKO, 1937) and *It's Always Fair Weather* (MGM, 1955).

ney, who lived in Gary, Indiana. He sold the show *No No Nanette* [1925] on the idea of metal taps. He was the only manufacturer of taps for one year. Well, then the tap business exploded—over a thousand patents! The next year, somebody invented taps that instead of being under the toe of the shoe, extended along under the little toe. And then somebody put lips and clips on, and others came along with a Jingle Tap in which a penny was put inside the tap. And then somebody else came along with a Car Check Tap, which you put your trolley-car token inside. And the tap started to become bigger and rounder and terrible. And Capezio, who only made ballet shoes, was forced into making tap shoes. An Irishman in New York by the name of Morgan came out with Morgan Taps, which most of the professionals preferred. Then Jimmy Selva, who had made ballet shoes, started manufacturing. It went wild. But the first taps I remember were Haneys.

Well, in the late 1920s, radio killed Dad's phonograph business, but it brought the Kelly Studio in strong. Right after the radio came in, just a couple years later, sound pictures started. Sound movies were great. By the mid-1930s, every time Shirley Temple made a movie, our studio enrollment doubled. We had one hundred girls in our studio who all looked exactly like Shirley Temple! They were all her age and all had curls just like Shirley Temple. We couldn't stop it. So we went with it. In one of our shows we did a big "Shirley Temple" finale number. Mother went down to the local department store in Johnstown and talked to the owner of the store. She bought a gross of dresses, different colors. When the finale of the show happened, every girl came out in a dress that had a big bow on the back, all with their hair in bouncing curls, and they all looked just like Shirley Temple!

We thought Shirley Temple was a remarkable dancer, and she was. I asked Bill Robinson in later years if Shirley was as good a dancer as she seemed to be in movies. He said, "Aw, Fred, that girl was so perfect it was embarrassing. I'd show her a step and the next day I come down and start to do the step and she'd say, 'Uncle Bill, yesterday you started that on the other foot!'"

In the early 1930s, Cab Calloway came to Philadelphia with his terrific Cotton Club musical re-

EXTRA-SPECIAL ADDED ATTRACTION

vue. In it were The Nicholas Brothers. Their next stop was Altoona, Pa. Well, The Nicholas Brothers had just got their first chance for a shot in a Hollywood movie, and they took it. The way they told Cab was, "You wouldn't want to see two of your dancers held back?" Cab agreed with them. "Fine, when are you leaving?" They said, "Right now. Bye, Cab!" And they ran out the door. They already had their suitcases in the taxi, California-bound!

So immediately, Cab had his manager telephone William Morris in New York, and the William Morris agency spent all Saturday-night-long trying to get hold of two black dancers, particularly brothers. You know, brother-and-sister teams were very in vogue in those days. So William Morris called ahead to Pittsburgh and asked if there were any tap teams that were great. They said, "Oh, yeah, we got two. We got The Three Fish Brothers—they're the three funniest little black dancers you ever want to see. My God, the one dresses like a girl and the other one pats him on the head every time he jumps up and they do Splits, they're just great." Then the agent said, "Well, what of the other act?" "Oh, The Kelly Brothers, they stop the show. They're great. They've played the Stanley and the Loews Penn in town. They're a very professional act." So the agent said, "Fine, let's book The Kelly Brothers."

Gene and I took the Pennsylvania Railroad and arrived in Altoona at ten A.M., and we went straight to the rehearsal at the theater. Across the front of the theater was a huge banner that read: CAB CALLOWAY AND HIS COTTON CLUB REVUE. Now, being just a Pittsburgh kid, I wasn't too familiar with night-

The Kelly Brothers reunite for their vaudeville-styled number in *Deep in My Heart* (MGM, 1954). Their uncanny resemblance is never in greater evidence than in this series of rehearsal shots.

clubs in New York. And I certainly didn't know much about the Cotton Club. All I knew was that Cab Calloway's music was hot, and I wanted to dance to it. But if we had any brains at all, we might have realized then that we were out of a job. We were two kids crazy to get on that stage and perform, and we didn't think anything of it. We just marched right backstage and asked for the manager. I remember this enormous black man came out, and that he was sporting a Derby hat. He looked down on us and asked, "You're The Kelly Brothers?" I said, "Yeah." He replied, "I'm gonna stop the rehearsal." So he went over to the door, held up his hand. Now Cab is in the middle of the music, and he stopped the orchestra. "What's so important?" he said, "what in the world is so important that you have stopped me in the middle of rehearsal?" The manager said, "Cab . . . meet The Kelly Brothers!" Cab walked in, took one look at us, looked at his manager, and in a real Amos and Andy put-on said, "Somebody done make a *big* mistake!"

So he asked us, "Did you know this was an all-black show?" And I said, "Yes, but I thought you needed a dance team." He said, "You don't mind working . . . ?" (In those days there wasn't the freedom, you know, to go back and forth.) "No, we've got your records at home, and you guys really play with a beat. It'd be great to dance to it!" So it looked like we were in.

We arrived at the theater for rehearsal and handed the musicians our arrangements. Then one of the guys looks at Cab and he said, "It'll take us a few minutes to dig some of this. But man, these arrangements are wonderful." So Cab said to us, "You kids got nice arrangements. Let's go through it. Now, which one of you is the fast dancer?" And I said that I was. He asked what number I dance to, and I replied "Stardust." Well, "Stardust" isn't a fast number at all. But I explained, "I start in half-time, and I go into full-time, then I double-time, then I quadruple-time for the finish." He said, "This is something I want to see!" Well, Cab Calloway's band played the thing, and Gene and I danced the thing, and as soon as it was over, they all stood up and clapped and cheered. That was really something. The guys we were nuts about were applauding us!

We told Cab that this would be our first appearance in Altoona. He said, "Well, you better get something to eat before the first show. There's a little restaurant right across the street. I'll have a table reserved for you up in front." So we sat at the front table in the window of the restaurant right across the street from the theater. We had just had this sensational rehearsal and we were high as kites. So while we were eating, we saw the guys from the theater bring out a ladder to change the marquee: EXTRA-SPECIAL ADDED ATTRACTION—GENE AND FRED KELLY—THE KELLY BROTHERS. That was it. Now we knew we had made it! And, we even got held over with Cab the next three days in Johnstown. What a time that was: just kids, and having the time of our lives.

In 1937, Gene left for New York to audition for a Broadway show. The show was closing so nothing happened. He went back the following year at the request of Bob Alton (Alton was a big Broadway dance director and later became one of the head choreographers in Hollywood), who put him in a show called *Leave It to Me* [1938], the same show that made Mary Martin an overnight sensation singing Cole Porter's "My Heart Belongs to Daddy."

When World War II broke out, I was brought into the *This Is the Army* unit as medical sergeant and choreographed the big "Mandy" number, as well as danced the lead in it. This run went on for quite a while, because after we did the U.S. tour and made the Warner Bros. movie of it, we toured the world. Two and a half years in unrecognizable makeup!

There's a funny story that happened when the unit was in London during the war in the early 1940s. They all wanted to hear "Easter Parade," but the army show was all set, and it didn't include "Easter Parade." Berlin came out onstage and they interrupted him while he was singing "Oh, How I Hate to Get Up in the Morning." Now, the English audiences are supposed to be very polite, but they cheered all through the thing, and of course, the music is all arranged and choreographed. He figured the applause would die down as he sang. But Mr. Berlin does not have a loud voice. I'm standing in the wings watching this pandemonium, and I hear somebody yell out of the audience, "Sing 'Easter Parade.'" Berlin turns around, and it was Her Royal Highness! So the English secret service equivalent ran down the aisle into the orchestra pit and says, "Stop the music. Play 'Easter Parade.' It's a Royal request." So the orchestra ad-libbed playing "Easter Parade," and the whole audience is singing it. And they get to the musical bridge, "you'll find that you're in the rotogravure," and the audience all sings, "you'll soon be seen in a smart magazine." Berlin stops and says, "What's that?" The English publisher comes running up onstage. Now, this is opening night of *This Is the Army* at the Palladium in London! Sixteen generals and the entire royal family! The Berlin publisher is onstage trying to explain to Berlin that he had forgotten to ask permission to change the lyric. There was no rotogravure section in the English newspapers, they wouldn't know what it was, so he changed the lyric to read, "you'll soon be seen. . . ." without changing the context. The two of them are having this discussion onstage in the middle of the show! And there's the royal family sitting up in the box, and I'm offstage going, "Berlin's going to die, he's just going to die." So Berlin finally cues the conductor to start "Easter Parade," and they come to the bridge, and Berlin points to the publisher, and the publisher sings the middle line all by himself in a terrible voice, and the audience goes crazy. It was the hit of the show.

Around 1954, Gene and I finally got to dance together on film in a movie called *Deep in My Heart* [1954]. We just had a little spot in the film—it was to be an old-time vaudeville-type number to Sigmund Romberg's "I Love to Go Swimmin' With Wimmen." We had a *lot* of fun because it was the first time we had danced together since Pittsburgh.

———————————————

So, there's a bit of it anyway. Gene and I started out as kids together dancing in Pittsburgh, then Broadway, then Hollywood. Sometimes together, sometimes separately. Whatever the case, we always got along great. It wasn't always that way with brothers. I personally saw two real-brother acts break up by physically fighting. In one act, both brothers changed their name. And I'll never forget one member of a tap trio taught the act's routine to a female trio, and a fight with knives ensued worse than any movie, because the physical chase lasted for a bleeding hour and a half back and forth for three blocks past the theater and back again the other way (dancing was worth fighting for!). They all stayed in the business, but never spoke to one another since. Another act both fell in love with the girl in the act, thus, a solo and a duo. But with The Kelly Brothers, that kind of stuff just never happened. We were never jealous of each other. Gene wasn't jealous of me. I've never been jealous. I've always been very proud of him, and he of me. You know, we worked too hard to waste time on comparisons.

January 26, 1989
Tucson, Arizona

19

DANCING WITH THE GREAT BILL "BOJANGLES" ROBINSON

EDDIE BROWN

Bill was a very fine man. He wanted everybody to recognize him as a big star. Which he was. You don't call him Bill Robinson, you call him *Mr.* Bill Robinson.

I t was every tap dancer's dream to see the great Bill Robinson. Watching the master tap out a melody of clear phrases from his feet sent chills up and down the backs of even the best hoofers. They said Bill Robinson had the cleanest taps around. They said that Bill Robinson could do the easiest routine in the world and get away with it because of his charm and charisma. They said that he could drive a dancer crazy with the complexity of a step that looked so easy. But when tap dancers talk about Bill Robinson, they talk of the greatest tap dancer of all time. There were others who could tap out a mean percussive piece. There were others who could flip and split. But, according to the best of them, nobody had Bill Robinson beat on sheer tap dancing ability.

Bill Robinson had an impressive career. When he was not starring in a Broadway show, he was starring in the Cotton Club, or starring in a Hollywood movie, or starring in vaudeville, or starring in a benefit. As a matter of fact, he appeared in more than five hundred benefit performances a year, during which time he was doubling in shows and at clubs. Bill

Eddie Brown, master of Rhythm Tap.

Sheet music cover of Bill Robinson's trademark song "Doin' the New Low-Down," 1928. From 1933—1939, young hoofer Eddie Brown shadowed the legend to this number in *The Bill Robinson Revue.*

Robinson was simply a star whenever and wherever he worked. And he was always working.

When not appearing in a regular show, or in a movie, Bill Robinson would throw together what was loosely called *The Bill Robinson Revue.* He would put together a chorus line of girls and a chorus of boys and make a show. The revue appeared in vaudeville. But not just any vaudeville—the Orpheum Circuit. And whenever Bill Robinson came to town in a show, tap dancers would flock to see him. Most just went away shaking their heads. They knew Robinson was great, but for the life of them, could not translate his artistry for themselves. He was a man standing alone in talent.

Bill Robinson was immortalized with his theme song/dance, "Doin' the New Low-Down." The words were perfectly suited to the master:

> I got a pair of feet
> That have found that low-down beat
> Low down, down around the spot
>   that's hot . . .
>
> Got my feet to misbehavin' now
> got a soul that's fit for savin' now
> Heigh ho! Doin' the new low-
>   down . . .
>
> Once you hear that haunting strain to
>   it
> I'd bet my life you'll go insane to it
> Heigh ho! Doin' the new low-down.*
>
>   *"Doin' the New Low-Down"

Bill Robinson was correct when he sang, "I'd bet my life you'll go insane to it," because that was precisely what happened every time tap dancers watched him dance. In 1929, Bill Robinson made a 78 rpm recording of that number, taps and all. For the first time, tap dancers could revel in the sounds of those Robinson feet right in their own home. And Bill Robinson's taps echoed through households all day long.

One tap-happy lad who never tired of winding up that old phonograph was Eddie Brown. Raised in Omaha, Nebraska, he learned to tap dance in his uncle's dancing studio at a very early age. But most of his tap schooling came off the corners, along with other hoofers. Like so many children of the era, Eddie Brown spent nearly seven days a week jamming on those street corners with the neighborhood kids, developing and refining his talents. He danced professionally through the 1930s and 1940s, as a single, as part of the tap trio Brown, Gibson and Reed, in nightclubs, and with the great swing bands, including Jimmie Lunceford, Duke Ellington, Count Basie, George Shearing, Dizzy Gillespie, and J. C.

Higginbotham. But the highlight of his tap dancing career was dancing with the great Bill "Bojangles" Robinson during the 1930s. Over a period of six years, Eddie Brown appeared in *The Bill Robinson Revue*, and not only got to watch Bill Robinson in action, he got to dance with him as well. While other tap dancers dreamed what it would be like to dance with the King of Taps, Eddie Brown had the rare opportunity to live that dream.

E D D I E   B R O W N — Bill Robinson came to Omaha when I was sixteen years old. He was having all the dancers sign up for a tap dance contest. I signed up and went down to the theater, and do you know, I won it!

I was the thirty-seventh contestant. Bill Robinson called out my name—"Eddie Brown! Well, what do you do young man?" "I dance." He said, "What kind of dance do you do?" I said, "I do the *same* thing you do." He laughed. The whole audience laughed! "What music do you use?" "The *same* music you use," I said, " 'Doin' the New Low-Down.' " The audience laughed again. I said, "I ain't jivin'." Dig it!

So the band played the thing, and I went through it. When I finished and walked up to Bill, he said, "Don't go. Wait. I want to talk to you." So I waited, and when he come off, he said, "Where did you learn my dance?" I told him, "I learned it off your records."

I had bought recordings of him tap dancing and listened to them on our Graphonola. Well, I'd slow it down *real* slow and listen to it over and over again. And then I'd go and see him in a picture, so I knew what tap steps he was doin'. And that's how I put that guy together! Step by step.

After the contest, he come over to my house and told my mother and father, "I would like to have your son in my show and take him to New York." My folks blew their stack. "What? He's in school. He can't go to New York!" So they wouldn't let me go.

Bill left town, but I knew where he was goin' —the Apollo Theatre in New York City, One hundred twenty-fifth and Lenox Avenue. I went to school, but boy, did I mope around. Two weeks I hung around there. I took it. But then I just couldn't stand it no longer knowin' *the* Bill Robinson wanted me in his show. So at the end of that two weeks, that Friday, I left to go to school, but I didn't go to school, dig it? Me and Kokomo and Teddy, they dancers too, went over to Sixteenth Street and got that train. Riding the rods!

We didn't know where we was goin'. Just going! Kokomo and Teddy were twins. But, Kokomo was *experienced*. He's the one that guided us to New York. Sure did. Took us a week to get there. Oh, boy! Because we had to be aware of the railroad dicks. They didn't want you hobo-ing. They would kick you off that train—you know what I mean? Yeah! I never will forget that trip as long as I live.

When we got to New York, we went directly to the Apollo Theatre. Went up to see Bill. I asked somebody to get him and ask him to come outside; we couldn't go in there, 'cause we just got off that freight train! Bill came out, took one look at us, and knew we done run off. See, I was still underage. He said to me that he could only take

Three views of the legendary West Coast tap dancer, Eddie Brown.

me in his show when I turned eighteen. He gave us some money so we could go and get cleaned up, get a place.

For the next year and a half, we had to duck. We couldn't work in no club or nothing, because police patrolled all the time. So we gigged, you know. Busked—danced in the streets—and people threw money to us. Do you know, we made twenty, thirty dollars a day doin' that. And this was durin' the Depression!

Well, I finally turned eighteen, and I had to hide no more. Bill Robinson brought me out to his show—*The Bill Robinson Revue*. Bill opened the show. He would do a little thing, a little chatter, a little dance. Then he'd call me out there. And I'd do this dance with him, this dance that I had learned, "Doin' the New Low-Down," in the back of him. Like a shadow. And I wore the same thing he wore. If he'd wear a suit, I'd wear a suit. If he'd wear tails, I'd wear tails.

That's the way it was. That was the only number I was in. And I was in that show for six years, from 1933 to 1939. We toured from New York out to the West Coast. San Francisco was the last deal, see. When we got to San Francisco, we played the Orpheum Theatre on Market Street.

Then Bill wanted to take the show to his hometown, Richmond, Virginia. You know what happened, don't ya? There was forty-five people in the show, and all of them left. You might as well say all of them. Those that stayed, ain't no way in the world he could make a show out of them! Richmond, Virginia? The South? No way! I *ain't* goin' down there. You kiddin'. Uh uh!

———————————

Bill was a very fine man. He wanted everybody to recognize him as a big star. Which he was. You don't call him Bill Robinson, you call him *Mr.* Bill Robinson.

He was a great cat!

July 12, 1988
San Francisco, California
(Died, December 28, 1992)

1940 –1955

PART 3

During the early 1940s, tappers danced as they never had before. America's involvement in World War II did nothing to reduce the country's thirst for entertainment, and tap dancers were enjoying a great popularity. The Swing Era had hit the nation full force, and the music perfectly suited the steps of the sensational tap stylists who worked throughout the era. Tap rhythms—steps as well as styles—led them forward into the next phase of tap's evolution.

When the war ended, America looked to the magic of show business to brush the years and many bad memories aside. Broadway brought forth its brightest collection of musical comedy in years. But now Broadway, and all live entertainment, had to battle for success in a highly unfavorable climate. Whereas the 1928–1929 Broadway season saw two hundred productions, only sixty-two major productions surfaced in 1949–1950. The reasons were plain and simple. As radio had done nearly twenty years earlier, now television was beginning to steal audiences, and the competition for entertainment dollars was fierce. By the early 1950s, television was coming into its own as America's major supplier of entertainment. And the figures dominating the television screens were generally vaudeville, stage, and radio stars. Many tap dancers were seen by the masses for the first time on such hit variety packages as *The Ed Sullivan Show.*

Despite it all, live entertainment did flourish for several more years, and tap dancers throughout the country, though working less than in previous decades, were still hitting the boards. Nightclubs were becoming smaller, vaudeville was practically gone, Broadway's season was diminutive compared to its past; still, tap dancers were finding new and exciting rhythms for their and the public's delight.

In the 1950s, perhaps the strongest influence on tap dancers was bebop. Charlie Parker and other contemporaries were putting out music that was something to be reckoned with, and there was a new generation of tap stylists who did: Baby Lawrence and Teddy Hale were the leaders among the many dancers grappling with this new musical form.

By 1955, tap dancing had been around for over one hundred years as an American art form. For the next two decades, it would slip quietly away from the public eye, as there were no longer ample performing venues for dancers to make a living. Some dancers went to Europe and continued to entertain with success; some tried different professions, as teachers and choreographers. But, during the next twenty years, tap dancing would hold its own only to emerge as strong and as versatile as it had ever been. Because Americans love rhythm. And that is what tap dancing is all about.

20

WWII'S *THIS IS THE ARMY*

GENE NELSON

The GI audiences were the greatest. . . . They were so glad to be there watching something that brought them closer to home. Our show was a jewel in the night.

When the United States entered World War II, the military ranks were filled with the nation's young and healthy men. The nation's male entertainment ranks, as a result, were nearly depleted. Off the stages and off to the boot camps went the singers, actors, comics, jugglers, and tap dancers. The country did not lose their good services altogether, though. Many of these talented men went into entertainment units. Their units toured the United States, Europe, the South Pacific—anywhere there were American military personnel. Most of these units were under the auspices of Special Services or the USO. However, there was another unit that was strictly army. It was a one-of-a-kind. And it was created by a most unlikely candidate—America's most prolific songwriter, Irving Berlin. The unit was called *This Is the Army*.

This Is the Army first appeared on Broadway in 1942, and then toured the United States. The unit made its way across the country all the way to Hollywood, where in 1943, *This Is the Army* was filmed (with a slightly filled-out cast that included George Murphy and Ronald Reagan). Then it went overseas, and by the end of the war, had literally gone around the world.

This Is the Army was a musical extravaganza loaded with tap dancing. Fred Kelly was there, Stumpy Cross was there, Billy Yates was there, and a young newcomer—Private First Class Eugene Leander Berg—was there. Through a series of lucky circumstances, Eugene Leander Berg found his way to the *This Is the Army* unit, and for the next three years, he helped bring much-needed entertainment to millions of servicemen and civilians alike.

After the war, Eugene Leander Berg returned to Hollywood where he became Gene Nelson—the last of the great screen tap dancers of the golden age of musicals; he made all of his major musical films in the 1950s. Had Gene Nelson appeared just ten years earlier, he would have hit the production peak of the movie musical rather than the tail end of it. Nonetheless, his ingenuity, grace, and amazing talent resulted in scores of classic tap dance numbers recorded for posterity on film. His movies included *Tea for Two* (1950), *The West Point Story* (1950), *Lullaby of Broadway* (1951), *She's Working Her Way Through College* (1952), and *So This Is Paris* (1955). Gene Nelson was immortalized in *Oklahoma!* (1955), where he brought the character of "dumb ol' " Will Parker to great tap heights.

Gene Nelson's style was smooth, rhythmic, and romantic. His work incorporated the best of tap

Three programs from *This Is the Army's* World War II tour: (left to right) Persian Gulf (Iran), Egypt (Cairo), Great Britain (London Palladium)

woven together with jazz, ballet, acrobatics, and gymnastics. Gene Nelson choreographed all of his dances so that each movement surpassed the last with a seeming effortlessness. When Gene Nelson danced, there was always a moment when his audience was left breathless.

GENE NELSON — I had just seen a guy named Fred Astaire in a movie called *Flying Down to Rio* [1933], at the Wilshire Theatre in Santa Monica . . . I was twelve years old. I had to learn to do that! He made it look so easy. So, in defense of my mother's hardwood floors—which I was scratching badly trying to emulate Mr. Astaire—I was enrolled in a class at the Miramar Hotel with Roy Randolph for Saturday classes in tap dancing.

I liked going to class. But, what I didn't realize was that I was required to *practice* what I'd

learned—every day. My dad laid down a linoleum floor in the garage for me to practice on. I truly hated practicing. It interfered with my after-school playtime. I began ducking practice with deliberate regularity. When my dad found out, he said, "No practice—no lessons!"

A couple of years later, and after seeing three or four more Astaire films, I went to my parents and told them I wanted to start tap lessons again—but seriously, this time. My first teacher at the Albright School of Dance was a wonderful guy from New York, Steve Granger. A real hoofer.

Gene Nelson flying high over the beach of Santa Monica, between movies and tours with Sonja Henie's *Hollywood Ice Revue*, 1939

I took private lessons from him, and the first routine he taught me was "Bojangles" Bill Robinson's routine to "Doin' the New Low-Down."

During this period, I teamed up with a fellow student named Ted Hansen. We got into a lot of flashy stuff like Toe Stands, Double Wings to Toe Stands, and a lot of challenge steps. We got pretty good and began doing free shows at the Veterans Hospital and the openings of markets where they used to do little promotional shows featuring local talent . . . wherever we could get in front of an audience.

When I got to high school, it was tough. Boys who took dancing lessons were automatic "sissies," and I spent a lot of time defending myself. But that began to change when the "macho boys" discovered I could be useful by performing at various school functions. Suddenly, I wasn't a "sissy" anymore. They needed me to make themselves look good.

After my first year in high school, I left Albright and went to the biggest professional school in Hollywood—Fanchon and Marco—where I got heavily into acrobatic training and advanced tap and adagio work. Fanchon and Marco were tied in with the Paramount Theatre in downtown Los Angeles, where they had a big chorus line called The Fanchonettes, similar to The Rockettes at Radio City Music Hall. There was a movie and four shows a day, including vaudeville acts—a big orchestra and all. This schedule was interrupted three times a year for *The Fanchon and Marco*

Juvenile Revue, which played for two weeks. My first professional job was in their revue at fifteen dollars a week. Wow! I was fifteen years old, and I learned a lot about show biz with them.

But by the time I was sixteen or seventeen, my school work began to suffer greatly, and with the distinct threat of not graduating with my class, my mom and dad pulled the plug on Fanchon and Marco so I could concentrate on my studies. They were right, of course.

And I graduated . . . barely.

I got interested in ice skating—in fact, I liked it so much that it became an obsession with me. In August of 1938, just three months after graduation, I was asked to audition for Sonja Henie's *Hollywood Ice Revue* at the Polar Palace in Hollywood. Bert Clark, Sonja's technical advisor and manager of the Polar Palace, had shown an interest in my skating and arranged it. I made the audition for the chorus and began immediate rehearsals for the winter tour. What a break! Seventy-five dollars a week! I must say that my dance training put me way ahead of the game, and I progressed very rapidly over the next two years. I had apparently found a new career. By the second year I was doing specialty work, and I understudied Sonja's tango partner, Stuart Reyburn.

I had abandoned tap and began taking ballet to improve my skating. I studied with Bert Prival, who was then teaching for Nico Charisse. He was marvelous to work with, and I treasure all the help he gave me.

I toured with Sonja for two years and did two of her films at Fox Studios—working both as a chorus skater and dancer.

The West Point Story (Warner Bros., 1950)

By late 1940, I was costarring in an ice show that Sonja produced at the Center Theatre in New York, *It Happens on Ice*. Catherine Littlefield choreographed the show and it was, to say the least, a unique and baffling experience for the New York reviewers. I remember *The New Yorker Magazine* called it "the frozen aquacade." Nevertheless, the novelty attracted the New York and tourist audiences.

On that fateful Sunday, December 7, 1941, we were just about to make our entrance for the matinee performance when the news of Pearl Harbor flattened us. I knew then and there I would be called for the draft—which I didn't want—so I enlisted in the Signal Corps at Fort Monmouth, New Jersey. With a report date in March of 1942, I promptly married the girl I was engaged to, Miriam Franklin, on December twenty-second. She was then appearing in the Ethel Merman show *Panama Hattie*, and was one of the great Broadway tap dancers, as well as assistant to Robert Alton, who choreographed the show. It was she who got me back on track with dancing during this time.

On my twenty-first birthday, I found myself a buck private in the Signal Corps and assigned to Company L of the fifteenth Regiment Officers Candidate School as a company clerk. What had I done to deserve this! It was so boring and tiresome: up at six—my buns glued to my desk chair poring over the records of these "ninety-day wonders," as they were called, and getting no exercise. God, I hated it! In desperation one day, I took my little portable Philco radio and went to the main administration building hall after work. In my fatigues, I began tap dancing to whatever music I would find on the radio. It felt so good

---

to be working out again. I took out all my anger and frustration on the wooden floor.

One afternoon while I was working out, a little bald private first class stuck his head through the door and watched for a while. It didn't bother me—an audience of one is better than no audience at all. Then he spoke: "You want to be in the post show next week?" Well, that was the best offer I'd had since I'd been there, so I accepted immediately. Now I had something to work for.

That little (five-foot-one-inch) PFC who was working in Special Services turned out to be the famous Irving "Swifty" Lazar, one of the most powerful agents in Hollywood—"the diminutive giant."

The post show went great. It felt so good to be performing again. What I didn't know was that Irving Berlin was in the audience with his army staff, which included Sergeant Josh Logan, Sergeant Ezra Stone, and Sergeant Robert Sidney. They were there scouting for talent for Berlin's all-army show, *This Is the Army*. Logan and Stone were the directors and Sidney was the choreographer.

The next morning, I sat poring over the reams of orders and transfers, preparing my morning report, and suddenly there, as big as life, was my name: "Private First Class Eugene Leander Berg, #12073731, transferred to Camp Upton, Long Is-

land on special duty with *This Is the Army* Company." I cut my own orders, took them into "old Jelly Beans," our captain—we called him Jelly Beans because he was a Chiclets and candy salesman before becoming a captain—for his signature, and I was out of there by noon. And that afternoon I joined a company of three hundred and sixty-five talented actors, dancers, singers, musicians, and technical crew members—all of us in the army—and an integral part of Irving Berlin's *This Is the Army*.

This was the "big time," boy. Josh Logan and Ezra Stone directing, and Bob Sidney and Nelson Barclift doing the choreography to Irving Berlin's music—what an experience! After a few weeks of rehearsing at Camp Upton, we were moved into New York City and were headquartered at the Broadway Theatre, where the show was to open. We were still in the army, and we had to stand muster every morning for roll call and duty assignments, and even some close order drill.

On July 4, 1942, we opened. It was an instant smash—magnificent! SRO for six months at the Broadway and then we went on a national tour,

While on tour in the United States, the *This Is the Army* unit paraded from the train station to the theater accompanied by full marching band in every city. Sgt. Gene Berg (soon to become Gene Nelson) leads the company forward, as depicted in this scene from the Warner Bros. 1943 film version.

By 1945, the Tour of Duty finds the *This Is the Army* company overseas in Leyte, Philippines. Here acrobat Angelo Buono and tap dancer Gene Berg point the way to happier times.

which ended in Hollywood. We traveled by train and paraded from the train station to the theater with full marching band in every city. The biggest thrill of the tour happened in Washington, D.C. For the first time since Lincoln was shot, a president attended a theatrical performance. FDR and Eleanor came to a special matinee performance. After our evening performance, the President invited the entire company for late supper at the White House, and we were all individually introduced to him. I'll never forget it.

Anyway, after closing in Los Angeles, we reported immediately to Warner Brothers Studios to commence working on the film version of *This Is the Army* (which starred Ronald Reagan and George Murphy). They built a full tent camp on the back lot, with an obstacle course and everything. All our nonpicture-related time was spent at the camp in military pursuits of all kinds.

As the filming began to wind down, we all kind of prepared ourselves for the return to our original army companies. It was a sad time—the thought of not doing the show anymore. But the War Department came to the rescue in the nick of time. The general of Special Services decided to send the show around the world to play for the troops wherever we could get to them. The company was reduced to one hundred and sixty-five members, and we began gearing up to become a self-sustaining unit under direct orders from the War Department.

We opened at the Palladium Theatre in London in November of 1943. We performed for the Queen of England and the princesses, General Eisenhower, General Bradley, Lord and Lady Mountbatten, and a load of other dignitaries, both military and civilian. Then off on a tour of the provinces —Scotland, Midlands, and Ireland. Our last stop before leaving the British Isles was Liverpool, where we boarded a troop ship bound for Italy by way of Algiers. March of 1943, we opened in Naples at the San Carlo Opera House and played for General Mark Clark and [over the next six months] the entire Fifth Army. Then we headed north and east, getting closer to the front-line action. Some camps had no theaters—just big stage platforms, and the troops sat on hillsides. Santa Maria, Foggia, Bari, and then we followed the Fifth Army into Rome as they chased the Germans out. Well, from there we headed east to Egypt, Iran, India. God, Iran was the *pits*. When we got there in September, it was around a hundred and twenty-

Coming ashore in New Guinea loaded down with show gear, including costumes, props, and sets. *This Is the Army*'s South Pacific Tour of Duty ship, *El Liberatador*, is at upper right, 1945.

Warner Bros.' 1943 motion picture version of *This Is the Army*. The show-stopping number "What the Well-Dressed Man in Harlem Will Wear" features the all-black contingent with Sgt. Joe Louis (center), Stumpy Cross (left), and Bill Yates (right).

This theater at a naval installation in the Marianas is typical of facilities built by enlisted men for *This Is the Army*'s unit. The tents to the right and left of the stage are the dressing rooms, 1945.

five degrees. We traveled from camp to camp, the length of Iran by truck convoy and finished in Hamadan, near the Russian border. We played for the Russian High Command there and for "Vinegar Joe" Stilwell, U.S. Commanding General of the China-Burma Command.

Then to the South Pacific. You got to remember that we were like a traveling circus. We were a self-sustaining unit and completely independent of all the commands in which we played. Each of us had two or three jobs to perform apart from doing the show. Some were cooks, some were in wardrobe repair and maintenance, others were electricians, carpenters, company clerical workers, or did set and prop maintenance. We did it all. I was assistant stage electrician—hanging lights and mounting spotlights, hauling generators and cable. We carried our own fifteen-hundred-pound generator on wheels.

When we got to the Pacific, we were assigned our own boat. It was a little converted Dutch interisland boat and had only a three-man navy crew. We slept in four-high wooden bunks that were built into the cargo hold. Our galley was four army field stoves lashed to the foredeck. The

show sets, boxes of electrical equipment, and the wardrobe, et cetera, were stored in the number-two hold. Now, being shorthanded in our navy crew, I volunteered for gun duty in emergencies. I was second twenty-millimeter gunner. I learned to operate the steam winch to unload our show onto trucks at each port o' call. I got to like that a lot—it was fun, and I got damn good at it.

We did ten one-night stands all the way up the coast of New Guinea, playing at army and navy installations that were sometimes fifty miles inland. We'd arrive at dawn, unload onto trucks, schlep to the camp, unload, set the show up, light it, and by that time it was showtime. We'd do the show, tear it down, load everything back on the trucks, and head back to the boat. The rest of the company hit the sack while the unloading crew and I winched the show back into the hold. The minute the last piece was in the hold, the skipper would weigh anchor and we were off to our next port o'call. It was then about two-thirty A.M.

I got to tell you, I learned more about theater and show business in those two years—it would have taken twelve years at home under normal conditions to accumulate that much experience. Hell, we performed in the rain, in thunder and lightning, under the wildest conditions you could ever imagine. Even if it was outdoors, we had to make it look just like Broadway for those guys.

Gene Berg and fellow *This Is the Army* **performers ankle deep in flood waters from an overnight torrential rain. Despite it all, tap shoes stay afloat. Tour of Duty, South Pacific, Island of Tinian, 1945.**

GENE NELSON

Most of them had never seen anything like it in their lives.

We had a black contingent in our company, and they were some of the greatest hoofers around. They did a number that never failed to stop the show cold. It was called, "What the Well-Dressed Man in Harlem Will Wear." It was a barn-burner, let me tell you! Stumpy Cross (of Stump and Stumpy) and Billy Yates led the number—it was just great!

The GI audiences were the greatest. We thought, at first, these combat guys would resent us, but not so. Some of them would come up and just want to touch us. You know what I mean? They were so glad to be there watching something that brought them closer to home. Our show was a jewel in the night.

One time, I'll never forget, they built our stage at the bottom of a natural hillside amphitheater. In back of the stage, they put up tents for our dressing room with long wooden benches. Well, the hillside was filling up with about two thousand guys and officers when it started to rain. When it rains in the Pacific, baby, it pours. Our stage manager, Alan Anderson, looked out front and the guys were getting under their ponchos. He came out and posed the question to the men, "Looks like it's going to get very wet. It's up to you—you want the show, we'll do it." In unison they all yelled, "*Go! Go! Go!*" They weren't about to move.

The orchestra put on their ponchos, someone futilely swept some water off the stage, and the overture began. By the end of the opening number, the stage was flooded and rivers of water were running in one end of our dressing-room tent and out the other. They laid planks from the

stage, and we had to stand on the benches to change wardrobe. We played the show straight through. In fact, they didn't even move when the show was over. They were spellbound.

In the daytime, those who didn't have assigned duties would accompany Irving Berlin and give a show at the field hospital wards. We covered more men in every category of the service. Total performances from July 4, 1942 to September 1945—1,238. Grand total attendance—2,468,005 armed forces and civilian. God, I wouldn't do it again for a million dollars. But I wouldn't take a million dollars for that experience.

We were on Guam when the war ended. A few more islands and many more shows later, we finished the tour in Honolulu for our final performance. Then it was all over—back to the States and discharge.

What now?

My wife, Miriam, had been working at Paramount Studios all during World War II. She worked with a very good Canadian tap dancer named Johnny Coy and appeared in a number of film musicals, like *Duffy's Tavern* [1945]. She had met a big agent named John Darrow who handled Gene Kelly, June Allyson, Van Johnson, and the directors Chuck Walters and Robert Alton, all of whom were at MGM. I met him, and he asked if I'd audition for him. I did, and he liked what he saw. I signed with him, and he arranged for an audition at Fox Studios where they made a screen test of my dancing and a dramatic scene. I signed a stock contract with them.

Supposedly, they signed me to be groomed as their dancing leading man for Betty Grable and June Haver. One of the executives, a little Jewish man, rather ironically decided my Swedish name, Berg, was "too Jewish" and ordered it be changed. I submitted a few suggestions, among which was

Hermes Pan and June Haver look on in wonder as Gene Nelson soars high above in full split. Rehearsal hall at 20th Century-Fox Studios for *I Wonder Who's Kissing Her Now*, 1946

the last name of Nelson, my mother's maiden name. They liked it, and my new identity began —Eugene Leander Berg became Gene Nelson.

It was June Haver who gave me my first break at the studio. I was doing my daily rehearsal in A Hall with the pianist they provided, and as Irving Lazar did at Fort Monmouth, June Haver stuck her head in the door and watched. I wasn't rehearsing anything in particular, just trying new combinations and rhythms and tricks—getting ready for whatever.

I didn't know who she was and didn't pay much attention. After a while she left. The next day I got a call to report to George Jessel's office at ten A.M. When I got there, there was June with Mr. Jessel, "the Toastmaster of America." "Junie tells me you're a pretty good dancer, and she wants to dance with you in my picture," Mr. Jessel said. It sounded great to me. No arguments. The film was *I Wonder Who's Kissing Her Now* [1947], and it was being choreographed by my idol, Hermes Pan, Fred Astaire's choreographer. That

was my start in films.

Later on, there was a movie coming up with Betty Grable called *Mother Wore Tights* [1947], a burlesque story. The lead was a burlesque song-and-dance man, and the casting office sent me to see the producer about the part. He took one look at me and started to laugh. I had no idea why. Then he apologized and told me, "We have no part for Betty Grable's *son!*" I was twenty-four years old, and I looked about eighteen. They hired Dan Dailey for the role, which ended my career at Fox. They soon dropped my option.

Then came *Lend An Ear* [1948], a neat little revue that Gower Champion directed and choreographed. Carol Channing was in the show too. We opened at Las Palmas Theatre in Hollywood and played to SRO for six months. We went to Broadway and became a big hit at the Broadhurst Theatre. Gower and Marge Champion were great, and I learned a lot from them about choreography. Then, after eight months, my agent was contacted by Warner Bros. to have me come to Hollywood and test for a film called *The Daughter of Rosie O'Grady* [1950]. What I didn't know was that June Haver was starring with Gordon MacRae, and she had told Bill Jacobs, the producer, that she wanted to dance with me in the picture. That's how the offer came about. I left *Lend an Ear* and came back home, tested, and signed for the film. It was great being with her again. Also in the film was a little sixteen-year-old contract

Gene Nelson and Yvonne Adair in a steamy moment from the "Who Hit Me" dance, featured in *Lend an Ear*. Broadhurst Theatre, New York, 1949.

Gene Nelson's dumb ol' cowboy Will Parker in "Everything's Up to Date in Kansas City" from *Oklahoma!* (Magna, 1955). Filming was done on location in—Nogales, Arizona.

player named Debbie Reynolds. It was her first film.

You see, Warner Bros. had just signed Doris Day and Virginia Mayo and were beginning to produce musical films again. I ended up doing ten musicals in three years for them. I choreographed all of my numbers myself with the expert help of a fine dancer named Al White, who assisted Leroy Prinz, the dance director at Warners. In most cases, I came up with the idea for the numbers, too. It was a great creative learning experience in many ways, including staging the dances for camera (which was very different from staging dances for theatrical productions).

=====

Somebody gave me a red T-shirt once with the inscription, I DIDN'T KNOW IT WAS IMPOSSIBLE WHEN I DID IT. I think that sums up my whole creative philosophy in dance choreography. If it isn't a challenge, it's not worth doing. Strangely enough, I didn't come by that philosophy by myself. It was Fred Astaire who planted the seed for me in 1942.

I first met Fred at Paramount Studios when I was on overseas furlough from *This Is the Army*, before we left for England. I was in uniform, and I snuck onto the lot—it wasn't hard in uniform— and made a private tour of all the soundstages.

No one would dare question a serviceman in those days. I wandered in to the dubbing stage. It was very quiet and lit only by a work light. Then I heard the sound of taps. I quietly moved around the bandstand and there he was, the King, himself. A towel around the neck, shirt open at the collar, and the traditional necktie around his waist as a belt. He was rehearsing a dubbing version of one of his numbers from The Sky's the Limit [1943], which he had just finished. I can't describe my feelings, except that I suddenly felt I was stealing something very valuable.

He finished the little section he was working on, and looked up and saw me watching. He was most charming, and greeted me warmly, and he graciously interrupted his rehearsal to chat with me for a few minutes. I told him how I loved all of his routines and asked him how he came up with all those wild ideas of using furniture, golf clubs, whatever was handy in his routines. And he said, modestly, "I don't know . . . you don't know if these things will work until you try them."

June 6, 1989
Los Angeles, California

21

THE JIVIN' JACKS AND JILLS

PEGGY RYAN

You only have two feet and four taps to make magic.

Okay Jackson, here it is!
Don't be a *square*!
Don't be *icky*!
Get hep, brother, to the sweet
   and hot singeroo musicals
starring Hollywood's liveliest aggregation
   of swing-steppers—
*The Jivin' Jacks and Jills!**
                    *Promotional ad 1942

It was the era of swing, and the entire nation went "Jive." And the jivin-est of them all were The Jivin' Jacks and Jills. Their story began in 1941, when the call went out to gather up the "heppest" tap feet in Hollywood. The result was the formation of The Jivin' Jacks and Jills, twelve teenagers, six boys and six girls, between the ages of twelve and seventeen. Their first film was *What's Cookin'?* (1942), which also starred Donald O'Connor, the Andrew Sisters, and Woody Herman. The picture clicked and Universal Pictures immediately set out on a series of movie musicals with The Jivin' Jacks and Jills. When most other movies had production schedules of six months to a year, The Jivin' Jacks and Jills cranked out fourteen films in two years.

The kids livened up every picture they were in with their incredible energy and talent. The films were loaded with scenes, like parties or rehearsals, that were really just excuses to put on big dance numbers. In a sense these dances were like challenges because the kids would be spotlighted for their specialty. This framework was a breakthrough in musical films. Previously, most dances were staged for an ensemble—everyone did the same thing, everyone had the same style, and everyone was the same height. In The Jivin' Jacks and Jills, everyone was unique, and everything they did was fresh and varied.

Although many of the pictures they performed in were B, low-budget, operations, they featured top choreographic and dancing talent. On many of the films, Hollywood choreographer Louis DaPron was brought in to work on the tap dance material. DaPron was considered one of the finest tap dancers and choreographers ever in the business. He danced in films himself throughout the 1930s and 1940s, and became Universal's choreographer throughout the 1940s. He continued his career as choreographer in movies, and then with the advent of television, found a new career choreographing for variety shows. The kids of The Jivin' Jacks and Jills worked extensively with this tap legend.

When The Jivin' Jacks and Jills were first put together, the kids were far from amateurs, despite their ages. Although the composition of the group would vary slightly from picture to picture, the initial aggregation consisted of a stellar lineup of youthful tap veterans: Jack McGee, Roland Dupree, Bobby Scheerer, Joe "Corky" Geil, David Holt, Dolores Mitchell, Dorothy "Dottie" Babb, Jean and Jane McNab, Grace McDonald, Donald O'Connor, and Peggy Ryan. A few of these kids had already had careers in movies as children: Donald O'Connor, David Holt, and Peggy Ryan.

Peggy Ryan started out tap dancing at the age of two and made her first break in pictures in Top of the Town (1937) with George Murphy. By the time she was selected for The Jivin' Jacks and Jills, she had years of film and stage work behind her. And she was one solid tap dancer—on The Jivin' Jacks and Jills' top roster.

The series came to an end in 1944, when some of the boys, including Donald O'Connor, came of age and were drafted. But during the previous two years, The Jivin' Jacks and Jills brought the Swing Era to life in fourteen musical feature films with titles that really resounded the times: Get Hep to Love (1942), Give Out, Sisters (1942), Private Buckaroo (1942), and What's Cookin'? (1942). The kids all got a chance to bring their tap jive to the screen: Bobby Scheerer did turns, Roland Dupree did splits, Dorothy Babb did spins, and Peggy Ryan did a little bit of everything—and did it with great exuberance and flair.

P E G G Y   R Y A N — My mother and daddy were a ballroom team, and when I came along in 1924, I interrupted their career. My mother then put all of her hopes and dreams that her daughter would be what she wanted to be. I think that was probably the reason I started dancing. There was a place called Ratliff's Dancing Academy—it was a ballroom at night and a dancing school in the daytime. My mother worked nights checking hats there for my dance lessons. I was two years and nine months old, and I guess I had the gift. Because who dances when they're three years old! I made my first professional appearance for an Elks benefit when I was three. I did the "Butterfly" dance, and I understand I danced with my back to the audience all the time.

Then my mother decided, when I was about five, that I was ready for the big time, and she took me on a train up to Hollywood. There was a big audition for Gus Edwards's Vitaphone Shorts at that time. It was a big call for little kid dancers, and I was picked out of a couple of hundred

Peggy Ryan seems entirely uninterested in Johnny Coy's overtures in *That's the Spirit* (Universal, 1945).

dancers and did the movie *Wedding of Jack and Jill* [1929]. After that, we had to go back to San Diego, because we had no more money.

When I was ten, my mother decided it was time to go back to Hollywood again. A little old lady called Granny Williams gave us ten dollars a month to cover my costs at the Hollywood Professional School, HPS. So Mother and I got on the train and went back to Hollywood. We got a little old apartment at Hollywood and Western, and HPS was right around the corner. As a matter of fact, that was the first time I met Donald O'Connor, in the fourth grade there. You see, he was in the fourth grade forever. Really and truly, because he was always on the road. So he'd come back to HPS and I would be in a higher grade, but he'd still be in the fourth grade!

There was a dance teacher by the name of Jimmy Muellett, and he had a little dancing school at the Professional School. He saw me dance and said, "You have got to go out to MGM with me and dance for the studio's dance director, Dave Gould." They were looking for a little girl to play Eleanor Powell as a child in the movie *Born to Dance* [1936]. He taught me an impression of Eleanor Powell, four steps, and I really was exceptionally good at this age. So they took me out to MGM, and I danced for Dave Gould. I did the impression, I did singing, and I did a crying scene. At that time, you had to do it all. They were so pleased and said "She's going to be signed for seven years!" I signed a contract, you know, like that day for seven wonderful years . . . I thought.

Dave Gould had Eleanor Powell come over to look at me dance. Well, she took one look and said, "She is not dancing in my movie." I was really good, you know. They say, "No children and animals," and until I got older, I didn't realize how true it was. Dave Gould, who was a wonderful, wonderful man, was so angry that he put me on a big Actors Fund Benefit show to make up for the disappointment I had suffered that day. He got the same hundred and eighty men that Eleanor was to dance with in the movie, put them behind me, and I did *her* dance in front of them. This was the same benefit show Gable and Colbert did their hitchhiking scene with real cars coming on the stage. It was a magnificent thing. That night I was signed for a movie called *Top of the Town* [1937]. I also got a big bouquet of flowers on stage, and it said "To my protégée, from Eleanor Powell." So that's show business. . . .

I did do *Top of the Town* over at Universal with George Murphy. It was a wonderful big musical, black and white and very Art Deco. I did my impression of Powell in that and then danced

THE JIVIN' JACKS AND JILLS

Eleven-year-old Peggy Ryan rehearsing for *Top of the Town* (Universal, 1937) with choreographer Gene Snyder, brought out to Hollywood from Radio City Music Hall to work with the Rockettes.

the finale "Jamboree" with George. Got marvelous reviews, "The little child prodigy" and all this. But by then, I was getting into an awkward age. My ears were always big—I had to grow into them! And then I didn't realize that in three months the studio could drop your option. I had called all my relatives in San Diego—my grandmother, my aunts, and my uncles—and they all decided to move to Hollywood because "little Peggy was going to be a star." But here I was, you know, ten, eleven years old, under contract to MGM,

Peggy Ryan and Donald O'Connor during their dance number "When You Bump into Someone You Know and Love" from *Patrick the Great* (Universal, 1945). This nifty Soft Shoe set by resident dance director Louis DaPron.

and there was no place to put me. So I went and did dramatic roles. There was a young actress named Virginia Weidler, and if she didn't get the part, I would get it. If there was a foil for Jane Withers, I would do it. You know, always the other kid, the brat. I was a big crier, and I did a lot of crying. I did *Grapes of Wrath* [1940] with John Ford.

I continued doing dramatic roles until I was fifteen, when I got a call to audition for the Broadway musical *Meet the People* [1940] that they were doing in Los Angeles. This was the forerunner of the musicals where you had to do it all: You were in the chorus, you were featured, you were a singer, you were a dancer. You couldn't just dance and you couldn't just sing. I am not a singer. I sing, but that is not where I'm best! For this audition, I had to sing. So I got a great friend of mine, Buddy Pepper, who was a wonderful singer, to come to the audition with me. He sang the whole thing of "Shadrack," and all I sang was

THE JIVIN' JACKS AND JILLS

Louis DaPron takes Peggy Ryan through the steps during rehearsal for an upcoming picture. Donald O'Connor looks on with awe at the two veteran dancers, 1940s.

shadrack. Somehow, I got the role. And it was in this show that I really cut my teeth on being on-stage. Because, remember, I had always been in films, never, you know, on any kind of a major stage, never vaudeville. I learned so many different kinds of crafts in this show, like comedy, timing, singing, speaking singing. All the things that I needed to do. We took the show to San Francisco and then to Chicago. And then on Christmas Eve, we opened opposite *Pal Joey* on Broadway. We had second-string critics opening night, but we did well.

We were in New York almost a year, and on my nights off I used to go and see other shows. Donald O'Connor was in town at the same time. I was at the Mansfield Theatre, and he was doing vaudeville with his family. He called and said, "I got an audition across the way for a show called *Best Foot Forward.* Let's do "Fellow and a Girl" from *Meet the People.* We're a shoo-in." So we practiced a little, and then we went across the street. Now, even though I was in a Broadway show, I'd never done a real audition before—it was all a first for me. We had to wait in the back, and we were given a number. I think we were a

hundred and ninety-something. When it was our turn, we walked onto the stage. There was nothing but the stage light, and we went into this [sings] "It seems there was a fellow . . ." and we thought we were wonderful. About halfway through, they say, "All right. Next!" We really bombed. We went outside, and we were so despondent—now here *I'm* in a show, *he's* doing well, and we couldn't even get past the audition! We got even though. A little later when we're at Universal doing our movies, they tried to borrow us to do the leads of *Best Foot Forward,* and we said, "No!"

After some more touring, I ended up back in Hollywood and finally got asked to do a screen test with a bunch of kids for The Jivin' Jacks and Jills—six couples were chosen for the best dancers in Hollywood of that age group, twelve through seventeen. I was seventeen then, Donald was sixteen. And that was the next time we met. We both got in The Jivin' Jacks and Jills, and I was partnered with him because we were the tallest ones. And believe me, I wanted to dance with Ronald Dupree. He could turn, he could do it all. But I got stuck with Donald . . . in the back! We did the movie *What's Cookin'?* [1942]. And no billing: It was "The Jivin' Jacks and Jills." We had a marvelous director on this picture named Edward Cline. Now, Edward Cline had been a Keystone Cop and loved comedy, and he loved Donald because of his vaudeville days. I just hap-

pened to be there. So when they'd finish a scene, Cline would come up and say, "Now this is what you say, and I won't cut until you say it." We'd done our dance, and we'd all be doing "bread and butter, bread and butter," you know, background talk. When the scene stopped, Donald and I rushed forth, and I'd say, "My, but your hair is getting thin." And he'd say, "Who wants fat hair!" Then Cline would say, "Cut!" Now these would be left in the rushes every day, which the heads of studios always saw. And they kept seeing the two of us doing all this junk—you know, "Have you taken a bath lately?" "Why? Is there one missing?" "Cut!" He would leave all of this stuff in it! So when it came to editing the picture, we were in it, but we had no billing. They used to preview the movies in Bakersfield, and they'd send out cards for the audience to fill out, what they liked, and so on. For *What's Cookin'*? the cards all asked, "Who are the dark-haired couple?" The next picture, we got billing!

Well, our movies were about an hour in length, and we usually had something like thirteen dance numbers. You know, you'd put a lamp shade on your head, there'd be a bath, anything to dance. And they just kept adding numbers with Donald and me, Donald and me, Donald and me, until he was seventeen and I was eighteen. Incidentally, our birthdays are the same. August twenty-eighth. See, he claims to be a year younger. He has never shown me his birth certificate. He said it was lost. But I'll go with it. Anyway, the studio

heads knew he was going to be eighteen, and that he would be drafted because this was during WW II. But we were on such a roll in these films. They were musicals. They were happy, and everybody wanted to see it. We were the "Judy and Mickey" of Universal. By the time Donald was sixteen till the day he went in the service, we made fourteen musicals in a row. Bam, bam, bam.

During that time, most of the conversation we had was in front of a camera. We were up at five o'clock, we were into makeup, and then on the set. "All right, take one!" And I'd say, "Hi Donald." And, "Hi Peggy." It was like that. But, you know, he would confide in me. I was like an older sister.

At first our pictures were B's, second-rate. Then they went to "B-pluses," and a little better budget with them. *The Merry Monahans* [1944] was to be our first big picture, so the studio brought in veteran actor Jack Oakie to play our father. Donald and I thought we were pretty good by then. We weren't really, you know, big-headed, but we were on a roll. So, we said to each other, "Now, we're *not* going to let Jack Oakie steal any of our scenes. We'll stick together." The very first scene we had to do was in our dressing room. We had just come off the stage, and our father (played by Jack) was talking to us. Donald and I kind of winked at each other, like we got this scene nailed—"He is not upstaging us." Pretty soon we hear laughter and we look around—*our* backs are to the camera and Jack Oakie is dead center between us. He had completely manipulated us around without our knowing it. And the entire crew was in on it!

During many of these Universal movies, our choreographer was the great Louis DaPron. Oh, what a dear Louis was. I always thought he was very shy, because he didn't come on real strong, you know—his feet talked for him. Ours was always a professional thing, because we didn't have time to get to know a person. I only knew Louis through dance. But I could pick up a step so fast. I *felt* like him, I *thought* like him. And once I got the step, you know, within five minutes, it was with me forever. Louis was wonderful. He did the most innovative things with his feet. Things I've never seen before or after. On the beat and off the beat. His gift was boundless. He was a dancer's dancer. And I actually got to dance with him in the film *Babes on Swing Street* [1944].

My idol growing up had been Astaire, because he brought it all together. All the style, the move-ment, the ballet. And Bill Robinson was another one, absolutely sensational. When I was very young, Bill Robinson came over to Universal and saw me dance, and he said to me, "You sure you haven't got any black blood in you? You dance like *us.*" It was a big compliment! Anyway, I think Louis was between an Astaire and a Robinson. He used the floor like black dancers. Because at that time, they used a lot of slaps, a lot of floor work—they didn't use the height and the turns and the lifts and the things that Astaire did. Louis could combine them both. With a barrel turn here and then get right down to the floor. But Louis—Louis should have been a star himself. But as he told me, "I don't have it from the waist up." And a lot of

With most of Universal's dancing leads drafted during World War II, Canadian dancer Johnny Coy was brought down to become a featured player. Here Peggy Ryan and Johnny Coy dance around the entire house in this fast-paced number from *On Stage Everybody* (Universal, 1945).

people don't, you know. He was great. He had the best legs and feet, I think, of anybody. I have danced with some wonderful people, but if I had a choice of just dancing with somebody, it would probably be Louis. We danced alike. Just picked up from each other. It was wonderful and it was a delight.

During The Jivin' Jacks and Jills series of films, Donald's love interest would be for either Susanna Foster or Gloria Jean. I would always be a sister or the girl that didn't get him. You know, the one chasing after him! One of the movies I finally did get Donald in was *Patrick the Great* [1945]. Anyway, Donald was kept so busy that he never really got a chance to learn the dances. We would shoot some of those movies in ten days, and shoot the dance numbers blind. They'd say, "All right, take one!" And we would dance, with Donald kind of following along. Donald and I knew how to fake together—and on film. For example, in *The Merry Monahans*, you'll see we're doing a big ballet sequence, and he loses his ballet shoe. He keeps running around trying to find it, and I'm ad-libbing. They left it in the movie!

We were very dedicated and very easy to work with. We were so thankful to be working. We felt this was it! At the end when Donald had to go in the service, I might have been making three hundred and twenty-five dollars a week, and he might have been making six hundred. We would get a bonus of five hundred dollars a movie. We thought that was the *world*. But anyway, Donald went in the service—he was eighteen and I was nineteen by then. Universal had fourteen movies that were released over the next two years. I was nineteen forever!

—————————————————

Tap dancing—you get out there and it goes. You have to do it from your toes to the last tips of your hair. You have to dance all over. I think the reason I loved tap dancing is that I love the music. And I hear the beat. I cannot dance to a piece of music I don't like. I think I would have been an excellent drummer, because that's what I do with my feet. It's all in the way you use them. It's the sound you get out of those taps, just combinations of sounds.

You only have two feet and four taps to make magic, you know. And you *can* make magic with it.

December 12, 1988
Las Vegas, Nevada

22

EIGHT FEET OF RHYTHM: THE FOUR STEP BROTHERS

MACEO ANDERSON

You may be nervous when you go on the stage, you anxious to get out there. But when you get out there, man, like you in heaven.

The Four Step Brothers was one of the greatest Flash Tap acts ever. The act was started in the mid-twenties by a group of eager teenage boys. Their formula for success was fast rhythm taps, acrobatic leaps, and boogie woogie jitterbug-style tap dancing, all put across through the electrifying mode of challenge. It was a style that came right off the street—the clapping of the hands, the encouraging yelps, the fast-paced tempos, and the ceaseless topping of tap steps. The Four Step Brothers played every nightclub and theater of importance in the United States and they were a sensation wherever they appeared. They toured extensively abroad where they were cheered by everyone who saw them, including kings and queens. From the 1930s on, they appeared in numerous motion pictures, including: *It Ain't Hay* (1943), *Rhythm of the Islands* (1943), *Greenwich Village* (1944), *That's My Gal* (1947), and *Here Come the Girls* (1953).

Unlike other brother acts of their day, The Four Step Brothers were not actually brothers. They were four incredibly talented hoofers. Through the years the names and faces changed, but the formula always remained the same: the challenge. Each dancer

The Four Step Brothers in *Greenwich Village* (20th Century-Fox, 1944), Sunshine Sammy, Freddie James, Al Williams, and Happy

strove to top the others, and as the complexity and speed of their steps heightened, audiences were rocketed from their seats. Of all the members of The Four Step Brothers, three were alive during the research for this book: Maceo Anderson (a founding member of the act from the mid-1920s), Prince Spencer (who joined the act in 1941), and Flash McDonald (who joined the act in 1942). Their experiences in the quartet were vast. Before each member joined the act, they had already chalked up extensive years on the stage as solo performers: They were involved with shows, with other partners, in burlesque, and in clubs. By the time they joined The Four Step Brothers, they were seasoned tap dancing professionals.

Maceo Anderson was a founding member of the The Four Step Brothers. And with them he made it to the top—he was a headliner.

MACEO ANDERSON — I was born on September third, 1910. When I was about three years old, livin' in Charleston, South Carolina, I can remember that I always wanted to come north. I see the train headin' up there, and I used to get on one of those brooms an' make like I was ridin' a horse after that train. And I would wave a hand as that train passed by, knowin' that's where I wanted to go.

When I finally did go north, it wasn't by train. I was about six years old, me and my mother went to New York City on a cotton boat. We got off that boat, went right up to Harlem, and got off at One hundred thirty-second and Lenox Avenue. We landed right on the main street in Harlem! Everything was happening there. And I went directly to the Hoofers Club. I didn't know it was the Hoofers Club, I just looked down in there and heard those taps. The Hoofers Club was right under the Lafayette Theatre. The Lafayette was One hundred thirty-second and Seventh Avenue. That's where the "Tree of Hope" was, right in the middle of the street. Entertainers used to put our hand onto the Tree of Hope and wish for work.

I used to sneak up into the balcony of the Lafayette Theatre to see all the shows. I was just a little kid, had to sneak in there. Between shows, I used to go from the Lafayette Theatre downstairs until the next show. All kind of famous acts came down there. Honi Coles. Leonard Reed. That's how you get the way of the dancers. And if you want to find a dancing act, you go down there and look the dancers over. Sometimes Bill Robinson come down there, the kids would shout, "Here come Mr. Robinson!" Bill would take off his coat and dance, then when he leave we used to all get up and try to do what he did. I remember The Condos Brothers came to the Lafayette Theatre. Well, someone said, "Hey, The Condos Brothers are upstairs in the Lafayette Theatre!" And we all ran up from that Hoofers Club and occupied the first row of the theater. All of us tap dancers. The Condos Brothers came onstage, and we sat there with our arms folded *watchin'*—their feet! The second they were done with their act, we all ran out of that theater and right back down into the Hoofers Club. "Did you see that?" "Was it this?" No! It was this!" Everyone was tryin' to steal their steps. Those Condos Brothers were hot! They was somethin' else! And that's how we learned dancin'. We used to dance down in this little room and we would smoke. We loved dancin' so much.

I lived on One hundred twenty-second Street. Down in the basement, we used to have like a dance place. I had a dance floor, and all the kids who lived in that area used to come down there and practice, see, instead of going down to the Hoofers Club. And I can remember a lot of kids came down there, like Bill Bailey. Even his sister, Pearl, used to come down there and learned how to tap. I never forget, my mother used to fix a big pot of beans and rice. We would eat that food and then stay up half of the night dancing, challenging each other. It was just like a Hoofers Club.

There used to be an amateur night up in Harlem at the Lafayette Theatre. Now, amateur night was the one when if you was no good, they put the hook on you and pulled you offstage. They blew like a horn, and the band all played, and the guy with the hook he'd pull you offstage. In the early twenties, I was watchin' the show and the two boys came on, one was a light-complected boy, and he'd try to dance, but he'd dance off time. When the other one played a tune, he would dance. But he was still off time, and the brother with the hook got him and brought him offstage. Everybody laughed and they boo'd him and everything, but I thought the guys was pretty good. So I goes back and I met them in the alley, and

---

This 1925 photo shows an eager quartet of young dancers. Pictured here are (left to right) Red, Happy, Al, and Maceo at the Cotton Club.

I said, "We ought to get together." So they said, "Well, all right. I'll tell you what—meet us down at the Hoofers Club tomorrow and we'll get together." And that's what we did.

Years ago, there was an act on the circuit called Williams and Walker. They was good. This was during the times when they don't allow no Negroes on the stage and the black-up stuff come up. Williams and Walker were light-complected. They had to black their face and put that white stuff around their mouths. That's what they had to do in those days. Anyway, Williams and Walker were quite a name then, so we used that name because everybody knew Williams and Walker. Our name was Anderson, Williams and Walker.

We went up to the Cotton Club—this was around 1925—and you know who was on the door at the Cotton Club? Jack Johnson, the heavyweight champion. I was born on the day he won the championship in 1910. Yeah, now he was all through with boxing and he was a doorman at the Cotton Club. He would bring the people into the Cotton Club, go to the sidewalk with an umbrella and bring them in. So we was trying to sneak past him. He run us down—"Hey, you kids, get outta here, they don't allow your kind, especially no black kids," you see. So what we did—we sneak around the back. I forgot how we got in there, but we got backstage. I saw all these guys come back there with guns and everything. You *know* I didn't know that was Owney Madden! I didn't know that was Dutch Shultz!. You heard of those gangsters? I didn't know, but that's the days at the Cotton Club in the twenties. We hid back of the little dressing room behind a rack of costumes. And then, finally Duke Ellington came out to get some water at the fountain.

We run out and said, "Mr. Ellington! Mr. Ellington! We want to get on and we want to dance—see, see this?" And we fell on our knees and jumped all around. He said, "Hey, you guys don't belong here. Get the heck out of here. Boy, you better don't let them see you here." And he says, "Get out of here—you can't dance in no show here. You know better than that." We said, "Mr. Ellington please—blah, blah, blah, blah, blah, blah, blah, . . ." So, anyhow, after we've been there three or four times, he said, "All right, I'll tell you what. I'll put you on at intermission. And you boys better be good." But then he looked us over and said, "Get something to put on!" He said. "What you got here? Get something and put it over your clothes—you can't go out like that." So we went and got a blouse and—we *stole* a blouse more like it. We went through that night, and do you know something? We stayed in the Cotton Club four years! And that's where The Step Brothers was made.

We decided that we wanted a fourth dancer, so we invited this kid that was dancing at the club. When we all were trying to think of a name for the group, he said, "Don't you know that they do a lot of brother acts? Seem to be a lot of brothers, all the cats named brothers." And he was right! There were tremendous brother acts then. There was The Condos *Brothers*. There was The Rich *Brothers*. There was Miller *Brothers* and Lois. Then the greatest, I'm going to tell you right now, was The Berry Brothers. The three Berry brothers. Then the next great act was The Nicholas Brothers. But The Nicholas Brothers was little kids then. Anyway, this guy goes on to list the brother acts, The Two Black Dots—these guys was so black you can't see nothing but the eyes. They were a great act and they was brothers. So now he said, "Well, what can we use—Step By Step. I said, "Oh . . . Step By Step." I just said, "Well, how 'bout The Step Brothers." So they—"Oh,

The Four Step Brothers—Eight Feet of Rhythm. Top to bottom: Flash McDonald, Maceo Anderson, Al Williams, and Prince Spencer, circa 1941.

yeah. All right!'' you know. And that's when we became The Four Step Brothers—Eight Feet of Rhythm.

The girls of the Cotton Club were beautiful! I remember a lady named Cora LaRedd—now, she could tap. And there was Lena Horne—when she came to the Cotton Club she was just in the chorus. I used to send her little notes upstairs. I tried to talk to her, but her mother was right behind her! The Nicholas Brothers came into the club in 1932, and we got all hot fired over them. And The Berry Brothers come over as a sensation. We had these tap acts coming in. But all the time, we were right there, see. Right there. And we stayed there longer than any dance act in the place. We would go from the Cotton Club, work other theaters and come back to this, see, like that. We played the Keith-Orpheum Circuit. We played—oh, God, I can't even remember all the circuit. We was breaking barriers down working places that those blacks had not worked. That's why they say we opened doors for the other people. Because we was doing this while they were at the Cotton Club. Oh, yeah, we worked the black circuits, too. We worked the "Chittlin' Circuit" ['Round The World]. All the Negro houses, see. It took up four weeks. Then we used to go around there, and next week go around, and then next week we would go back around. And like that.

We worked a lot with Duke Ellington, not only

in the Cotton Club, but on tour, too. I remember someone once wrote: "The Step Brothers are to dancing what Duke Ellington is to music." And that was quite some compliment! In those days —who can be a greater man than Duke Ellington? There's a man who can play music for two days and two nights of his own creation! He don't stop and start putting nothing between—he play a song one after another that's his own. That's the greatness of him, see.

So, we would take all this jazz we were hearin' and turn it into tap steps, you see. The rhythm of tap. That's what gets you. [Sings] "Rhythm is my business. Rhythm's what I do. Rhythm is my business." You'd use that. Rhythm is your business. You do your rhythm; it's about rhythm and tap dancing and creating. You want to create something. And once you know your craft and know something about your craft, then you want to create. Because you can't stand still and see somethin' goin' down! You got that in your heart. Your heart is in that thing, and nobody can stop you. And you don't care how much time or how hard it is, you goin' to do it. Because you trying to create something.

When I'm dancing, it's like I'm in heaven. That dancing kept me from worrying—it looked like it took my worries away. Of course, a lot of people say as long as you're busy—but I'm talking complete—you got the greatest happening. You may be nervous when you go on the stage, you anxious to get out there. But when you get out there, man, like you in heaven. Everything cool right down. And when my feet are goin', automatically they go. One time I danced off the stage! I don't know what the heck happened to me, but I found myself down in the audience. That show you how my mind was going, see!

There was just so much rhythm churnin' inside me. Music happenin'. Dancers happenin'. There were just so many great tap dancers out there,

all kinds! Nick Condos, he's the one that come to Harlem, boy, and he licked them colored guys, they run back and hide. That man danced so much. He was the dancin'est white guy I ever seen in my life. And so was Donald O'Connor. I mean he can really dance. Gene Kelly's good, but Gene Kelly is not outstanding as a tap dancer, but as a entertainer and a dancer he's one of the greatest. Now Fred Astaire, he took ballet and put tap in it. He is the first one that did that. He never was one that goes in for no hard, hard, real hoofing, you see. What made him so great was the poise he had, see. That man used to *walk* beautiful! There were King, King, and King, one of the greatest dance acts you *ever* seen. They used to dance with chains tied to each other's leg! You ain't never seen precision like them. Buck and Bubbles was my top pride, then The Berry Brothers. The Berry Brothers wasn't tap dancers, they was more like acrobatic dancers and jazz dancers. You see, it's hard to get an acrobatic act in a tap act. That's why we became so good at it, because we did both. We didn't really know what we was doing, but we did both. And we were good at what we was doing. But as far as I am concerned, nobody can top those people I just told you about. I hold pride in saying that The Four Step Brothers, *we* can *touch* those people, you see. I'm not bragging about it, but it's the truth.

===

I mean, it's so great the career we had, oh yeah. When I look back I say, "It can't be *I* did those things," you see. Our concern was tryin' to give the public something else, somethin' different. In the meantime, we was giving them entertainment.

July 17, 1988
Los Angeles, California

DANCING AT
THE APOLLO

FLASH McDONALD

Whenever we finished our dance, that applause in your ear, you wouldn't believe it. Oh, that's what would win you over. That's the sweetest thing in the world.

23

"

It's showtime at the Apollo!" Those words ushered in some of this century's finest acts, from singers to dancers, comedians to bands; the Apollo was a mecca for entertainment for nearly half a century. The Apollo Theatre was christened in 1934 (having formerly operated under other names and operators). Located at 253 West 125th between Seventh and Eighth Avenues in the midst of Harlem, it had, from the very start, the reputation of being the "warmest, most critical cold house that ever lived." If an act came in there with the right attitude, with the right material, and the right talent, they could make it. It was said that if an act could make it at the Apollo, it could make it anywhere—because the audiences at the Apollo were extremely strict. They were kind-hearted, but strict. They knew a good act when they saw one, as they had seen the best of them. On the other hand, the audience could tell a phony in a minute, and if an audience did not favor an act, they would let it know. By the same token, if they liked it, the performers could do no wrong. The theater originally sat two thousand. The second balcony was very high up and had the cheapest seats. Three to four

A jam session with four of the eight feet of rhythm, Prince Spencer and Flash McDonald, 1950s

hundred people could sit in that second balcony, and there sat a cluster called the "world's greatest critics." When they booed an act off, they really booed it off! The act either got good, or "got the business."

The Apollo was initially run by Frank Schiffman. According to those who worked with him, Schiffman was an absolute genius. His success was in making elaborate shows available to those living in the immediate area. Schiffman had a sense of the community, and an awareness of community problems. Through his genius, he was able to produce and, at the same time, show a profit. Consequently, a love-hate relation developed between him and many of the artists playing the theater. Schiffman was the "Tsar"—he ruled the roost. He told the acts what they would get paid; oftentimes less than they had gotten at other theaters. However, if the act drew, they were paid accordingly. Frank Schiffman was the consummate businessman, and made the Apollo the number-one theater in Harlem.

The doors of the Apollo opened at ten A.M., and by eleven, the stage show was already on. The show lasted seventy-five minutes—an hour and fifteen minutes of sock entertainment. Then came the movie, after that the trailers, a newsreel, and possibly a short subject. Then the stage show again. And the minute that curtain came down on the show, the screen came down and the picture went on. From eleven A.M., until eleven P.M., that was the routine. The Apollo normally ran four shows a day: eleven A.M., three P.M., six P.M., and nine-thirty P.M. On Saturdays, an extra midnight show was added, and on Sunday, there were only three shows, beginning at three P.M. However, this formula was altered according to the attraction. If an act really drew, the Apollo could run as many as seven shows a day. In this event, the feature picture was cut, and the entertainers only got a half an hour off between shows. To say the least, it was a tumultuous experience for the thousands involved.

One twenty-two-year-old who cut his teeth at the Apollo was Flash McDonald. He had been performing professionally for only a few years when he first stepped on that stage, but he learned in the week that he appeared at the Apollo what made an act good. Flash McDonald moved out to the Coast in 1942, where, shortly thereafter, he was asked to join The Four Step Brothers. He spent the next thirty years of his life performing with the act, traveling throughout the United States and Europe.

FLASH McDONALD — I was like a kid when I started. And we started the old way. I guess I was about twelve years old, and I learned to tap dance on the street corner. I was born in Saint Louis, March sixteenth, 1919. And all the kids used to hang around the corner, and each one would cut a step. We'd try to do somethin', and each one would try to outdo the other one. And every time a new dance would come out or some kind of a step, or we'd see someone in the show come out and do it, we'd go try to do it. We got so that tap dancin' to us was like singin'. We'd tap the rhythm out just like we heard it. We didn't do tap dancing rough, we kept it real smooth. Like you would sing a song —it would tell a story. When we were kids, our story was plain, it was like a song; you could hear it dancing, and it would come out beautiful.

That's how I got started. I didn't intend to dance professionally. It was by accident. I started out sellin' newspapers. I would stop by the tavern to sell papers, and the customers in the place say, "Can you dance? You dance, I'll buy a paper from you." So I said, "OK." I sold them more papers dancing than just sellin' papers. I was thinking, "I'm just going to start around and just dance for the people and get the money that way." See, back then you made tips. A person could make in several hours thirty-five, forty, fifty dollars a night—tips, just tips. The biggest night was Friday, Saturday, and Sunday night—that was like eighty a night! And so I did that, I guess, till I was about fifteen.

Then I wanted a job in a club. A lot of people liked me and wanted me to work. And they would say, "Why don't you come work for me? I do three shows a night, and I give you fifty dollars a night and all the tips you make." You know, I went out and danced, and the owner'd throw twenty-five or thirty dollars himself to get the people started. When you get through, you got a pocketful of money. So you know when you dancing that on the floor that night, the boss is going to throw you at least a hundred dollars in tips! That's when I got the bug. I begin to want to dance.

I learned to tap dance by the way it sounded to me. I loved that sound. I thought that was the best sound I ever heard in my life. It got me. That won me over. From then on, I wanted to dance. When I got onto the stage, the people loved me so, they didn't want me to stop. That spoiled me! Then I begin to see other dancers that were terrific. Like I'd go to the movies and see Fred Astaire, Ginger Rogers, and Bill Robinson. My favorite was Bill Robinson. Now, there's a man that talked with his feet. I looked there and thought, "I can do that." I quit the kind of dancin' I was doing and went strictly in for that. But I had to have a mixer. Dancing like Bill Robinson wasn't enough, I couldn't give the people enough for their money. I'd get only so good a hand, you know. So I said, "Well I'll fix that." I started variety, acrobat, all kind of dancin' mixed up together. And all the time I was on the stage I kept my taps going. My taps would ring. The tappin' was what kept the melody goin'. And there never was a slow spot. I'd keep a nice beautiful step going, then after I'd do it for so many bars, I'd do exciting steps. I got so I had lots of steps. I could do at least twenty-five steps in a routine. Different, not the same ones. And I would save my best ones for the last. I had wind then! *The Post Dispatch* wrote me up and said, "He danced that one hour and a half within stopping, and never did the same step twice."

Around 1940, I left Saint Louis and went to Chicago and started mixing with real performers—the professionals. I got in with the agent Burle Adams. He was big then, represented Louis Jordan. So I traveled with Louis Jordan, and got lots of work. Burle Adams put me in theaters that did only evening shows, seven and nine, like the Fox. And then he got me in the Apollo Theatre, in New York. Now, I had never worked the Apollo. I was innocent. I was only about twenty-two, something like that. Well, the Apollo would start at ten o'clock in the morning, and they're doing seven shows a day! Seven shows a day. I'd say, "Oh, my God. Well, OK, I'll try."

[Frank] Schiffman ran the Apollo Theatre. Schiffman had a hot show there. I think I got there on Thursday night, and they had rehearsal Thursday night. I didn't know it, see. I went and got me a room in the hotel and went to sleep. Then I got up the next morning and went to the movie and saw me a picture. The show was on, and I was watching pictures! So about eleven o'clock the picture's over, I come out of the theater and walked to the stage door. And they said, "Who are you?" I said, "I'm Flash." They said, "You not in this show, I ain't got nothing about you." I say, "Yes, I am. I'm in this show!" He said, "This show been on!" I said, "Oh, my God!" The show was about over, you see. Schiffman come back there—ooh, he was mad! Schiffman could have killed me! He

looked at me, he was so mad he couldn't hardly talk. He called me everything but "child of God." He thought I was gonna be, you know, a smart aleck, you know, smart guy. Give a lot of lip and all that. I didn't say a word, I just let him talk. For I done missed the show, and I wanted the work! So I sit there, and finally my agent, who was there, come back. My agent carried a lot of weight,— he had the star of the show. So, he said to Schiffman, he says, "He's a nice kid. See, he just got into show business. He won't do it anymore." Schiffman say, "Well Lord, my show, my show, my show!" And then to me he said, "OK. What can you do?" I said, "I'm a dancer." He said, "What's the band going to play for you?" I said, "Play me a jumpin' song, like "One O'Clock Jump," you know, "a swingin' song." Well, I didn't have no taps on, no nothing. But I went out there, and I tore that show up! I *stopped* the show. So, when I come off the stage, I was standing backstage where I could hear Schiffman saying, "Well, I guess you think you're great now." And that was my first meeting with Schiffman! But after that, he

Flash McDonald joined the famous Flash act, The Four Step Brothers, and with his fast footwork, fit right in with the current members, Prince Spencer, Al Williams, and Maceo Anderson, 1940s.

became my friend. Me and Schiffman—we was like that [crosses his fingers]. He was my buddy.

The shows at the Apollo were booked for week stands—and that was enough! That was around seven shows a day. Shoot, my God! The picture would only play about maybe an hour. They timed it when the show go over, the picture's gettin' ready to start again. Like every half an hour, every forty-five minutes they were playin' the music for the new show. Oh, boy! But it's an experience. It's an experience. And that was my start to gettin' with the big boys.

I didn't like cold weather, so about '42, I come out here [Hollywood], yeah. And that's when I met The Four Step Brothers. At that time, Central Avenue used to be quite jumpin'. I mean, when I say jumpin', quite a lot happening then, yeah. The neighborhood was quite popular for entertainers and all the people around. It was lot happening to keep me busy. I won a foothold out here dancing. One of The Step Brothers died, and they were looking for a new member. Someone told them, "They got a little kid down working at the Jungle Room. Go down there and catch him." I was the last new member to come in that act.

We made a picture, had a lot of club dates, and then we went to Las Vegas. Then Las Vegas only had a gravel road!—the Las Vegas Boulevard —and they had three hotels on it—the Thunderbird, the El Rancho Vegas, and the Last Frontier, and that was it! Well, we went over good. The show clicked, and I kind of fittin' right in. A lot of our friends saw the act and said, "That kid fits right in the act. He belongs with the act." Well, I was glad to hear that, you know. Because I had always been a single, and never with a set routine. But working with The Step Brothers was different, and it all work out well.

Les Step Bros wow Parisian connoisseurs at the Medrano Stadium in France. The Four Step Brothers traveled the world for over fifty years, entertaining audiences with their high-powered Flash tap act, 1952.

They said, "Seeing that we got a new fellow in the act"—a new blood they call it—"a new blood in the act—we got to go back to New York and show 'm what we are doing." We went to New York and played the Paramount. That stage couldn't have been no wider than a few feet. And that was small. From the rear it looked like it was just big enough for you to stand on. And they had a band,—the band got so much space behind you. Now at rehearsal, they got it all drawn out on the floor. And it looks like it's big—plenty of room. I could dance and all that, but with four guys—can you imagine four out in that little space!

We rehearsed the act about—oh, I guess about five times we rehearsed it. When we finished, the fellow there said, "You did a nice show, 'cept you did the last part of your act out in the aisles where the people are!" We done danced all over that stage. He say, "You got to cut that down." But it worked good for us, and we proved ourselves in New York City, which is what you had to do in those days! And from then on, every job we got was terrific. This went on, and jobs just kept piling up. In other words, we couldn't look back. Everything we touched was good.

I think it was about 1947—we signed a contract to go to Europe—Paris. We went over on the *Queen Mary*! Yeah. Listen, that was the greatest thrill—I mean it was a *ship*. About a block long. The biggest ship I ever seen in my life! We had about ten trunks! People said, "What are ya all doin'?—movin' America to Paris?" We did a dance on the boat for the captain, and we won the whole ship over. The captain gave us the run of the ship—First Class, Second Class—said, "Anywhere you want to go, you can go. Nobody going to stop you." Oh, boy, that was something. They made us so welcome we didn't feel any prejudice. If the people were, they didn't show it. We'd go into First Class and they mingled just like they been minglin' with you all the time. In a way, you had to stop and look at it, you know. You really did. It made a difference, yeah. We saw a lot of boys that got out of the army, stayed over there [in Europe] just on account of that reason, see. That was the way of things then. All in all, it took us nine days to cross on the *Queen Mary*. That was nine days of happiness.

We got to Paris, France and played the Lido Club for six months. It was fabulous! That's where I saw Errol Flynn and Bogart and Ingrid Bergman, John Wayne, Buster Crabbe—I met all the guys. Paris was real popular at that time. We just saw stars on top of stars, and we liked it. But at first, we were a little afraid how they would react to us. They called us "claquette" dancers, and we didn't think they would understand. We didn't think they'd like it. They was always a bit behind us in the styles in the jazz and all of that. So we figured we was too far ahead of them for them to like it. But they went for it! They were up on bands a little more than we thought. Yeah, they loved Les Step Brothers. After the Lido, we freelanced all over Europe—Paris, Italy, and Spain. It became fun, it really did. We started having a ball. Yeah, oh yeah, we was the hit then. This was a great time to be in Europe. It was the end of the war. Because, you know, after the war and that, everybody seemed to be uncertain. The war made a lot of changes and did a lot of damage, too. At that time, it was like a new adventure. Everything seemed like it was starting over again.

Our act was a good twenty minutes of tap dancin'! A fast twenty minutes. We done a lot of dancing in that twenty minutes, yeah. See, we had four men who could use each one's breath; while I'm dancin', they can be resting. And after I do so much, I can step back and be fresh for later on. That's the way we did it. And by the time each guy dance, you did a lot of time! Twenty minutes of knock-out tap dancin'. The audiences loved us, and whenever we finished our dance, that applause in your ear, you wouldn't believe it. Oh, that's what would win you over. That's the sweetest thing in the world.

July 15, 1988
Hollywood, California
(Died March 20, 1991)

DANCING AT THE APOLLO

24

THE "STORY" OF TAP

PRINCE SPENCER

They called me "On-Too-Long," because I would go on the stage and never know when to leave! I was stagestruck.

A book can tell a story. A song can tell a story. A ballet can tell a story. And, a tap dance can tell a story. It may be hard to imagine, because it is a wordless story, but the tale is there just the same. Taps are laid down with precision and beauty, with delicacy and harmony. The soul of the dancer is conveyed through cold metal plates on the bottom of shoes. A happy story can be told with brisk staccato taps; a sad story with sliding melancholy taps. The story is transferred to the "sole"—and tap dancers have been telling their stories for over a hundred years.

The story changed as America changed. Tap dancing has accompanied every phase of music from the earliest days of minstrel shows. The styles and story of tap have evolved with the "Tempo of America." There were rhythm dancers who got right in the heart of the beat and moved it around with their syncopation. There were Buck and Wing dancers who skittered on top of the melody. There were flash dancers who electrified the melody to near hysteria. All of these dancers had a method of telling their stories. Some ad-libbed as they went along. Others had a set routine, a series of steps to a set

Nattily dressed, The Four Step Brothers pose for a sharp publicity shot. (Top, left to right) Happy and Al; (bottom left to right) Prince and Freddie, 1940s.

piece of music. Others had a combination of ad-lib and routine. In this event, the beginning and the ending of the routine were set, and the middle was the ad-lib section—storytelling time. Here, a dancer could roam freely around the tune, through the age, through the feeling of the day, into the hearts and emotions of the people there, and create a tap dance sensation.

Flips, splits, Over the Tops, kick outs, Wings—those were the territory of The Four Step Brothers. Others did them too, but not like these four fellows. In 1941, The Four Step Brothers acquired a new member who was just as adept as their legacy—Prince Spencer. He was born October 3, 1917 in Jenkinsville, South Carolina. The family moved to Boston, Massachusetts six months later, and then migrated to Toledo, Ohio where Prince Spencer grew up. He started dancing at the age of eight, and was influenced by the many great tap dance artists who came through Toledo on the vaudeville circuits and burlesque shows of the time. He saw the great Bill Robinson. But even before that, he saw

King Rastus Brown—Mister Tap himself. King Rastus Brown never became a star. However, he was certainly a star in the eyes of those who saw him and heard his tap "story" (primarily black dancers). Not much is known of him. What is known is that he had the finest pair of feet a dancer could ever wish for. When King Rastus Brown came through Toledo during the 1920s, he left an indelible impression on young Prince Spencer; Spencer heard a tap dancer, and realized that tap was much more than just "beating the boards." Tap dancing was a song in itself. It was a story. And Prince Spencer's story would be filled with life, with flash, and exhilaration.

PRINCE SPENCER — One particular man come to our hometown, a black dancer named King Rastus Brown. He was an old man by this time, and he danced with a cane. King Rastus Brown just impressed me so much, because his tap was so clear and profound. I didn't have any idea that feet could make this kind of a sound. I had seen the movie dancers—guys Buck dancing and Shuffling and what not. And I remember the Waltz Clog and Pat Rooney. But King Rastus Brown danced so impressively that I began to see what dancing was about. His dancing told a story. When I saw Bill Robinson years later, I understood what he was doing, and I said, "That's what this fellow, King Rastus Brown, was doing years ago."

THE "STORY" OF TAP

I remember once I went to see King Rastus Brown, and people were upset because they couldn't see his feet from the stage. King Rastus Brown made the remark, "You don't have to see my feet to enjoy my dancing. My dancing tells a story. If you can't see my feet, and you hear this—*ah bedle bedle dum, dedle dop dop, dedle deh dop*—well, now, that's just not a lot of noise going on." He said, "This is a definite rhythm and it tells a story." And then he did it with his feet to show what he meant—*ah bedle bedle dum, dedle dop dop, dedle deh dop.* Bill Robinson said the same thing years later, and that was like the master putting the touch on a story and saying, "Yeah this is where it's supposed to be." I was a little boy and I read where it said, "Bill Robinson is the greatest exponent of rhythm." Yeah, tap dancing was an art—to excel in dancing, your feet had to have a great sense of rhythm where you couldn't afford to lose time or lose rhythm or miss a beat, or you weren't in that category of greatness. That's what Bill Robinson brought about.

Well, I was too poor to go to the dancing school, so when the white kids around my neighborhood would go to dancing school, they would come back home and show me what they did. Their mothers would get at them, because I begged them to show me what they learned in school— and I'd have it part of my dance routine the next day or the *same* day!

It was around 1932, I got in a show in Toledo called *Get Goin' Louisiana Hayride*, and I did very well. Some scouts came to the Rivoli Theatre and had me to do an audition for Ben Bernie's band. That's when Ben Bernie used to say, "Yowsah! Yowsah! Yowsah!" He took me on the road with him during the summer. Then Major Bowes had some shows coming out, and someone told me to go see him. What the job really was, it was unknown professionals. You weren't really ama-

teurs, if you weren't good he wouldn't take you. *Major Bowes' Amateur Hour* was on the radio, and I won first prize. So that's when he invited me to be with his show. I left Ben Bernie and went with Major Bowes on his show *Major Bowes' Dixie Jubilee*—an all-black show of talented youngsters. We traveled throughout the country, starting in Washington, D.C. at the Fox Theatre. In those days, blacks could come in upstairs, but weren't allowed in the front. So we were all dressed up in our tails and everything, and we were so good that they took us out of our tails

Prince Spencer, 1940s

and put us in overalls and jeans and bandanas! And we had to come in the back door, you know, couldn't come in the front. I stayed with Major Bowes, oh, I guess, maybe four years. I would go from one show to another: *Major Bowes' World's Fair Revue, Major Bowes' Second Anniversary Dixie Jubilee.* Every time a show would fold or disband, he would put me with another show. I became like a favorite of his. And in fact, they called me his "protégé."

In those days, I used to do a solo tap, everything Bill Robinson used I tried to use. I used to dance to the tune "Nagasaki," a real up-tempo number. We'd broadcast live from 1697 Broadway. That's where the *Ed Sullivan Show* originated. They had a portable stage, like a flat board, for me to tap dance on, and laid down a microphone—one of the great big mikes. In those days, every dancer sang some kind of song in addition to dancing. I think I either sang "Nagasaki" or "Wrap Your Troubles in Dreams."

Doing radio in those days was quite something. We didn't have no say so, it was all set up for us. We were children at the time, or youngsters. It was like you're doing an audition in the audition room. The band was there, most likely in front of you. They had the microphone set up, and you didn't see all the audience. It was like a recording room almost. So it wasn't a thing like you were being nervous or excited, it was like you were dancing in a rehearsal hall. But it was exciting, because there was a tremendous listening audience! They had telephone lines for people to call in and vote on their favorite amateur—"If you want to vote now, here's your numbers to call." They had different spot cities where you would call in, like New York, Philadelphia, Chicago, or Detroit. And then the votes were tallied up. Well, we really knew before the show who was going to win. I always knew if I was going to win or not, you know. Major Bowes would announce me as the winner and then that I was opening in Washington, D.C. at the Fox Theatre that Friday, you know! Later, Ted Mack replaced Major Bowes, and I joined his show called *Youth on Parade.* Ted Mack took all the cream from Major Bowes's amateur shows and made this show.

After working with Major Bowes and Ted Mack, I went out on my own. At first I had a partner, but just for a short time, and that was Henry Colemen. But he died real young, I think of pneumonia. After that, I stayed by myself and did a single. I had a good single. I worked the B. F. Keith Circuit. That's when I met Sammy Davis—he was about twelve years old—with The Will Mastin Trio. We were working on the same bill in Detroit where I was doing a single. And they called me "On-Too-Long," because I would go on the stage and never know when to leave! I was stagestruck. I

The caricaturist's view of The Four Step Brothers, 1944

got on the stage, and the floors would be good or something, I'm goin' over good, and I didn't know when to come off, you know! I had a set three-minute act that consisted of my music and my exit step, "going out" step. And I never forget The Will Mastin Trio saying, "We don't want to follow Prince, because he's on too long!"

In those days, whatever you did while you were dancing, it was acceptable. They didn't cut you off. If you told a joke while you were dancing, if you sang a song before you started dancing, it was good. Dancing was the forte. I sang and told one-liners. Whoever told a joke in front of me in some other town, I told it in my act! I sang everything I could think of. I had guide charts for the bands. The opening thing was either staff music or written for me. Then the piano player could play stop time. During the stop time, I'd ad-lib as long as I was going over—and I usually felt good and stayed out there!—that's why they called me On-Too-Long! Opening and in between was everything I could think of or whatever would come to me that night. "I think I'll do a little Pat Rooney." I go OK. Waltz Clog. I do a little Bill Robinson. And I do whoever I liked. But if I felt like I was losing them, I'd give em' this cue— "Let's go home" or "Take me out," and the band would start to play the sixteen bars to take me out. That got you off the stage. For my exit step I did flips, splits and the Russian kick-out. Four Trenches. A double hand flip. A split, Over the Top. That was a good "going out," you know. Yeah. You may die in between, but "going out" was set completely. All sixteen bars.

Not only did I do imitations of tap dancers like Robinson, I also did imitations of nondancers. I did President Roosevelt, and I did Ned Sparks! I did the double-talk comedian Roy Atwell. "My name is Roy Atwell, no Inkwell, no Stinkwell . . ." In those days, you knew Roy Atwell because he was with Fred Allen. I never forget this: "My name

was Roy Atwell, no Inkwell, no Stinkwell. You saw my dame in tights, I mean my name in lights . . ." And I did a Buck and Bubbles thing—[sings]:

Years ago a certain sage said this whole
    world was a stage,
and we were the players from the start.
Now, for they say that colored folks with all
    their songs and laughs and jokes,
and the show must play a special part.
All the world is rhythm mad.
All the world wants rhythm bad,
and colored folks are mighty glad.
We've got rhythm. Yeah, man.
All the good things on this earth come from
    rhythm, joy, and mirth.
And colored folks are rich from birth.
We've got rhythm. Yeah, man.
Up in Harlem, boy, we're doing swell.
    Nature gave us something, something that
    we could sell.
Laugh, sing, joy, and mirth.
Colored folks are rich from birth.

I was determined to be successful, and I had a good single act. I worked mostly the white clubs. The only one black club I worked at was the Club Alabam. I don't want to put this without sounding—well, I'll tell you what—you worked the white clubs then, you were accepted. I worked the high-class white clubs. I worked the Music Box on Hollywood Boulevard. In the white clubs, the show was all white. I was the only black in the show. A lot of times when I was traveling, they had to go out and get me food. Down South, I could go in the hotel but couldn't come out! So all the kids in the show had to bring me food back to the hotel. I was the baby of the group, had all the sympathy going for me and everything, and I milked it pretty good!

But it was in 1941, at the Club Alabam on the Coast, that Freddie James came up to me regarding joining The Four Step Brothers. I had known of him. I always admired him. He was the world's greatest dancer, Freddie James. And he asked me did I want to join The Step Brothers. See, Maceo Anderson was being inducted into the army, and that only left Freddie, Al, and Happy. They needed a fourth. So I joined up. Maceo came out of the Army '45 or '46. Sadly, Happy died, but then Maceo got back in the act. When Freddie James died, I got Flash to join. Just how

Three of The Four Steps doing their "Bottle Dance." Prince Spencer (center) madly dances out the rhythms while Flash McDonald (left) and Maceo Anderson (right) encourage him with alternating time-setting hand clapping and foot stomping. This technique, taken from the infamous street corner Challenges, was incorporated into The Four Step Brothers' act so successfully that it became their trademark, 1940s.

things were then.

I was with The Four Step Brothers for twenty-nine years. Yeah. Everything you can think of we did. We went around the world four times. We danced for the Queen of England. We danced for Hirohito. We danced for the Queen of Cambodia. We danced for the Prince of Laos. We danced for the King of Thailand; he was a jazz enthusiast, he played the saxophone. I think we were one of the most, I guess, lovable acts, because everyone could relate to it, you know. We each had a step that someone in the audience could probably do or tried to do. The audience picked out their favorites—like a baseball team. Each member would have something the audience in particular would like to see him do. We put dancing first. Always on time. Did a good act. Neat and clean. We did something the public could relate to. Good rhythm that they could hear and understand, you know. Not above their head. And the excitement of watching flash dancers—there's nothing like it!

We worked Radio City Music Hall. That was a *beautiful* theater. I remember before we played

THE "STORY" OF TAP

there, I had seen Raymond Winfield, from Tip, Tap and Toe do all those slides in his routines. So I went out to perfect them. And when we played Radio City Music Hall, I would sneak out on the stage early before the shows and rub a little boric acid into the floor to make the floor slippery. And I could slide real good in it. But then one day, one of the Rockettes slipped! And that put an end to my slide "secret."

In 1946, we were at the Paramount on a show with Frank Sinatra and The Pied Pipers. This was six shows a day, seven days a week. Yeah. There was no days off. Our act was thirteen minutes, and whatever dance we did, it was a Challenge. If it was the waltz, it was a waltz challenge. He did a Double Wing, I did a move that was harder. Each guy had to do an outstanding step. You couldn't use a mediocre step, because the routine wouldn't build. First guy did a step, we'd get a hand on that. The next guy come on had to do a step even harder. The third guy did a step even more so. And the last guy had to bring the dance to a pinnacle. And when one guy was dancing, we'd always be kind of a picture on the stage. Like a frame around him. We were standing behind him, either clapping our hands in time, or we might have our canes down and our hats on top of the canes. But nothing could detract from the one in front. For the finish, we always did a closing step together. At the end, we used to make a speech with a little kind of comedy. Something like, "We appreciate your appreciation very appreciably . . ."

Maceo danced first, then Al, then Flash, then me. And then at the very end of my routine, we'd count *one, two, three, four, five, six, seven*—that's when the band would come in. And the band would play sixteen bars to take us off again. We incorporated a lot of acrobatics into our tap dancing. The hard part of all our acrobatics was doing it in rhythm. Yeah! You have to do a flip

Prince Spencer flies high over the heads of his cohorts in Rhythm, Al Williams, Maceo Anderson, and Flash McDonald. At the time the photo was taken, The Four Step Brothers were appearing in Paris, France, at the Medrano Stadium, 1952.

and a split into that beat. Either one beat or a beat and a half, and you took another half beat to be on time for the next step: *Di-di-di-dop, BAM.* A flip! You had to go Over the Top and you had to do a flip within the next two beats and get up. If you couldn't, you took that stuff out. You had to make your timing precise to the beat and never off the beat. We had two and a half choruses of swing music where the four of us challenged each other.

For my part of the challenge, I'd jump across their backs, or I'd do the flips and splits or I'd do Over the Top. I did flips, one-hand flips, split into split. I did Over the Tops, Double Wings, kick-outs—Russian kick-outs on the floor, mule kicks. That's what always made me think that I was an exceptional dancer, because I could do a variety of dancings, you know, not just rhythm on the floor. I could do hand springs, flips, splits, spins, Double Wings, Five Tap Wings, Over the Tops, everything. I was good in everything. If I did a flip and split, it was good. If I Pulled Trenches, it was good. If I did a Wing, it was good. I only did what I did good. And I had to be good to dance last, after the three guys were on. Those were *great* dancers, you know. And we did this thirteen-minute act six times a day! But each guy was not dancing for thirteen minutes completely, because of the challenge—see what I mean? The opening was together, and the time we talked in between, this guy danced, and this guy danced, and this guy danced, and I did this, and by then, you could catch your breath. But doing six shows a day—we was young and full of ambition. I don't know. We were full of energy. It wasn't hard at all. I enjoyed every minute of it. And the audiences at that time—oh, my goodness. It sounded like thunder! Each time we were out on that stage, it sounded like thunder. When you're young, that alone would give you enough energy to do two more shows!

Each one of The Four Step Brothers had their own style, something that the people could relate to. And over the years, we went from Radio City Music Hall to the Roxy to the Paramount to around the world to the kings and queens. If I had to describe The Four Step Brothers, let's say in just a few words, I would say we were the most *exciting* rhythm dancers. Four guys dancing—there was a force of excitement that is hard to explain. Each guy challenging the other. Just forceful excitement.

December 13, 1988
Las Vegas, Nevada

25

TAPPING INTO
THE CLASSICS

PAUL DRAPER

I was a very serious type of dancer. I didn't sell the steps to the audience. I was anxious to *do* the dance, not to sell it. I wanted to be part of the art.

The music of Bach, Tchaikovsky, and Brahms are not genres that readily bring to mind a connection with tap. However, to one fleet-footed dancer, the work of these composers offered up a symphony of possibilities. When Paul Draper entered the tap dance scene in the 1930s, the composition of the art changed forever.

Paul Draper was born in Florence, Italy on October 25, 1909. His parents were Americans living abroad. During his early childhood years there, he was embraced by the classical music of Europe—just when ragtime and jazz music were newly entering the American domain. Paul Draper's home was filled with classical music, and his family was visited by many great classical artists of the day; they left an indelible impression on the youngster.

The family moved back to the United States when Paul was four years old. He began tap dancing as a young man and was very soon absorbed by it. From the start, however, he was altogether unimpressed by what seemed to him the cacophony of sounds other tap dancers clattered out with their metal-plated shoes. During the 1930s, the vernacular expression "laying down iron" meant that a tap dancer had really laid down some rhythms. To Paul Draper this same phrase meant just a lot of noise. His ear was tuned to another musical and rhythmic concept.

After spending time in New York, Paul Draper traveled back to Europe in order to develop his art. Most of his tap contemporaries were executing wildly exciting and flashy steps to the weird "tattoos" of the jazz age. Meanwhile, Paul Draper was tuning his taps to the classics. In 1941, he joined up with classical harmonica player Larry Adler, and together they embarked on a series of highly acclaimed concert tours. These concert engagements continued to play before packed houses in the United States and abroad until 1949. Paul Draper, like many of America's eminent artists, was blacklisted during the McCarthy era. He moved to Geneva, Switzerland in 1950, and in 1954, he returned to the United States.

Paul Draper wove together classical music and tap dance. And, in this, he brought a new understanding—and new respect—to tap. In the 1940s, the world was watching and loving tap dance, but still considered it, simply, a novelty dance form. Over the years, legions of tap dancers had attempted to change the prevailing attitude. Paul Draper, in the 1940s and 1950s, succeeded by being the first to bring tap dancing into a concert setting.

Paul Draper appeared in two films that give a rare glimpse of his artistry: *Colleen* [1936] and *The Time of Your Life* [1948].

PAUL DRAPER — I don't know how it happened. I was at Arthur Murray's working as a ballroom dancing instructor. I had always known how to ballroom dance pretty well. One of the other teachers was able to do a Time Step, and I was fascinated with it and got him to teach me. He was a pretty good dancer. I learned to do about a half a step.

I took to tap dancing. Never had lessons. I was very bad, but I was fascinated with it. Never had lessons? That isn't altogether true; I had about three lessons from a fellow called Tommy Nip. I think it cost fifty cents a lesson, or something like that. And he told me I should stop tap dancing, because I was such a long time learning. Nip said it was a waste, really, of my time!

Anyhow, I went on tap dancing on my own and made up four dances to four tunes by Duke Ellington, "Black and Tan Fantasy," "Mood Indigo"—I don't remember the other ones. What I made up was not altogether tap dancing; it had a lot of movement in it and some tap dancing, because I didn't know much then. I got no work, but I made up a lot of numbers!

I rehearsed at Phil Waiman's on Broadway somewhere in the Fifties. There were many rehearsal halls then in that area. Theater rehearsal halls. You could hire a hall for a dollar an hour at the most. Anyhow, I made up these dances, and I decided to go to London, because I was having no success at selling them in New York. And I thought to myself, "I know what. I'm just not appreciated here. I'll go someplace where they will like it right away." And I went over to London. I had letters of introduction to everybody you could hand an introduction to: C. B. Cochran, Noel Coward, Lady Colfax, Samuel Cortauld. And they all were very sweet to me. They all asked what could they do. And I said, "Well, here I am, I'm a dancer." And they all saw me dance or sent me someplace where I could be seen dancing. But I got no work, because I wasn't very good!

By the 1940s, Paul Draper's tap phrasing and dancing form successfully blended with the dramatic stylings of classical music, 1943.

I went up into a rehearsal hall over there for six pence an hour. There was a show rehearsing preparatory to a road tour, called *Sensations of 1932*. A girl in it had lost her partner; he decided to leave show business. She either heard me or saw me tap dancing; it was a fairly open rehearsal hall. We didn't necessarily shut doors. She asked me if I would like to dance with her. Yes! I went out with this show, which was kind of a vaudeville entertainment show, all over England. But it came to an end. All this time, I was getting a little bit better. Not much. Still had not had lessons of any significance. Well, after leaving them, I went over to Paris and got a job in a famous Parisian night-club, Le Boeuf Sur Le Toit.

I was, at the time, dancing on a round marble pedestal about three feet high, a couple of feet wide. I'd learned this from an act called Chilton and Thomas, an excellent American tap dancing act. Man and wife, they were in vaudeville in England. I went back after seeing them and asked them to show me a few steps. He danced on pedestals—he had three of them, each one higher than the other. He'd hop from one to the next. The last one was up about seven or eight feet. The actual top on the last one was probably about a foot and a half wide, so it was very small foot work. He had a very neat step, did very good Pullbacks. I paid for a lesson, learned them, and added them to my own little act. My pedestal had a very heavy base so it wouldn't tip, but I think people expected I might fall off. I didn't.

By this time, I no longer had the Ellington numbers. I had one slow dance, and one fast dance, "Bye Bye Blues." I did most of my work on the pedestal; my tap shoes made a lovely sound against the marble. An excellent sound, a very clean, short, dry sound. And I liked that very much. I was pretty good by this time; I had an idea of what I was doing.

I was in Europe altogether about two and a half years, from the spring of 1929 to 1932. Le Boeuf Sur Le Toit was quite an experience. I'm trying to remember the whole flavor of that time in Paris. Jean Cocteau was the designer, or maybe even part owner, of that nightclub. And his influence on all things cultural in Paris, if not all of France, was significant. Picasso was just beginning to emerge. And Gauguin, Rousseau, Matisse, Monet, Man Ray, Stravinsky, Debussy, Ravel were the people who were discussed at the Café Des Deux Magots, and the Café Des Fleurs, famous left-bank restaurant cafés. All this was grist to the mill of a young person starting in any form of art. All these things had a profound influence on me. And, of course, I thought I knew everything.

However, I got stranded in the South of France; I had no more work, had no more money. Wired home for money, the reply was: "You've sown wild oats for long enough. Will send fare. Come home. Undertake some responsible profession." Yes. Glad to. Glad to. I came home, pedestal with me, and went right on rehearsing. It was not to undertake "some more serious profession." I went on sowing wild oats! Rehearsed at Erving Plummer's rehearsal hall at Forty-five West Forty-fifth Street in New York City.

Agents used to come around to rehearsal halls and look in and see what was there, hoping to find an act. By this time, I had quite a few numbers. I was a medium-good tap dancer. I had very fast feet, and I was pretty clean, and I was very imaginative. I had much more interesting music than anybody else had, though it was not classical music at that time. Ferde Grofé, George Gershwin, stuff like that.

Anyhow, around 1933, an agent saw me rehearsing. He had some girl tap dancers, and he had a fellow whom I'd never heard of before— Jack Albertson (the very same one!), a dear, sweet, lovely artist. A good pool player, too! And a very good Soft Shoe dancer. He and I made up a

number together. We had, I think, three girls, and it was called Paul Draper and Company. We got booked in Long Island, Brooklyn, the Bronx, playing "break-in dates" in vaudeville theaters. A break-in date meant that you were not paid your full salary, as stipulated in the contract you signed. You seldom ever were paid it! Because in order to be paid that, you had to have a settled act. An organized, known, settled act. Well, if the agent-manager kept changing the act a little bit, or bringing a new girl in, or letting a girl go, then you had a succession of what were called break-in dates. You could be hired for those at half or maybe three-quarter salary. So we did a whole lot of that. We weren't super good, but we weren't awful, either. This went on, I guess, about eight or nine months.

Ruby Keeler and Paul Draper in the film *Colleen* (Warner Bros., 1936)

TAPPING INTO THE CLASSICS

I was learning all the time. I was very determined, and I was sure I could make something out of this thing. Finally, the agent-manager came back one night after some show. He handed me back the contract that I had signed with him at the start of this enterprise. He held it up and moved it up and down under my chin and looked at me and said, "No puss, no puss." That meant I had no personality. I was deadpan. This came because I was a very serious type of a dancer. And I didn't sell the steps to the audience. I was anxious to *do* the dance, not to sell it. I wanted to be a part of the art. So anyhow, that was the end of the act, and we all went our separate ways. I went out on my own as a single. I had an act now, because I had enough numbers to make an act. I was still on the pedestal then, though I did some things off of it as well.

Some theaters had certain amateur nights, professional tryout nights, or whatever—like what happened and was made so famous up at the Apollo Theatre, where all of the hoofers at one time or another worked. I saw many of them up there. One of the most famous was called "Wild Bird." He wasn't known by another name. And when he got high, he did things nobody has ever done. He wasn't the most dependable act in the world. Sometimes he would show up late, and sometimes he wouldn't show up at all. But when he showed up, and he was on, he was untouchable.

There were many other theaters that followed much the same format that had been so successful and long used at the Apollo. They had nights when acts would audition, and they'd either get thrown off the stage, or they would have a success. And then if the bookers and theater managers liked them, they might sign them up to six weeks' or six months' work, depending on how many theaters were in that chain. Sometimes I would get some work, and sometimes I wouldn't!

I got off onto a few things; the Paramount chain had me on once, and I went around with them with my own act. And some of the Loews Circuit. The vaudeville circuits were fun to do. We did four or five shows a day. I did a whole lot of vaudeville as a single, just under my own name, Paul Draper.

At this point in time, I was dancing to "Bye Bye Blues," "Lazy River," "Tea for Two," stuff like that. "Manhattan Serenade," parts of the Gershwin "Concerto," "Rhapsody," but shortened versions, not the whole thing, naturally. You never danced over three minutes for one dance. The audience were like little kids; you couldn't hold them, they couldn't concentrate.

"Laying down iron." You ever heard that phrase used? Laying down iron. Well, that was what tap dancing was considered. It was a much-used term for an act. And if you could lay down enough iron, you were a successful act. And if you laid down a whole lot of iron, you might indeed put grooves into the stage. And if you put them in an inch deep, you had to be worth something! I didn't lay down iron. I was trying to dance. I was a dancer trying to make a difference as an artist, trying to make something that hadn't existed before, and trying to change the lives of whoever saw it.

But I gradually became rather successful. There were almost no solo dancers then. So there was very little competition. There were only what were called Ballroom Dancing acts. There were a whole lot of those. Almost nobody danced alone. I was one of the few people. So I made more money, in a sense, because I could fill the same spot and I was just one person. I would get almost the same salary that the ballroom team would get,

Paul Draper dances with Ruby Keeler down the panel of this sheet music cover from the film *Colleen* (Warner Bros., 1936). As the song title aptly puts it, "You gotta know how to dance." Draper's and Keeler's tap number to that song showed that indeed they did know how.

because I would use up the same amount of time! But I always had an accompanist. I never appeared anyplace without an accompanist. Even with the orchestra in a vaudeville house, I had my own man in the pit at the piano. Sometimes he made more money than I did! But it was essential for me to have the music played the way I had made up the number. Since I had made it up with that accompanist, it would be played the same way all the time.

So that happened well and easily, and as I say, I kept going around and got hired in a couple of nightclubs. They were little spots. I was getting, I don't know, I think a hundred fifty, maybe two hundred dollars a week.

About this time, I had an idea to do a couple of Handel minuets, a little Bach gigue, and started making them up. Now, I had always heard and always liked classical music, but never thought of it for tap dancing. As a matter of fact, I had been brought up with classical music. My father sang, and we had music in the house in England. I can remember Arthur Rubinstein, Pablo Casals, Ysaye, Cortot, Thibault playing in the house in London. The first tune I ever learned to hum, the first tune I ever learned, was the theme of the first movement of Beethoven's Violin Concerto! So, I had this as a background. But I'd never dreamed I could use anything like that to tap dance to. But I began to have an idea that maybe these things

might make good music for tap dancing. So, I began to make them up, and I began to do the same steps that I always had done. The only steps I knew, really. And somehow they didn't seem to fit. The arms didn't look right. I just wasn't satisfied with it. I thought to myself, "Arms, arms, arms, head, body, upper body. Yes, must move, must move, must move."

I thought and thought. I said, "Maybe I ought to go *learn* how to dance!" So I went up to the School of American Ballet, which had just come to New York. I knew Lincoln Kirstein. I had met George Balanchine. And so I went up to the school and had lessons. I was a rank beginner in ballet, though I was a fairly experienced tap dancer at the time and making a living at it. I was about twenty-three by this time, and I started studying with the little kids, nine, ten, eleven years old. I was never, ever going to become a ballet dancer, but I started to learn how to move around so that I was able to do the things I had wanted to do—make sounds which were rhythmically appropriate and sensible, and imaginative and inventive, and still look something like a dancer. This was my first experience ever, really, with learning how to dance. And it was a revelation to me! A brand new experience.

I got hired to be in a nightclub show at the Hotel Pierre, which was experimenting in "serious" nightclub entertainment. Mario Braggiotti's Orchestra, eight girls and myself. It was a very chic and smart place—very expensive, big cover charge, excellent food, splendid wine list, very refined atmosphere. I was doing quite a few numbers by this time, though not on the pedestal. I still was not doing much classical stuff at this point, but I was starting to learn.

I was hired at the Persian Room in the Plaza Hotel, and that was really a success. We'd open with "It Was Just One of Those Things." Then I danced to the Handel minuet, Debussy's "Golliwog's Cake Walk," "The Blue Danube Waltz," "It Ain't Necessarily So," "Malagueña," "Asturias," and a little fun number at the end, a little jazz. Eddy Duchin had the orchestra, and Eddy and I worked there for about sixteen weeks each year for about three years, and that was great fun. I had an advantage over many dancers then. I did about forty minutes as a solo act. That meant six or seven dances, all quite different, and a couple of minutes for introducing each one. Very economical for a nightclub.

My manager was one of the office boys in Harry Rogers's office (Harry Rogers, who had fired me). The office boy was Jack Davies, a dear, beautiful Welshman who became one of the leading the-atrical agents on Broadway. He was my exclusive agent from that time till the day he died, and we never had a contract. He handled me throughout the halcyon days at the Plaza, the Waldorf in the Empire Room, the Rainbow Room, the Cocoanut Grove in Los Angeles, Chez Paree in Chicago . . . I was now earning a lot of money. Things were successful. I had a valet and accompanist, and I was making about twenty-five hundred a week, which was an exceedingly high salary in those days!

It was shortly after that, about 1940, Larry Adler

Paul Draper brought the classics to high society at the Plaza's Persian Room, 1937.

and I met. We got hired at Radio City Music Hall. They had a huge set that had three forty-foot doors facing the audience. They had one girl singer, one harmonica player, and one tap dancer. She came out of the middle door and sang—I don't know—"Stormy Weather," or "Can't Help Lovin' Dat Man," or whatever the song was. She came out and sang it—Larry came out and played it—I came out and danced it. Then we all three did it ensemble. It was a big success. And what followed the stage show was a Walt Disney cartoon, *The Pied Piper*. The opening song was "The rats, the rats, we gotta get rid of the rats." Larry and I were going up in the elevator in Radio City Music Hall after the opening. Well, the loud-speaker system in this elevator was on all day, so that everybody would know if it were near the time when they had to appear. We're standing opposite each other. We have, of course, met, and we hear this thing, "The rats, the rats, we gotta get rid of the rats." He looked over at me and he said, "You think they mean us?" And we became fast friends.

We used to sell each other at any theater we played. I would say, "Have you heard Larry Adler play the harmonica?" And he'd say, "Have you seen Paul Draper dance?" We would bump into each other at various independent theaters, one of which was, for instance, Grauman's Chinese out in Hollywood—which was a famous theater. And we decided to give a concert. We hired a hall up in Santa Barbara. The whole thing cost us about a thousand dollars to put on, I guess. We

Paul Draper and Larry Adler formed a uniquely prosperous union, and performed in a series of highly acclaimed concert tours.
Program photo of Paul Draper and Larry Adler reproduced with permission from the Dance Collection, the New York Public Library at Lincoln Center, Astor, Lenox, and Tilden Foundations.

did everything we knew. He did four numbers. I did four numbers. He did four numbers. I did four numbers. We had an intermission. He did four numbers. I did four numbers. He did four numbers. And then we did four numbers together! I did every dance I'd ever made up! And it was a long, long show. It was tedious and long! But we made a little money, and it was very successful.

About a year after that, I asked Columbia Concerts to see me at the Waldorf with a view to doing concerts with Larry. They sat in a stone-

faced array watching me dance to Bach, Liszt, Brahms, Chopin, etcetera. And all of it being successful. Boy, the audience was mouse quiet. They broke out into ovations at the end of each number! It was lovely living. Larry did much the same thing as I did: He played classical music on the harmonica. And they hired us, made up an act, and sent us out. We did thirteen dates. And they gave us an account sheet at the end of the thirteen dates—we'd made seventy-one fifty, or something, apiece! But they invested money in it, because we'd had a success. And we really took off after this. For about eight or nine years we averaged about a hundred thousand dollars a year. That's out of the concerts. Until the blacklisting.

We had a success with the concert tours. We did nightclubs and odds and ends like that. When we were not doing the concert tours, I was still studying ballet, enabling myself to do things a little better than I had before. We played every hall large enough to hold us: Carnegie Hall, San Francisco Opera House, Los Angeles Philharmonic, Symphony Hall in Chicago. The big places—we were there.

Larry would start out our program. He'd do two or three numbers: a Mozart, a Bach. I would come out and do a Handel minuet, a Vivaldi or Scarlatti sonata. I would go off, Larry would come back, and he would do a Brahms or Kol Nidre. I would come back, and I did "A Sonata for Tap Dancer," which was an unaccompanied work. It took about seventeen minutes and had four movements. It was a serious evening! And we'd end up the first half doing an ad-lib and improvisation—"à la manière de" anybody that the audience called out. We would ask, "Who do you want?" Naturally, if you get enough people asking, you can always find something you'd like to do. It might be Scarlatti. It might be Scriabin. It might be Debussy, Ravel, Tchaikovsky. And according to what mood Larry was in, or I was in, we'd select one that we liked, and he'd start off with it, and that would be that. I would make up what I hoped was an appropriate dance. Intermission. Second half, we would start to get into the jazz thing. Larry would do "It Ain't Necessarily So," or "When Day Is Done." I would do "Surrey with the Fringe on Top," "Ain't Necessarily So," a folk medley that I had made up, ending up with "Three Blind Mice," "I've Been Working on the Railroad," "Yankee Doodle," a lot of stuff like that. Then we would get together at the end and have an ad-lib, which consisted of more requests from the audience. At which Larry was phenomenal. He could play anything, and the object of it was for him to throw me! He would switch from classical into jazz. . . . They'd ask for all sorts of things! "Beethoven's Fifth." And we'd say, "Do you want the whole thing, or will just one movement be enough?" And the audience was in fine form by this time. We always ended up with "I Got Rhythm." That was the only set thing we had. That would take about eight, ten minutes! I'd be exhausted at the end of it! I'd look at Larry as I whirled by and say, "Make this the end! Make this end!" And off we'd go.

We had a wonderful time. And that went on very well right up to the blacklisting. The thing started in '48. Took us about a year before it came to trial. It was early in 1950 before it actually became a court case. And that went on for about six weeks. A hung jury. But I don't think it would have made any difference whether it had been in our favor. Neither of us had any work. And that stayed right like that, you know, right on through.

That thing had nothing to do with dancing, it was more something of the times than it was of anything else. Coming down from earning a whole lot of money to not making anything at all, it's not earthshaking. It's at least annoying, you know. It's upsetting, shall we say. But nobody ever stopped me from dancing. If they'd been smart, they'd have found some way to make me unable to dance. But that never occurred to anybody. Economic disenfranchisement is considered the worst thing that can happen to one in a capitalist society. So it didn't occur to them to break a leg or something like that; render one incapable of doing the thing that they love to do—that never stopped.

It is all within one context, one flavor—trying to create, trying to make a difference, trying to be a piece of the art. A dancer shapes space. He envisages and dreams and conjures up the space he wants. The way the universe makes its shape, a dancer does exactly that same thing.

I've had great fun. I think that I have earned a little tiny piece of the art, that I have held on to one corner of it, and helped make the fabric and the color and the shape of it just a little bit. To do something—that's really what you dance for.

December 5, 1988
Woodstock, New York

26

DANCE DIRECTORS WHO DO NOT DANCE

ANN MILLER

When [performers] came under contract [at MGM], they were asked if they sang and danced. And if they didn't, they didn't get hired!

When the movie musical really hit it big in the 1930s, a typical credit sheet contained the following listings: Director, Producer, Scenarists, Story, Music and Lyrics, Gowns, Director of Photography, . . . and Dance Director. If it did not read "Dance Director," it read "Dances Staged By . . ." Because those were the days when screen dances *were* staged and directed. They were musical numbers featuring scores, if not hundreds, of chorus boys and girls, moving in militarylike formations to the hot tunes of the day. The most famous purveyor of the formation dance number was Busby Berkeley, known as "Buz" to his friends and working cohorts. His precise geometric extravaganzas are unrivaled to this day. However, there were other remarkable dance directors: Bob Alton, Nick Castle, Bobby Connolly, Louis DaPron, Seymore Felix, Sammy Lee, Hermes Pan, LeRoy Prinz, Chuck Walters. Their combined efforts have left a legacy of musical numbers from Hollywood's Golden Age of musical films.

However, of all the dance directors, only a small number could actually dance. The vast majority were technicians more than anything else. They were tech-

Ann Miller dances her famous number "I've Gotta Hear That Beat," from *Small Town Girl* (MGM, 1953), which was choreographed by Willie Covan and directed by Busby Berkeley.

nicians with an artistic vision, and they were able to combine the two and accomplish glorious results. Their formula for success worked perfectly with an ensemble piece. But when these technicians found themselves confronted with actual tap dancers, it was another story. Busby Berkeley could give the tap dancers concepts, direction, movement, but he could not give them tap steps. A tap dancer had to be brought in to work with the star. In Hollywood, there were four outstanding tap "coaches": Nick Castle, Willie Covan, Louis DaPron, and Hermes Pan. These were the real hoofers. Even though they were the brains behind the feet, they often went uncredited in a film. Eventually, though, they were considered the legendary choreographers of Hollywood's film industry.

During the 1930s and into the 1940s, many dancing stars were frustrated working with dance directors who could not dance. It made no sense to them, as accomplished dancers, to find themselves faced with such a situation. No sense at all. They were greatly relieved when a hoofer was brought in to pinch-hit on the tap for the dance director. In *Small Town Girl* (1953), in her most famous tap number, "I've Gotta Hear That Beat," Ann Miller worked with dance director Busby Berkeley. He had the scheme for the number, the concept of the musicians' hands and instruments coming through the floor, and of Ann ricocheting through and past them. However, Busby Berkeley could not dance, and even if he could, he never could have contributed to the style of such an outstanding and dynamic dancer as Ann Miller. So MGM's ace in the hole was brought in to work with her—Willie Covan. Together they created one of the most riveting tap dance numbers ever filmed. Willie Covan had had

fifty years' experience by the time he worked with Ann Miller. He had been the founding member of the smash quartet The Four Covans during the 1920s. In the 1930s, Covan was brought to MGM personally by Eleanor Powell. Through his years at MGM, he not only coached stars in dance, but also worked with them on their film routines—uncredited.

Nick Castle, Louis DaPron, and Hermes Pan were not so overlooked in the credit department. Each came strongly into their own as dance directors, and eventually as "choreographers." (The word was introduced into the vernacular by Agnes De Mille in 1942, when she "choreographed" *Oklahoma!* on Broadway. It took on such strong connotations, that Irving Berlin even parodied the concept in his uproarious number in *White Christmas* (1954), suitably featuring Danny Kaye and a chorus of "modern"

DANCE DIRECTORS WHO DO NOT DANCE

dancers: "Chaps who did taps, aren't tapping anymore—they're doing 'Choreography.'") Nick Castle worked extensively with The Nicholas Brothers, The Condos Brothers, and Betty Grable. Louis DaPron choreographed for The Jivin' Jacks and Jills, and Donald O'Connor and Peggy Ryan. Hermes Pan worked with Fred Astaire and Ginger Rogers, and Betty Grable. And Ann Miller had the good fortune to work with all three men.

She was born Johnnie Lucille Collier in Houston, Texas, on April 12, 1923. When she was still a child, her parents selected a stage name for her, and she became Anne Miller, later simplified to Ann Miller.

Ann Miller went on to become one of America's top female tap dancing stars. She followed Ruby Keeler, then Eleanor Powell on film. Other women tap dancers of the time, though featured primarily in B pictures, were Dixie Dunbar, Jeni LeGon, Mitzi Mayfair, Peggy Ryan, and Eleanore Whitney. Each of

the women had her own outstanding style. Ann's was "machine gun" taps that came exploding in a hail out of her shoes. She even received notoriety in Ripley's *Believe It or Not* as the world's fastest tap dancer: A speedometer attached to her feet recorded five hundred taps per minute! However, Ann Miller's dancing was not speed alone; she danced with sheer energy, bursting with joy, vigor, and wild excitement. Because Ann Miller appeared extensively in movies, a wealth of her tap dancing has been captured for posterity in such film classics as *Stage Door* (1937), *Easter Parade* (1948), *On The Town* (1949), *Small Town Girl* (1953), and *Kiss Me Kate* (1953).

A N N   M I L L E R — I really wanted to be a ballet dancer! I started out dancing when I was—oh, between six and seven. I took ballet and tap, like most young little girls do. My dance teacher in Houston used to have a drummer come in and play with the piano player. I've got some Indian blood in me, and I used to hear that drum, and I tell you, I don't know whether it was the Indian blood or what, but I just took off and started tapping. I just lost all interest in ballet!

When I was still a little girl, my mother took me backstage at the Majestic Theatre in Houston, Texas, where I was born—and introduced me to Bill Robinson, "Bojangles." And she asked Bill, would he watch me dance, and if he thought I had a lot of rhythm, and would it be worth following the career—because my dancing teacher was so impressed with me. I danced for him, and he thought I was terrific and taught me three or four steps backstage. I came back to him later when

I was ten years old, and he worked with me again when he came through Houston. He really was the one that kind of inspired me to tap dance. Of course, there were wonderful people like Fred Astaire—I used to sit in the movie houses and watch him and Ginger Rogers and Eleanor Powell. They were all my idols, you know.

I started dancing professionally when I was eleven when I came out to Hollywood. I finally got a job at the Bal Tabarin Club, which was a big theater restaurant in San Francisco. They had talent scouts two nights in a row come in, one from Columbia Studios and one from RKO. And I was doing my own little style of dancing. It was like a machine-gun style that I developed at a very young age. I got offers from both studios. My mother turned Columbia down and took RKO, and I was over there for three years. I danced in my first picture that I did, a big picture called *New Faces of 1937*. Did a big tap number in that.

Ann Miller, the girl with the "machine gun" taps, sets a record tapping 598 per minute, 1942.

Ann Miller and her mother inspecting one of the dancer's tap shoes, 1940s

DANCE DIRECTORS WHO DO NOT DANCE

And then I did *Stage Door* [1937] with Ginger Rogers and Katharine Hepburn. I got my first speaking part in that. And I danced with Ginger Rogers. Oh, honey, I was like fourteen years old at the time and involved with a classic, marvelous movie. Then, by the time I was fifteen, I was starring in *You Can't Take it With You* [1938], with Jean Arthur and Jimmy Stewart. I played a ballerina in it who's supposed to be really lousy, which was kind of fun, because Misha Auer was my ballet master. That was a terrific picture that won the Academy Award for Best Picture of 1938. From there I did *Room Service* [1938] with the Marx Brothers.

When I was fifteen years old, I left RKO and went and did *George White's Scandals* [1939] on Broadway. I had two big tap numbers, and I was a smash hit. I had my picture in the front of *The Daily News* in New York, in front of *The Daily Mirror* in New York. *George White's Scandals* was a revue. We had Ella Logan, who was a terrific singer, Ben Blue, who was tremendous—very funny comic. We had the Three Stooges. We had Willie and Eugene Howard, who were a great comedy team. And, of course, the very beautiful and glamorous George White Show Girls. It was a tremendous show and a big hit, and it ran for a year on Broadway. I was two years on the road with it. It was really exciting, you know, for a kid of fifteen, who everybody thought was eighteen. I had to lie about my age. Even when I was under contract to RKO, I fibbed. But I had to in order to keep my contracts. They didn't want juveniles. They really didn't.

After the *Scandals*, I came back to Hollywood for my first big one-picture deal at RKO. I left RKO at a hundred and fifty dollars a week, and then I came back to RKO at three thousand dollars a picture—that's what one Broadway show did for you! Eleanor Powell was at her height and really going great guns. RKO, you know, kind of kept

me as a threat to Eleanor Powell, because she was getting two hundred and fifty thousand a picture, and I was getting a hundred and fifty dollars a week! I was doing my type of dancing, which was different from hers. Hers was more acrobatic. I never was very interested in acrobatic-type things—I'd say I was more of a hoofer than Eleanor. I was such a great admirer of hers. I met her actually at a premier of a film, though I can't remember which one it was. She came

Fourteen-year-old Ann Miller steps lively on the sheet music cover for *Tarnished Angel* (RKO, 1938).

over and said hello to me, and we just started talking and hit it off. Eleanor was a wonderful lady, and we became great friends.

I developed my style of tap dancing when I was just a little girl. It's funny how life is. My style of dancing was faster and more, well—machine-gun-type of taps than—I don't know, than Fred Astaire or Eleanor Powell. Because of my style, whenever I was shooting a movie or in a stage show, I would always have to make sure the floor was absolutely without any nails or any screws popping up, and make sure that the seams of the masonite was laid properly. Before every show, I went out with a carpenter and checked that floor before I started to warm up. And that was a big responsibility. I always made sure that that floor was in order, not too slippery and all that sort of thing.

Throughout my career, I never really got a chance to see too many other women tap dancers, because I was so busy working myself. I do remember there was a girl called Eleanore Whitney. She was a very pretty girl, very attractive. She was at Paramount, if I remember correctly. And she tapped, and she was terrific! She had her own little style. You know, everybody had their own style. And Peggy Ryan, she was very pert and very flip and cute as hell. She tapped. And she was good! She worked with Donald O'Connor. Louis

DaPron set a lot of their stuff. Louis DaPron did a lot of movies with me. He was wonderful. Oh, yes. And we worked very well together. I mean, Louis was terrific!

I worked with most of the great tap choreographers: Nick Castle, Louis DaPron, Willie Covan, Hermes Pan . . . Nick Castle was a fantastic tap dancer. He used to work a lot with The Condos Brothers and The Nicholas Brothers. Nick Castle was a great dance director, he really was. And he danced! Buz Berkeley was one of the greatest of all dance directors, but he couldn't tap. He couldn't dance. He had to hire somebody to come in and do the work for him. That's how he happened to hire Willie Covan. Buz had the ideas, but he would have somebody else work on the tap and the actual dancing. I worked with Willie Covan once, and it was probably the best thing I've ever done: "I've Got to Hear That Beat" [*Small Town Girl*, 1953]. It was a Busby Berkeley number, but Willie Covan worked with me on some of the tap stuff. I think he was wonderful. He made a

In a contest to decide who could tap—or type!—faster, Ann Miller defeated expert typist Ruth Myers with 627 taps per minute to the typist's 584 taps per minute. In doing so, Ann Miller broke her own record of four years earlier, 1946.

Three tap dancing greats and a swimmer (left to right), Nick Castle, Esther Williams, Ann Miller, and Hermes Pan, 1951.

primitive jazz things. He absolutely rejuvenated dancing. Totally revitalized it and redid it. When I worked with him, because he couldn't tap, I used to get Nick Castle to come in and work with me, and then we'd do a lot of Jack Cole's ideas. Bob Alton is another one who never danced. And he was at MGM. I did "Shaking the Blues Away" with him in *Easter Parade*. Nick Castle worked with me on the tap, and Bob Alton worked with me on the song and the arms and the movements and, you know, designed the set and did all these things. He was an incredible man. But he didn't dance. Buz Berkeley didn't dance either. That kind of upset me. It's better to work with a dance director that dances. They can tell you their ideas better and all. I think that Hermes was great because he could dance, you see. Hermes really was terrific. Because he would give me a style and a line, you know, like to do a turn and to come out in a certain way with a line of the body just right. And he worked with me on a lot of tap steps. Oh, what a darling man. Anything that you did with Hermes Pan—it was like going to a party on the set. He was always so cheerful and full of fun and happy hearted, and he was terrific.

As a matter of fact, Hermes Pan was my first "Hollywood date." He took me to the Academy Awards in 1938. I wore my first long evening dress. It was bright-yellow taffeta, I'll never forget it. Hedy Lamarr was very, very "in" at that time. She had just done *Algiers* [1938], and she had black hair and [a] very pale face and dark hair and dark eyebrows. I came to the door with all this white makeup on, dark-red lipstick, and he

lot of contributions. Gave me a lot of little extra steps here and there that helped me along, because that number was a fantastic number. With all those arms through the floor and the rows and rows of saxophones, rows and rows of trumpets, rows and rows of trombones. You know, it was incredible. There was just nobody like Busby Berkeley. He was a taskmaster. But Willie Covan helped me a lot. He was terrific. I just adored him. When I was doing it, did I realize that it would stand out? Well, it was certainly was different!

I also worked with Jack Cole. I did two or three pictures with him. Oh, honey, he was fantastic. He wasn't a tap dancer, he was a dance director. He did a lot of East Indian work. The lady from the ballet, Agnes De Mille—everybody got tired of that after a while, and Jack came along and made everybody bend over and do a lot of real

made me go in and wash my face before he would take me to the Awards! He made me wipe off all that pancake makeup. And he said, "Now you go in there and fix your face and put some rouge and lipstick—you don't need all that stuff." Oh, honestly. See, I was trying to look sophisticated because I was only fifteen years old—no, at that time—no, at the time he took me out I was fourteen. And he didn't know that. He thought I was eighteen. He said, "I'm not taking you with all that *junk* on your face." I was just devastated. I tell you, I thought I was going to die. But I went and took it all off and put on a regular face. He had to sit and wait and pat his foot while I was changing my face!

In 1948, I was signed with MGM. I did *On the Town* [1949], which was the first musical to be filmed on location and not on a soundstage. Gene Kelly, Frank Sinatra, Betty Garret, Vera-Ellen, and Jules Munshin were all on that picture. Being at MGM, it was like going to a big party every day, I mean it was just like having a party with good friends. They were terrific. So I loved it. And during those days, we all used to go around the lot and watch each other making films. At RKO, when I first started out, Fred Astaire would come over and watch if I was doing a tap number. Marlene Dietrich used to come and watch me dance during the shooting of *Time Out for Rhythm* [1941] over at Columbia Studios. A lot of the people used to come over. Rita Hayworth used to come and watch me. Then I used to go over on her set and watch her with Gene Kelly—oh, it was wonderful, you know. You hear all this stuff about stars fighting and being bitchy and all, we *weren't*! I mean—at MGM, I had the best fun with Debbie Reynolds and Janie Powell and Kathryn Grayson and Esther Williams. They're chums of mine. They were wonderful girls. And there was never any hateful jealousy and all that stuff. At least there wasn't in the musical world. Everybody was of the highest caliber. Look who was around! Fred Astaire, Gene Kelly—and everybody had to dance to be under contract at MGM. Didn't matter who they were—Clark Gable, Greer Garson, Lana Turner, Ava Gardner—they all danced. Yeah. Joan Crawford, she tapped too. They all had to tap. They all had to sing. They all had to move. When they came under contract, they were asked if they sang and danced. And if they didn't, they didn't get hired!

I finally got to work with Fred Astaire in 1948 in *Easter Parade*. I had known him on and off for so many years socially, you know, but to finally get to work with him was a real thrill for me. He was a great, great gentleman. Very much a perfectionist, and he worked hard. But I was really too tall for him. And so was Rita [Hayworth] and so was Cyd [Charise]. The only one that was really right for him was Ginger Rogers. She was five foot four, and she looked so pretty with him with her high heels. The other girls were five six, five seven and they had to work in ballets because they were too tall! But I'll never forget working with Fred—oh, it was fun. Yes. He was lovely, you know, he was really such a sweet man.

Of all the fun we had, making films was hard work though. You had to get up at five o'clock in the morning, and get out there to be into makeup at six in the morning, and have your hair done at seven, and body makeup put on at eight A.M., and be down on the set not later than eight-thirty—out there standing up in front of the cameras, *and* you had to know your lines! And you had to sit around so long between shots. By the time they get around to doing it, you're already tired and worn out and bored and, you know, feel like you want to go home! I like stage in a way, because you get out there and you do it, and the audience, if they love you, they clap, clap, clap and you know, "Oh, my God, they loved me." At least you know where you stand when you're onstage. It is so exciting when you walk out in front of that audience and you know

that that audience is a challenge. Every show is different. The same people don't sit out there. They're all different. Some audiences are smilers, some are clappers, some are laughers. But when you walk out on that stage, you walk out like every night's an opening night. There's an excitement there that you would never get in film. But I adore film, and the good thing about film is you have a permanent record of it all. On the stage it's just all lost.

===

Well, I think tap dancing is very *electric*. The minute a tap number comes on, you sit up and listen. It's exciting. You know, you can be going along and seeing a lot of that ballet and seeing a lot of that jazz that they do. But the minute a tap dancer comes on, or a tap number comes on, you sit up and listen!

I guess that I've always tried to make all my dancing very happy-hearted and very fresh and very with it. About all I can say. I don't know. It wasn't dull! I tell you, I've danced—I looked at my feet tonight, I thought, "Feet, you've danced me millions of miles!"

February 9, 1989
Beverly Hills, California

27

NIGHTCLUB CHORUS GIRL

FRANCES NEALY

I always could tap dance. I loved tap dancing. And they always had tap dancers in the shows.

Before silent films, Hollywood was a quiet conservative town. During the 1910s, dancing to jazz bands was actually forbidden within the city limits. So those wishing to have an evening of dancing and entertainment simply motored outside the city's confines to its outlying areas. There they could try out their feet to the newest and greatest dance crazes such as the Chicken Shuffle.

In 1912, a man named Baron Long opened the Vernon Country Club. It was located in one of the independent towns where activities such as drinking and dancing were not subject to the legal bindings of Los Angeles. Though not situated in Hollywood, it was Hollywood's first bona fide nightclub. Fatty Arbuckle, Mary Pickford, Gloria Swanson, Wallace Reid, Mabel Normand, and Tom Mix were just some of the early Hollywood personalities who streamed in night after night. Before he became the reigning Sheik of silent films, Rudolph Valentino got thirty-five dollars a week as a tango dancer there.

Like many of the early southern California nightclubs, Vernon was very unglamorous compared to the later clubs. As a matter of fact, it was situated

in the middle of a beet field. However, this inauspicious roadhouse was to become the birthplace for Hollywood night life, being the first club to introduce jazz to southern California. But Baron Long's most significant contribution to nightclub life was his innovation of orchestra, dancing, chorus girls, and floor show interwoven for an evening's entertainment. This novelty became standard for nightclubs and was responsible for employing thousands of specialty dancers, tap dancers, and girls in the line. Chorus lines of tap dancing beauties were only just originating with Long's nightclub. In the years ahead, many a "sweet young thing" would get to test out her charm and rhythm in a sleek and glamorous chorus line.

If in the teens, nightclubs were cropping up throughout the Hollywood area, by the 1920s, Hollywood was replete with them. Despite the introduction of Prohibition on June 30, 1919, nightclub life continued to prosper, and so did its entertainers. By this time, Hollywood was firmly established as the movie capital of the world, and the fortunes it created had to be spent. The "Great White Way" of the West Coast established itself right outside Hollywood, in Culver City. The Kit Kat Club, the Sneak

Inn, Tommy Ryan's Diner, King's Tropical Inn liberally supplied bootleg hootch in addition to their "socko" floor shows.

But the ultimate Los Angeles nightclub during Prohibition was Sebastian's Cotton Club. Frank Sebastian, "The King of Cabarets," was one of Hollywood's top entertainment brokers and was the first to exclusively feature "sepia" entertainment. Lionel Hampton, Cab Calloway, Duke Ellington, and Louis Armstrong were just a few of the club's headliners.

The 1930s brought in the Depression. With millions out of work, it hardly seemed the time to go out on the town. But the Depression just did not seem to hit Hollywood as hard as it did the rest of the country. The movie industry was reveling in the introduction of sound, and new millionaires were popping up right and left. Hollywood simply became more glamorous, and so did the nightclubs. There was the Cocoanut Grove, the Trocadero, Sardi's, and the Colony Club. There seemed no end to the creative concepts for putting across a night spot. Club openings continued at a manic pace, and by the mid-1930s, Hollywood night life was boundless. Movie stars went out in throngs, enjoying the most fabulous and dazzling entertainment a club could offer. And they were entertained. Every club had a band, a singer (or two), a dancing act (or two), and, of course, its bevy of beauties—the chorus line.

The 1940s may have meant world war for the rest of the world, but for Hollywood it meant economic health and vigor. Clubs continued to thrive. Swing was all the rage, and top bands like Tommy Dorsey, Benny Goodman, Glenn Miller, and Harry James entertained the masses seeking night life. The Mocambo, the Stork Club, and the wartime Hollywood

Canteen were host to some of the greatest entertainment of the land.

Many "Colored Revues" were popularized around Hollywood at this time, as they had been on the East Coast. The Swanee Inn, Little Eva, Café Society, and the Bal Tabarin, were all clubs featuring all-black shows; and like their East Coast counterparts were shows fabricated for all-white audiences. Anyone interested in the "real thing," though, headed out to Central Avenue in Los Angeles to clubs like the Last Word, the Plantation, and the Club Alabam, which showcased top black entertainment. It was said that these shows far outdid any of the shows in the white clubs. And of course, they too had their chorus lines. Every club had them. Lines were part and parcel of nightclub life, and a terrific opportunity for a chorus girl to be seen.

One of these talented "terpers" was Frances Nealy. She tap danced her way through the 1930s and 1940s, working chorus lines in some of the top Hollywood clubs, including the Club Alabam, Slapsy Maxie's, Shep's Playhouse, and the Nightlife. Though she was well versed in all chorine dance basics, Frances's specialty was tap. She was often brought out of the line to do her syncopated stair dance.

Aside from her club work, Frances Nealy also danced in the chorus of two Bill Robinson revues, in San Francisco and Philadelphia. She stepped out of the chorus occasionally to team up with other tap dancers, including Ike Parrish and Frank James. But it was primarily her work in the chorus lines of Hollywood-heyday nightclubs that kept her busy as a tap dancer through the years. In those glamorous and exciting times, at any given moment a star like Duke Ellington or Fred Astaire might just walk in and see the show. And that might just be the night when a chorus girl got her chance to step out of the line and tap her stair dance. It was for those moments that a chorus girl lived.

FRANCES NEALY — I was born on October the fourteenth, 1918, in San Diego, California. When I was a kid, tap dancing was sort of a way of life. Every parent sent their kid to dancing school to take tap lessons. Now I *thought* that every parent did. But I found out later many of the black people back then in the 1920s and 1930s didn't have money for dancing school. I took it for granted that everybody was doin' what I was doin'.

I started out with dance lessons, doin' little recitals and what have you. And then my mother and father separated. My mother sent me to a woman in Berkeley, where I was sort of boarded out. She used to give tap shows, so I was around musicians and dancing. I was always tall for my age, and when I was about twelve or thirteen years old, I was up there dancing with women who were

twenty-five, thirty-five, and forty years old.

I guess you'd say my first professional job was in Sacramento, at the Club Eureka. That's where I ran into a dancer who came in there, by the name of Juanita Pitts. The name of the act was *Pitts and Pitts*. Well, she was such a terrific dancer. I'd never seen a woman dance like she did before. She danced like the guys. She was good. She almost made me feel like I couldn't dance! Because I was still doin' more or less the Buck and Wing dancing. Meanwhile, they had come out with what they called the close rhythm. That was what bebop was to the music world. It was a new, sort of different way of dancing. They came off the ball of their foot, and started dropping their heel, and making sounds close to the floor. There was a variation between West Coast dancers and East Coast dancers. I think the East

Coast dancers were always better. Things were happening on the East Coast that weren't happening out here. That put them a little ahead of us. It was like, I learned the Shim Sham Shimmy in 1936. But from what I understand, the dance came out in the twenties. We didn't do it out here. There was a girl came from New York, and she had danced in the Cotton Club in New York on summer vacations when she was still a young girl. Anyway, she said, "You don't know the Shim Sham Shimmy?" I'll never forget it! I said, "No." She said, "Well, everybody does the Shim Sham Shimmy!" And she taught me that dance, which was then already ten or twelve years old.

I came to Los Angeles from Sacramento, and had my twenty-first birthday there. The only way I could get a job was as a chorus girl, because I didn't have a regular act. I was by myself as a dancer. So I danced from the late thirties like '38 and '39, all through the forties as a chorus girl. I *always* could tap dance. I *loved* tap dancing. And they always had tap dancers in the shows.

During the forties, I worked for Leonard Reed at Shep's Playhouse. It was one of the leading clubs in the city at that time for black shows. The shows usually consisted of a male singer, a female singer, an exotic dancer with chorus girls, a comic—and you had your tap dancers. The show would open up with the chorus girls. Then you had your male or female singer. Then you had the tap dance act. Somewhere in there, they had an exotic dancer. Usually, the chorus girls would do maybe a little number. And then you would come back with your other vocalist, who was either a man or a woman. And then whoever was the big act would take over. It was well rounded. Shows were anywhere from forty-five minutes to an hour long. The chorus girls, we opened and closed the show and usually did a middle number. They called that "the production."

In the clubs, you would always work with your back to the orchestra. The floor was center, and the people were all around at tables. The show would take place on the dance floor. Sometimes floors were elevated. The band was usually raised on a stage. The band would play in between shows and people would get up and dance. There would be two or three shows a night. It

The Reedettes, Leonard Reed's chorus line at the Lincoln Theatre, "L.A.'s Little Apollo." Frances Nealy right in step (fourth from left), 1944

In this glamorous "lobby," Frances Nealy's got it all, including tap shoes, 1951.

Nightclub act James and Nealy, 1940s. Frank James was a one-legged dancer and consequently the act soon dissolved: "They weren't too in favor of handicapped people in those days."

wasn't a tiring job, because I got the chance to be with all the greatest musicians. I loved the music. It's what inspired me to dance.

The clubs would always keep the band, keep the chorus girls, but bring in new principals. We'd change our chorus numbers every two weeks. If it was a slow season or right after the holidays or something like that, a lot of times the bosses wouldn't bring in a star attraction. And that's when the chorus girls got a chance to step out of the line and do their little specialty. Some of the chorus girls could sing pretty good. Some could do exotic dancing. When I stepped out of the line, I tap danced.

In looking for something to do in one of these particular shows, I had learned a stair dance from a dancer called Eddie Redman, when I was about fifteen years old up in Sacramento. Whenever I was ready to do a single, that's what I would always do—the stair dance.

I worked Slapsy Maxie's, on Wilshire Boulevard. That was a good job. Now, you'll have to think —back in those days they didn't have mixed lines. I worked with all black girls. Although there was a thing with black girls; they liked them fair with long hair. I mean, I used to look up sometimes and find that I was the darkest one. A real dark girl had a hard time finding work; she wasn't too popular at that time. For example, when I was nineteen, I came to Los Angeles. I went to this fella, Mr. Weldon, to get into movies. When I went there, the first thing he said was, "You're the wrong color." I couldn't believe it. He said I was too light. They liked them a *little* darker. Well, when I went to New York in 1945, I went to Atlantic City, and I was layin' out in the sun. And Ziggy Johnson, who had all the shows, he came down and said, "You better get out of that sun, or you won't be able to get a job! Because they really like *lighter* girls." I said, "My God, I'm too light for Hollywood and too dark for New York. Where am I gonna go?!" That was kind of rough for a nineteen-year-old.

Most of the shows I worked were black shows—but white clubs. I worked very, very few black clubs. In some it was a mixed crowd, but never a mixed show. Now, the Nightlife was pretty well mixed. That's why, I think, they started callin' em "black and tan," because your audience was mixed.

Frances Nealy joins with comedic tap dancer Ike Parrish. Parrish and Nealy worked clubs in Los Angeles, 1943.

Frances Nealy, 1953

In the early 1940s, I worked with Bill Robinson in his show called *Born Happy*. I was in San Francisco at the time. It was a musical revue, either at the Curran or the Geary. One of the girls in the show had to go back to New York, and I heard there was an openin' in the show for a chorus girl in the line. So I went down there and got the job. I worked with *Born Happy* for the run in San Francisco. Then I had the pleasure of working with Bill Robinson again in Philadelphia at a club called the Shangri-la.

During this time, I also teamed with a one-legged dancer, Frank James. We did a jitterbug routine and comedy. And we did a challenge: I would do a step, and Frank would try to do the step with his one leg. We had a good success. But at that time they weren't too cool on handicapped people. Because we got together up in San Francisco at the Champagne Supper Club when Linda Hopkins was there. And when I came down here and wanted to do the show, they said they couldn't use Frank because he was handicapped.

I also worked with Count Basie at the Orpheum Theatre in Los Angeles. That was when they had vaudeville. But I wasn't workin' the chorus. I was doin' a tap act with a fella named Ike Parrish. I always wanted to be with a good act so I could work all those big houses like the other acts were doin'. The name of our act was *Parrish and Nealy*. We did fifteen minutes—Parrish sang and did a little comedy. But it was basically a tap act.

During the 1930s and 1940s, there were always plenty of clubs to work at. We used to go to one club from the other. When one show closed, there was always another club to go to. Maybe it was in Arizona, maybe it was San Francisco. Sometimes I'd work right here in Los Angeles on one job, maybe six or eight months. If you saw a club that you liked, you would go there and find out who was producin' the show, or talk to the boss, and he'd bring you in. There were always shows. There was just always shows. And all the shows had tap.

June 6, 1988
Los Angeles, California

NIGHTCLUB CHORUS GIRL

DANCING WITH
THE BIG BANDS

JIMMY SLYDE

And what I can say is, it's been a
wonderful way of life.

B y the mid 1930s, vaudeville was on its way
out and a new form of entertainment was
taking its place—Presentation. Whereas
vaudeville consisted of a lineup of variety
artists, Presentation focused on the music.
The musicians were taken out of the orchestra pit
and placed right up on the stage. And the bands
were no longer any old rag-tag pit bands, they were
top-drawer swing orchestras. Names like Dorsey,
Barnet, Ellington, Goodman, and Calloway flashed
on theater marquees. These swing bands played all
across the country throughout the 1930s and 1940s,
but when they played the big 1,700–2,000-seat East
Coast theaters, they put together a tidy show that
was called a unit. The unit was comprised of a
chorus line of girls, a singer, a comic, and a dance
act—a tap dance act. That entire package was called
Presentation.

One of the circuits popular for Presentation was
the "'Round the World" circuit. Its heyday was
1930–1934. 'Round the World was a four-week tour
playing black houses. It began with a week in New
York at the Lafayette, then on to a week in Philadelphia at either the Earle, Standard, Uptown, or

Benny Carter, 1926

Jimmy Slyde dances at the Shirley Club in Everett, Mass., 1950.

With vaudeville on the way out, the Swing Era ushered in a new form of tap entertainment—Presentation. Big bands traveled with a chorus line, singer, comic, and tap dance acts. Jimmy Slyde (not pictured) danced with Louis Armstrong, 1942.

Pearl, then off to Baltimore at the Royal for a week, and then finishing up with one week in Washington, D.C. at the Howard. After this four-week tour was completed, the unit would lay off a week in New York, rehearse a new show at the Lafayette Hall, and then start off on the circuit once again. By the time a show played the same city the next time, it would be at least five weeks later.

Presentation was exciting entertainment. Its reign lasted for well over a decade. And in those days it was bandied about that, "Every band had a tap dance act," and "every tap dancer had a band." Certain tap dancers became associated with certain bands, though this was not always the case. A tap dancer might be booked with several different bands over a period of time. And those who had this good fortune were able to dance accompanied by all musical genres of the day.

Miller Brothers and Lois danced with Cab Calloway and Jimmie Lunceford; Coles and Atkins tapped with Cab Calloway and Count Basie; The Condos Brothers traveled with Benny Goodman, both Jimmy and Tommy Dorsey, Count Basie, Duke Ellington, Sammy Kaye; Bunny Briggs tapped with Duke Ellington, Charlie Barnet, Earl Hines, and Count Basie; Bill Bailey danced with Duke Ellington; Teddy Hale was with Count Basie; Baby Lawrence worked with Count Basie; Ralph Brown toured with Cab Calloway, Duke Ellington, and Jimmie Lunceford; The Four Step Brothers were with Tommy Dorsey and Benny Goodman; Jeni LeGon danced with Fats Waller and Count Basie; The Four Blazers worked with Don Redman, Tiny Bradshaw, and Benny Carter; The Four Flash Devils were with Duke Ellington and Count Basie; and Peg Leg Bates, perhaps the most ubiquitous of all, danced with Jimmy Dorsey, Charlie Barnet, Duke Ellington, Cab Calloway, Count Basie, Erskine Hawkins, Jimmie Lunceford, Claude Hopkins, Louis Armstrong, and Billy Eckstine—just to name a few.

During the Swing Era, there was another young tap dancer coming up who brought in a beautifully lyrical style—slides. His name, Jimmy Slyde. Jimmy Slyde began tap dancing in the early 1940s, in his teens. Through the influence of an early teacher, he began incorporating elaborate sliding into his tap dancing, which soon became his trademark. He joined together with another slide dancer, Jimmy "Sir Slyde" Mitchell, and together they formed the tap dance duo, The Slyde Brothers. They played nightclubs, burlesque, and theaters. Jimmy Slyde danced with the big bands throughout the United States, including those of Count Basie and Duke Ellington. Slyde's style of improvisation was fitting for the various styles that he encountered throughout the 1940s and 1950s. His deep sense of the music, combined with his near-poetic dance style, produced some of the most enchantingly tuned taps ever to hit the boards.

J I M M Y   S L Y D E — I was born in Atlanta. But I left Atlanta when I was about two, three years old. I was raised really in Boston, and went to school there. My mother always wanted me to play the violin. At ten years old the violin was my first introduction to music and the arts. And I was doing very well with it. But I just got so I wanted to become a dancer. 'Cause there were many theaters at the time, and they had great floor shows. You know, stage shows, vaudeville and like that.

In Boston the RKO Boston was a good theater. They had the Orpheum theaters, the Keiths, the Metropolitan Theatre. They had burlesque houses, they had the Globe. Boston was always a good show business city. Many people came to break in their acts. They had a lot of good clubs around, and theaters. The whole New England area, Maine,

Presentation shows traveled the " 'Round the World" circuit, which included black theaters in New York, Philadelphia, Baltimore, and Washington, D.C. The Count Basie band, pictured here, carries tap acts Miller Brothers and Lois, the Condos Brothers, Bunny Briggs, Bill Bailey, Baby Lawrence, Jeni LeGon, the Four Flash Devils, Peg Leg Bates, and Jimmy Slyde, among others, 1941.

New Hampshire, Rhode Island, was very big with show business.

I saw many acts. The great acts like Pops and Louis, The Chocolateers, Stump and Stumpy. Great dance acts, you know. Willie Covan, of The Four Covans, I mean—they were great acts. They weren't just great dancers, they were *acts!* And they worked. And a lot of people were very happy to see them, just to know that that part existed and there was some importance put on it at one time.

I started studying tap dancing when I was about twelve years old at the Stanley Brown Dance Studio. It was Two-ninety-five Huntington Avenue, in a place called the Gainsveld Building. Which is right across the street from the New England Conservatory where I was studying violin. Stanley Brown had a great school. That's where I met Bill Robinson, Derby Wilson, Bubbles. These were all friends of his. So, Stanley Brown started me off. He taught us all of the basics. And he gave his recitals every year in the New England Conservatory, in a place called Brown Hall. I remember it just like it was yesterday. 'Cause it was really my introduction into performing, so to speak. You know, these recitals and things.

I learned to slide from a guy named Eddie Ford. Eddie "School Boy." He was teaching at Stanley's at the time. What a great dancer. Another student,

Jimmy Mitchell ("Sir Slyde") and I started getting together, and Eddie started working on a slide routine for us. So we started calling ourselves The Slyde Brothers. And we were pretty *good!* I mean, *I* thought we were *great!* Other people just thought we were good. But, that's a matter of opinion.

In the late 1940s, we did a good solid eight-minute act. Which was all they wanted from a tap dancer in those times. And we were in many shows. The Florence Club, the Golden Anchor, just really great clubs. There were a couple of burlesque theaters and things like that that we worked. Everything that was available, we worked it. A lot of clubs. Burlesque was great, because it was the closest thing to vaudeville in show business at that time.

I also danced with some big bands. Danced with Basie's band and Duke Ellington. I grew up around good musicians and oftentimes played with them in California. Working the circuit with Basie's band, you were working theaters, probably had six or seven shows [a day] to do. First one was probably around ten-thirty A.M. The next one was the afternoon show, twelve to one P.M. Then you do something from four to six P.M. After that, you do the night shows, probably seven-thirty 'till nine P.M.

During a song, I would tap about three choruses up front. And then the band would come back in, and I'd do another two and a half, three choruses. Then I'd close it up and whip it out. With the bands, for the most part, I tried not to get too mired in routines, you know. I'm not a routine man. 'Cause dancing is a translating thing, especially if you're tapping. You're making sounds yourself, you know what I mean? Well, it is the sound. I think it's like instrumentation in the music business. Some things you go for the sound. The sound to me is always important. That's how I dance—by sound. I think that's probably my bebop influence. 'Cause I like bebop jazz.

But the sound is so important. Not just your "tonation." Tonation is important too. But it takes a long time to get aware or become aware of your tonation. Different dancers have different sounds. Some dance heavy, some dance light. I'm *strictly* sound-oriented. It's important. Me, myself, I'm not a great dancer or anything like that. People like Baby Lawrence and Teddy Hale, these were fantastic dancers. They could do anything. I'm a more of a tonation—I'm a musical dancer.

When I was dancing with the bands, people loved it. 'Cause dancing is a translating thing, especially if you're tapping. 'Cause you're making sounds yourself. Tap dancing fits with the music—it's like a summation there. Like I said, to me it's just a total pleasure. Not a bad way of life. I loved it. And what I can say is, it's been a wonderful way of life.

June 16, 1988
Boston, Massachusetts

29

THE "CLASS ACT": COLES AND ATKINS

CHOLLY ATKINS

There were so many Class Acts, I can't remember most of them. Because back in the late twenties and early thirties . . . it was class all the way.

The Class Act. It was everything it implied. And tap dancers who were part of Class Acts were just about the classiest thing around. Class Acts were more than just dress and manner; they were a combination of elegance mixed with grace—each ingredient being equally essential. Tailored suits, tuxedos, and white tie and tails were standard fare for the ordered attire of the three-a-day. From head to toe this special breed of performers was immaculate, sophisticated, and the last word in style. They could strut around the stage as though floating on air, and they carried themselves with abounding polish and charm. Dancers could have class, but to be part of a Class Act was something else altogether.

The Class Acts began developing in the teens and continued on into the middle of the twentieth century. These acts were made up of two, and oftentimes three, dancers. The formula consisted of precision dancing—executing identical steps together—and class—class from head to toe. Dress was impeccable and each movement a work of art. The term *picture dancing* was coined to describe this phenomenon of tap dance artistry that made

Cholly Atkins and Honi Coles dance on the stage of Philadelphia's Latin Casino, 1948.

Rhythm Pals. In 1939, he landed in New York City, and through a tip from Honi Coles, auditioned for the great World's Fair show *The Hot Mikado*, featuring the legendary Bill "Bojangles" Robinson. Honi Coles and Cholly Atkins first met in 1939; however, they did not dance professionally as a team until after World War II, when they formed their act Coles and Atkins.

Coles and Atkins—the definition of a Class Act. It ran twelve minutes. This was unusually long for a tap act, but then again, this was no ordinary tap act. Most tap acts of the time lasted anywhere from three to eight minutes, and they were just expected to tap. Any singing or comedy was considered an invasion of the other entertainers' territory. However, Coles and Atkins broke through that barrier with their delightful twelve-minute act comprised of singing, comedy, and of course, excellent tap dancing. It was a blend that was ultimately pleasing to the audience and proved to ensure their longevity as an act. Coles was the rhythm dancer, creating poetry with his feet; Atkins was the flash dancer, combining balletic moves with tap. Their confidence as individual dancers, and their rapport as a team, was winning. Their most outstanding number was their Soft Shoe. The Soft Shoe had been performed for nearly a century before Honi and Cholly began working on theirs. What set their version apart was the seemingly perilous slowness of it. Each step was executed in graceful symmetry that was absolutely breathtaking. Never before had such precision and style been brought to this tempo of Soft Shoe. The "slow Soft Shoe" became a favorite in their repertoire.

Honi Coles and Cholly Atkins were not the first to bring class to tap. But by the 1950s, they were definitely the last word in it.

"every motion as pretty as a picture!" In a Class Act, the dancers' very appearance on a stage could elicit sighs of delight from an audience. They were the peak of aesthetic entertainment.

One of the greatest class acts of all time was Coles and Atkins, Charles 'Honi' Coles and Charles "Cholly" Atkins. They met in a show business hotel in Harlem in 1939, and spent much of the next two decades dancing together. Honi Coles was unusually tall for a tap dancer, and his lanky build simply enhanced the graceful tap style he was then developing. His good looks and sparkling eyes exuded a rare joy beyond the charm he possessed. During the 1930s, Honi Coles was known as having the fastest feet in the business. His main interest was rhythm tap, that lyrical, percussive tap form that was developing rapidly in the 1920s and 1930s by many tap dancers, including the "father" of rhythm tap, John Bubbles. It was said that Honi Coles could do everything Bubbles did, but faster.

Cholly Atkins cut his teeth performing in nightclubs throughout the country with the duet The

CHOLLY ATKINS — I was born in Birmingham, Alabama, September 30, 1913. My parents moved to Atlanta, Georgia when I was two, and when I was four, the lady that my mother was working for moved to Buffalo, New York. She asked my mother to come along with her, and that's where I went to school, and that's where I got started in the show business. See, in high school our physical education teacher was a Russian, and he used to put on little recitals. He would teach us to do dance steps, like Soft Shoes and things of that type. That was the beginning of my tap dancing.

In 1933, I met a young boy named Bill Porter, who was a good tap dancer. We became good friends, and he started to teach me how to really tap. I picked up so fast until eventually we built an act together called The Rhythm Pals. At first, I used to do mostly singing in the act. Then we

Newspaper advertisement for Cholly Atkins and Bill Porter, The Rhythm Pals, who performed in Burlington, Ontario, Canada, in July, 1938

The famous six Cotton Club Boys on tour with Cab Calloway (center) and His Orchestra at the Chicago Theatre. Cholly Atkins (far right) shaped the Cotton Club Boys into one of the "hottest" precision tap sextets ever seen, 1940.

THE "CLASS ACT": COLES AND ATKINS

In 1939, Bill "Bojangles" Robinson brought *The Hot Mikado* to Flushing Meadows for the New York World's Fair. Cholly Atkins joined the show that year. This program cover illustrates the tap—and the panache—in this smash Broadway show.

Bill Robinson leads the chorus girls through some fancy hoofing in *The Hot Mikado* (lower photo), 1939.

Cholly Atkins and Dotty Saulters strike a snappy pose from their successful act Cholly and Dotty, 1941–1943.

did a couple of little elementary dance routines together. He did most of the heavy dancing at this time. In 1935, we went to New York, back to Buffalo, then to California, where we stayed until about 1938 doing nightclub stuff. We worked at Sebastian's Cotton Club, which was one of the biggest spots in California. Acts like Rochester and The Berry Brothers worked there. It was frequented by most of the movie stars.

In 1939, I moved back to New York and into a real show business building up in Harlem, Twenty-forty Seventh Avenue. It was real show business—The Mills Brothers, Honi Coles, Cook and Brown were all living there. Honi and I used to play softball together almost every day, because we weren't working steady at that time. Somebody mentioned to Honi that the Cotton Club was looking for a replacement for one of the Cotton Club Boys, and he suggested that I check it out. So I did, and secured the position. Two days later, I was working in the show. The Cotton Club Boys were not only working at the Cotton Club at that time, they were also doubling in *The Hot Mikado*, the show featuring Bill Robinson at the New York World's Fair.

The Hot Mikado was a takeoff on Gilbert and Sullivan's *Mikado*. The show was pretty much the same, with the exception that the music was swing! Michael Todd was the producer, and Bill Robinson was the star. It was a very colorful show. We must have had almost fifty people in the cast—a great choir, a lot of wonderful singers and dancers. We constantly played to capacity crowds, and it was great fun doing it! But the biggest thrill about the show was the last half hour—that was strictly Bill Robinson. The entire cast stood onstage, in heavy enormous costumes, while he did his regular vaudeville act. He told jokes, sang, and did several dances. That was the finale of the show every night. Did I ever enjoy that—oh, yeah! It was an education for any young tap dancer to stand behind the tap master himself on a nightly basis and just see how perfection really was. His right foot was just as true as his left foot. His taps were so clean and impeccable that he didn't miss anything, ever. And he was a very nice person. Insecure in many cases, you know, because he was not well educated as far as formal education was concerned. But he was very streetwise. It was a pleasure to have the opportunity to spend a couple of years working with him.

During all this time with *The Hot Mikado*, we

were doubling at the Cotton Club downtown. Cab Calloway and his band were at the Cotton Club then, and we were in the latter part of the show. We would do *The Hot Mikado* at the World's Fair, and then at nine-thirty P.M., cars were waiting for us to hop in, and they would race us over to the Cotton Club. When we got there it was around ten P.M.—we'd do that show, and then a second show. That meant three shows a night, and that went on for two years! Oh, we were all young, and it was exciting!

In the early 1940s, Honi and I had an opportunity to produce a show at the Paradise Club in Atlantic City. We put a little young starlet in the act, Dotty Saulters. I did a couple of numbers with her. Some producers and agents happened to come in and see us, and they made us offers to book the act after we closed Atlantic City during the summer. In September, when the show closed down, Dotty and I went on the road with The Mills Brothers, and Honi Coles went on the road with Cab Calloway. Dotty and I continued to work, especially out west, in the Midwest, Detroit, Chicago, St. Louis, Kansas City. I remember we were in Kansas City on tour with Louis Armstrong when Pearl Harbor was bombed. Not too long after that, Honi Coles got Cab Calloway to put us into his revue so that we could all be together again. Then April of 1943, Honi was inducted into the service, and in September of 1943, I was inducted. Cab kept my partner and wife, Dotty, as his band vocalist. But that was the end of our dancing for a few years.

World War II ended, and in late 1945, both Honi and I were finally discharged. We decided that we'd open up a dancing school. Coming out of the service we had no money, so we said, "We'll throw some little routines together and do an act for a while to make some money, and then we'll open a dancing school," which never really happened, because the act was so successful!

Honi was a real lyrical rhythm dancer. His tap dancing was smooth as silk. My style of tap dancing? I tried to mix up some nostalgia dancing, like the things that Eddie Rector did up on the toes, and some of the rhythm things that John Bubbles did, all along with some balletic things. You know, just create a style—because I wasn't really a great rhythm dancer like a Honi Coles or a Baby Lawrence or a John Bubbles. These great dancers really created complex dancing. I was a good dancer, but these gentlemen were *great* dancers.

Cholly and Dotty tear it up at New York City's Strand Theatre in *The Cab Calloway Revue*, 1943.

I was mostly a performer. I could do singing, dancing, talking, whatever was required. The same thing applied to Honi. That's why I think we did such a fine act together. Because we were versatile. That's the way I would basically describe my style—versatile.

Honi and I did a very interesting act. It was unusually complex, as far as talents were concerned. We drew on each other's talents—what we could do best individually and collectively. And we did a lot of good tap dancing. We sang well together, too, and we had some good humor. Not belly laughs, but just nice little snickers, and just enough to break up the dancing. It was a very wonderful variety act. But our forte was tap dancing. We had one number in the show that became quite a standard number—it was

our Soft Shoe. This particular dance was exceptionally slow and very well choreographed. We spent a lot of time on it, and it came across as a masterpiece. The dance looked so easy, but it was very difficult. We did it so slowly that the balance was very important. In other words, you couldn't get drunk and do it! When we started working on the number we didn't have a tune in mind, just started makin' it up. Ethel Waters was a good friend of ours, and she used to periodically come to our rehearsals. She came by one day while we were working on this number, and she began humming "Taking a Chance on Love," which was one of her famous numbers. We said, "That's a good tune," and so we kept it! That really made her very happy, and then we were pleased too, because it fit so well. The slow Soft Shoe became our trademark—two and a half minutes of beautiful tap dancing.

Our whole act was twelve and a half minutes. That was quite a lot for a tap act. Sometimes we would even stretch it, because when we got into our individual solos, if it felt good, we might do an extra eight or sixteen bars. Basically, we had what you call a get-on—it was an up-tempo thing. We'd get on, and we would do about sixteen bars of dancing before we would break the tempo down just about in half. Then we would go into a song, and after that we would do a little jazz chorus, strictly jazz dancing, and then we did a rhythm dance together. About two and a half choruses of dancing. It was done to "I Love You Truly." Then we did the Soft Shoe, and after that, Honi did his solo. He would always finish on the stage left, and at the very end of it, I would step out in front of him and take his bows! So, here

After World War II, Cholly Atkins (right) joined forces with veteran tap dancer Honi Coles (left). Together they formed Coles and Atkins, and mesmerized audiences around the country with their signature routine—the slow Soft Shoe, 1947.

This composite shot, taken at the world-famous Apollo Theatre in Harlem, New York City, captures the variety of Coles and Atkins's tap styles—Comedy, Flash, Soft Shoe, and Precision, 1954. Photo by Gordon Anderson, Apollo photographer.

we would do several jokes. You know, add a little humor. Then I'd get into my single. I did a lot of Wings. See, Honi did a lot of close intricate tap in his solo, and I did a lot of balletic flash stuff in my solo. At the end of my single, Honi would come back and join me. It was up-tempo, real fast, you know. I would do eight bars, he'd do eight bars, and we'd do eight bars together. We'd break the tempo down and do our exit material, which was a lot of big movements, not acrobatics, but just big movements like big Charleston steps. Then we'd get all the way over on stage right, and we would just run holding on to each other, and we'd just slide off the stage!

Throughout the late 1940s, we went on tours with big bands, night clubs, and finally a European tour in 1948. In '49 we auditioned for *Gentlemen Prefer Blondes*, were accepted, and stayed in that show until '52. We opened the second act to a tune called "Mamie is Mimi." It was one of the highlights of the show. Well, it

came in a very ideal spot. It was a cabaret scene, a Parisian nightclub, and all of the cast were seated, men in their tuxedos, and women in fine evening gowns, jewelry, and tiaras. A master of ceremonies would introduce the character Mimi—"And she will be supported by the very famous American team of Monsieurs Coles and Atkins." We came on to a very bright tempo [snaps fingers]. It was only about, I guess, maybe six minutes, a song and a dance. You see, the story was about a young girl from the South who went to Paris. Her name was Mamie, but when she got to Paris, they called her Mimi, and she was the toast of the Rue de la Paix:

> She was a gal, they called her Chippy.
> There was a gal we knew so well.
> She was a girl from Mississippi.
> But now she's a Mademoiselle.
> Her name was Mame.
> To France she came.
> Now Mamie is Mimi,
> the toast of the Rue de la Paix.

After we finished singing the song we did a tap routine while she was doing an exotic dance. We were like a picture frame around her. Then we did a finish together. It stopped the show every night. We would just come back and take bows and take bows until finally the people would sit down!

Actually, Agnes De Mille was supposed to stage our number in *Gentlemen Prefer Blondes*, but she didn't really know what to do with tap dancers

Throughout their partnership, Honi Coles (left) and Cholly Atkins (right) epitomized the Class Act, 1950s.

After *Gentlemen Prefer Blondes*, we had good contacts in the legit field of entertainment, and we ended up doing quite a bit in summer stock. We did a *Gentlemen Prefer Blondes*—they were doing that a lot of places. We did *Kiss Me Kate* and *Girl Crazy*. The first time we did *Kiss Me Kate* was in Dallas, Texas, 1953. We did the "Too Darn Hot" number. Originally, they had a singer sing it and two dancers dance it. But since Honi and I could both sing and dance, we did the vocal and the dance. In summer stock they were very creative, they would do things a little different than on Broadway. Like in *Girl Crazy*, they created a spot for us. We did our Soft Shoe while Margaret Whiting sang "The Man I Love." This was quite an attraction in the show, having two major things happening. They had her spotlighted on one side of the stage, and they had us on another side of the stage. It was very, very effective.

Finally Jule Styne, who composed the music, came to us and said, "Look, get yourself a piano player, sit down and figure out what you should do on this number—because you'll sit here until the show opens and nobody will know what to do with you!" And then he said, "When you get it all together, call me and let me look at it, and then I'll get her to come and look at the dance and put her stamp of approval on it." That's what we did. She came in and said, "Lovely, lovely. Wonderful. I've done a great job on this." And who got credit in the program? Yeah, she did! Honi did some things with her later, and they used to talk about it a great deal. She said it was the first thing that she took credit for that she didn't have anything to do with. It was very big of her to admit that.

Throughout the years, Honi and I developed our style of being a Class Act. We were both very tall, we dressed very well, and we carried ourselves. We didn't do all the acrobatic things other acts did. Most of our stuff was presented in a sophisticated manner. There had been a lot of great Class Acts: Pete Peaches and Duke, Three Little Words, and The Giants of Rhythm, which Honi was a part of for a while. There were just so many class acts, I can't remember most of them. Because back in the late twenties and early thirties, all of the acts were impeccable as far as dress was concerned. It was walking suits, tuxedos, full-dress suits, and all different colors, with the shoes to match. And it was beautiful. It was just part of the show business. Class all the way.

December 12, 1988
Las Vegas, Nevada

30

ON THE ROAD TO BEBOP

BRENDA BUFALINO

When you read the Charlie Parker charts, they're very complicated rhythmically, but, in fact, nowhere near what we do still. It's pretty sophisticated, what a tap dancer can do.

Something happened in the 1940s. Music changed. And it did not just go through some tidy evolutionary stage, it went through a wild revolution that affected anybody who had anything to do with dance.

When Charlie Parker and Dizzy Gillespie first took their band to the South, they stopped their audiences dead in their dancing shoes with their music. The crowd had come to dance; they loved to dance. It was the Swing Age, or so they thought. But they could not dance to *this* music—the music had started, and the dancers just stood there. Their faces fell in utter bewilderment. They were frozen by the rhythms emanating from the bandstand. Parker and Gillespie continued playing their music, but the crowd just never got the point.

What they heard from Charlie Parker and Dizzy Gillespie was about to become a national sensation. They had come to hear swing, and what they got was a new beat which their ears could not understand. That beat was called bebop.

Bebop's definition is "jazz characterized by rhythmic and harmonic complexity and innovation, lengthened melodic lines, executed with loud bra-

vura." But to most early listeners, it was just plain confusing. Dance fanatics suffered, but the tap dancers, in particular, struggled the most. The rest of America realized soon enough that they were not going to dance to bebop—bebop was something to listen to, to get 'into the groove' with. But tap dancers were resolved to conquer it. So they followed these new players around and listened for hours on end.

It was a struggle that, in retrospect, seems difficult to understand. But the musical chasm from jazz to swing to bebop was so vast, that it took great leaps of understanding for many. Some never got it. But the determined listened, and listened, and listened to this music until it seeped into their pores and became a part of their rhythmic existence. If they stuck it out long enough, they got it. Baby Lawrence got it. So did Bunny Briggs. So did Jimmy Slyde. And there was a girl who got it, too. Brenda Bufalino became one of the major figures to bring tap right on through this musical revolution. She was a keg of dynamite, and she had a pair of feet that just would not quit.

Brenda Bufalino grew up learning the traditional tap shtick of the 1930s: suitcase tap, jump-rope tap, hula tap. There was a lot of shtick in the 1930s. Brenda was the youngest member of a group called The Strickland Sisters, the "sisters" being her mother and aunt. They sang and recited, and she tapped. They came in on the tail end of vaudeville, so there was not much work there. However, there were plenty of USO and club dates to keep them busy. In the early 1940s, a tap act could really work.

By the time Brenda was fifteen years old, she began hearing a new rhythm inside her soul that was to become her obsession. She made her way to Boston to study with Stanley Brown. Stanley Brown's studio was *the* place to learn tap in Boston,

and many of the great tap dancers of the forties and fifties went through Brown's school. Brenda joined his company of dancers, and, after a time, moved on to New York City. It was in New York that she, like many other tap dancers, really encountered the revolution of bebop.

She spent every free hour of her day and night in smoky jazz clubs listening to all the great players of the age, not just of bebop, but of every form of jazz music that was happening. She listened to Max Roach, Clifford Brown, Wilber DeParis—jazz clubs dotted the island of Manhattan. For a young person interested in music, it was jazz heaven.

Through this immersion in the world of music, Brenda Bufalino conquered the phenomenon of tap dancing to bebop and modern jazz. More important, she became part of the music—she became another great jazz player.

BRENDA BUFALINO — I used to sit under the piano for four or five hours a day when I was a little kid. My aunt was preparing for her master's degree, and I would sit under there doing my school work. Even though I don't play an instrument—other than I play the concertina badly—music was obviously my biggest influence as a tap dancer. It really wasn't the dancers.

I was born in 1937 and grew up in Swampscott, Massachusetts. My family was a musical family. My grandfather had been a ballroom teacher, played the fiddle. My grandmother played the piano and sang. My aunt was a coloratura soprano and concert pianist. My mother was a lyric soprano and elocutionist. And my father was a contractor! He didn't have too much to do with all this, except he paid the bills.

I started dancing when I was about four. The school that I studied in was Professor O'Brien's Normal School of Dancing, which was a kind of an esoteric school. He taught interpretive, Egyptian, Spanish, acrobatic, and tap; and that was every day. He had about forty people in the room—all ages. There were no children's classes. And they were not allowed to have any recitals or any flash, anything that wasn't really serious. Most of the older girls went on to be Rockettes. I always thought I would be a Rockette. That would be what I did, you know. 'Cause that's where they all went. But that did not happen!

I guess I started with Professor O'Brien there when I was about six, and soon after, was incorporated in my mother and my aunt's show called The Strickland Sisters. And we did a lot of club dates in the New England area. It was a pretty great show, because they would have their Dutch medley, their Hawaiian medley, and then their Spanish medley. And I would do tap dancing to all that different music. My mother would do the monologue, and they would sing. They had beautiful voices! So it was pretty terrific. It was very atmospheric. My mother used to do Tennyson, Hiawatha, you know—it was heavy as well as entertaining. I came after vaudeville, but there were many examples for them. They were kind of vaudeville and classical. It's funny, though, my mother always kept wanting to be a jazz singer! But she was so trained, she could never make the switch!

During those early years, I was like the tap dancing kid. Aside from our nightclub work, I did a lot of USO, because that was during the war period. We would go to hospitals and army camps and traveled with a guy named "Pop" in a great big bus. And at that particular time, I think my specialty was roller-skating tap. I had a roller-skating act and a Hawaiian tap act! I mean, it was pretty strange. My Hawaiian number was, I think, "Lovely Hula Hands." I know I did a very big number to "Slow Boat to China." That was a big number, that was acrobatic tap. I used to do a lot of acrobatic things on stage, too.

By this time I had switched to a lady called Alice Duffy. She was much more theatrical. Mr. O'Brien had been very purist. It was all about "the dance," and "the spirit of the dance." Alice Duffy was about costumes! The more glitzier stuff that I did came from her. Jump-rope tap that I did, and the Hawaiian number, came from Alice Duffy. The more classical numbers, like suitcase dances to "I'm Alabamy Bound," came from Professor O'Brien. Tap dancing on suitcases was classical, in a way. The mixture of genres—Alice Duffy was into that.

In 1952, when I was around fifteen years old, I decided I wanted a "primitive" dance. I didn't even know what a primitive dance was. You know, when you're in Swampscott! But I wanted something primitive. So I used Ravel's "Bolero." I had a leopard-skin costume, and a hat with horns and fuchsia ostrich feathers, and claws, and I danced on this great drum. My mother's agent was sitting in the audience at a recital, and he said, "I think she should go to Stanley Brown. I think that's where she belongs."

My mother, of course, didn't know who Stanley Brown was. But the agent could see from what I was doing what I was after. My folks were divorced by then, so I kind of wandered into Stanley's studio by myself. I was wearing my pink dress, my white hat, my white shoes, and my white gloves. Because, you know, if you're from Swampscott, you *always* wore gloves, and you *always* wore a hat! And I remember standing downstairs at Stanley's—I heard the drums upstairs. The contrast was quite shocking. And I just fell in love with it. Stanley tried to send me home. He said, "You don't belong here. If you come here, you are going to be very unhappy. You're turning your back on your own tradition. And you will never be happy if you try to do this. There is no place for you in this world." And of course, that was all I needed to hear. That made it even more desirable!

And so, I went into Stanley Brown's, and that really was the turning point for me. 'Cause, although I had heard my mother a lot playing jazz in the house and trying to sing jazz herself, I never was in the world of it. Between the modern primitive that was taught there, and the jazz dance, and the jazz tap dance, which I had never heard before, that was probably the beginning of my style of dancing.

So I stayed there and joined the troupe from Stanley's very quickly—in which we did these great galas. Then we started working in nightclubs. I was very much underage, only fifteen, and we opened up in a sailor bar. It was really seedy! There was sawdust on the floor, you know. We stayed there for nine months. We were so successful, they redid the whole club. By the time we left they had lights, a new bar, and a new floor! Needless to say, the sawdust was off the floor.

Stanley's was a big dance group. We all did solos as well as the group work. It was *outrageous*, you know, it was really outrageous stuff —the one I remember the best was doing the "Red Shoes" on point with Afro-Cuban body work!

I don't know too much about Stanley's background, but Stanley was one of the major teachers of tap dancing in the country. [Jimmy] Slyde came out of Stanley's. A lot of people came through Stanley's. It was a very hip place. He really turned out a polished professional. It was a great time, and there was a lot of jazz music there. He had Sandy Sandiford, a fine arranger who was a mentor to a lot of future arrangers. And so it was the first time for me that I really was able to work with arrangements and musicians—although all the stuff that I did with my family was live—my aunt sang or we had another accompanist. But this was when I really began to understand jazz arranging.

Stanley gave me a number to "I Like New York in June" ["How About You?"]—I *hated* that song.

At age fourteen, Brenda Bufalino is the sweet image of a girl from Swampscott, with no hint of the explosive percussive dancer lurking within, 1951.

And I *cried*! I was very temperamental. Terribly temperamental. And I went to Sandy in tears and said, "I hate this song!" But, that's when I learned that a tune is only a tune—it's what you do with the arrangement that counts. And he made the most smashing arrangement for me.

At that time, there was a lot of jazz in Boston. I would go from high school, take the bus into Boston, take classes, and either work or go to the jazz clubs. Then I'd go home late, late, late, and get up and go to school. Needless to say, I didn't

---

Brenda Bufalino as caricatured by Jerry Jennings, circa 1955

do too well in school! Because I was really seriously in training and listening to music. It was a great time. Modern music was beginning to come through. There was a musical change. And that's how it happened that I was a "cusp" dancer, I was right on the cusp of the change. The old influences were there; I learned the old stuff, but I was very excited about the new music that was coming out. But I didn't figure there was any way to incorporate modern jazz and tap. It took me a long time to figure out how to use the newer music when I was tapping.

By the time I got to New York, which was soon after joining Stanley's troupe, I got really involved in Max Roach and Clifford Brown, that great group [Max Roach and Clifford Brown Quintet]. In fact, I used to listen to them every night, because it upset me. I didn't understand it. I didn't understand what they were doing. I was really trying to grapple with it. And I have a funny sort of mind—everything goes in the back door. Things don't hit me frontally. I can't tell you who I heard, or any particular moment when the light went on. It's just that I was there at that cusp period. And I think, probably, the biggest turning point for me musically, where I really began to understand where I was going, was the period I was studying Max Roach. You know, where I would just go every night.

I didn't have much opportunity to play with these players who were stretching. I was playing with much less, you know, club bands who weren't particularly great. I never had that wonderful opportunity of traveling with a Cab Calloway. My opportunity with music was always to have a terrible band! That was my good fortune! Which is not altogether bad. Because you learn how to deal with music. To make bad music good.

I used to go to the 125 Club up in Harlem every night after I finished my shows and listen to the jam sessions up there. There were after-hour jam sessions from four till seven or eight o'clock in the morning. I was really saturating myself with music, and my ear got very developed at that particular time. It kind of stayed with me. I was fortunate enough to work later on in my life with great players in the avant-garde. I went even past the modern jazz and just completely into the avant-garde.

I also got interested in how pieces were put together. I lived upstairs over Jilly's Black Magic Club. So I would listen to the cocktail lounge players. And they played very sophisticated songs. My lyrical sense also got very titillated, and I started putting things in my act at that time like Billy Strayhorn's "Lush Life." My arranger, Sandy, said, "What are you doing with this song? You're too young to use this song!" But at that time, I was into a lot of dissonance. I would find songs that were pretty out there and fairly dissonant and complicated to dance to.

I liked dissonance, and I liked a certain amount of chaos and cacophony. The degree of it that was coming out of bebop—the kind of splitting, the splitting of phrases, the harmonics—was getting more complicated. It sounded quite frenetic and wild. Now, it doesn't. Now, we say, "Well, what was the big deal about that?" It seems quite tame by comparison. But at the time, it was pretty unsettling what they were doing. And it was a time that musicians were really exploring. So anyway, it was pretty hot. Pretty wild.

I lived down on Fifty-second Street, so I could go to Birdland, I could go to Basin Street. I used to go to Jimmy Ryan's on Monday nights, and that was New Orleans jazz. There was Wilber DeParis, and Sydney DeParis. They were wonderful players. They used to take all the chairs and everything out, and I could dance with them on Monday nights, because that was the slow night. And so I was just *in* it. You know, I was right on the street,

I was living on the street, and I was a kid. So the people were pretty nice to me.

It was a very hot moment for jazz, 'cause as I said, the mix was still being done. You had the really modern players, like Basie would come in—and then you would have Wilber DeParis playing the New Orleans—and the Australian Jazz Quartet would come in—so that it was a big wonderful creative mix of music that really, I think, took me for the rest of my life. Plus, it was still a time when people were jamming. To be able to go to the clubs uptown and hear jam sessions for hours on end was something else. They were just playing nonstop.

And as much as I listened to music, I'd have to say that a lot of times the tap dancers did know more about music and the rhythms than the musicians did. I was studying tap with Honi Coles for a short time when he had his studio on Fifty-second Street with Pete Nugent. Honi's phrasing seemed revolutionary to me—as much so as the music of the time. His influence on both tap dancers and musicians was tremendous. I think musicians were stymied by the rhythms that tap dancers were laying down. I could definitely see a few of the dancers of that time influencing the transition of music. It's very logical, because the tap dancers were there before the changes happened. And everything comes in to everyone through the back door. I don't imagine that someone would say, "Well, I think I'll take that from that tap dancer." I don't think that's the way it's done. I think it just kind of evolves. 'Cause a tap dancer's rhythms are much more sophisticated, even to this day, than the drummer's rhythms. When you read the Charlie Parker charts, they're very complicated rhythmically, but, in fact, nowhere near what we do still.

It's pretty sophisticated what a tap dancer can do. Which is why, I think, the public has such a hard time with its form, because it is so sophisticated. Unless it's the traditional three steps and a break. Then it can be heard! You know, that's part of the reason, I think, that it's hard to get tap across. 'Cause it's still ahead of its time. I think tap is a very visceral form. There's a double-edge problem, because people identify tap dancing personalities so strongly, that a lot of times the art of it will get lost behind the personality. And yet, that's what it is. But even the great jazz players could play their figures with wit. And those are the ones that are really remembered. An audience is subliminally waiting for the wit, as well as the rhythm. They don't want to be disturbed with glitches. Rhythmic glitches disturb an audience without any of them knowing why. So if something's steady, they can relax behind it and really get into it. I think audiences expect a certain degree of wit in presentation. And part of the reason the personality is so important is because it is also a way of executing a figure with a certain wit. It will help describe the figure clearly.

I learned that an audience will also go along with the narrative of tap. They will go along with an indeterminate narrative, if the emotional substance is correct that's behind it—what is being said emotionally is what is being done rubato with the taps, the poetic figure of tap. They feel it, yet it's very rare that they're gonna know *why* they're feeling it. It's a very educated audience that says, "That's so interesting the way that figure played against the other figure."

I've spent a lot of time thinking about how the audience perceives the form. It's really important for us to do that. Why certain things work and others don't. I'm always telling dancers when they're learning tricks [complicated, difficult steps or rhythms], "If you learn to walk four steps in the right way, you'll get a hand. You do your tricks and you'll get nothing, if they're not done in the right way and in the right place. Some other guy will come in and just walk across the stage and he'll get all the applause, and you just *killed* yourself!"

======================================

It's all very complex, the business of tap. And I think what drew me to it was the ability to be a musician—what the form implies musically—that I can compose. Because I'm not that much of a visual person, I'm a much more oral person. And I *love* music. That gives me the opportunity to arrange and compose, to write music for it. So it's quite perfect. I never lose my interest in it. And I think rhythm is magic. One day I have a wish to take a roof off of a building with rhythms. I have a very strong feeling that rhythm is the magic component. You know—that it can change things. That rhythm can really change levels of other people's energy—this is a very exciting thing. And if you can make it in just the right connection, you can take a roof off a building! I'm waiting for that day!

May 25, 1989
Washington, D.C.

(On the day of this interview, Congress declared May 25, Bill Robinson's birthday, National Tap Dance Day. The bill was signed into law by the President of the United States.)

ON THE ROAD TO BEBOP

GLOSSARY

ACROBATIC: Tumbling, splits, etc., often incorporated into tap routines.

AD LIB: To dance as one wishes without regard to a set pattern of movements—to improvise.

AROUND the WORLD: A popular 1920s movement. The dancer puts both hands down on the floor in an open position while at the same time squatting down, using one foot to balance, then swinging the free leg out over stationary leg and hands (having to lift hands and drop them again as leg goes around).

ARTHUR MURRAY: Popular dance instructor since the 1920s. The Arthur Murray Dance Studios have taught thousands of students in the art of ballroom dancing.

BAMBALINA: Traveling Time Step, invented by Eddie Rector.

BLACK BOTTOM: Dance craze of 1926, which followed the Charleston; contained black influence; strictly a theatrical form of dance and rarely ever used in social dancing.

BLACK-UP: Theatrical term for putting burnt cork on the face. White actors in minstrel shows blacked-up. And later, black performers blacked-up, so the audience would not know they were black.

BREAK: A two-measure dance movement that follows a six-measure movement; to complete an eight-measure phrase.

BUCK and WING: An American clog dance marked by winglike steps, done mostly on the balls of the feet. Forerunner of rhythm tap.

CAKE WALK: Originally, a form of entertainment among African Americans in which the prize of a cake was given for the most accomplished steps and figures in walking; later, a stage dance developed from these movements.

CHALLENGE: A tap challenge occurs when tap dancers attempt to top each other with tap steps.

CHARLESTON: A twisting movement turning the toes inward and then outward; dance craze of 1925, considered to be of black origin, from Charleston, South Carolina. Performed both onstage and in social dancing, the dance has been revived numerous times.

CHITTLIN' CIRCUIT: See "'Round the World."

CLASS ACT: The Class Act consists of a tap team (or trio) that performs precision dancing, executing identical steps together. The act makes the dance a thing of beauty and sophistication, laced with taps. High-style, grace, sleekness.

CLASSICAL TAP: Use of ballet and/or ballroom with tap; use of upper-body movement; complete dancing. Used extensively in movies. (Not to be confused with tapping to classical music.)

CLOG DANCING: Dancing with wooden clog shoes.

CLOSE RHYTHM: Style of tap dancing introduced in the 1920s, popularized by John Bubbles, and carried on through the present. It employs close footwork, including many heel drops to bring in a rhythmic beat. Also called heel and toe, jazz tap, and rhythm tap.

COMEDY: Use of comedy movement in dance. Also known as legomania and eccentric.

CRAMP ROLLS: Movement employing steps and heel drops in specific patterns.

CUTAWAY. Cinema term meaning cutting away from the main action.

ECCENTRIC: Misdirection rooted to the ground. Angular work, fooling the eye.

ESSENCE: A basic movement associated with Soft Shoe dancing containing many and varied rhythm patterns.

FANCHON and MARCO: A brother and sister team that formulated motion picture prologues (units) that traveled to a circuit of theaters. 1920s–1930s.

FLASH: Wildly exciting dance movements incorporating acrobatics. Often used to finish a dance.

FLASH ACT: A dance act that incorporated flash as the main component.

FLIP: An acrobatic move accomplished by jumping in the air and spinning the body in a circle, head over heels. This move was used extensively by top flash tap acts from the 1930s to the 1950s.

FREEZE and MELT: The sparkling contrasts between posed immobility and sudden flashing action.

HEEL and TOE: Style of tap dancing introduced in the 1920s, popularized by John Bubbles, and carried on through the present. It employs close footwork, including many heel drops to bring in a rhythmic beat. Also called close rhythm, jazz tap, and rhythm tap.

HEEL DROP: A forceful dropping of the heel to the floor while the weight is placed on the ball of the same foot.

HOOFER: A tap dancer who concentrates on the per-

cussion of tap as opposed to incorporating upper-body movement.

HOOFING: Tap dancing with no other dance influence.

IMPROVISATION: To perform without dancing to a set pattern of steps or routine. See "Ad Lib."

JAZZ TAP: Style of tap dancing introduced in the 1920s, popularized by John Bubbles, and carried on through the present. It employs close footwork, including many heel drops to bring in a rhythmic beat. Also called close rhythm, heel and toe, and rhythm tap.

JIG TOP: The black tent show at a carnival. Circa 1900s to 1920s.

JINGLE TAP: A metal tap containing a loose washer within, worn on the heel. It produces extra sounds when tap movements are executed.

JIVE SPLIT: Also known as a jazz split, a split where the dancer drops to the floor, fully extending the front leg straight forward, but bending the back knee. A much easier move to accomplish than a full split.

JUMP ROPE TAP: A novelty tap dance form that incorporated jump roping with tap dancing. Popular during the 1920s and 1930s.

LAYING DOWN IRON: Straight-forward hoofing.

LEGOMANIA: A form of "rubber legs." Use of wild and wiggly leg movements in the air.

MAXIE FORD: A fast-paced shuffle step with leaping from one foot to the other.

MAXIES: See Maxie Ford.

MESS AROUND: A stationary step, hands on hips, feet apart, bouncing up and down on heels, hips rotate in a circular motion.

MULE KICKS: Russian dance, kicking out the legs.

NOVELTY: Novelty tap dances incorporated specialty props such as jump ropes, suitcases, stairs, et cetera.

ONE MAN DANCE: Several dancers pressed up against each other, front to back, dancing in exact unison.

OVER the TOP: A flash step consisting of bending forward, springing up, and bringing each leg, in turn, around from the back and across the front of the other leg.

PADDLE and ROLL: Close floor work using heel and toe, alternating feet back and forth.

PICKANINNY (aka: PICK): Black children performers who often accompanied white female singers as insurance for a "sock" finish.

PALACE, THE: The pinnacle theater of American vaudeville. Located in New York City on West Forty-seventh Street and Broadway.

PASS: An individual of mixed racial heritage who could pass for white.

PASSING: see Pass.

PRESENTATION: Followed vaudeville. Swing bands were taken out of the orchestra pit and put on the stage as featured entertainment. In big cities the bands expanded their show by putting together a package including singers, tap dancers, and comics.

PROLOGUE: A short musical revue featured before the showing of the movie. Popular during the early 1930s, and tied in to the theme of the movie (e.g., if the movie was set in China, it would be an Oriental revue).

PULLBACK: A hopping back-brush-step movement: With the weight on one foot, extending the other foot in the air, usually to the rear, executing a back brush with the supporting foot, landing on the ball of the same foot.

PULLING the TRENCHES: A flash step of the old school consisting of long backward slides on the outside edge of the foot, alternating each leg, while the body is bent forward at the waist and swinging the arms 180 degrees in a windmill fashion.

RHYTHM TAP: Style of tap dancing introduced in the 1920s, popularized by John Bubbles, and carried on through the present. Also called heel and toe, jazz tap, and close rhythm. It employs close footwork, including many heel drops to bring in a rhythmic beat.

RHYTHM WALTZ CLOG: A modified form of the Waltz Clog introduced with Ragtime when syncopation became the vogue in music. This resulted in more complex rhythm patterns for the dancers compared to the simple rhythms of the first forms of Waltz Clog.

RIFF: A movement combining a forward brush and heel scuff on the same foot.

'ROUND the WORLD: Popular during the 1920s–1930s, 'Round the World was a four-week vaudeville tour playing black houses. The tour began with a week in New York at the Lafayette, then on to a week in Philadelphia at either the Earle, Standard, Uptown, or Pearl, then off to Baltimore at the Royal for a week, and then finishing up with one week in Washington, D.C. at the Howard.

ROUTINE: A set series of steps to a set piece of music.

RUBBER LEGS: A form of movement usually associated with eccentric, legomania, or comedy dancing, wherein the legs are used in a loosely exaggerated fashion.

RUSSIAN: A style of ethnic Russian dance employing exciting kicks and turns. Popularized and incorporated into tap dance at the turn of the century. The moves were used in flash routines extensively even up until the 1950s (e.g. The Four Step Brothers, Gene Kelly).

SHIM SHAM SHIMMY: A four-step routine created in the 1920s by Leonard Reed and Willie Bryant, originally called Gofus. Shimmying of the shoulders added. (The four steps are: 1. Shim Sham, 2) Push Beat and a cross over, 3) Tack Annie, 4) Half Break, and then the Walk Off is tagged on.)

SHUFFLE: A front brush followed by a back brush using the ball of the foot, executed to the front, side, or back.

SLIDE: A pushing of the free foot forward or in any desired direction with or without weight. A slide may be executed from numerous approaches.

SNAKE HIPS: A form of rolling hip movements used extensively in the 1920s by burlesque and shimmy dancers.

SOFT SHOE: A dance performed in a slow 4/4 time; originally was danced with sand on the floor or without the use of metal taps. The most common step or movement to be associated with Soft Shoe dancing is the Essence.

SPLIT: Dropping to the floor with legs fully extended out, either to the sides, or front leg forward and back leg back.

SRO: Standing room only.

STOP TIME: A melody broken by the irregular flow of notes through the use of rests. In a simplified form, chords played on the first beat of each measure with a rest on the following three beats.

STRUT: Movements derived from Cake Walk. Attached to elegance. Strutters held shoulders erect, head up, brought their knees up high when moving forward, pointing their toes while doing so. Best described as imitation of a peacock or chicken.

SYNCOPATION: A temporary displacing or shifting of the regular metrical accent. The common varieties occur when a sound is begun on an unaccented beat and continued through the following accented beat.

TAB SHOW: see Tabloid Show.

TABLOID SHOW: An abbreviated vaudeville show, also known as a Tab show.

TAP CHARLESTON: Incorporation of tap dancing into the Charleston dance. Popularized in 1925.

THEATRE OWNERS BOOKING ASSOCIATION: see T.O.B.A.

THROUGH the TRENCHES: see Pulling the Trenches.

TIME STEP: One of the most common of tap steps. An eight-measure step placed at the beginning of a dance routine. A total of six Time Steps was usually executed, followed by a break. Originally used to establish the tempo of a routine for the musicians, as rehearsals were rarely held in small-time vaudeville.

T.O.B.A.: Theatre Owners Booking Association (aka: Tough on Black Asses). The Black vaudeville circuit; black entertainers performing in black theaters.

TOE STANDS: A movement of the old school of tap wherein the dancer is on the points of both feet. Can also be done on one foot at a time—Toe Stand.

TRADE EIGHTS: Two or more dancers, or a dancer and musician(s), each taking (playing or dancing) eight bars of music alternately.

TRENCHES: see Pulling the Trenches

TRIPLETS: A group of three tap sounds performed on each beat of music, e.g., "one and a, two and a, etc."

WALTZ CLOG: A dance in 3/4 time. Originally performed in clogs (wooden soles and heels of maple) that beat out a rhythm upon the floor or stage. This form of dance today is usually performed in shoes with metal taps attached; it has become a form of tap dancing.

WINGS: A movement executed on one foot while the other foot is in the air: With the toe of the supporting foot turned inward, throw the foot outward in a swishing movement, executed on the outer edge of the sole. On the outward swishing movement, the ankle rolls out. The arms are oftentimes thrown out in a circular movement, in a flapping motion, thus, the term "wings." The foot hits the floor a number of times, the number determines the name of the step, i.e., a Three-Tap Wing, means that each foot tapped the floor three times. The Five-Tap Wing was invented by Nick Condos.

APPENDIX A

TAP DANCERS AND TAP ACTS, 1900–1955

AARON, CHARLIE: 1930s–1940s. West Coast (San Francisco) teacher; produced some of the best nightclub tappers. Called The Tap Dancing Master of Ceremonies of San Francisco. (W)

ALTON, BOB: 1930s. Dance director in films. (W)

ANDERSON, MACEO: 1920–present. Acrobatic, flash, tap. Part of Four Step Brothers. Clubs, movies, theaters. (B)

ASTAIRE, ADELE: 1905–1930s. Classical tap, comedy. Sister of Fred Astaire. Part of team The Astaires. vaudeville, Europe, Broadway. (W)

ASTAIRE, FRED: 1905–1970s. Classical tap, comedy,. Brother of Adele Astaire. Part of team The Astaires. vaudeville, Europe, Broadway, Movies, radio, records, television. (W)

ASTAIRES, THE: 1905–early '30s. Adele and Fred Astaire, brother and sister tap dance act. Appeared in vaudeville, Europe, Broadway shows. (W)

ATKINS, CHARLES "CHOLLY": 1930–present. Rhythm, Soft Shoe. Cotton Club Boy. Part of team Coles and Atkins. (B)

*There were literally thousands of tap acts between 1900–1955. The list presented here is a compilation of acts and information remembered by those interviewed in this book. Ethnicity of act has been noted for historical perspective and record: (A) = Asian, (B) = black, (W) = white.

Fred and Adele Astaire

AUSTIN, VIVIAN: 1940s. Movies. (W)

BABB, DOROTHY: 1940s. Spins. Jivin' Jacks and Jills. (W)

BAILEY, BILL: Late 1920s–1950s. Flat-footed board beater. Pearl Bailey's brother. (B)

BARNES, MAE: 1920s. Appeared in *Runnin' Wild* (1923) (B)

BARTO AND MANN: 1920s–1930s. Dewey Barto and George Mann. "Dumb" act, Dewey Barto was very small, and George Mann was very tall. Comedy, knockabout. Vaudeville, movies. (W)

BARTON, JAMES: 1920s–1930s. Top Clog dancer. (W)

BATES, PEG LEG: 1920s–1970s. Top one-legged tap dancer. Rhythm tap. Appeared in vaudeville, clubs, Broadway, television. (B)

BRANT, PEG E.: 1930s–1950s Jivin' Jacks and Jills. (W)

BELL, GENE: 1940s–present. Silas Green Revue (1945). (B)

BERRY BROTHERS, THE: 1920s–1940s. Ananias, James, and Warren. Top Flash Act, sensation, strut, cane. Performed in Cotton Club, in Paris, appeared in films. Never wore taps. (B)

BERRY, ANANIAS: 1920s–1940s. King of the strut. Part of The Berry Brothers. (B)

BERRY, JAMES: 1920s–1940s. Comedy tap, acrobatic; cane. Part of The Berry Brothers. (B)

BERRY, WARREN: 1930s–1940s. Tap, acrobatic; cane. Part of The Berry Brothers. (B)

BILLY AND MILLY: 1940s. Soft shoe, stomp routines. (B)

BLAKE, ATTA: 1920s–1930s. Originated Tap Charleston. (B)

BLUM, AL AND GUSSIE: 1925–1936. Brother and sister act. Rag doll dance. Al eccentric. Headliners on the Orpheum Circuit. (W)

BLUM, BEA: 1950s–present. Part of the Tommy Conine Trio. West Coast teacher. (W)

BOLGER, RAY: 1930s–1980s. Legomania, comedy, eccentric tap. Appeared on stage and screen. (W)

BRADLEY, CLARENCE "BUDDY": Early 1920s–1960s. Tap teacher. Created dance routines for many Broadway musicals in the late twenties and early thirties.

Coached some of the tap greats, including Pat Rooney, Jessie Matthews, Ann Pennington, Eddie Foy, Ruby Keeler, Jack Donahue, Adele and Fred Astaire, Tom Patricola, Eleanor Powell, Paul Draper. Choreographed in Europe during 1920s–30s. (B)

BRIGGS, BUNNY: 1920s–present. Paddle-and-roll tap. Child society dancer. Big Band dancer. (B)

BROWN BUDDIES, THE THREE: 1930s–1940s. Flash, tap. Curly, Happy, and Smiley. (B)

BROWN, EDDIE: 1930s–present. Rhythm tap. Danced with Bill Robinson Revue 1933–39. West Coast nightclubs 1940s. (B)

BROWN, ERNEST: Part of team Cook and Brown. (B)

BROWN, KING RASTUS: 1920s. One of the first and foremost Buck and Wing dancers. (B)

BROWN, RALPH: 1930s–present. Cotton Club solo act. Dancer with Cab Calloway orchestra. (B)

BROWN, STANLEY: 1930s–1940s. Renowned Boston

Ray Bolger

tap teacher. The Stanley Brown Dance Studio was located at 295 Huntington Avenue in the Gainsveld Building. (B)

BROWNS, THE THREE: early 1930s. Flash and tap. (B)

BRYANT, MARIE: 1930s–1950s. Popular chorus girl. Clubs, movies. (B)

BRYANT, WILLIE: 1920s–1930s. Class Act. Vaudeville. (B and W)

BUBBLES, JOHN (JOHN W. SUBLETT): 1920s–1950s. Father of rhythm tap, brought in the heel. Top strut dancer. Part of top Class Act Buck and Bubbles. Originated the role of Sportin' Life in Gershwin's *Porgy and Bess*. Opened the door for modern jazz-tap percussion. Bubbles contributed the sounds that prepared America's ear for bebop. Vaudeville, theaters, movies. (B)

BUCK AND BUBBLES: 1920s–1950s. Top Class Act. Buck played the piano, Bubbles danced. Comedy, singing, and dancing. Vaudeville, theaters, movies. (B)

BUCK (FORD LEE "BUCK" WASHINGTON): 1920s–1950s. Part of top Class Act Buck and Bubbles. Played piano, comedy tap. Vaudeville, theaters, movies. (B)

BUCKNER, CONRAD "LITTLE BUCK": 1950s. Acrobatic tap. (B)

BUDDY AND JUDY: late 1930s–1940s. Clubs, theaters. Swing tap. (W)

BUFALINO, BRENDA: late 1940s–present. Clubs, teacher, one of the greatest exponents of jazz tap. East Coast. (W)

BUSINESSMEN OF RHYTHM, THE: 1950s. Acrobatic, Flash, Tap. Danced with trays: Flew over chairs, caught trays in midair, went directly into splits. (B)

BURNS AND ALLEN: 1920s–1930s. George Burns and Gracie Allen. Soft Shoe dancers. Vaudeville, movies. (W)

BURNS, SAMMY: 1920s–1930s. Teacher (1755 Broadway, NYC). (W)

CAGNEY, JAMES: 1920s–1950s. Buck and Wing. Teacher. Broadway 1920s–1930s. Hollywood movies 1930s –1950s. (W)

CARLOS, ERNEST: 1930s. Top NYC teacher, Ernest and Madison. (W)

CARPENTER, LOUIS SIMMS: 1920s–1945. Part of Four Flash Devils 1930s–40s. Later part of Copasetics. (B)

CASTLE, NICK: 1930s–1940s. Top movie tap choreographer. (W)

CHANEY, ISAIAH "LON": 1940s–present. Comedian and dancer. (B)

CHEFS, THE THREE: 1930s–1940s. Flash Act. Dressed as chefs, held trays with food on them. Movie Shorts. (B)

CHILTON AND THOMAS: 1920s–1940s. Tap Charleston. Danced on pedestals. Played white theaters, Fanchon and Marco, Europe. (B)

CHOCOLATEERS, THE: late 1930s–1940s. Comedy, acrobatic tap; knockabout, kneefalls. Originally from West Coast. Originated "Peckin'" dance craze. (B)

CHOCOLATE STEPPERS, THE: early 1930s. Flash Act. (B)

CHOLLY AND DOTTY: 1940s. Cholly Atkins and Dotty

Saulters. Toured with Cab Calloway. (B)

CHUCK AND CHUCKLES: 1940s. Comedy tap. Child act styled after Buck and Bubbles. (B)

CLARK, JUDY: 1940s. The "B" Betty Hutton, movies. (W)

CLAYTON, LOU: 1910s–1940s. Classy hoofing. Performed in vaudeville, on Broadway, and with Clayton, Jackson, and Durante (Lou Clayton, Eddie Jackson, Jimmy Durante) at Club Durante, at the Palace Theatre. (W)

CLIFF AND RADCLIFF: 1920s. Tap, Soft Shoe. Radcliff played trumpet, sang like a man and woman, appropriately changing hats. (B)

COHAN, GEORGE M.: 1900–1930s. Stiff-legged Buck and Wing. Broadway star, writer, composer, director, producer. (W)

COLES AND ATKINS: mid-1940s–1950s. Honi Coles and Cholly Atkins. Danced with Big Bands; Europe, Broadway, theaters, clubs. Class Act, Soft Shoe, Rhythm. (B)

COLES, CHARLES "HONI": 1930s–1980s. Class Act. Soft Shoe, rhythm. Part of Coles and Atkins. (B)

COLLINS, DEAN: 1940s. Choreographer, dancer. Movies. (W)

COLLINS, LEON: late 1930s–1987. Rhythm tap. Out of Boston. (B)

COMPTON, BETTY: 1930s. Movies.

CONDOS BROTHERS, THE: late 1920s–1950s. Top rhythm tap dancers. Movies. (W)

CONDOS, FRANK: late 1920s–1930s. Oldest of Condos Brothers. Acrobatics, tap. (W)

CONDOS, NICK: late 1920s–1950s. Middle member of Condos Brothers. Credited with inventing the five-step Wing. (W)

CONDOS, STEVE: 1930s–1989. Youngest member of Condos Brothers. A top rhythm and improvisation dancer. (W)

CONINE, TOMMY: 1935–1960s. Jazz tap. Tommy Conine Trio. (W)

CONNOLLY, BOBBY: 1930s. Dance director. Films. (W)

COOK AND BROWN: 1920s–1930s. Knockabout tap team. (B)

COOK, CHARLES "COOKIE": 1920s–present. Knocka-

bout tap. Part of Cook and Brown and later Copasetics. (B)

COPASETICS, THE: 1950s–present. Rhythm, Buck and Wing, Soft Shoe, jump-rope tap. Performing group founded upon Bill Robinson's death. Comprised of veteran tap dancers. (B)

COSTELLO, GRACIE: 1940s. Jivin' Jacks and Jills. (W)

COTTON CLUB BOYS, THE: 1930s. Soft Shoe, tap, some flash. Six male dancers. Performed at the Cotton Club and on tour with the Cab Calloway Orchestra. (B)

COVAN, DEWEY: 1900s–1920s. Rhythm, Soft Shoe, Class Act. Brother of Willie Covan. Part of The Four Covans. Pick in Minstrel shows, T.O.B.A., vaudeville, Broadway (*Shuffle Along*, 1922). (B)

COVAN, FLORENCE: 1910s–1920s. Rhythm, Soft Shoe, Class Act. Wife of Willie Covan. Part of The Four Covans. T.O.B.A., vaudeville, Broadway (*Shuffle Along*, 1922). (B)

COVAN, WILLIE: 1900s–1970s. Rhythm, Soft Shoe, flash, Buck and Wing, acrobatic, Class Act. Founding member of The Four Covans. Invented Around the World with no hands, Rhythm Waltz Clog. Brought class, style, and total dance movement to tap. Pick in minstrel shows, early contests, partner with Slow Kid Thompson, T.O.B.A., headliner in vaudeville, Broadway, Europe, international, movies, choreographer, head dance instructor at MGM studios. (B)

COVAN AND RUFFIN: 1910s–1920s. Willie Covan and Leonard Ruffin. First to bring black Class Act to the top circuits in the North. Eccentric, Russian, tap. Act was subtitled, "Every Move a Picture." (B)

CROSS, JIMMY: 1930s–1940s. Stump of Stump and Stumpy. (B)

CUTOUT AND LEONARD: 1920s. Leonard Reed and Maceo Ellis. (B and W)

COY, JOHNNY: 1940s. Classical tap. Canadian tap dancer, came to Hollywood during WWII. Universal Pictures. (W)

DAILEY, DAN: 1940s–1950s. Classical tap, comedy. Movies. (W)

DALE and LEAN: 1937–1950. Eddie Dale and Scotty Lean. Acrobatic tap. Nightclubs western New York, New York City: Town Casino, Club Rhapsody, Glen Park Casino. (W)

DaPRON, LOUIS: 1920s–1987. Rhythm, legomania, comedy, classical tap. Vaudeville, clubs, 1930s movies (Paramount), choreographer (Universal, 1940s), choreographer Television, teacher. (W)

DAVIES, MARION: 1920s–1930s. Movies. (W)

DAVIS, JR. SAMMY: 1930s–1990. Child star with The Will Mastin Trio. Stage, Movies. (B)

DAY, DORIS: 1950s. Classical tap. Movies (Warner Bros). (W)

DIAMOND, JOHN: 1840s. Top white "jig" dancer in the world. (W)

DIANE, DOLORES: 1940s. Jivin' Jacks and Jills. (W)

DIXON, HARLAND: 1897–1962. Character Dancing (imitations of different nationalities), comedy, Soft Shoe, eccentric, Class. Minstrels, vaudeville, Broadway, choreographer (Broadway and Hollywood). Part of Dixon and Doyle. (W)

DIXON, LEE: 1930s–1950s. Classical tap, rhythm. Movies (Warner Bros, 1930s). Broadway (originated Will Parker in stage production of Oklahoma!, 1940s). (W)

DONAHUE, JACK: 1920s–1930s. Clog dancer, comedy, tap. One of the top dancers of his time. (In the 1928 Buck-dancing contest for performers in Broadway musicals, Bill Robinson and Jack Donahue won first and second, while Will Mahoney and Fred Astaire tied for third.) (W)

DOTSON, CLARENCE "DANCING": 1920s–1943. Eccentric, Soft Shoe. One of the few black dancers to hit the top in the twenties, soloing on the Keith Circuit. (B)

DOWLING, EDDIE: 1915–1920s. "The Rainbow Man." Had a hill on stage with a rainbow point on it. Danced on a rainbow. (W)

DOWNS, JOHNNY: 1930s. Comedy, legomania. Movies (Paramount Studios) with Dixie Dunbar. (W)

DOYLE, JIMMY: 1910s–1920s. Tap, Legomania. Part of Doyle and Dixon. (W)

DOYLE AND DIXON: 1910s. Jimmy Doyle and Harland Dixon. Character, Class, Soft Shoe, eccentric, comedy. "Classiest two-man hoofing act in show biz." Vaudeville. (W)

DRAPER, PAUL: 1930s–present. Tapped to classical music and American classical jazz (Gershwin, Grofé). Danced concert tours with classical harmonica player Larry Adler. (W)

DRAYTON, THADDEUS: 1906–1930s. Russian, acrobatic, Soft Shoe. Part of Greenlee and Drayton. (B)

DUDLEY, BESSIE: 1920s–40s. Chorus girl. Theaters. (B)

DUKES, THE THREE: late 1930s–1940s. Tap dancing trio; splits, kneefalls. (B)

Lee Dixon

The Dunhills

DUNBAR, DIXIE: 1930s. Dancing doll of Paramount Studios. College pictures with Johnny Downs. (W)

DUNCAN, ARTHUR: 1950s–present. Buck and Wing, Rhythm. Popular on *Lawrence Welk Show* in 1960s. (B)

DUNHILLS, THE: 1930s–1960s. Great rhythm trio; Wings, ballet-inspired flash steps. Vaudeville, movies. (W)

DUPREE, ROLAND: 1930s–1980s. Splits. Teacher. Biggest tap school in Los Angeles. Jivin' Jacks and Jills movies. (W)

EBSEN, BUDDY: 1930s–present. Legomania, eccentric, comedy. Part of The Ebsens. Vaudeville, Broadway, movies. (W)

EBSEN, VILMA: 1930–present. Tap, Ballroom, comedy. Part of The Ebsens. Vaudeville, Broadway, movies. (W)

EBSENS, THE: 1930–1942. Comedy, legomania, tap, eccentric. Buddy and Vilma Ebsen, brother and sister act. Vaudeville, Broadway, movies. (W)

EDDIES, THE THREE: 1933. Tap, legomania. Precision Class Act. Dressed in tuxedos. (B)

EDWARD SISTERS, THE: Late 1930s–early 1940s. Two sisters. Apollo, theaters, clubs. (B)

ELLEN, VERA: 1940s–1950s. Classical tap. Movies. (W)

EVANS AND EVANS: 1920s–1930s. Famous for "Whiskbroom" tap dance (later taught to George Burns and Gracie Allen and featured by them and Fred Astaire in *Damsel in Distress*.) Vaudeville. (W)

FAYE, ALICE: 1930s–1940s. Screen star. Tap danced in many films with Shirley Temple, Jack Haley, others. (W)

FIVE KELLYS, THE: Sibling act fashioned after The Seven Little Foys. Joan, James, Gene, Louise, Fred. Pittsburgh shows. (W)

FRED AND SLEDGE: late 1930s–1940s. Acrobatic, Flash. (B)

FOX, BEBE: 1940s. Jivin' Jacks and Jills. (W)

FAGAN, BARNEY: late 1880s. Leading Clog dancer. (W)

FIVE HOT SHOTS: late 1930s–mid-1940s. Flash, comedy. (B)

FORD, MAX: 1910s–1920s. One of the Four Ford Broth-

The Four Flash Devils

rope. Member Copasetics. (B)

GARLAND, JUDY: 1930s–1940s. Musical comedy actress. Tapped danced in many movies with Mickey Rooney [MGM]. (W)

GEIL, JOE "CORKY": 1940s. Jivin' Jacks and Jills. (W)

GIANTS OF RHYTHM, THE THREE: late 1940s–1950s. Snake Hips, legomania, comedy. (B)

GILBERT, GLORIA: 1930s. Toe tapper. Put ballbearings into her pointe shoes to spin faster. Vaudeville. (W)

GOBS, THE THREE: 1932. Tap, Legomania. Dressed in sailor suits. (B)

GORDON AND ROGERS: 1930s–1940s. Timmy Rogers and Freddie Gordon. Knee falls, splits, Soft Shoe, tap, and eccentric. (B)

GRABLE, BETTY: 1930s–1950s. Classical tap. Movies (with Condos Brothers and Hermes Pan). (W)

GRANGER, STEVE: 1930s–1980s. West Coast teacher (Gene Nelson). First tap dancer to use screws and countersink the taps. (W)

GREEN, CHUCK: 1930s–present. Child tap dancer. Comedy and rhythm. Part of Chuck and Chuckles. (B)

GREEN, WILLIE: 1929–1930. Legomania. (B)

GREENLEE, RUFUS: 1910s–1936. Russian, acrobatic, Soft Shoe. Part of Greenlee and Drayton. (B)

GREENLEE AND DRAYTON: 1910s–1930. Rufus Greenlee and Thaddeus Drayton. Pioneering Class Act. Russian, acrobatic, Soft Shoe. Europe, vaudeville (played Palace in WWI when Bert Williams and Bill Robinson were the only other black dancers to appear there), Broadway, Cotton Club. (B)

GREENWOOD, CHARLOTTE: 1910s–1950s. Eccentric (straight-leg kick to head). Stage and movies. (W)

GROSS, ETTA: 1910s. Champion female Buck dancer. (B)

GROUNDHOG: 1930s–1950s. Acrobatic, Wings, Rhythm. (B)

HALE, TEDDY: 1940s–1950s. Rhythm tap. Outstanding,

ers. Wing dancer. Invented the Maxie Ford. (W)

FORDYCE, LORNA: 1940s. Classical tap. West Coast clubs. (W)

FOUR BLAZERS, THE: 1930s. Flash. Wore big wide shirts (blazers). (B)

FOUR COVANS, THE: 1920s–1930s. Eccentric, flash, tap, Soft Shoe, Russian. One of the first black Class Acts. One of the top acts to headline vaudeville in the 1920s. T.O.B.A., vaudeville, Broadway, movies, international. (B)

FOUR FLASH DEVILS, THE: 1930s. Flash Act. Toured Europe. (B)

FOUR FORDS, THE: 1910s–1920s. Maxie, Johnny, and two others. Vaudeville. (W)

FOUR ROCKETS, THE: 1930s–1940s. Flash, tap. (B)

FOUR STEP BROTHERS, THE: 1920s–1960s. Flash, acrobatic. Top act through the years. Cotton Club, nightclubs, vaudeville, movies. (B)

FOY, EDDIE, JR.: 1910s–1930s. Part of the Seven Little Foys. Vaudeville. (W)

FRED AND GINGER: 1930s. Cotton Club, Europe. (B)

GAINS, BUBBA: 1920s–1930s. Tap dance with jump-

exciting, note-for-note dancer. Improvisation. (B)

HALEY, JACK: 1930s–1940s. Comedy. Straight-forward hoofing. Movies. (W)

HAYWORTH, RITA: 1930s–1940s. Classical tap. Movies. (W)

HIGH HATTERS, THE: 1940s–1950s. West Coast. Nightclubs, movies. Bernard Bradley, Clarence "Frenchy" Landry, Eudell Johnson. (B)

HIGHLANDERS, THE: 1933. Tap, eccentric. Dressed in Scotch attire. (B)

HILL, FLORENCE: 1930s. Chorus girl, Shake dancer. (B)

HILLMAN BROTHERS, THE: 1930s–1940s. Class Act. (B)

HOLDER, ROLAND: 1934–1936. Tap, Buck and Wing. Added new dimension to the Tango Twist and called it the Holder Twist. (B)

HOLT, DAVID: 1940s. Jivin' Jacks and Jills. (W)

HOOKER, DYNAMITE: late 1920s–early 1930s. Eccentric, "Tap Charleston gone wild." Probably only dancer to always open the Cotton Club show. (B)

HOPE, BOB: 1920s–Present. Buck and Wing, Rhythm. Vaudeville, Broadway, movies.(W)

HORNE, JOYCE: 1940s. Jivin' Jacks and Jills. (W)

HUMPHREYS, DICKIE: 1940s. Jivin' Jacks and Jills. (W)

HUTTON, INA RAE: 1930s. Energetic Big Band leader of her all-female orchestra. Often tap danced in front of the orchestra during selections. Nightclubs, band shorts (W)

HYDE AND SEEK: mid-1930s–1940s. Hoofers. Walter Hyde and Syd. Theaters, clubs. (W)

INKY: 1924–1926. Acrobatic tap. Mostly T.O.B.A. Part of Pen and Ink. (B and W)

JACKSON, "BABY" LAWRENCE see LAWRENCE.

JAMES, FREDDIE: 1920s–1940s. Acrobatic, tap. Part of The Four Step Brothers. (B)

JASON, SYBIL: 1930s. Child star Warner Bros. musical shorts. Vaudeville, British and South African vaudeville. (W)

JESSE, JAMES, AND CORNELL: late 1930s–1950s. Dancing waiters. Tap, Wings, acrobatics. Would spin trays on fingers, throw in the air, and catch trays in a split. (B)

JIVIN' JACKS AND JILLS: 1940s. Teenage tap dance sensations. Danced in Universal movies. (W)

JOHNSON, DARIEL: 1940s. Jivin' Jacks and Jills. (W)

JOHNSONS, THE: late 1930s–early 1940s. Brother and sister act. (B)

KAY, MARILYN: 1940s. Jivin' Jacks and Jills. (W)

KEAN, BETTY: 1940s. Broadway, vaudeville, Hollywood. (W)

KEELER, RUBY: 1920s–1970s. Buck and Wing dancer. First tap dancing star of moving pictures. Clubs, Broadway, movies (Warner Bros.). Brought tap "back" in the 1970s with No No Nanette. (W)

KELLY BROTHERS, THE: 1920s–1930s. Fred and Gene Kelly. (W)

KELLY, FRED: 1920s–Present. Classical tap, acrobatic, roller-skates tap, Soft Shoe. Vaudeville, radio, Broadway, movies. Choreographer and teacher. (W)

KELLY, GENE: 1920s–1980s. Classical tap, acrobatic, roller skate tap, Soft Shoe. Vaudeville, Broadway, movies (MGM). (W)

KING, KING, AND KING: 1920s. Sensational act of the 1920s. Dressed in convict outfits complete with ball

Hal Leroy

and chain. Did total synchronized dancing. Famous for toe stands. (W)

LANG, HAROLD: 1950s. Broadway dancer. (W)

LANE, WILLIAM HENRY (MASTER JUBA): 1840s–1852. In 1845, Lane was acknowledged as the world's greatest tap (then known as "jig") dancer. (B)

LA REDD, CORA: late 1920s–1930s. Buck dancer, lots of eccentric work. Greatly admired Cotton Club tap dancer. (B)

LAWRENCE, "BABY": (sometimes spelled Laurence): 1930s–1950s. Rhythm dancer, improvisation. (B)

LEE, BILLY: 1930s–1940s. Child star. Movies; vaudeville. (W)

LEGON, JENI: mid-1930s–Present. Buck and wing, acrobatic, flash. Theater, movies (partnered Bill Robinson). (B)

LEONARD, EDDIE: 1870–1940. Soft Shoe dancer. Composer who composed for his own tap dances, including his signature song "Ida." (W)

LEROY, HAL: 1930s–1980s. Legomania, comedy, eccentric, Tap Charleston. One of the few white dancers to see the inside of the Hoofers Club. Broadway, movies (circa 1930s). (W)

LESLIE, JOAN: 1940s. Movies. (W)

LeTANG, HENRY: 1930s–Present. Tap instructor, Manhattan. For years connected with the best of black tap shows and dancers. (B)

LONG, WALTER: late 1930s–early 1940s. Film, clubs. (W)

MACK, LAVINIA: 1920. Appeared in Runnin' Wild (1923). (B)

MACREE, MAXIE: 1920s–1930s. Famous for knee falls. One of the first blacks to get in a white show (George White's Scandals 1929 and 1930). (B)

MADISON, JOHNNY: mid-1930s–1940. One of the all-time great tap teachers. (W)

MAHJONGS, THE: 1934–1936. Helen Toy, Dorothy Toy, and Paul Wing. Song and dance act. West Coast clubs and Fanchon and Marco. (A)

MAHONEY, WILL: 1920s–1930s. Famous for pratfalls and tap-dancing on a giant xylophone. In a Buck-dancing contest for performers in 1928 Broadway musicals, he tied for third with Fred Astaire, with Bill Robinson and Jack Donahue winning first and second. Vaudeville, Broadway. (W)

MANNING, JACK: 1920s–1930s. Novelty. Broadway dancer. School. (W)

MATTISON, ETHLYN: 1940s. Jivin' Jacks and Jills. (W)

MATTISON, JOHNNY: 1940s. Formed the Jivin' Jacks and Jills at Universal. (W)

MAYFAIR, MITZI: 1940s. Broadway, musical shorts. (W)

MAYO, VIRGINIA: 1940s–1950s. Classical tap. Movies (Partnered Gene Nelson in some Warner Bros. movies). (W)

McALLISTER, BLUE: 1920s–1930s. Eccentric and tap. In Blackbirds of 1928. (B)

McCABE, BETTY: 1940s. Movies. (W)

McDONALD, FLASH: 1920s–1970s. Acrobatic, Flash, Rhythm. Part of The Four Step Brothers. Vaudeville, clubs, movies. (B)

McDONALD, GRACE: 1940s. Movies, Broadway. Sister of Ray McDonald. (W)

McDONALD, RAY: 1940s–1950s. Classical tap. Brother of Grace McDonald. Broadway, movies (Universal). (W)

McGEE, JACK: 1940s. Jivin' Jacks and Jills. (W)

McNAB, JEAN AND JANE: 1940s. Jivin' Jacks and Jills. (W)

MIDNIGHT STEPPERS: 1930s. Acrobatic tap. First to do One-Man Dance. For exit, one did flip over other two, picking up a handkerchief from the floor as going off. Dick, Ace, and Eddie. (B)

MILLER, ANN: 1930s–Present. Noted for her precise fast-paced rhythm tapping, and remarkable tapturns. One of the most famous screen tap dancers. Movies. (W)

MILLER BROTHERS, THE: 1932–1933. Three brothers: George, Danny, Duke (Honi Coles was with the trio for a while). Danced on pedestals. Flash, Soft Shoe. (B)

MILLER BROTHERS AND LOIS: 1933–1940s. Worked on pedestals. Trenches, turnovers, Over the Tops. (B)

MILLER, CURLY: 1938–1946 Comedy, acrobatic, tap. Part of Reds and Curly, variety act (B)

MILLER, MARILYN: 1920s. Broadway dancing star. (W)

MILLER, TAPS: 1930s–1940s. Buck, rhythm dancer. (B)

MILLS, SHIRLEY: 1940s. Jivin' Jacks and Jills. (W)

MITCHELL, DOLORES: 1940s. Jivin' Jacks and Jills. (W)

MOKE AND POKE: late 1940s–1950s. Knockabout tap,

falling in rhythm. (B)

MONTGOMERY, JACK: mid-1930s. Coast tap dancer. (B)

MONTGOMERY, SAMMY: 1935–56. Flash, tap, Wings. (B)

MURPHY, GEORGE: 1920s–1940s. Graceful, debonair tap dancer. Clubs, theaters, movies. (W)

NEALY, FRANCES: late 1930s–Present. Famous for her stair dance. West Coast chorus girl. (B)

NELSON, GENE: 1930s–Present. Classical tap, acrobatic, rhythm. Broadway, army, movies (Warner Bros.), records, television. (W)

NICHOLAS BROTHERS, THE: 1930–Present. Classical tap, acrobatic, rhythm. Famous for bringing flash and acrobatic dancing to a stylized form. One of the only acts to do a full split (most acts did a jazz split, aka jive split). Cotton Club, Broadway, radio, records, movies, television, clubs, Europe. (B)

NICHOLAS, FAYARD: 1920s–Present. Classical tap, acrobatic, rhythm. Half of The Nicholas Brothers. Famous for bringing flash and acrobatic dancing to a stylized form. Noted for his beautiful hand movements. Coined the term Classical tap to describe their form of tap dancing. Cotton Club, Broadway, radio, records, movies, television, clubs, Europe. (B)

NICHOLAS, HAROLD: 1930–Present. Classical Tap, acrobatic, rhythm. Famous for bringing flash and acrobatic dancing to a stylized form. First dancer to do a run up the wall into a backward flip directly into a split on the floor (Orchestra Wives) Cotton Club, Broadway, radio, records, movies, television, clubs, Europe. (B)

NIT, JOHNNY: 1920s. First black tap dancer to be celebrated by Broadway critics. (B)

NOLAN, O'NEILL: 1940s. Jivin' Jacks and Jills. (W)

NUGENT, PETE: 1920s–1952. Class Act par excellence. Part of Pete Peaches and Duke. T.O.B.A., Broadway, Duke Ellington's Jump for Joy, Billy Eckstine's band. Staged many black Class Acts. (B)

OAKIE, JACK: 1920s–1950s. Hoofer. Vaudeville, stage, screen. (W)

O'CONNOR, DONALD: 1920s–Present. Acrobatic, Comedy. Part of O'Connor Family. Vaudeville, movies, Jivin' Jacks and Jills. (W)

O'CONNOR FAMILY, THE: 1920s–1930s. Acrobatic, Buck and Wing. Vaudeville. (W)

O'CONNOR, PATSY: 1930s–1940s. Vaudeville. O'Connor Family. Jivin' Jacks and Jills. (W)

PALMER, AARON: early 1920s. Class, Soft Shoe. Married Alice Whitman, father of Pops Whitman. (B)

PAN, HERMES: 1920s–1970s. Classical and rhythm tap. Choreographer. Teamed with Fred Astaire for all RKO Astaire-Rogers pictures. Broadway, Movies. (W)

PATRICOLA, TOM: 1920s–1940s. Comedy tap, legomania. Billy Rose's star tap dancer at the 1939 World's Fair. Wore wooden shoes. Did rhythms of top of his toes. "A mop gone crazy," played ukulele as he danced. (W)

PATTERSON AND JACKSON, "THE TWO TONS OF RHYTHM": 1930s–1940s. Rhythm tap. Weighed about 250 pounds each. (B)

PAYNE, JIMMY: late 20s–1940s. Teacher. Out of Chicago. (W)

PEN AND INK: 1927–1928. Acrobatic, wings. Leonard Reed and Inky. T.O.B.A. (B)

PENNINGTON, ANN: 1920s. Soubrette. Classical tap. Broadway. (W)

PETE AND PEACHES: 1920s. Class Act. Pete Nugent, Irving "Peaches" Beaman. (B)

PETE, PEACHES, AND DUKE: 1931–1937. Pete Nugent, Irving "Peaches" Beaman, and Duke Miller. Class Act. Attributed with establishing a new kind of continuity of interweaving rather than episodic: During each man's solo, the other two joined in for the middle third of his performance. Could pass for white or black, but never played a white hotel or night club. (B)

PETERSON, PETE: 1930s–Present. Rhythm tap. Part of Taft, Boon and Peterson. Fanchon and Marco, movies, clubs. (W)

"PIANO": 1920s. Famous down in Hoofers Club. Could only dance holding on to the piano. (B)

PITTS, JUANITA: late 1930s–1940s. Extraordinary girl tap dancer. Pitts and Pitts. Nightclubs. (B)

POPS AND LOUIE (LOUIS): 1930s. Turns, flips, splits, Soft Shoe. Albert "Pops" Whitman and Louis Williams. Left U.S. in 1930s, went to Europe, never came back. (B)

PORKCHOPS AND GILLESPI: mid-1930s. Porkchops Patterson (fat) Billy Gillespi (skinny). Comedy, tap. (B)

POWELL, ELEANOR: 1930s–1940s. Top female screen

tap dancer. Known for her precision, rhythm, grace, style, exuberance. Teamed with Astaire in *Broadway Melody of 1940*. Movies. (W)

PRIMROSE, GEORGE: 1870s–early 20th century. Leading exponent of Soft Shoe. Minstrel. (W)

RADCLIFF, FRANK: 1920s–1950s. Tap, singer, comedian. (B)

RADIO CITY ROCKETTES: 1930s–Present. All female. Line work, tap. Radio City Music Hall. (W)

RALL, TOMMY: 1940s–1950s. Acrobatics. Jivin' Jacks and Jills. (W)

RAY, PETER: 1920s–1930s. Danced with a tray. T.O.B.A. Butterfield Circuit. (B)

RECTOR, EDDIE: 1920s–1930s. Of all Soft Shoe dancers, unquestionably the greatest soloist and major influence on the Class Act teams. Introduced what became known as stage dancing. Famous for Sand Dance and for his Waltz Clog. Credited with the Bambalina (Traveling Time Step). Pick, T.O.B.A., carnivals, vaudeville. (B)

RED AND CURLY: 1937–1946. Tap, eccentric, acrobatic. (B)

RED AND STRUGGLES: 1920s–1930s. Comedy tap. (B)

John Bubbles

REED AND BRYANT: 1930–1933. Class Act. Stair dance (two man) Willie Bryant, rhythm; Leonard Reed, Wings. Invented Shim Sham Shimmy. (B and W)

REED, LEONARD: 1920s–Present. Tap Charleston, acrobatic, rhythm. Part of Reed and Bryant, Pen and Ink, Cutout and Leonard. Choreographer, producer, including two Cotton Club shows; Apollo; *Rhythm Bound* (1934); chorus lines. Gillies, carnivals, T.O.B.A., vaudeville, Broadway. (B, Choctaw Cherokee, and W)

RICE, THOMAS DARTMOUTH, DADDY "JIM CROW": 1820s–1840s. White dancer who borrowed movement and song from black individuals. World-famous as a virtuoso dancer whose individual flair escaped definition. Minstrels. (W)

RICHMAN, HARRY: 1920s. The song and dance man of the 1920s. Elegant performer. Introduced song "Puttin' on the Ritz." Broadway, Movies. (W)

RITZ BROTHERS: 1930s. Comedy tap, stage, movies. (W)

ROBINSON, BILL "BOJANGLES": 1880s–1949. One of the greatest and most beloved tap dancers of all time. Brought tap up on its toes from flat-footed Buck and Wing. Famous for neat, clean footwork. Danced with a hitherto-unknown lightness and presence. His pattern of using three two-bar musical phrases, followed by a two-bar contrasting phrase (called a Break), became classic in tap dance structure. Vaudeville, Broadway, clubs, movies (teamed extensively with Shirley Temple—became the first interracial "couple" to appear in movies). (B)

ROBINSON, LaVAUGHN: 1930s–Present. Rhythm. Street dancer, band dancer, teacher. (B)

ROGERS, GINGER: 1920s–1950s. Classical tap. Teamed with Fred Astaire in ten major motion pictures. Broadway, movies.

ROONEY, ANNE: 1940s. Jivin' Jacks and Jills. (W)

ROONEY, MICKEY: 1930s–1950s. Classical tap, comedy. Child star, juvenile star of pictures. Movies. (W)

ROONEY, PAT, SR.: 1920s. Originator of the Waltz Clog. Vaudeville. (W)

RUTLEDGE AND TAYLOR: 1920s–1930s. Juny Rutledge

---

and Johnny Taylor. Tap Charleston. Sebastian's Cotton Club. (B)

RYAN, PEGGY: 1930s–Present. Classical Tap, Comedy, Rhythm. Child star, juvenile star of pictures (Universal). Stage, movies. 1940s. Jivin' Jacks and Jills. (W)

RHYTHM PALS, THE: 1935–1938. Bill Porter and Cholly Atkins. Clubs. (B)

SADIE MONTGOMERY AND LEONARD: 1928. Tap, Soft Shoe, Wings. Vaudeville. (W)

SALT AND PEPPER: late 1930s. Two girls. (B)

SAULTERS, DOROTHY (DOTTY): 1930s. Soubrette. Part of Cholly and Dotty. Night clubs. (B)

SAMMY, SUNSHINE: 1920s–1930s. Child tap star. Vaudeville. (B)

SCHEERER, BOBBY: 1940s. Jivin' Jacks and Jills. (W)

SHIPLEY, GLENN: 1920s–1980s. Classical Tap. West Coast Teacher, Choreographer. (W)

SIMS, HOWARD "SANDMAN": 1950s–Present. Taps on sand. (B)

SINATRA, FRANK: 1940s–1950s. Comedy, Classical tap. Movies. (W)

SLATE BROTHERS, THE: 1930s–1940s. Eccentric tap. Three dancers. (W)

SLYDE, JIMMY: 1940s–Present. Most famous slide dancer. (B)

SMALL AND MAYES: 1920s–1930s. Harry Mayes (like John Bubbles, strong rhythm tap) and Danny Small (played piano). Vaudeville. (B)

SMITH, ALMA: 1929–1930. One of the best female tap dancers. Strong dancer, with the power of a male dancer. (B)

SMITH, JIMMY: 1930s. Danced on a giant piano keyboard, played "The Man I Love" and "I Got Rhythm" while tap dancing. (B)

SNEAKS & EMIL: late 1920s–early 1930s. Comedy tap. Wore taps on sneakers. Clubs, T.O.B.A. (B)

SPENCER, PRINCE 1930s–1960s. Rhythm, acrobatic, flash. Part of Four Step Brothers. Clubs, movies. (B)

STAMPER, GEORGE: 1920s. Lazy Man's Dance in slow motion, including splits. Featured dancer in *Runnin' Wild* (1923). (B)

STANTON, RONNIE: 1940s. Jivin' Jacks and Jills. (W)

STEWART, RICHARD (aka DICKIE LOVE): 1940s. Jivin' Jacks and Jills. (W)

STUMP AND STUMPY: 1930s–1940s. Comedy tap; Billy Yates and Stumpy Cross. Featured act with Woody Herman Orchestra. (B)

SUBLETT, JOHN "BUBBLES" (see BUBBLES).

SUNNY AND EDDIE: 1928–29. Eccentric, legomania. (B)

SUNNY, EDDIE, and EDDIE: 1930–31. Eccentric, legomania. Also sang excellent three-part harmony. (Note: Same as Sunny and Eddie, The Three Gobs, The Three Eddies, and The Four Highlanders. The act was the same, only the name and costumes changed.) (B)

TAPPS, GEORGIE: 1930s–1940s. Classical tap. Broadway star. Clubs, movies. (W)

TAYLOR, WINSTON, AND HOWARD: 1925–1927. Dynamic exponents of Charleston, Flying Charleston, and Tap Charleston. From Kansas City, MO. (B)

TEMPLE, SHIRLEY: 1930s. Number-one child star of the 1930s (number-one box office attraction above Astaire/Rogers and Clark Gable for three years). Tapped

Bobby Scheerer

her way through feature films with Bill Robinson, George Murphy, Buddy Ebsen, Jack Haley. Movies (20th Century-Fox). (W)

THOMPSON, ULYSSES S. "SLOW KID": late 1880s–1950s. Part of Covan and Thompson. Comedy, Slow Soft Shoe. Appeared in *Dixie to Broadway*. Vaudeville. (B)

THREE LITTLE WORDS: 1929–1930s. Soft Shoe. Connie's Inn. (B)

THREE SPARKS OF RHYTHM: 1920s–1930s. Danced on a metal table; when they tap danced there were sparks. (B)

TOP HATTERS, THE: 1940s. West Coast Team. Class Act, flash. (B)

TIP, TAP AND TOE: 1930s–1950s. Rhythm, slides. Danced on a giant drum. Clubs, movies (B)

TOMMY CONINE TRIO, THE: 1950s–1961. Bea Blum, Andine Kanights, and Tommy Conine. One of the last tap acts to work regularly in the 1960s. (W)

TOY AND WING: 1936–1955. Dorothy Toy And Paul Wing. Toy did toe dance, Wing did tap, acrobatic, legomania. Ballroom tap. Vaudeville, clubs, theaters, and at country's first Oriental nightclub, Forbidden City. (A)

TYLER TWINS, THE: 1940s. Hollywood. Classical tap. (W)

VECCHIO, JIMMY: 1940s. Played xylophone while tapping. 1940s. Jivin' Jacks and Jills. (W)

VIRGINIA LEE AND LATHROP BROTHERS: 1930s. Among the best Class Acts. (W)

WASHINGTON, FORD LEE "BUCK" see BUCK.

WAYBURN, NED: 1920s. First school that taught tap dancing (1919, NYC). Teacher (the Astaires, Eleanor Powell, etc.), Choreographer (*Ziegfeld Follies*) (W)

WEBER, LOVE JEAN (aka JEAN DAVIS, aka LIZA PALMER, aka LIZA ARMS): 1940s. Jivin' Jacks and Jills. (W)

WEINGLASS, DEWEY: 1920s–1930s. Russian, legomania. Attributed with inventing the Double Around the World with no hands. (B)

WELLS, MORDECAI, AND TAYLOR: ("THE THREE KLASSY KIDS"): late 1920s–1930s. Soft Shoe. Famous for a routine "Hittin' the Bottle," where each dancer performed a bewildering variety of steps around a bottle without ever knocking it over. Class Act. Jimmy Mordecai, Dickie Wells, Ernest Taylor. (B)

WEST, BUSTER: 1920s. Tap, eccentric. Danced with Tom Patricola. (W)

WHITE, GEORGE: 1910s–1920s. Started career as a straight hoofer, gave up to produce his *Scandals*. (W)

WHITING, JACK: 1920s–1940s. Suave tapping leading man in American and British musical comedies. Vaudeville, movies. (W)

WHITMAN, ALBERTA: 1920s. Dressed as man. Part of Whitman Sisters. (B)

WHITMAN, ALICE: 1920s. One of the best female tap dancers of the era. Part of Whitman Sisters. (B)

WHITMAN, "POPS": 1920s–1940s. Alice Whitman's son. Rhythm, Wings, acrobatic. T.O.B.A. (B)

WHITMAN, SISTERS: 1920s–early 1930s. Musical revue. Lots of tap. (B)

WHITNEY, ELEANORE: 1930s. Rhythm, classical tap. Bill Robinson protégé. Teamed with Louis DaPron in Paramount features. Movies. (W)

WIGGANS, JACK: 1910s–1920s. Soft Shoe. Brought the Class Act to T.O.B.A. Credited with inventing and popularizing the Pull It, the Bantam Twist, and the Tango Twist. (B)

WILL MASTIN TRIO, THE: 1940s–1950s. Rhythm tap. With Sammy Davis, Jr. Played big-time white houses. (B)

WILLIAMS, FRANCES: 1930s. Rhythm, classical tap. Stage, movies. (W)

WILLIAMS, JACK: 1930s. Toe tapper. Stood on toes and danced (had taps on toes) Featured dancer in *Rhythm Bound* (1934). Upset New York, which had never seen male toe tap dancer. (B)

WILSON, DERBY: 1920s–1940s. Imitated Bill Robinson. (B)

WILSON, IRON JAW: 1930s. Tap danced, picked up tables and chairs in his teeth, and danced while spinning. Nightclubs. (B)

WINFIELD, RAYMOND: 1920s–1940s. Slides. Nucleus of Tip Tap and Toe. Clubs, movies. (B)

WING BROTHERS, THE: 1945. Paul Wing and Lorry Long (Chinese-Australian). Comedy, legomania tap. Fashioned after Nicholas Brothers. Up and down West Coast, East Coast, and at country's first oriental nightclub, Forbidden City. (A)

WING, TONY: 1945–Present. Close-to-floor work, combination of tap and ballet together. Performed at famous all-Chinese club in San Francisco, Forbidden City, and all over West Coast in clubs and theaters. (A)

WITHERS, JANE: 1930s–1940s. Hoofer. Child star. Movies. (W)

WOODS, TOMMY: 1920s. Acrobatic tapper. Featured dancer in Runnin' Wild (1923). (B)

WORTHEY AND THOMPSON: late 1920s. Tap, Soft Shoe. Danced on double stairs (wide enough for two people). Appeared in Blackbirds of 1928. Went to Europe, never came back. (B)

YATES, BILLY: 1930s–1950s. Comedy tap. Part of Stump and Stumpy. (B)

YO YO AND RAYE PEARL: mid-1930s–1940s. Yo Yo played the yo yo while dancing Soft Shoe. Raye Pearl sang and danced. (B)

ADDENDUM

ACKERMAN, JACK: 1940s-present. Bebop tap dancer. Musical comedy, television, in acts (with Tommy Conine and Ray Malone), as a solo, and in concert circuit, including three appearances in Carnegie Hall. (W)

AMES, JERRY: 1945-present. Dancer, teacher, choreographer. The only Caucasian in original legendary cast of The Hoofers. Founder of the Jerry Ames Tap Dance Company. Performs Morton Gould's Concerto for Tap Dancer and Orchestra with symphony orchestras. Co-author of The Book of Tap with intro by Eleanor Powell. (W)

ARNTE, DIAMOND TOOTH BILLY: circa 1920s. Rhythm tap dancer with the Harley-Sadler (travelling road show) in Texas. Had diamonds set in his teeth; would begin dancing and then smile, the spotlight sending off a dazzling light from the diamonds. (B)

BELFER, HAL: 1940s-present. Eccentric. MGM, Universal and 20th Century-Fox studios' dance choreographer. Choreographed "The Cane Dance Opener" for the Four Step Brothers. (W)

CARROLL, MICKEY: 1929-1940. A Munchkin in The Wizard of Oz, he first had a career as a tap dancer in Vaudeville, nightclubs, and theaters. Circa 1934, he held the record for "fastest taps" in Ripley's Believe It Or Not column. (W)

DANIELS, DANNY: 1930-present. Performer, choreographer, teacher. Performed in Broadway shows. 1950s-present, choreographed extensively for television, films, and Broadway. 1952, collaborated with Morton Gould and premiered the Concerto for Tap Dancer and Orchestra and later the Hoofer's Suite. (W)

FLETCHER, BEALE: 1940s-1994. Vaudeville, nightclubs, USO. Leading teacher in North Carolina. Along with wife, Peggy, performed as "The Dancing Fletchers, America's Most Versatile Dance Team." (W)

FURMAN, JAAKKO: 1930s-present. One of the first known tap dancers in Finland. (W)

GILBERT, AL: 1940s-present. Master teacher. 1947 opened Al Gilbert's Hollywood Theatrical Dance School. In late '50s, his company, Stepping Tones, began producing spoken dance records with vocal instruction and rhythmic tapping sounds, becoming one of the largest manufacturers and distributors of dance records. Brother, Pat Rico. (W)

GREEN, WALTER: 1930s-1940s. From Indianapolis, worked in New York nightclubs. Fast paddle and roll tap dancer. Had a "machine gun" slow walking step containing approximately thirty-two taps in a four-bar phrase. (B)

HARBERT, CARITA: 1930s. One of the Four Co-vans. (B)

HOCTOR, DANNY: 1939-present. High Style Rhythm. With wife, Betty, Hoctor and Byrd; shows, television, Soundies, nightclubs. 1940s, has the largest dance mail-order company; promotes his books, records, videos, original songs. 1959, formed Dance Caravan, tours the United States bringing tap to hundreds of thousands of students. (W)

HORN, PAT: 1950s. Often partnered Gene Nelson in movies and television. (W)

JOHNSON, FOSTER: 1925-1981. Fluid, paddle and roll, combined with leaps and spins. Danced with the big bands of Benny Moten, Lionel Hampton, Louis Armstrong, Count Basie. Teamed with Pops Whitman in 1940s. Important West Coast teacher in late '70s until his death at age 65 in 1981. (B)

KAHN, STANLEY: 1930s-present. Classical, Rhythm, Legomania, Buck and Wing. West Coast choreographer, prominent teacher. Inventor "Kanotation"—tap notation shorthand. (W)

KING, EVELYN: 1940s-present. Performed with sister as The Tiffany Twins during the early '30s throughout Europe and the United States. Married Jimmy King of King King and King. Performed knock-about adagio act with them during the '30s and '40s. (W)

LANDRY, CLARENCE: 1930s. Member of the West Coast tap group, The High Hatters. Theaters, nightclubs, movies. (B)

LEDGIN, CY: 1919-1994. Vaudeville from 1919-1924. Dubbed "Young Joe Frisco." Tapped and twirled a rope. Taught from 1930 up until his death in 1994. (W)

LEE, MABLE: 1930s-present. Performed at nightclubs and in shows. In many chorus lines; one of the original Apollo Girls. (B)

LYONS, CARNELL: 1940-1990s. Performed with trio Jesse, James, and Carnell during '40s-'50s. He then settled in Germany where he became a prominent teacher until his death at age 75 in 1992. (W)

NELSON, MIRIAM: 1930s-present. Performer, choreographer, director, producer, teacher. Broadway, movies, television. Los Angeles-based choreographer for television, movies, and shows. Dance assistant to Gene Nelson on many of his pictures. Staged, directed, and choreographed acts for Donald O'Connor and Ann Miller among many others. Choreographed and staged Agnes de Mille's Broadway revival of Oklahoma! (W)

PAYNE, JIMMY: 1930s-1990s. Chicago-based teacher. (B)

RICO, PAT: 1940s-present. Performer, teacher, choreographer. Performed throughout the nightclub circuit in Los Angeles, appeared in movies. Originator of "Computer Tap" and "Hi-Tech Tap," a scientific approach to teaching tap. Brother, Al Gilbert. (W)

STEWART, NICK: Vaudeville, nightclubs, stage, radio, television, movies. Began his career in New York and entertained at the original Cotton Club. (B)

STOREY, LLOYD: 1930s-present. Shows, Soundies, nightclubs. Famed Detroit tap teacher. Began as one of the Apollo Boys at Apollo Theatre 1938, in Gay New Orleans during '39 Worlds Fair, toured with Hot Mikado starring Bill Robinson. Acts include: Harry and Fats, Kenny and Lloyd, Al and Lloyd, The Sultans featuring Lloyd Storey and Frank Colvard. (B)

SULTANS, THE: 1959-present. Lloyd Storey and Frank Colvard. (B)

SUTTON, JIMMY: 1930s-present. Performed billed as "Dixie's Dancing Demon." During his long career as a teacher, he produced twelve Radio City Rockettes. He is the author of Fascinating Rhythms, a highly acclaimed manual for tap teachers. (W)

TURNBULL, GLENN: 1939-present. Rhythm Legomania. Performed on Broadway, summerstock, television, movies. (W)

WILLIAMS, JACK: 1936-1960. Theaters, nightclubs, Broadway, films. Nine Broadway shows, with over 1500 performances. Played with big bands, including Harry James, Tommy Dorsey, Raymond Scott. Wore split-sole wooden shoes, style heavily influenced by Lancheshire Clog with ballet and eccentric mixed in. (W)

WILLS, JR. , LOU: 1940s-present. Performer, choreographer, teacher. One of the greatest acrobatic Rhythm tap dancers. Clubs, Broadway, Las Vegas, television. (W)

WONDER, TOMMY: 1930s-[died 1993]. Tap danced with a full-size doll attached to his feet. Nightclubs, movies, and Broadway. (W)

ZERBY, JON: 1920s-present. Vaudeville. West Coast teacher. (W)

APPENDIX B
FILMOGRAPHY

TAP DANCERS ON FILM, 1900–1955

1900–1920

UNCLE TOM'S CABIN
Early examples of Time Step,
Breaks, the Strut, and Cakewalk
Thomas A. Edison (21 min),
1903.

1920–1928

AFTER SEBEN
James Barton (performing in
blackface)
Paramount, 1928

DANCING COLLEENS, THE
Erin's Famous Tap Dancers
Rayart Pictures ca. 1928

REB SPIKES BAND
Four unknown black tap dancers
Vitaphone (1 reel), 10/17/27

RUBY KEELER
Tap dance, two minutes
Movietone (1 reel), 6/4/28

1929

BLACK AND TAN
Five Hot Shots
RKO (2 reels), 12/8/29

BLACK NARCISSUS
Buck and Bubbles
Pathe (2 reels), 8/17/29

BROADWAY MELODY
Bessie Love, Anita Page
MGM, 3/9/29

DANCE OF LIFE, THE
Nancy Carroll, Hal Skelly
Paramount, 9/7/29

FOWL PLAY
Buck and Bubbles
Pathe (2 reels), 11/16/29

GLORIFYING THE
AMERICAN GIRL
Mary Eaton, Dan Healy
Paramount, 12/7/29

GOLD DIGGERS OF BROADWAY
Ann Pennington
Warner Bros., 9/12/29

GREAT GABBO, THE
Marjorie "Babe" Kane
SonoArt-Worldwide, 10/29

*From the 1920s–1950s, there were very few
musical films made that did *not* have tap
dancing in some form. This appendix concentrates on "featured" tap dancers—solo,
and groups. There are some entries listed
here that have not been viewed since their
original release. In these cases it is assumed
that the tap dancer did perform a tap number in the film. Release dates are noted: month,
day, year, when available.

HAPPY DAYS
Ann Pennington, Slate
Brothers
Fox, 12/23/29

HALLELUJAH!
Esvan Mosby
MGM, 11/30/29

HOLLYWOOD REVUE OF 1929
Joan Crawford
MGM, 8/18/29

IN AND OUT
Buck and Bubbles
Pathe (2 reels), 10/8/29

IS EVERYBODY HAPPY?
Ann Pennington
Warner Bros, 10/6/29

MARKIN' TIME
Rooney Family with
Pat Rooney, Sr.
Universal (2 reels), 10/3/29

NIGHT PARADE
Ann Pennington
RKO, 10/27/29

ON WITH THE SHOW
Four Covans
Warner Bros, 6/19/29

SALLY
Marilyn Miller
First National, 1/12/30

ST. LOUIS BLUES
Jimmy Mordecai
Radio Pictures (2 reels), 9/8/29

SHOW OF SHOWS
Dancers, two choruses—one
    black, one white
Warner Bros., 11/24/29

SUNSHINE SAMMY AND HIS
BROTHERS
in STEPPIN' ALONG
Sunshine Sammy and his
Brothers
MGM Movietone (1 reel), 2/4/29

SWEETIE
Helen Kane, Jack Oakie
Paramount, 10/27/29

THUNDERBOLT
Nina Mae McKinney
Paramount, 6/22/29

WEDDING OF JACK
AND JILL, THE
Johnny Perrone, Peggy Ryan
Warner Bros.-Vitaphone (short),
    1929

1930

CHASING RAINBOWS
Bessie Love, Anita Page
MGM, 1/19/30

CHECK AND DOUBLE CHECK
Four Step Brothers
RKO, 10/25/30

DARKTOWN FOLLIES
Buck and Bubbles
Pathe (2 reels), 2/4/30

DIXIANA
Bill Robinson
RKO, 8/16/30

FOLLOW THROUGH
Zelma O'Neal and chorus
Paramount, 9/27/30

HAPPY DAYS
Dixie Lee, Richard Keene,
Tom Patricola, Ann Pennington,
Slate Brothers,
Martha Lee Sparks,
Fox, 2/27/30

HELLO BABY
Ann Pennington
Vitaphone (2 reels), 6/9/30

HIGH TONED
Buck and Bubbles
Pathe (2 reels), 1/18/30

HONEST CROOKS
Buck and Bubbles
Pathe (2 reels), 2/8/30

JUST IMAGINE
Frank Albertson, Marjorie White
Fox, 10/29/30

KING OF JAZZ
Chorus tap
Universal, 8/17/30

LEGACY, THE
Betty Compton
Warner Bros., ca. 1930

LET'S GO NATIVE
Jack Oakie
Paramount, 8/16/30

MAMMY
Corbet Brothers
Warner Bros., 5/31/30

MARCH OF TIME, THE
Barney Fagan
MGM, 1930
(never released as a whole)

MUSICAL BEAUTYSHOP
Sammy Lewis
Twickenham Studios, 1930

PARAMOUNT ON PARADE
Nancy Carroll, Mitzie Mayfair,
Jack Oakie
Paramount, 5/10/30

PEACH-O-RENO
Dorothy Lee, Bert Wheeler
RKO, 12/25/31

PUTTIN' ON THE RITZ
Harry Richman, white and
black choruses
United Artists, 3/1/30

SUNNY
Marilyn Miller
First National, 11/23/30

THEY LEARNED
ABOUT WOMEN
Nina Mae McKinney
MGM, 7/6/30

TOP SPEED
Joe E. Brown, Inez Courtney
Warner Bros., 12/24/30

U.S.S. TEXAS
Tap dance to music made
on a tin can Issue 81.
Paramount (newsreel), 1930

UNDERDOG, THE
James Barton
Vitaphone (2 reels), 1/15/30

WHOOPEE
Eddie Cantor
United Artists-Goldwyn, 9/27/30

1931

BLUE RHYTHM
Mickey and Minnie Mouse
Walt Disney (cartoon), 8/25/31

CAUGHT PLASTERED
Bert Wheeler, Robert Woolsey
Radio Pictures, 9/5/31

LAUGHING SINNERS
Joan Crawford (tap charleston)
MGM, 5/30/31

1932

DANCERS IN THE DARK
Lyda Roberti
Paramount, 3/11/32

GIRL CRAZY
Mitzi Green, Dorothy Lee,
Bert Wheeler
RKO, 3/25/36

HARLEM IS HEAVEN
Bill Robinson, and chorus tap
Lincoln, 1932

MIDSHIPMAID, THE
Jessie Matthews
Gaumont-British, 1932

NIGHT WORLD
Mae Clark
Universal, 5/5/32

PIE, PIE BLACKBIRD
Nicholas Brothers
Warner Bros. (1 reel), 1932

SPORT PARADE, THE
Uncredited black tap dancers
and chorus line tap
RKO, 1932

TEN MINUTES TO LIVE
Chorus line tap
Micheaux, 1932

1933

BARBER SHOP BLUES
Four Step Brothers
Vitaphone (1 reel), 9/23/33

BROADWAY THRU A KEYHOLE
Barto and Mann, Frances Williams
United Artists Fox, 10/27/33

BROADWAY TO HOLLYWOOD
Mickey Rooney
MGM, 9/15/33

BUNDLE OF BLUES
Florence Hill and Bessie Dudley
Paramount (1 reel), 9/1/33

DANCING LADY
Fred Astaire, Joan Crawford
MGM, 11/27/33

EMPEROR JONES, THE
Harold Nicholas
United Artists, 9/29/33

FOOTLIGHT PARADE
Ruby Keeler, James Cagney
Warner Bros, 11/21/33

42ND STREET
Ruby Keeler, Eddie Nugent,
Clarence Nordstrom
Warner Bros., 3/29/33

FLYING DOWN TO RIO
Fred Astaire, Ginger Rogers
RKO, 12/29/33

GOING HOLLYWOOD
Marion Davies
MGM, 12/22/33

GOLD DIGGERS OF 1933
Ruby Keeler
Warner Bros., 6/17/33

GOOD COMPANIONS
Jessie Matthews, Uncredited
Dancer
Fox Great Britain, 1933

HELLO EVERYBODY
Kate Smith
Paramount, 2/17/33

MILLS BLUE RHYTHM BAND
Possibly Blues McAllister,
Jump-rope dance,
Three Dukes
Warner Bros., 1 reel, 1933

MR. BROADWAY
Hal Leroy, Joe Frisco
Broadway-Hollywood
Productions, 1933

MYRT AND MARGE
Donna Damerel, Eddie Foy, Jr.
Universal, 12/4/33

RUFUS JONES FOR
PRESIDENT
Sammy Davis, Jr.,
Will Vodery Girls chorus line tap
Warner Bros. (2 reels), 1933

SCANDAL
Uncredited solo tap dancer,
chorus tap
Unidentified production
  company
(connected to Jack Goldberg),
1933

SLOW POKE
Bunny Briggs, Cotton Club Girls
Skibo Productions, for
Educational Film Corp. released
  through Fox, 1933

SMASH YOUR BAGGAGE
Ace and Eddie, Danny Alexander
(jump-rope tap),
Smalls' Paradise chorus line,
"Rubber Legs" Williams
Vitaphone 1 reel, 4/22/33

SOURCE UNKNOWN
Johnny Dunn
Unidentified Dutch production
Feature film, ca. 1933–34

STOOPNOCRACY
Harold Nicholas
Max Fleischer/Paramount (short),
  1933

THAT'S THE SPIRIT
Cora La Redd
Vitaphone, 3/13/33

USE YOUR IMAGINATION
Hal Leroy, Mitzi Mayfair
Vitaphone (2 reels), 9/12/33

WAY OF ALL FRESHMEN, THE
Hal Leroy
Vitaphone (2 reels), 3/18/33

1934

BABY TAKE A BOW
James Dunn, Shirley Temple
Fox, 1/22/34

DAMES
Ruby Keeler
Warner Bros., 10/3/34

DON REDMAN AND HIS
ORCHESTRA
Red and Struggles
Warner Bros. (1 reel), 1934

EVERGREEN
Jessie Matthews, Barry McKay
Gaumont-British, 1934

FLIRTATION WALK
Ruby Keeler
Warner Bros., 11/16/34

GARDEN PARTY, THE
Ina Ray Hutton
Paramount, 1 reel, 1934

GAY DIVORCEE, THE
Fred Astaire, Ginger Rogers
RKO, 10/11/34

GEORGE WHITE'S SCANDALS
Dixie Dunbar
Fox, 3/16/34

HAPPINESS AHEAD
Paul Wing and Dorothy Toy and
the Mahjongs
Warner Bros., 1934

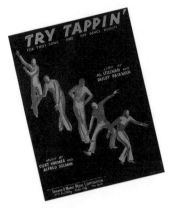

HAROLD TEEN
Hal Leroy
Warner Bros., 3/7/34

HARLEM AFTER MIDNIGHT
Ralph Brown
Micheaux, ca. 1934–35

HIPS, HIPS, HOORAY!
Bert Wheeler
RKO 2/2/34

KID MILLIONS
Nicholas Brothers
United Artists, 12/8/34

KING FOR A DAY
Bill Robinson
Vitaphone (2 reels), 6/28/34

MURDER AT THE VANITIES
Chorus line
Paramount, 5/25/34

NIGHT IN A NITECLUB
Buck and Bubbles, Martha Raye
Universal, 1934

PAREE, PAREE
Paula Stone
Warner Bros. (short), 1934

PICTURE PALACE
Hal Leroy
Vitaphone (2 reels), 1/29/34

PRIVATE LESSONS
Hal Leroy
Vitaphone (2 reels), 3/18/34

RHYTHM ON THE ROOF
chorus tap
Paramount (short), 1934

SHE'S MY LILLY, I'M HER WILLIE
Will Mahoney
Two uncredited tap dancing
roller skaters
Educational Productions,
released through
Fox, 1934

STAND UP AND CHEER
James Dunn, Shirley Temple
Fox, 5/4/34

SYNCOPATED CITY
Hal Leroy
Vitaphone (2 reels), 10/20/34

WHOLE SHOW, THE
James Barton
Universal (2 reels), 12/17/34

WONDER BAR
Hal Leroy
Warner Bros., 3/31/34

1935

ALL-COLORED VAUDEVILLE
SHOW
Nicholas Brothers
Vitaphone (short subject), 9/6/35

BIG BROADCAST OF 1936
Bill Robinson, Nicholas
Brothers
Paramount, 9/26/35

BROADWAY HIGHLIGHTS NO. 4
Cora La Redd
Paramount (1 reel), 9/27/35

BROADWAY MELODY OF 1936
Eleanor Powell, Buddy and Vilma
Ebsen, Nick Long, Jr.
MGM, 9/16/35

BY REQUEST
Tip, Tap and Toe
Warner Bros, 1935

CORONADO
Betty Burgess, Johnny Downs,
Nicholas Brothers
Paramount, 11/29/35

CURLY TOP
Shirley Temple
Fox, 7/26/35

DON'T GAMBLE WITH LOVE
The Nicholas Brothers
   (uncredited)
Columbia, 2/15/35

FIRST A GIRL
Jessie Matthews
Great Britain, 1935

GEORGE WHITE'S 1935
SCANDALS
Eleanor Powell
Fox, 3/29/35

GO INTO YOUR DANCE
Ruby Keeler
Warner Bros., 6/5/35

GOLD DIGGERS OF 1935
Chorus (uncredited male trio)
Warner Bros., 3/16/35

HARLEM AFTER MIDNIGHT
Uncredited tap and chorus line
Micheaux Pictures, 1935

HOLLYWOOD RHYTHM
Uncredited white tap duet
Paramount (short), 1935

HOORAY FOR LOVE
Bill Robinson, Jeni LeGon
RKO, 6/14/35

IN PERSON
Ginger Rogers
RKO, 11/22/35

IN OLD KENTUCKY
Bill Robinson
Fox, 9/6/35

LITTLE BIG SHOT
Sybil Jason
Warner Bros., 9/7/35

LITTLE COLONEL, THE
Bill Robinson, Shirley Temple
Fox, 2/22/35

LITTLEST REBEL, THE
Bill Robinson, Shirley Temple
20th Century-Fox, 12/27/35

MAIN STREET FOLLIES
Hal Leroy
Vitaphone (2 reels), 7/6/35

MAJOR BOWES'S AMATEURS
IN VARIETY REVUE
Al Reynolds, other unidentified
    tap dancers
Commonwealth, released
    through
RKO (2 reels), 1935

MILLIONS IN THE AIR
Eleanore Whitney
Paramount, 12/13/35

MUSIC IS MAGIC
Two white, two black men
Fox, 11/1/35

MUSICAL MEMORIES
Ruby Keeler, Hal Leroy
Paramount (short subject),
11/14/35

NITWITS, THE
Betty Grable, Bert Wheeler
Radio Pictures, 6/7/35

OLD MAN RHYTHM
Betty Grable, Sonny Lamont
RKO, 8/2/35

PADDY O'DAY
Jane Withers
Fox, 1/17/35

REDHEADS ON PARADE
Dixie Lee
Fox, 8/30/35

ROBERTA
Fred Astaire, Ginger Rogers
RKO, 2/26/35

SHIPMATES FOREVER
Ruby Keeler, Meglin Kiddies
Warner Bros., 10/16/35

SWEET MUSIC
Ann Dvorak and chorus
Warner Bros. 2/23/35

SYMPHONY IN BLACK
"Snakehips" Tucker
Paramount (1 reel), 1935

THANKS A MILLION
Ann Dvorak, Patsy Kelly
Fox, 11/15/35

THIS IS THE LIFE
Jane Withers
Fox, 10/18/35

TOP HAT
Fred Astaire, Ginger Rogers
RKO, 8/29/35

VAUDEVILLE REEL NO. 4
Pat Rooney, Sr., Pat Rooney, Jr.
Vitaphone (short), 1935

1936

ACCENT ON GIRLS
Ina Ray Hutton
Paramount (1 reel), 1936

BANJO ON MY KNEE
Buddy Ebsen
20th Century Fox, 12/4/36

BIG BROADCAST OF 1937, THE
Louis DaPron and Eleanore
Whitney
Paramount, Oct. 9, 1936

BLACK NETWORK
Nicholas Brothers
Vitaphone (2 reels), 5/5/36

BORN TO DANCE
Buddy Ebsen, Eleanor Powell
MGM, 11/23/36

BY REQUEST
Tip, Tap and Toe
Vitaphone (1 reel), 3/2/36

CAN THIS BE DIXIE?
Jane Withers
20th Century-Fox, 11/13/36

CAPTAIN JANUARY
Buddy Ebsen, Shirley Temple
20th Century-Fox, 3/17/36

CHANGING OF THE GUARD
Sybil Jason
Warner Bros. (short), 10/10/36

COLLEEN
Paul Draper, Ruby Keeler
Warner Bros., 3/26/36

COLLEGE HOLIDAY
Louis DaPron, Johnny Downs,
Eleanore Whitney
Paramount, 12/25/36

DANCING FEET
Nick Condos, Joan Marsh,
Eddie Nugent
Republic, 2/28/36

DANCING PIRATE
Charles Collins
RKO, 5/22/36

DEVIL IS A SISSY, THE
Jackie Cooper
MGM, 9/18/36

DIMPLES
Shirley Temple
20th Century Fox, 10/16/36

EVERYTHING IS RHYTHM
Johnny Nit, Harry Roy
Rock Studio (GB), 1936

FIRST BABY, THE
Johnny Downs, Dixie Dunbar
20th Century-Fox, 5/15/36

FOLLOW THE FLEET
Fred Astaire, Ginger Rogers
RKO, 2/20/36

GOING NATIVE
Bill Bailey
Skibo Productions, released by
Educational Pictures (1 reel),
    1936

GOLD DIGGERS OF 1937
Lee Dixon
Warner Bros., 12/26/36

GREAT ZIEGFELD, THE
Ray Bolger
MGM, 3/19/36

HIDEAWAY GIRL
Louis DaPron
Paramount, 11/20/36

IT'S LOVE AGAIN
Jessie Matthews, Cyril Wells
Gaumont-British, 1936

IT'S LOVE AGAIN
Jessie Matthews
Great Britain, 1936

JACK OF ALL TRADES
Jack Hulbert
Gainsborough, 1936

JIMMY LUNCEFORD AND HIS
DANCE ORCHESTRA
The Three Brown Jacks
Warner Bros. (1 reel), 1936

KING OF BURLESQUE
Dixie Dunbar, Nick Long, Jr.
20th Century-Fox, 1/3/36

LITTLE MISS NOBODY
Jane Withers
20th Century-Fox, 6/12/36

LUCKY STARLETS
David Holt, Lois Horne
Paramount (short), 1936

MUSIC GOES 'ROUND, THE
Eddie "Rochester" Anderson
and Johnny Taylor, Ananias Berry
Columbia, 2/25/36

OH, EVALINE
Hal Leroy
Vitaphone (2 reels), 2/17/36

ON THE WRONG TREK
Charlie Chase, Rosina Lawrence
Hal Roach, 1936

PIGSKIN PARADE
Johnny Downs, Dixie Dunbar
20th Century-Fox, 10/23/36

POOR LITTLE RICH GIRL
Alice Faye, Jack Haley, Shirley
Temple
20th Century-Fox, 7/24/36

RED NICHOLS AND HIS WORLD-
    FAMOUS PENNIES
Two black tap dancers
Warner Bros. (short), 3/21/36

RHYTHMITIS
Hal Leroy
Vitaphone (2 reels), 8/10/36

SHOWBOAT
Irene Dunne, Hattie McDaniel
Universal, 5/17/36

SING, BABY, SING
Dixie Dunbar
20th Century-Fox, 8/4/36

STAR REPORTERS
Betty Jane Cooper and
Lathrop Brothers
Paramount (1 reel), 1936

STOWAWAY
Uncredited Chinese woman
20th Century-Fox, 12/25/36

STRIKE ME PINK
Unidentified girl
Goldwyn, 1/24/36

SWING TIME
Fred Astaire, Ginger Rogers
RKO, 9/27/36

THREE CHEERS FOR LOVE
Louis DaPron, Eleanore Whitney
Paramount, 6/26/36

WASH YOUR STEP
Hal Leroy
Vitaphone (short), 3/30/36

THE STAR REPORTER SERIES
Louis DaPron and Vera Marshall
source unknown, probably
Paramount (1 reel), 1936

1937

ALI BABA GOES TO TOWN
Jeni LeGon, Peters Sisters
20th Century-Fox, 10/29/37

ARTISTS AND MODELS
Rhythm Pals
Paramount, 8/13/37

BROADWAY MELODY OF 1938
Buddy Ebsen, Judy Garland,
George Murphy, Eleanor Powell
MGM, 8/16/37

CAIN AND MABEL
Marion Davies, Sammy White
Warner Bros., 9/22/36

CALLING ALL STARS
Buck and Bubbles,
Nicholas Brothers
British Lion (England), 1937

CLARENCE
Johnny Downs, Eleanore Whitney
Paramount, 2/12/37

CLEAN PASTURES
Bill Robinson (cartoon)
Warner Bros. Merrie Melodies,
5/22/37

DAMSEL IN DISTRESS, A
Gracie Allen, Fred Astaire,
George Burns
RKO, 11/19/37

DEVILED HAM
Toy and Wing
RKO (1 reel), 1937

52ND STREET
Cook and Brown, Pat Paterson,
Rocco and Saulter,
Georgie Tapps
Walter Wanger Productions,
released through
United Artists 11/19/37

GANGWAY
Jessie Matthews
Gaumont-British, 1937

HEAD OVER HEALS
Jessie Matthews
Gaumont-British, 1937

HOLY TERROR, THE
Jane Withers
20th Century-Fox 2/5/37

JIMMIE LUNCEFORD AND HIS
DANCE ORCHESTRA
The Three Brown Jacks
Vitaphone (1 reel), 2/18/37

LIFE OF THE PARTY, THE
Ann Miller
RKO, 9/3/37

LOVE AND HISSES
Chilton and Thomas
20th Century-Fox 12/31/37

MANHATTAN MERRY-GO-
    ROUND
Possibly Cook and Brown
Republic Pictures, 11/13/37

MEET THE BRIDE
Pat Rooney, Jr., and Herman
    Timberg, Jr.
Educational Films, 1937

MELODY FOR TWO
Donald and Jack O'Connor
(dance deleted)
Warner Bros., May 5/1/37

MURDER IN SWINGTIME
Two uncredited black tap
   dancers
Condor Pictures, released
   through
RKO (1 reel), 1937

NEW FACES OF 1937
Ann Miller
RKO, 7/1/37

ONE MILE FROM HEAVEN
Bill Robinson
20th Century-Fox, 8/13/37

POTLUCK
Three Rhythm Boys
Educational Films, 1937

READY, WILLING AND ABLE
Lee Dixon, Ruby Keeler
Warner Bros., 2/5/37

ROSALIE
Ray Bolger, Eleanor Powell
MGM, 12/20/37

SHALL WE DANCE?
Fred Astaire, Ginger Rogers
RKO, 5/7/37

SINGING MARINE, THE
Lee Dixon
Warner Bros., 7/3/37

SOMETHING TO SING ABOUT
James Cagney, Harland Dixon,
Johnny Boyle
Grand National, 9/1/37

STAGE DOOR
Ann Miller, Ginger Rogers
RKO, 9/18/37

START CHEERING
Hal Leroy
Columbia, 3/3/37

SWEETIES
Pat Rooney, Jr. and Herman
   Timberg, Jr.
Educational Films, 1937

SWEET SHOE
Four Specs
Nu-Atlas, released through
RKO (1 reel), 12/31/37

SWING
Tyler Twins
Micheaux ca. 1937

SWING FOR SALE
Hal Leroy
Vitaphone (2 reels), 5/3/37

SWING HUTTON SWING
Ina Ray Hutton
Paramount (1 reel), 1937

THIS'LL MAKE YOU WHISTLE
Jack Buchanan, Elsie Randolph
Wilcox, 1937

THIS WAY PLEASE
Betty Grable
Paramount, 9/15/37

TOP OF THE TOWN
Ella Logan, George Murphy,
Peggy Ryan
Universal, 3/6/37

TURN OFF THE MOON
Johnny Downs, Eleanore Whitney
Paramount, 5/14/37

UNDERWORLD
Raymond Collins, Dorothy Salters
Sack Amusement, ca. 1937

UPS AND DOWNS
Hal Leroy
Vitaphone (2 reels), 10/18/37

VARSITY SHOW
Buck and Bubbles, Lee Dixon
Warner Bros., 7/14/37

WAKE UP AND LIVE
Condos Brothers
20th Century-Fox, 4/23/37

WALTER WANGER'S VOGUES
of 1938
Dorothy "Dotty" Saulters,
Four Hot Shots,
Georgie Tapps, Wiere Brothers
United Artists, 8/7/37

WAY OUT WEST
Laurel and Hardy
MGM/Hal Roach, 4/16/37

WHEN LOVE IS YOUNG
Nick Long, Jr.
Universal 4/4/37

WILD AND WOOLLY
Jane Withers
20th Century-Fox, 9/10/37

YOU CAN'T HAVE EVERYTHING
Tip, Tap and Toe
20th Century-Fox, 8/6/37

YOU'RE A SWEETHEART
Alice Faye, George Murphy
Universal, 12/17/37

FUN IN FUN
(title uncertain)
Three Gobs
Production company unknown,
probably short subject, ca. 1937

1938

ALEXANDER'S RAGTIME BAND
Dixie Dunbar, Wally Vernon
20th Century-Fox, 8/11/38

CAFE RENDEZVOUS
Samuels Brothers and Edith
Fleming
RKO (1 reel), 12/28/38

CAMPUS CONFESSIONS
Eleanore Whitney
Paramount, 9/16/38

CAREFREE
Fred Astaire, Ginger Rogers
RKO, 9/2/38

CARNIVAL SHOW
Three De Loveliers
RKO (1 reel), 6/24/38

COLLEGE SWING
Jackie Coogan, Betty Grable,
Slate Brothers
Paramount, 4/8/38

DOWN ON THE BARN
Danzi Goodell
Mentone, released through
Universal (2 reels), 1938

DUKE IS TOPS
Willie Covan, chorus Line
Million Dollar Productions, 1938

FRESHMAN YEAR
Dixie Dunbar
Universal, 9/2/38

HAL KEMP AND HIS
ORCHESTRA
Patsy Starr
Paramount (1 reel), 1938

HAPPY LANDING
Condos Brothers
20th Century-Fox, 1/28/38

HAVE YOU GOT ANY CASTLES?
Bill Robinson (cartoon)
Warner Bros. Merrie Melodies,
6/25/38

HOLD THAT CO-ED
George Murphy, Johnny Downs
20th Century-Fox, 9/16/38

INTERNATIONAL RHYTHMS
Princess Chiyo
Nu-Atlas/RKO, 1938

JUST AROUND THE CORNER
Joan Davis, Bill Robinson,
Shirley Temple
20th Century-Fox, 11/11/38

KEEP SMILING
Jane Withers
20th Century-Fox, 8/12/38

KNIGHT IS YOUNG, THE
Hal Leroy
Vitaphone (2 reels), 12/5/38

LITTLE MISS BROADWAY
George Murphy, Shirley Temple
20th Century-Fox, 7/29/38

PRISONER OF SWING, THE
Hal Leroy
Vitaphone (short), 6/11/38

RADIO CITY REVELS
Ann Miller, Buster West
RKO, 2/11/38

RADIO HOOK-UP
Charles Collins
RKO (1 reel), 1/28/38

RASCALS
Jane Withers
20th Century-Fox, 5/30/38

REBECCA OF SUNNYBROOK
FARM
Bill Robinson, Shirley Temple
20th Century-Fox, 3/18/38

ROAD DEMON
Bill Robinson
20th Century-Fox, 12/2/38

SAILING ALONG
Jessie Matthews, Jack Whiting
Gaumont-British, 1938

SALLY IRENE & MARY
Joan Davis, Alice Faye,
Marjorie Weaver
20th Century-Fox, 5/4/38

SKYLINE REVUE
Billy and Milly with Sugar Nichols
RKO (short), 4/1/38

STYLES AND SMILES
Marion Daniels
Nu-Atlas/RKO, 1938

SWEETHEARTS
Ray Bolger
MGM, 12/30/38

SWING
uncredited male and female
tap dancers
Micheaux Pictures, 1938

SWING, SISTER, SWING
Johnny Downs and
Kathryn "Sugar" Kane
Universal, 12/20/38

TARNISHED ANGEL
Ann Miller
RKO, 10/26/38

THRILL OF A LIFETIME
Johnny Downs, Eleanore Whitney
Paramount, 1/21/38

UP IN LIGHTS
Pat Rooney
Vitaphone (2 reels), 8/13/38

UP THE RIVER
Bill Robinson
20th Century-Fox, 12/9/38

WALKING DOWN BROADWAY
Dixie Dunbar
20th Century-Fox, 3/11/38

1939

ARIZONA WILDCAT
Jane Withers
20th Century-Fox, 2/3/39

BABES IN ARMS
Judy Garland, Mickey Rooney
MGM, 10/13/39

BOYFRIEND
Jane Withers
20th Century-Fox, 5/19/39

BROADWAY BUCKAROO, THE
Condos Brothers
Vitaphone (short), 6/3/39

DANCING CO-ED
Ann Rutherford, Lana Turner
MGM, 9/29/39

HAWAIIAN NIGHTS
Johnny Downs
Universal, 9/8/39

HONOLULU
Gracie Allen, Eleanor Powell
MGM, 1/31/39

IT'S SWING HO—COME TO THE
FAIR!
Bill Robinson
Paramount (newsreel), 10/1939

MAL HALLET AND HIS
  ORCHESTRA
Buddy and Claire Green
Vitaphone (short), 1939

MY SON IS GUILTY
Nicholas Brothers (uncredited)
Columbia, 12/28/39

ON YOUR TOES
Donald O'Connor
Warner Bros., 10/14/39

PACK UP YOUR TROUBLES
Jane Withers
20th Century-Fox, 10/20/39

PUBLIC JITTERBUG NO. 1
Hal LeRoy
Vitaphone, 1939

SAMOVAR SERENADE
Karavaeff, "Russian tap"
Nu-Atlas, released through
RKO (1 reel), 1939

SEEING RED
Louis DaPron
Warner Bros. (2 reels), 1939

STAR MAKER, THE
Dorothy Babb, Roland Dupree
Paramount, 8/25/39

STORY OF VERNON AND
IRENE CASTLE, THE
Fred Astaire, Sonny Lamont
RKO, 3/30/39

1940

ARGENTINE NIGHTS
Andrews Sisters, Ritz Brothers
Universal, 9/6/40

BROADWAY MELODY OF 1940
Fred Astaire, George Murphy,
Eleanor Powell
MGM, 2/9/40

BUCK BENNY RIDES AGAIN
Eddie "Rochester" Anderson,
Theresa Harris
Paramount, 5/3/40

DANCING ON A DIME
Grace McDonald, Robert Paige
Paramount, 11/1/40

DOWN ARGENTINE WAY
Nicholas Brothers
20th Century-Fox, 10/11/40

HIGH SCHOOL
Jane Withers
20th Century-Fox, 6/26/40

HIT PARADE OF 1941, THE
Ann Miller
Republic, 10/15/40

I CAN'T GIVE YOU ANYTHING
BUT LOVE, BABY
Johnny Downs (possibly),
Jeni LeGon
Universal, .5/20/40

IF I HAD MY WAY
Eddie Leonard
Universal, 5/3/40

LITTLE NELLIE KELLY
George Murphy
MGM, 11/20/40

MELODY RANCH
Ann Miller
Republic, 11/15/40

NAUGHTY NINETIES, THE
Possibly The Three Castles
Universal (1-½ reels), 1940

SHOOTING HIGH
Jane Withers
20th Century-Fox, 4/26/40

SING, DANCE, PLENTY HOT
Johnny Downs
Republic, 8/10/40

TIN PAN ALLEY
Nicholas Brothers
20th Century-Fox, 11/29/40

TOO MANY GIRLS
Hal LeRoy, Ann Miller
RKO, 11/1/40

TWO GIRLS ON BROADWAY
George Murphy
MGM, 4/19/40

VARSITY VANITIES
Dennet and Dae,
Dorothy Roberts
(number with Buddy Pepper
and Peggy Ryan deleted)
Universal (short), 1940

YOUNG PEOPLE
Charlotte Greenwood,
Jack Oakie,
Shirley Temple
20th Century-Fox, 8/30/40

YOUTH WILL BE SERVED
Jane Withers
20th Century-Fox, 11/27/40

1941

ALL-AMERICAN CO-ED
Johnny Downs
United Artists, 10/30/41

BALLET DANCERS'
NIGHTMARE
Slate Brothers
Soundies Corp., 8/4/41

BUCK PRIVATES
Andrews Sisters
Universal, 1/31/41

BY AN OLD SOUTHERN RIVER
Bill Robinson
Panoram Soundies, 1941

FOUR JACKS AND A JILL
Ray Bolger
RKO, 12/18/41

GO WEST, YOUNG LADY
Ann Miller
Columbia, 11/22/41

GOLDEN HOOFS
Jane Withers
20th Century-Fox, 2/14/41

GREAT AMERICAN
BROADCAST, THE
Nicholas Brothers
20th Century-Fox, 5/9/41

IN THE NAVY
Condos Brothers
Universal, 5/30/41

JAZZ ETUDE
Billy Burt
Soundies Corp.
(short), 12/31/41

KATHLEEN
Shirley Temple
MGM, 12/1941

LADY BE GOOD
Berry Brothers,
Eleanor Powell
MGM, 7/2/41

LET'S SHUFFLE
Bill Robinson
Panoram Soundies, 1941

MANHATTAN
Grace McDonald
Soundies Corp.
(short), 5/19/41

MELODY LANE
Louis DaPron
Universal, 12/19/41

MOONLIGHT IN HAWAII
Johnny Downs, Sunnie O'Dea
Universal, 8/1/41

MOON OVER MIAMI
Condos Brothers, Betty Grable,
Hermes Pan
20th Century-Fox, 7/4/41

PARACHUTE BATTALION
Buddy Ebsen
RKO, 12/12/41

RISE AND SHINE
George Murphy
20th Century-Fox, 11/21/41

ROOKIES ON PARADE
Louis DaPron
Republic, 4/17/41

SAN ANTONIO ROSE
Louis DaPron
Universal, 6/20/41

SECOND CHORUS
Fred Astaire, Paulette Goddard
Paramount, 1/3/41

SHADOWS IN SWING
Louis DaPron
Universal (2 reels), 5/5/41

SING ANOTHER CHORUS
Joe Brown, Jr., Johnny Downs,
Sunnie O'Dea
Universal, 9/19/41

SMALLTOWN DEB
Jane Withers
20th Century-Fox, 11/7/41

SUN VALLEY SERENADE
Dorothy Dandridge, Nicholas
Brothers
20th Century-Fox, 8/29/41

SUNNY
Ray Bolger, Anna Neagle
  (possibly)
RKO, 5/30/41

SWEETHEART OF THE
CAMPUS
Ruby Keeler
Columbia, 6/26/41

TIME OUT FOR RHYTHM
Ann Miller
Columbia, 6/20/41

TOOT THAT TRUMPET
Cook and Brown
Soundies Corp. (short) 12/22/41

WASHINGTON MELODRAMA
Dan Dailey, Virginia Grey
MGM, 4/26/41

WITH A TWIST OF THE WRIST
Grace McDonald
Soundies Corp., 7/7/41

YOU'LL NEVER GET RICH
Fred Astaire, Rita Hayworth
Columbia, 9/25/41

ZIS-BOOM-BAH
Roland Dupree
Monogram, 11/7/41

1942
—————————————
BABES ON BROADWAY
Judy Garland, Ray McDonald,
Richard Quine, Mickey Rooney
MGM, 1/2/42

BEHIND THE EIGHT BALL
Johnny Downs, Grace McDonald,
Ritz Brothers
Universal, 9/28/42

BORN TO SING
Ray McDonald
MGM, 3/42

BROADWAY
Chorus
Universal, 5/8/42

BY AN OLD SOUTHERN RIVER
Bill Robinson
Soundies Corp. (short) 1/12/42

FLEET'S IN, THE
Cass Daley, Betty Hutton
Paramount, 1/42

FOOTLIGHT SERENADE
Betty Grable, Hermes Pan
20th Century-Fox, 8/1/42

FOR ME AND MY GAL
Judy Garland, Gene Kelly,
George Murphy
MGM, 9/11/42

GET HEP TO LOVE
Jivin' Jacks and Jills,
Donald O'Connor, Peggy Ryan
Universal, 8/25/42

GIRLS' TOWN
Peggy Ryan
Producers Releasing,
3/6/42

GIVE OUT, SISTERS
Dan Dailey, Jivin' Jacks and Jills,
Grace McDonald,
Donald O'Connor, Peggy Ryan
Universal, 7/27/42

HARLEM RHUMBA
Chocolateers
Soundies Corp., 12/21/42

HI YA CHUM
Ritz Brothers
Universal, 1942

HOLIDAY INN
Fred Astaire, Virginia Dale,
Marjorie Reynolds
Paramount, 6/12/42

IT COMES UP LOVE
Gloria Jean, Jivin' Jacks and Jills,
Donald O'Connor
Universal, 9/21/42

JIVIN' JAM SESSION
Louis DaPron
Universal (2 reels), 7/20/42

JOHNNY DOUGHBOY
Jane Withers
Republic, 12/31/42

LET'S SCUFFLE
Bill Robinson
Soundies Corp.
(short), 1/12/42

MAISIE GETS HER MAN
Uncredited white and
black tap dancers
MGM, 5/42

MAYOR OF 44TH STREET, THE
George Murphy
RKO, 5/15/42

MOONLIGHT MASQUERADE
Three Chocolateers,
Eddie Foy, Jr.,
Betty Kean, Erno Verbes
Republic, 6/10/42

MY GAL SAL
Rita Hayworth, Hermes Pan
20th Century-Fox, 5/8/42

ORCHESTRA WIVES
Nicholas Brothers
20th Century-Fox, 9/4/42

PANAMA HATTIE
Berry Brothers, Dan Dailey
MGM, 7/21/42

PARDON MY SARONG
Tip, Tap and Toe
Universal, 7/21/42

PECKIN'
Chocolateers
Soundies Corp.
(short), 11/9/42

PRIORITIES ON PARADE
Ann Miller
Paramount, 7/22/42

PRIVATE BUCKAROO
Jivin' Jacks and Jills, Donald
O'Connor, Peggy Ryan
Universal, 5/29/42

RIDE 'EM COWBOY
Uncredited
Universal, 2/13/42

ROXIE HART
Ginger Rogers
20th Century-Fox, 2/20/42

SHIP AHOY
Eleanor Powell,
Stump and Stumpy
MGM, 4/23/42

SING YOUR WORRIES AWAY
Buddy Ebsen
RKO, 1/30/42

SIX HITS AND A MISS
Paul Draper, Ruby Keeler
Warner Bros. (short), 11/9/42

SPRINGTIME IN THE ROCKIES
Betty Grable
20th Century-Fox, 11/6/42

STRICTLY IN THE GROOVE
Grace McDonald
Universal, 11/20/42

SWING FROLIC
Peggy Ryan
Universal (2 reels), 2/24/42

TRUE TO THE ARMY
Ann Miller
Paramount, 3/17/42

TRUMPET SERENADE
Jivin' Jacks and Jills, Grace
MacDonald
Universal (2 reels), 6/18/42

TWEED ME
Chocolateers
Soundies Corp. (short) 12/31/42

WHAT'S COOKIN'?
Jivin' Jacks and Jills,
Donald O'Connor,
Peggy Ryan,
Susan "Tag-a-long" Levine
Universal, 2/24/42

WHEN JOHNNY COMES
MARCHING HOME
Four Step Brothers, Gloria Jean,
Donald O'Connor, Peggy Ryan
Universal, 11/24/42

YOU WERE NEVER LOVELIER
Fred Astaire, Rita Hayworth
Columbia, 11/19/42

1943

AIN'T MY SUGAR SWEET
Probably Argalie "Tommy"
Thompson
Panoram Soundies, 1943

ALL BY MYSELF
Tip, Tap and Toe
Universal, 4/30/43

ALWAYS A BRIDESMAID
Patty Andrews, Dean Collins,
Jivin' Jacks and Jills
Universal, 11/24/43

BEST FOOT FORWARD
Uncredited tap dancer
MGM, 10/43

BREAKFAST IN RHYTHM
Three Chefs
Panoram Soundies, 1943

CABIN IN THE SKY
Bill Bailey, John Bubbles
MGM, 4/43

CALLING ALL KIDS
Dickie Love, others (Our Gang)
MGM (short), 4/24/43

CHATTER
Cook and Brown
Soundies Corp.
(short), 11/29/43

CHOO CHOO SWING
Nicholas Brothers
Universal (2 reels), 11/12/43

CONEY ISLAND
Betty Grable, Hermes Pan
20th Century-Fox, 6/18/43

CRAZY HOUSE
Uncredited tap dancer
Universal, 10/8/43

DANCEMANIA
Harris and Hunt
Soundies Corp.
(short), 10/29/43

DANCE REVUE
Pat Rooney III
Soundies Corp.,
(short), 3/1/43

DU BARRY WAS A LADY
Gene Kelly
MGM, 8/13/43

FOOLIN' AROUND
Harris and Hunt
Soundies Corp.
(short), 11/1/43

FLYING FEET
Rita Rio
Soundies Corp.
(short), 6/28/43

GALS, INCORPORATED
Betty Kean, Grace McDonald
Universal, 7/9/43

GIRL CRAZY
Busby Berkeley Girls,
Judy Garland, Mickey Rooney
MGM, 11/26/43

HARLEM HOTCHA
Tops and Wilder
Soundies Corp.
(short), 12/21/43

HE'S MY GUY
Louis DaPron, Lorraine Kreuger
Universal, 3/15/43

HI, BUDDY!
Marilyn Day, Four Step
Brothers, Dickie Humphreys
Universal, 1/4/43

HIT PARADE OF 1943
Pops and Louis, Jack Williams
Republic, 3/16/43

HIYA SAILOR
Pops and Louis
Universal, 11/2/43

HONEYMOON LODGE
Tip, Tap and Toe
Universal, 7/28/43

HOW'S ABOUT IT
Patti Andrews, Dorothy Babb,
Louis DaPron, Bobby Scheerer
Universal, 2/3/43

I DOOD IT
Eleanor Powell
MGM, 7/27/43

IT AIN'T HAY
Lou Costello, Four Step Brothers,
Grace McDonald, Patsy O'Connor
Universal, 3/25/43

JIVEROO
Harry Day and Della
Soundies Corp.
(short), 6/28/43

JUMPIN' JACK FROM
HACKENSACK
Tommy Thompson
Soundies Corp.
(short), 10/25/43

MOONLIGHT IN VERMONT
Vivian Austin, Jivin' Jacks and
Jills, Ray Malone, Betty
McCabe
Universal, 12/24/43

MR. BIG
Jivin' Jacks and Jills,
Donald O'Connor, Peggy Ryan
Universal, 5/28/43

MY BEST GAL
Jane Withers
Republic, 1943

NEARLY EIGHTEEN
Bebe Fox, Gale Storm
Monogram, 11/12/43

NEVER A DULL MOMENT
Ritz Brothers
Universal, 11/19/43

NORTH STAR
Jane Withers
RKO-Goldwyn, 10/43

PARDON ME, BUT YOU
LOOK JUST LIKE MARGIE
Three Chefs
Soundies Corp., 6/28/43

POPPIN' THE CORK
Billy and Ann
Soundies Corp.
(short), 6/21/43

REVEILLE WITH BEVERLY
Ann Miller
Columbia, 2/4/43

RHYTHM OF THE ISLANDS
Four Step Brothers
Universal, 4/7/43

RHYTHMANIA
Harris and Hunt
Soundies Corp.
(short), 10/29/43

SHE'S FOR ME
Louis DaPron, Grace McDonald
Universal, 11/12/43

SKY'S THE LIMIT, THE
Fred Astaire, Joan Leslie
RKO, 8/21/43

SONG AND DANCE MAN, A
Taps Miller
Soundies Corp., 11/22/43

STAGE DOOR CANTEEN
Ray Bolger
United Artist, 6/43

STORMY WEATHER
Nicholas Brothers, Bill Robinson
20th Century-Fox, 7/16/43

SWEET JAM
Louis DaPron
Universal (2 reels), 9/27/43

SWEET ROSIE O'GRADY
Betty Grable, Hermes Pan
20th Century-Fox, 10/1/43

TAP HAPPY
Slim and Sweets
Soundies Corp.,
(short), 12/31/43

THIS IS THE ARMY
Stumpy Cross, George Murphy,
Fred Kelly
Army Chorus
Warner Bros., 8/14/43

THOUSANDS CHEER
Gene Kelly, Eleanor Powell
MGM, 9/22/43

TOP MAN
Donald O'Connor, Peggy Ryan
Universal, 9/24/43

WHAT'S BUZZIN' COUSIN?
Ann Miller
Columbia, 7/8/43

YANKEE DOODLE DANDY
James Cagney, Jean Cagney,
Rosemary DeCamp,
Walter Huston, Joan Leslie
Warner Bros., 1/2/43

1944

ATLANTIC CITY
Buck and Bubbles
Republic, 8/16/44

BABES ON SWING STREET
Peggy Ryan, Louis DaPron
Universal, 10/27/44

BEAUTIFUL BUT BROKE
Judy Clark, Joan Davis
Columbia, 1/28/44

BOWERY TO BROADWAY
Jack Oakie, Donald O'Connor,
Peggy Ryan
Universal, 10/26/44

BRING ON THE GIRLS
Johnny Coy
Paramount, 3/1/44

BROADWAY RHYTHM
George Murphy, Walter Long
MGM, 1/4/44

CAROLINA BLUES
Marie Bryant,
Four Step Brothers,
Ann Miller, Harold Nicholas
Columbia, 9/26/44

CHIP OFF THE OLD BLOCK
Donald O'Connor, Peggy Ryan
Universal, 2/25/44

COVER GIRL
Rita Hayworth, Gene Kelly,
Phil Silvers
Columbia, 4/6/44

DANCE IMPRESSIONS
Bobby Davis
Soundies Corp.
(short), 11/20/44

FILM VODVIL (series 2, no 2)
Douglas Brothers
Columbia (1 reel), 1944

FOLLOW THE BOYS
Donald O'Connor, Peggy Ryan
Universal, 3/31/44

FOUR JILLS IN A JEEP
Mitzi Mayfair
20th Century-Fox, 3/44

GHOST CATCHERS
Bobby Scheerer,
Love Jean Weber
Universal, 6/16/44

GREENWICH VILLAGE
Four Step Brothers
20th Century-Fox, 8/3/44

HEY, ROOKIE
Judy Clark, Condos Brothers,
Roland Dupree, Joyce Horne,
Ann Miller
(dances with Jimmy Vecchio
and Varmere Barman deleted)
Columbia, 3/9/44

HI, GOOD LOOKIN'
Tip, Tap and Toe
Universal, 3/17/44

JAM SESSION
Ann Miller
Columbia, 3/22/44

JUMPIN' AT THE JUBILEE
The Swing Maniacs
Panoram Soundies, 1944

MERRY MONAHANS, THE
Jack Oakie, Donald O'Connor,
Peggy Ryan
Universal, 9/15/44

MINSTREL MAN
Judy Clark, Benny Fields
PRC, 8/1/44

MY BEST GAL
Jane Withers
Republic, 3/28/44

PENTHOUSE RHYTHM
Judy Clark, Louis DaPron
Universal, 11/20/44

PIN-UP GIRL
Condos Brothers
20th Century-Fox, 5/10/44

RECKLESS AGE
Harold Nicholas
Universal, 10/26/44

SENSATIONS OF 1945
Eleanor Powell
United Artists, 6/30/44

SEVEN DAYS ASHORE
Uncredited female dancers
RKO, 4/44

SHINE ON HARVEST MOON
Four Step Brothers
Warner Bros., 4/8/44

SHOW BUSINESS
Eddie Cantor, Joan Davis,
Constance Moore,
George Murphy
RKO, 4/22/44

SING A JINGLE
Dean Collins, Betty Kean
Universal, 1/7/44

SINGING SHERIFF, THE
Iris Adrian, Louis DaPron,
Pat Starling
Universal, 9/15/44

SLIGHTLY TERRIFIC
Ray Malone
Universal, 5/5/44

SONG OF THE OPEN ROAD
Condos Brothers
United Artists, 6/2/44

STEP LIVELY
George Murphy
RKO, 6/26/44

STEPPING FAST
Burch Mann Dancers
Soundies Corp.
(short), 11/13/44

SWINGTIME JOHNNY
Harriet Hilliard, Andrews Sisters
Universal, 2/4/44

TAKE IT OR LEAVE IT
Nicholas Brothers
20th Century-Fox, 1944

THIS IS THE LIFE
Donald O'Connor, Peggy Ryan
Universal, 11/17/44

1945

ANCHORS AWEIGH
Gene Kelly, Frank Sinatra,
Tom and Jerry (cartoons)
MGM, 7/9/45

BIG TIMERS
Rocky Brown
All-American News (featurette),
1945

BILLY ROSE'S DIAMOND
HORSESHOE
Betty Grable
20th Century-Fox, 5/45

DOLLY SISTERS, THE
Betty Grable, Alice Faye
20th Century-Fox, 11/45

DUFFY'S TAVERN
Johnny Coy, Miriam Nelson
Paramount, 9/28/45

EADIE WAS A LADY
Ann Miller
Columbia, 1/23/45

EAGER BEAVER
Jean Ivory
Soundies Corp.
(short), 12/30/45

EVE KNEW HER APPLES
Ann Miller
Columbia, 4/12/45

GEORGE WHITE'S SCANDALS
Beverly Wills
RKO, 8/45

HERE COME THE CO-EDS
Peggy Ryan
Universal, 2/2/45

HER LUCKY NIGHT
Andrews Sisters
Universal, 2/9/45

HONEYMOON AHEAD
Grace McDonald
Universal, 5/11/45

MURDER WITH MUSIC
Alston and Johnsons
Johnson and Johnson
Century, ca. mid-1940s

NAUGHTY NINETIES
Uncredited Irish jig number
on showboat
Universal, 7/6/45

NIGHT CLUB GIRL
Vivian Austin, Billy Dunn
(aka Billy Lechner)
Universal, 1/5/45

ON STAGE, EVERYBODY
Johnny Coy, Peggy Ryan
Universal, 7/27/45

PATRICK THE GREAT
Jivin' Jacks and Jills,
Donald O'Connor,
Peggy Ryan
Universal, 5/4/45

RHAPSODY IN BLUE
Johnny Downs, Joan Leslie,
Tom Patricola
Warner Bros., 9/22/45

SANDIN' JOE
Two tap dancers
Soundies Corp.
(short), 9/10/45

SEE MY LAWYER
Grace McDonald, Ronnie Stanton
Universal, 5/25/45

SENSATIONS OF 1945
Eleanor Powell
United Artists, 6/30/45

SING YOUR WAY HOME
Peggy Brant
RKO, 12/45

SWING OUT SISTER
Jacqueline de Wit,
Arthur Treacher
Universal, 5/18/45

THAT'S THE SPIRIT
Johnny Coy, Jack Oakie,
Peggy Ryan
Universal, 6/1/45

TONIGHT AND EVERY NIGHT
Marc Platt
Columbia, 2/22/45

TWICE BLESSED
Jimmy Lydon, Lee Wilde
MGM, 7/45

WONDER MAN
Vera-Ellen, Danny Kaye
Goldwyn, 4/45

YOLANDA AND THE THIEF
Fred Astaire
MGM, 11/15/45

1946

AFFAIRS OF GERALDINE
Jane Withers
Republic, 11/18/46

BEALE ST. MAMA
July Jones
Sack Amusement, ca. 1946

BLACK ANGEL
Louis DaPron, Pat Starling
Universal, 8/7/46

BLUE SKIES
Fred Astaire
MGM, 12/27/46

DIXIELAND JAMBOREE
Nicholas Brothers
Vitaphone (short) 4/24/46
(footage is ca. 1934)

EARL CARROLL'S SKETCHBOOK
Dorothy Babb, Johnny Coy
Republic, 8/22/46

HARVEY GIRLS, THE
Ray Bolger
MGM, 1/18/46

JUNIOR PROM
Judy Clark, Dean Collins
Monogram, 5/11/46

KID FROM BROOKLYN
Vera-Ellen
Goldwyn, 3/21/46

LOVE IN SYNCOPATION
Tops and Wilda,
Ronnell and Edna
Astor, ca. 1946

LYING LIPS
Clyde "Slim" Thompson,
Teddy Hale
Sack Amusement, ca. 1946

MIDNIGHT MENACE
"Lollypop" Jones
Jimmy Walker
All-American News (2 reels),
1946

ROAD TO UTOPIA
Four Step Brothers
Paramount, 3/22/46

SLIGHTLY SCANDALOUS
Louis DaPron
Universal, 8/2/46

SOLID SENDERS
Clyde "Slim" Thompson
Sack Amusement, ca. 1946

TALL, TAN AND TERRIFIC
Thelma Cordero
Astor, 1946

TARS AND SPARS
Marc Platt
Columbia, 1/11/46

THREE LITTLE GIRLS IN BLUE
Vera-Ellen
20th Century-Fox, 10/46

THRILL OF BRAZIL, THE
Ann Miller
Columbia, 9/30/46

TILL THE CLOUDS ROLL BY
June Allyson, Ray McDonald
MGM, 1/46

TIME, THE PLACE AND THE GIRL,
THE
Condos Brothers
Warner Bros., 12/28/46

ZIEGFELD FOLLIES
Fred Astaire, Gene Kelly
MGM, 1/15/46

1947

DOUBLE RHYTHM
Lee Dixon, Nilsson Twins
Paramount, 1947

DOWN TO EARTH
Marc Platt
Columbia, 7/17/47

GOOD NEWS
Joan McCracken, Ray McDonald
MGM, 12/26/47

HI-DE-HO
Miller Brothers and Lois
All-American Pictures, 1947

I WONDER WHO'S KISSING HER
NOW
Gene Nelson
20th Century-Fox, 8/47

JIVIN' IN BE-BOP
Ralph Brown, Ray Sneed
Alexander Productions, 1947

LADIES' MAN
Dorothy Babb, Johnny Coy
(Dance cut, but used in a
Paramount short the same
year)
Paramount, 2/7/47

LIVING IN A BIG WAY
Gene Kelly
MGM, 6/47

MOTHER WORE TIGHTS
Dan Dailey, Betty Grable
20th Century-Fox, 9/47

MY WILD IRISH ROSE
The Dunhills
Warner Bros., 12/27/47

PITCH A BOOGIE WOOGIE
Cleophus Lyons
Lord-Warner (2 reels), 1947

SOMETHING IN THE WIND
Donald O'Connor
Universal-International, 8/12/47

SONG IS BORN, A
Buck and Bubbles
(Goldwyn Productions,)
RKO, 12/31/47

SWEET AND LOW
Sammy Davis, Jr. with
the Will Mastin Trio
Paramount (short) 4/28/47

THAT'S MY GAL
Four Step Brothers
Republic, 5/7/47

1948

APRIL SHOWERS
Jack Carson, Ann Sothern,
Robert Ellis
Warner Bros., 3/27/48

ARE YOU WITH IT?
Louis DaPron, Donald O'Connor,
George O'Hanlon
Universal-International, 6/8/48

BOARDINGHOUSE BLUES
Berry Brothers,
Stump and Stumpy
All-American Pictures, ca. 1948

BUDDY RICH AND HIS
ORCHESTRA
Louis DaPron, Buddy Rich
Universal-International (short),
11/23/48

EASTER PARADE
Fred Astaire, Judy Garland,
Ann Miller
MGM, 5/26/48

FEUDIN, FUSSIN'
AND A-FIGHTING
Louis DaPron, Donald O'Connor
Universal-International, 7/48

GIVE MY REGARDS TO
BROADWAY
Dan Dailey
20th Century-Fox, 6/8/48

IF YOU KNEW SUSIE
Eddie Cantor, Joan Davis,
Dick Humphreys, Margaret Kelly
RKO, 2/7/48

JUNCTION 88
"Pigmeat" Markham
Sack Amusement, ca. 1948

KILLER DILLER
Patterson and Jackson
Clark Brothers
All-American News, 1948

PIRATE, THE
Gene Kelly, Nicholas Brothers
MGM, 3/16/48

THRILLS OF MUSIC:
BUDDY RICH AND HIS
ORCHESTRA
Steve Condos
Columbia (1 reel), 1948

TIME OF YOUR LIFE
Paul Draper
United Artists, 9/3/48

WHEN MY BABY SMILES AT ME
Dan Dailey, Betty Grable
20th Century-Fox, 11/5/48

WORDS AND MUSIC
June Allyson, Hal Bell,
Blackburn Twins,
Vera-Ellen, Gene Kelly,
Ann Sothern
MGM, 12/7/48

YOU WERE MEANT FOR ME
Dan Dailey
20th Century-Fox, 1/16/48

1949

ALWAYS LEAVE THEM
LAUGHING
Milton Berle, Bert Lahr
Warner Bros., 11/26/49

BARKLEYS OF BROADWAY,
THE
Fred Astaire, Ginger Rogers
MGM, 3/15/49

KISSING BANDIT, THE
Ann Miller
MGM, 1/49

LOOK FOR THE SILVER LINING
Ray Bolger, June Haver
Warner Bros., 7/30/49

ON THE TOWN
Vera-Ellen, Betty Garrett,
Gene Kelly, Ann Miller,
Jules Munshin, Frank Sinatra
MGM, 12/1/49

SHAMROCK HILL
Ray McDonald, Peggy Ryan
Eagle Lion, 2/49

TAKE ME OUT TO
THE BALL GAME
Gene Kelly, Frank Sinatra
MGM, 3/1/49

YES SIR, THAT'S MY BABY
Donald O'Connor
Universal-International, 9/8/49

YOU'RE MY EVERYTHING
Berry Brothers
(Ananias and Warren Berry),
Dan Dailey
20th Century-Fox, 7/16/49

1950

DAUGHTER OF ROSIE
O'GRADY, THE
James Barton, Gene Nelson
Warners, 4/29/50

DUCHESS OF IDAHO
Eleanor Powell
MGM, 7/14/50

KING COLE TRIO WITH
BENNY CARTER
AND HIS ORCHESTRA
Bunny Briggs
Universal-International (2 reels),
   6/9/50

LET'S DANCE
Fred Astaire, Betty Hutton
Paramount, 11/24/50

MILKMAN, THE
Donald O'Connor
Universal, 8/31/50

MY BLUE HEAVEN
Dan Dailey, Betty Grable
20th Century-Fox, 8/23/50

RAY ANTHONY AND HIS
ORCHESTRA
Jimmy Vecchio
Universal-International (short),
ca. 1950

SUMMER STOCK
Judy Garland, Gene Kelly
MGM, 8/7/50

TEA FOR TWO
Doris Day, Gene Nelson
Warners, 9/2/50

THERE'S A GIRL IN MY HEART
Ray McDonald, Peggy Ryan
Allied Artists, 1/6/50

THREE LITTLE WORDS
Fred Astaire, Vera-Ellen
MGM, 7/6/50

WABASH AVENUE
James Barton, Betty Grable
20th Century-Fox 4/50

WEST POINT STORY, THE
James Cagney, Gene Nelson
Warner Bros., 11/18/50

1951

AN AMERICAN IN PARIS
Gene Kelly
MGM, 9/5/51

CALL ME MISTER
Dan Dailey, The Dunhills,
Betty Grable
20th Century-Fox, 1/31/51

CAVALCADE OF BANDS
Bobby "Tables" Davis
Dumont Television, (½ hour),
1951

DOUBLE CROSSBONES
Donald O'Connor
Universal-International, 4/51

LULLABY OF BROADWAY
Doris Day, Gene Nelson
Warners, 3/24/51

MEET ME AFTER THE SHOW
Jerry Brandow, Steve Condos,
Betty Grable
20th Century-Fox, 8/15/51

PAINTING THE CLOUDS
WITH SUNSHINE
Virginia Mayo, Gene Nelson
Warners, 10/6/51

ROYAL WEDDING
Fred Astaire, Jane Powell
MGM, 2/5/51

STARLIFT
Gene Nelson
Warner Bros., 12/1/51

TEXAS CARNIVAL
Ann Miller
MGM, 9/10/51

TWO TICKETS TO BROADWAY
Janet Leigh, Tony Martin
(Bobby Scheerer was Tony's
dance-in), Ann Miller
RKO, 11/5/51

1952

APRIL IN PARIS
Ray Bolger
Warner Bros., 1/3/52

BELLE OF NEW YORK, THE
Fred Astaire, Vera-Ellen
MGM, 2/12/52

EVERYTHING I HAVE IS YOURS
Marge and Gower Champion
MGM, 10/5/52

INVITATION TO THE DANCE
Gene Kelly
MGM, (made in 1952, released
   3/1/57)

LOVELY TO LOOK AT
Ann Miller
MGM, 6/2/52

MEET ME AT THE FAIR
Dan Dailey
Universal, 11/3/52

ROCK'N ROLL REVUE
Conrad "Little Buck" Buckner,
Coles and Atkins
Studio Films, ca. 1952

SHE'S WORKING HER WAY
THROUGH COLLEGE
Virginia Mayo, Gene Nelson
Warner Bros., 7/12/52

SINGIN' IN THE RAIN
Gene Kelly, Donald O'Connor,
Debbie Reynolds
MGM, 4/11/52

WHERE'S CHARLEY?
Ray Bolger
Warner Bros., 8/16/52

1953

ALL ASHORE
Ray McDonald, Peggy Ryan
Columbia, 3/53

BAND WAGON, THE
Fred Astaire, Jack Buchanan
MGM, 8/3/53

CALL ME MADAM
Vera-Ellen, Donald O'Connor
20th Century-Fox, 3/5/53

GIRL NEXT DOOR, THE
Dan Dailey
20th Century-Fox, 5/13/53

HERE COME THE GIRLS
Four Step Brothers
Paramount, 12/1/53

I DON'T CARE GIRL, THE
Mitzi Gaynor
20th Century-Fox, 1953

I LOVE MELVIN
Donald O'Connor, Debbie
Reynolds
MGM, 5/20/53

KISS ME KATE
Jeanne Coyne, Bob Fosse,
Carol Haney, Ann Miller,
Tommy Rall, Bobby Van
MGM, 11/26/53

SHE'S BACK ON BROADWAY
Condos and Brandow,
Virginia Mayo, Gene Nelson
Warner Bros., 3/14/53

SMALL TOWN GIRL
Ann Miller
MGM, 4/18/53

THREE SAILORS AND A GIRL
Gene Nelson
Warners, 12/26/53

WALKING MY BABY BACK
HOME
Janet Leigh, Donald O'Connor
Universal, 12/2/53

1954

BRIGADOON
Van Johnson, Gene Kelly
MGM, 9/2/54

DEEP IN MY HEART
Fred and Gene Kelly, Ann Miller
MGM, 12/24/54

GIVE A GIRL A BREAK
Marge and Gower Champion,
Bob Fosse, Debbie Reynolds
MGM, 1/1/54

THERE'S NO BUSINESS
LIKE SHOW BUSINESS
Dan Dailey, Donald O'Connor
20th Century-Fox, 12/54

TOP BANANA
Johnny Coy
United Artists, 2/54

1955

DADDY LONG LEGS
Fred Astaire
20th Century-Fox, 5/5/55

HARLEM VARIETY REVUE
Businessmen of Rhythm
Coles and Atkins
Bill Bailey, Little Buck
Studio Films (series of 30-minute
shorts), 1955

HIT THE DECK
Ann Miller
MGM, 2/24/55

IT'S ALWAYS FAIR WEATHER
Dan Dailey, Gene Kelly,
Michael Kidd
MGM, 8/8/55

MY SISTER EILEEN
Bob Fosse, Betty Garrett,
Janet Leigh, Tommy Rall
Columbia, 10/55

OKLAHOMA!
Gene Nelson
Magna, 1955

SEVEN LITTLE FOYS, THE
James Cagney, Bob Hope
Warner Bros, 7/55

SO THIS IS PARIS
Tony Curtis, Paul Gilbert,
Gene Nelson
Universal, 1/55

ADDENDUM

HEART O' THE HILLS
John Gilbert, Mary Pickford
First National, 11/10/19

BUTTERFLY
Ruth Clifford
Universal Pictures, 8/12/24

STRONG MAN, THE
Harry Langdon
First National, 9/12/26

EXILE, THE
Unidentified black male dancer
and chorus
Micheaux, circa 1928

GUS EDWARDS' INTERNATIONAL
COLORTONE REVUE
GUS EDWARDS' KIDDIE REVUE
toe-tap trio, contortionist tapper
MGM, short subject, 3/5/29

METRO MOVIETONE REVUE #2
Rose Marie Sinnett
MGM, short subject, 6/10/29

GOOD NEWS
Dorothy McNulty (aka Penny
Singleton) and Company
(including Ann Dvorak)
MGM, 8/25/30

PARDON MY GUN
unidentified girl
Pathe Exchange, 6/29/30

VOICE OF VAUDEVILLE
"CLIFF NAZARRO'S MODERN
MINSTRELS"
Four Covans, The
Fowler Studios, 1930

VOICE OF VAUDEVILLE
"THE FOUR COVANS"
Four Covans, The
Fowler Studios, 1930

HIGH SCHOOL HOOFER
Hal Leroy
Vitaphone (1 reel), 1931

SHE LOVES ME NOT
Eddie Nugent
Paramount, 1932

TIP TAP TOE
Hal Leroy
Vitaphone (1 reel), 1932

WOOPEE PARTY, THE
Various cartoon characters
and inanimate objects
Walt Disney (cartoon), 09/17/32

MICKEY'S GALA PREMIER
Mickey Mouse
Walt Disney (cartoon), 7/1/33

SEASONED GREETINGS
Sammy Davis, Jr.
Vitaphone (2 reels), 1933

SO THIS IS AFRICA
Bert Weeler, Robert Woolsey
Columbia, 2/8/33

TOO MUCH HARMONY
Grace Bradley
Paramount, 9/23/33

WILD BOYS OF THE ROAD
Dorothy Coonan
First National, 9/22/33

COLLEGE RHYTHM
Chorus
Paramount, 11/23/34

IN THE SPOTLIGHT
Hal Leroy
Vitaphone (2 reels), 1935

OH, EVALINE
Hal Leroy
Vitaphone (2 reels), 1935

MERRY MANNEQUINS
Various cartoon characters
Columbia Pictures (cartoon),
3/19/37

BOSKO BAGDAD
Bosko, Bill Robinson
MGM (cartoon), 1/1/38

BUGLE WOOGIE
Danny Hoctor, Susan Miller
Soundies Dist. Corp., 3/9/41

KISS THE BOYS GOODBYE
Eddie "Rochester" Anderson
Paramount, 6/23/41

ZIG ME WITH A GENTLE ZAG
Danny Hoctor, Gai Moran
Soundies Dist. Corp., 3/2/41

COLLEGE QUEEN
Noel Neill, Pat Phelan
Paramount (short subject), 2/15/42

SLICK HARE
Bugs Bunny
Warner Bros. (cartoon), 11/1/47

APPENDIX C
DISCOGRAPHY

TAP DANCERS ON RECORD, 1900–1955

FRED ASTAIRE

Accompanied by George Gershwin, piano
WA-3185-4 The Half of It Dearie, Blues

London, April 20, 1926
Columbia 3969
WRC 124, M-E 7136

Accompanied by Jacques Fray and Mario
Braggiotti
on two pianos
WA-8170-1 My One and Only

London, December 4, 1928

Columbia 5173
WRC 125, M-E 7037

Accompanied by a small jazz band
WA-10227-1 Puttin' On the Ritz

London, March 26, 1930
Columbia DB-96, FB-2207, FB-1257
WRC 124, M-E 7036

WA-10228-2 Crazy Feet

London, March 26, 1930

Accompanied by studio orchestra
CA-14213-2 Music Makes Me

London, December 12, 1933
Columbia DB-1329, FB-1256, 2912-D
WRC 124, M-E 7036, Epic L2N6072

Accompanied by Leo Reisman and His Orchestra
B-17733-1 No Strings

New York, June 26, 1935
Brunswick 7486, RL-296, Columbia DB-1825
Epic FLM 13103, Harmony 30549
Col SG 32472

Accompanied by Johnny Green and His Orchestra
B-17736-2 Top Hat, White Tie and Tails

New York, June 27, 1935
Brunswick 7487, RL-298, Col SG 32472

Los Angeles, January 30, 1936
LA-1095-A Let Yourself Go
Brunswick 7608, Columbia DB-1633
LA-1096-A I'd Rather Lead a Band
Brunswick 7610, Columbia DB-1635
Epic FLM 13103 Col SG 32472

Los Angeles, July 26, 1936
LA-1136-D Pick Yourself Up
Brunswick 7717, 02384, Vocalion 501
LA-1137-A Bojangles of Harlem
Brunswick 7718, 02385, Vocalion 500
Epic L2N 6064, Col SG 32472

Los Angeles, July 28, 1936
LA-1138-A Waltz in Swing Time (with tap dancing)
(Unissued)

Los Angeles, March 21, 1937
LA-1276-D Shall We Dance?
Brunswick 7857, 02425, Columbia 3166-D,
Epic FLM 13103, Col SG 32472
LA-1277-B Slap That Bass
Brunswick 7856, 02424, Columbia 3165-D,
Epic FLM 13105, Col SG 32472

Accompanied by Ray Noble and His Orchestra
LA-1467-C Nice Work if You Can Get It

Los Angeles, October 19, 1937
Brunswick 7983, 02533, Columbia DB-
Epic FLM 13103, Col SG 32472
LA-1468-A-B I Can't Be Bothered Now
Brunswick 7982, 02532
Epic FLM 13103, Col SG 32472

Los Angeles, March 26, 1938
LA-1610-A The Yam
Brunswick 8190, Columbia DB-1810
LA-1611-A The Yam Step Explained (with Ray Noble)
Epic FLM 13103, Col SG 32472

Accompanied by Benny Goodman and His Orchestra

Los Angeles, May 9, 1940

26809-A Just Like Taking Candy from a Baby

Columbia 35517, DB-1943, <u>CSM 891</u>

Accompanied by orchestra directed by Perry Botkin
LA-2359-A Me and the Ghost Upstairs
LA-2360-A (I Ain't Hep to That Step but I'll) Dig It

Los Angeles, September 22, 1940
Columbia 35815, C-173, DB-2018
Columbia 35852, C-166, DB-2014
<u>Epic FLM 13103</u>

Accompanied by Bob Crosby and His Orchestra
DLA-2996-A I'll Capture Your Heart (with Bing
                Crosby and Margaret Lenhart)
Let's Say It with Firecrackers

Los Angeles, May 27, 1942
Decca 18427, Brunswick 03358

Unissued

JACK BUCHANAN

Accompanied by orchestra directed by ?
Percival Mackey
WAX-2023-2 Let's Say Goodnight Till the Morning
                (with Elsie Randolph)

London, October 15, 1926

Columbia 9147

Accompanied by Harry Perritt and the London
Hippodrome Orchestra
WA-11453 Night Time

London, April 14, 1931

Columbia DB-484

Accompanied by Ray Noble and His Orchestra
OB-6327-1 Yes, Mr. Brown

London, March 8, 1933
HMV B-4398

EMELYNE (Evelyn) COLLIER

Accompanied by Gus Arnheim and His Orchestra
54731-3 Dancing to Save Your Sole
                (with vocal trio)

Culver City, March 30, 1930
Victor 22384

EDNA HOLDT Tap Dance Instructress

Accompanied by Casper Reardon, piano
75226-1 Beginner's Tap
75227-1 Soft Shoe Routine
75228-1 Waltz Clog
75229-1 Advanced Tap
75230-1 Advanced Tap Routine
75231-1 Professional

New York, February 15, 1933
Victor 24288
Victor 24288
Victor 24289
Victor 24289
Victor 24290
Victor 24290

JACK HULBERT

Accompanied by orchestra
——— Tap Your Tootsies

London, ca. March 1936
HMV BD-335, <u>EMI SH 217</u>

ELLIS JACKSON, Tap Dancing Trombonist

Accompanied by Billy Cotton and His Band
CAR-1435-1 How'm I Doin'? (Hey-Hey)
        (vocal by Cyril Grantham)

London, September 15, 1932
Regal MR-674

FREDDIE JENKINS

Accompanied by Duke Ellington and His
Orchestra
M-179-1-2 I've Got To Be A Rug Cutter
        (vocal by Ivie Anderson)

New York, March 5, 1937

Master 101, Brunswick 7989

EVELYN KUNNEKE

Accompanied by orchestra directed by Michael
Jary
Hokuspokus (Eins, Zwei, Drei . . .)

In Tirol Steht ein Berg

Berlin, September 30, 1942

Odeon 0-26551

Berlin, June 28, 1943
Odeon 0-26613

JESSIE MATTHEWS

Accompanied by Louis Levy and His Orchestra
TB-2123-1 Tony's in Town (vocal with
        the Three Ginx)
TB-2125-1 Got to Dance My Way to Heaven

London, April 17, 1936
Decca F-5982, Decca ECM2168

Decca F-5983, Decca ECM2168

Accompanied by Jay Wilbur and His Orchestra
DTB-3194-1 When You Gotta Sing, You Gotta Sing

London, August 7, 1937
Decca F-6470, <u>Decca ECM2168</u>

CLIFF NAZARRO

New York, September 18, 1939

042676-2 How to Learn to Tap Dance

Bluebird 10433

FAYARD NICHOLAS

Accompanied by orchestra directed by George
Scott Wood
OEA-4052-1 Keep a Twinkle in Your Eye
         (vocal by Harold Nicholas)

London, September 15, 1936

HMV BD-373, <u>PMC 7154 (British)</u>,
<u>EMI SH 265</u> (British)

Accompanied by orchestra directed by Frank
Signorelli
62858-A Wrap Your Cares in Rhythm and Dance
         (vocal by Harold Nicholas)
62859-A They Say He Ought to Dance
         (vocal by Harold Nicholas)

New York, December 6, 1937

Decca 1604, Brunswick 02588

Decca 1604, Brunswick 02588

ELEANOR POWELL

Accompanied by Tommy Dorsey and His
Orchestra
95379-1 You Are My Lucky Star
95380-1 I've Got a Feelin' You're Foolin'
95381-1 Got a Bran' New Suit

New York, October 11, 1935

Victor 25158, HMV B-8396
Victor 25158, HMV B-8396
Victor 25173, HMV B-8406

95505-1 That's Not Cricket
95506-2 What a Wonderful World

New York, October 14, 1935
Victor 25173
<u>RCA Victor LPV-560, AXM2-5521</u>

BILL ROBINSON

Accompanied by Irving Mills' Hotsy-Totsy Gang
E-30526 Ain't Misbehavin'
E-30527 Doin' the New Low Down

New York, September 11, 1929
Brunswick 4535, 7706, 01112
Brunswick 4535, 7706, 01112, also Columbia 30183

Accompanied by studio orchestra
E-36833 Keep a Song in Your Soul
E-36834 Just a Crazy Song (Hi-Hi-Hi)

New York, May 27, 1931
Brunswick 6134, 7705, 01168, Columbia 30183
As above, except Columbia 30184

Accompanied by Don Redman and His Orchestra   New York, December 29, 1932
B-12810-A Doin' the New Low Down   Brunswick 6520, 01521, Columbia 30184, <u>Co1 0L 6770</u>

The numbers to the left of each title indicate the matrix and the issued "take(s)" of each recording. If a flaw in the recording or performance necessitated a rerecording, a subsequent take number was assigned. The numbers to the right of each title indicate the catalog numbers of the records as issued, including foreign issues pressed from the original matrices. Long-play reissues are underlined. —Eric D. Bernhoft

REFERENCES:
BOOKS,
FILMS/VIDEOS

BOOKS

Ames, Jerry and Siegelman, Jim. *The Book of Tap, Recovering America's Long-Lost Dance.* New York: David McKay, 1977.

"Astaire to Run Tap Schools." *Dance News*, December, 1946.

Astaire, Fred. *Steps in Time.* New York: Harper & Brothers, 1959.

Atwater, Constance. *Tap Dancing.* Rutland, Vt.: E. E. Tuttle, 1971.

Audy, Robert. *Tap Dancing: How to Teach Yourself to Tap.* New York: Vintage Books, 1976.

Balliette, Whitney. *Such Sweet Thunder.* New York: Bobbs-Merrill, 1966.

———. Collected writings for *The New Yorker* on jazz. See especially his remembrance of Baby Lawrence in *New York Notes: A Journal of Jazz*, pp. 142–145. Houghton-Mifflin Co., 1976.

Ballwebber, Edith. *Tap Dancing.* New York: Clayton F. Summy, 1930.

———. *Illustrated Tap Rhythms and Routines.* New York: Clayton F. Summy, 1933.

Berson, Misha. "Syncopated Feats: The Rhythmic Roots of Jazz Dance on Film," *Image Magazine—San Francisco Chronicle/Examiner*, August 17, 1986.

Black, Shirley Temple. *Child Star.* New York: McGraw-Hill, 1988.

Blum, Daniel. *A Pictorial History of the American Theatre, 1900–1950.* New York: Greenberg, 1950.

Bogle, Donald. *Toms, Coons, Mulattoes, Mammies, and Bucks: An Interpretive History of Blacks in American Films.* New York: Viking, 1973.

Burchill, Kenneth. *Step Dancing—A Course of Twenty Lessons.* London: Sir Isaac Pitman and Sons, 1948.

Burns, George. *Gracie, A Love Story.* New York: Penguin Books, 1988.

Burns, George. *All My Best Friends.* New York: Putnam, 1989.

———. *Blue Book of Hollywood Musicals.* New York: Century House, 1953.

Butcher, Margaret J. *The Negro in American Culture.* New York: Knopf, 1956.

Cadwell, Grace. *How to Tap Dance.* St. Louis: B. Simon, 1931.

Caffin, Caroline. *Vaudeville.* New York: Mitchell Kennerley, 1914.

Caffin, Caroline and Charles. *Dancing and Dancers of Today.* New York: Dodd, Mead, 1912.

Calvin, Kenneth W. "The Big Idea of Fanchon and Marco, Part I," *The Dance Magazine*, March, 1929.

———. "The Big Idea of Fanchon and Marco, Part II," *The Dance Magazine*, April, 1929.

Cantor, Eddie and Freedman, David. *Ziegfeld*. New York: Alfred H. King, 1934.

Carlos, Ernest. *Tips on Tap*. New York: Edward B. Marks Music Corp., 1937.

Castle, Irene. *Castles in the Air*. Garden City, New York: Doubleday, 1958.

Castle, Nick. *How to Tap Dance*. Hollywood, Cal.: 1948.

Castle, Mr. And Mrs. Vernon. *Modern Dancing*. New York: Harper & Brothers, 1914.

Cholerton, Judy. *Hints on Tap Dancing*. Derby, England: The Association of American Tap Dancing and Modern Art Group, 1936.

Clark, Mary. *Presenting People Who Dance*. London: Paul Hamlyn, 1961.

Connor, Jim. *Ann Miller, Tops in Taps*. New York: Franklin Watts, 1981.

Croce, Arlene. *The Fred Astaire and Ginger Rogers Book*. New York: Vintage, 1977.

Cropper, Dorothy Horman. *Dance Dictionary*. New York: Dancers Book Publishers, 1935.

Dance Masters of America, Inc. *ABCs of Dance Terminology*. Washington, D.C.: Dance Masters of America, Inc., 1949.

Dance Masters of America, Inc. *Graded System of Tap*. Washington, D.C.: Dance Masters of America, Inc. 1974.

Daniels, Don. "Secular Tap," *Ballet Review*, pp. 82–90, Winter, 1982.

Davis, Sammy, Jr., Boyar, Jane and Burt. *Yes I Can*. New York: Farrar, Straus and Giroux, 1965.

Denby, Edwin. *Looking at the Dance*. New York: Pellegrini and Cudahy, 1949.

Dickens, Charles. *American Notes*, Vol. I. London: Chapman and Hall, 1842.

Donahue, Jack. *Letters of a Hoofer to His Ma*. New York: Cosmopolitan Book Corp., 1930–1931.

Draper, Paul. *Dance Magazine*. Numerous articles from August, 1954, through September, 1963, including: 8/54, 1/57, 7/57, 2/62, 5/62, 6/62, 8/62, 9/62, 11/62, 3/63, 8/63, 9/63.

———. *On Tap Dancing*. Marcel Dekker, 1978.

Duggan, Anne Schley. *Tap Dances*. New York: A. S. Barnes, 1933.

———. *Tap Dances for Schools and Recreation*. New York: A. S. Barnes, 1936.

———. *Complete Tap Dance Book*. New York: A. S. Barnes, 1947.

Ellison, Ralph. *Shadow and Act*. New York: Random House, 1964.

Emery, Lynne Fauley. *Black Dance in the United States from 1619 to 1970*. Dance Horizons, 1980.

Ewen, David. *The Story of America's Musical Theater*. Philadelphia: Chilton, 1961, rev. ed. 1968.

Farnsworth, Majorie. *The Ziegfeld Follies*. New York: Bonanza, 1956.

Feather, Leonard. *The Book of Jazz*. Paperback Library, 1961.

Felix, Seymour. "Dance Director's Grief," *The Dance Magazine*. January, 1929.

Ferguson, Katherine. *Elementary Tap Dances*. New York: Women's Press, 1930.

Fletcher, Beale. *How to Improve Your Tap Dancing*. New York: A. S. Barnes, 1957.

Fletcher, Tom. *100 Years of the Negro in Show Business*. New York: Burdge, 1954.

Fox, Ted. *Showtime at the Apollo*. New York: Holt, Rinehart and Winston, 1983.

Frost, Helen. *The Clog Dance Book*. New York: A. S. Barnes, 1921.

———. *Clog and Character Dances*. New York: A. S. Barnes, 1924.

———. *Tap, Caper and Clog*. New York: A. S. Barnes, 1931.

Gilbert, Douglas. *American Vaudeville*. New York: Whittlesey House, 1940.

Givens, Ron. "An Exultation of Hoofers," *Newsweek*, July 11, 1988.

Goldberg, Isaac. *Tin Pan Alley*. New York: John Day Co., 1930.

Goldberg, Jane. "The Lady Has Style," *Quincy Patriot Ledger*, July 28, 1973.

———. "It's All in the Feet," *Quincy Patriot Ledger*, April 24, 1974.

———. "An Interview with Paul Draper," *Ballet Review*, Vol. 5, #1, 1975–76.

———. "Taps for Ginger Rogers," *The Village Voice*, March 15, 1976.

———. "Tapping Back Into View," *Jazz Magazine.* Winter, 1978.

———. "A Hoofer's Homage: John Bubbles," *The Village Voice,* December, 1978.

———. "A Tap Festival," *Dance Scope.* 15:3, pp. 62–68, 1981.

———. *Foot Print: News on Tap.* New York: Changing Times Tap Publication, Fall 1983.

Hannah, Judith Lynne. *The Performer-Audience Connection.* Texas: University of Texas Press, 1983.

Haskins, Jim. *The Cotton Club: A Pictorial and Social History of the Most Famous Symbol of the Jazz Era.* New York: Random House, 1977.

———. *The Cotton Club.* New York: New American Library, 1977.

Haskins, Jim and Mitgang, N. R. *Mr. Bojangles.* New York: William Morrow, 1988.

Heimann, Jim. *Out with the Stars: Hollywood Nightlife in the Golden Era.* New York: Abbeville Press, 1985.

Hering, Doris, editor. *25 Years of American Dance.* New York: Rudolf Orthwine, ca. 1954. Anthology of articles from *Dance Magazine.*

Hillas, Majorie. *Tap Dancing.* New York: A. S. Barnes, 1930.

Hillas and Knighton. *Athletic Dances and Simple Clog.* New York: A. S. Barnes, 1926.

Hirschhorn, Clive. *The Hollywood Musical.* New York: Crown, 1981.

Hoctor, Danny. *Graded Exercises for Tap Dancing.* Aldwick, N.J.: Dance Records, 1971.

Horosko, Marian. "Tap, Tapping and Tappers." *Dance Magazine,* October, 1971.

Horowitz, Timna. "Hoofers Old and True and New," *Theatre LA.* Los Angeles: Vol. II, No. 1: December 1983/January 1984.

Hughes, Langston and Meltzer, Milton. *Black Magic: A Pictorial History of the Negro in American Entertainment.* New York: Prentice Hall, 1967.

Hungerford, Mary Jane. *Creative Tap Dancing.* New York: Prentice-Hall, 1939.

Jay, Leticia. "The Wonderful Old-time Hoofers at Newport," *Dance Magazine,* August, 1963.

Jessell, George. *Elegy in Manhattan.* New York: Holt, Rinehart and Winston, 1961.

Johnson, James Weldon. *Black Manhattan.* New York: Atheneum, 1968.

Jones, LeRoi. *Blues People.* New York: William Morrow, 1963.

Judd and Stuart. *Tap Dancing.* New York: The Women's Press, 1935.

Kehl, Leo. *Dances of Today.* Madison, Wisc.: ca. 1930s.

———. *Forma-Dance Tap System.* Madison, Wisc.: ca. 1930s.

———. *Progressive Course in Tap Dancing.* Madison, Wisc.: ca. 1930s.

———. *Tap Dances.* Vols. 1,2,3. Madison, Wisc.: ca. 1930s.

Kirstein, Lincoln. *The Book of the Dance.* Garden City, N.Y.: Garden City Pub. Co., 1942.

Kislan, Richard. *Hoofing on Broadway.* New York: Prentice Hall, 1987.

Knight, Arthur. "Dancing in Films." *Dance Index,* August, 1947.

Kobal, John. *Gotta Sing, Gotta Dance, a Pictorial History of Film Musicals.* London/New York/Sydney/Toronto: Hamlyn, 1971.

———. *Gotta Sing Gotta Dance.* Great Britain: Spring Books, 1988.

Laurie, Joe Jr. *Vaudeville.* New York: Henry Holt, 1953.

Leaf, Munro. *Isles of Rhythm.* New York: A. S. Barnes, 1948.

Little, Elise A. "A History of Tap," *The Dance Encyclopedia.* Anatole Chujoy, ed. New York: A. S. Barnes, 1949.

Manning, Betty. "Tap Marches On." *Dance Magazine,* October, 1944.

Martin, David. *The Films of Busby Berkeley.* San Francisco: David Martin, 1964 (monograph).

Martin, John. *The Dance.* New York: Tudor, 1964.

Marx, Trina. *Tap Dance: A Beginner's Guide.* New York: Prentice-Hall, 1983.

McLean, Albert F. Jr. *American Vaudeville as Ritual.* Lexington: University of Kentucky Press, 1965.

Mingus, Charles. *Beneath the Underdog.* New York: Penguin, 1980.

Moody, Richard. *America Takes the Stage.* Bloomington: Indiana University Press, 1955.

Moore, Lillian. "John Durang: The First American Dancer," *Chronicles of the American Dance.* Paul Magriel, ed.

New York: Da Capo Press, 1978.

Mueller, John. *Astaire Dancing: The Musical Films.* New York: Knopf, 1985.

Murray, Albert. *The OmniAmericans: Some Alternatives to the Folklore of White Supremacy.* New York: Vintage, 1983.

Murray, Kathryn. *My Husband, Arthur Murray.* New York: Simon and Schuster, 1960.

Nash, Barbara. *Tap Dance.* Dubuque, Wm. C. Brown, 1969.

Nathan, Hans. *Dan Emmett and the Rise of Early Negro Minstrelsy.* Oklahoma: University of Oklahoma Press, 1962.

Nettl, Paul. *The Story of Dance Music.* New York: Philosophical Library, 1947.

Nevell, Richard. *A Time to Dance: American Country Dancing from Hornpipes to Hot Hash.* New York: St. Martin's Press, 1977.

Noble, Peter. *The Negro in Films.* London: British Yearbooks, ca. 1949.

O'Gara, Sheila. *Tap It.* New York: A. S. Barnes, 1937.

Orchards, Theodore. "Tap Dancing—What of It?" *The Dance Magazine,* May, 1929.

Ormonde, Jimmy. *Tap Dancing at a Glance.* New York: Brewer, Warren, and Putman, 1931.

Parish, James Robert. *The Fox Girls.* New Rochelle, N.Y.: Arlington House, 1971.

Parker, David L. and Siegel, Esther. *Guide to Dance in Films.* New York: Gale Research, 1978.

Petsch, James. *Modern Tap Dance.* Hollywood, Ca.: James Petsch, 1937.

Ramsey, Rita. *Home Lessons in Tap Dancing.* New York: E. P. Dutton, 1932.

Randall, Skip. *Modern Tap Dancing.* New Jersey: Kimbo Music, 1967.

Raye, Zelia. *American Tap Dancing.* London: Zelia Raye, 1936.

Rice, Edw. LeRoy. *Monarchs of Minstrelsy.* New York: Kenny, 1911.

Rivers, Bobby. *Intermediate Rhythms.* New York: J. I. Phillips, ca. 1930s.

Rivoli, F. *How to Tap Dance.* New York: Kamin Book Shop, date unknown.

Roberts, W. Adolphe. "Jazz Dancing—A New Color in the American Rainbow," *The Dance Magazine,* May, 1929.

Ronna Dance Supplies. *Creative Tap Dancing.* Author unknown, 1954.

Rowland, Mabel, ed. *Bert Williams, Son of Laughter.* New York: The English Crafters, 1923.

Russell, Eddie. *The Art of Buck and Wing Dancing Simplified.* New York: Eddie Russell, 1924.

Ruyter, Nancy Lee Chafla. *Reformers and Visionaries: The Americanization of the Art of Dance.* New York: Dance Horizons, 1979.

Sachs, Curt. *World History of the Dance.* New York: Seven Arts Publishers, 1952.

Sampson, Henry T. *Blacks in Blackface: A Sourcebook on Early Black Musical Shows.* Metuchen, N.J.: Scarecrow Press, 1980.

Samuels, Charles & Louise. *Once Upon a Stage: The Merry World of Vaudeville.* New York: Dodd, Mead, 1974.

Sautoff, Hermine. *Tap Dance for Fun.* New York: A. S. Barnes, 1941.

Schiffman, Amy. "Tap is Back," *San Francisco Focus,* September 1985.

Schiffman, Jack. *Uptown: The Story of Harlem's Apollo Theatre.* Cowles, 1971.

Sennett, Ted. *Warner Brothers Presents.* New Rochelle, N.Y.: Castle Books, 1971.

Shipley, Glenn. *Modern Tap Techniques.* San Francisco: Glenn Shipley, 1951.

———. *Modern Tap Dictionary.* Los Angeles: Dance Publications, 1963.

———. *Tiny Tot Tap Technique.* San Francisco: Glenn Shipley, 1973.

———. *The Formulation of Tap Technique.* San Francisco: Glenn Shipley, 1974.

———. *The Complete Tap Dictionary.* San Francisco: Glenn Shipley, 1980.

Shomer, Louis. *Tip Top Tapping.* New York: Louellen Publishing, 1937.

Springer, John. *All Talking! All Singing! All Dancing!* New Jersey: Citadel, 1972.

Smith, Bill. *The Vaudevillians.* New York: Macmillan, 1976.

Smith, Cecil. *Musical Comedy in America.* New York: Theatre Arts Books, 1950.

Smith, Ernie. "Recollections and Reflections of a Jazz Dance Film Collector," *Dance Research Journal.* 15:2, pp. 46–48, Spring 1983.

Sobel, Bernard. "1,2,3,—Kick!: Sammy Lee, Dance Director of Many Hits, Explains His Methods of Increasing the Effectiveness of Ensemble Work," *The Dance Magazine*, January, 1929.

———. *A Pictorial History of Burlesque.* New York: Citadel, 1961.

———. *A Pictorial History of Vaudeville.* New York: Citadel, 1961.

Sommer, Sally. "Tap and How It Got That Way: Feet, Talk to Me!" *Dance Magazine*, September 1988.

———. "Tap Happy: Hines on Tap," *Dance Magazine*, December, 1988.

Southern, Eileen. *The Music of Black Americans.* New York: W. W. Norton, 1971.

Stearns, Jean and Marshall. *Jazz Dance, The Story of American Vernacular Dance: A history of dancing to jazz, from its African origins to the present.* New York: Shirmer Books, 1968.

Stearns, Marshall. *The Story of Jazz.* New York: Mentor Books, 1958.

Stein, Charles W., ed. *American Vaudeville as Seen by its Contemporaries.* New York: Knopf, 1984.

Stirling, June and Don. *A Modern System of Tap Notation.* Newark, N.J., Fairyland, U.S.A., Inc., 1958.

Stryker, Daisy Murrmann. *Tap Dancing Volume 1. U.S.A.:* Allied Institute of Dance, 1933.

———. *Tap Dancing Volume 2.* South Bend, Indiana: First National Institute of Dance, 1939.

Tamaroff, Alexander. *Taps.* New York: H. & T. Co., 1929.

Temin, Christine. "Dance Showcase Taps the Best to Demonstrate an Art Form," *The Boston Globe*, June 18, 1988.

Terry, Walter. "Tap Dance Trend." *New York Herald Tribune*, August 31, 1941.

———. *The Dance in America.* New York: Harper & Brothers, 1956.

Thompson, Howard. *Fred Astaire, A Pictorial Treasury of His Films.* New York: Falcon Enterprises, 1970.

Time-Life Books, ed. *This Fabulous Century 1930–1940—Volume IV*, New York: Time-Life Books, 1969.

Todd, Arthur. "From Chaplin to Kelly: The Dance on Film." *Theatre Arts*, August, 1951.

Toll, Robert C. *Blacking Up: The Minstrel Show in Nineteenth-Century America.* Oxford University Press, 1974.

———. *On with the Show: The First Century of Show Business in America.* Oxford University Press, 1976.

Tucker, Henry. *Clog Dancing Made Easy.* New York: DeWitt, 1874.

Vallance, Tom. *The American Musical.* New York: Castle, 1970.

Wade, Rosalind. *Tap Dancing in 12 Easy Lessons.* Philadelphia: David McKay, 1936.

Wayburn, Ned. *The Art of Stage Dancing.* New York: Ned Wayburn Studios of Stage Dancing, 1925.

Wheelock, Julie. "Tapping the Source of Inspiration," *Los Angeles Times*, June 26, 1988.

Wilkinson, W. C. *The Dance of Modern Society.* New York: Funk & Wagnalls, 1884.

Williams, Martin. *Jazz Heritage.* Oxford University Press, 1985.

Wilmeth, Don B. *American and English Popular Entertainment: A Guide to Information Sources.* Gale Research, 1980.

Winter, Marian Hannah. "Juba and American Minstrelsy," *Chronicles of the American Dance.* Paul Magriel, ed. New York: Henry Holt, 1948.

Wood, Philip Emerson. "At Last—The Native American Dance," *The Dance Magazine*, June, 1928.

Worsham, Doris G. "Gregory Hines succeeds in two-steps and 37 years," *The Oakland Tribune*, April 23, 1986.

Wright, Dexter. *Tap Dancing.* New York: Dexter Wright, 1931.

FILMS / VIDEOS

About Tap: 28 minutes, color, 1985. Hosted by Gregory Hines, with Chuck Green, Steve Condos, and Jimmy Slyde. Contact: Direct Cinema Ltd., P.O. Box 69799, Los Angeles, CA 90069.

By Word of Foot: 40 minutes, color, 1980. Features excerpts from The Village Gate Production. Contact: Times Tap Dancing Co., 65 E. 4th Street, New York, NY 10003.

Cookie's Scrapbook: 30 minutes, black and white, 1987.

Features Charles "Cookie" Cook and James "Buster" Brown reminiscing about vaudeville. Contact: Susan Goldbetter, 635 Carroll Street, Brooklyn, NY 11215.

Great Feats of Feet: 120 minutes, black and white, 1967. Documentary produced by Brenda Bufalino of a week in New Paltz, New York, with members of the Copasetics. Contact: Brenda Bufalino, 211 Thompson Street, #4K, New York, NY 10012.

The History of Jazz Dancing. 56 minutes, black and white, 1970. Lecture demonstration by Les Williams presenting the black man's role in the history of jazz dancing. Contact: New York Public Library, The Performing Arts Research Center, Lincoln Center, New York, NY 10023.

Jazz Hoofer: The Legendary Baby Lawrence. 29 minutes, color, 1973. Produced and directed by Bill Hancock. Contact: Rhapsody Films, 30 Charlton Street, New York, NY 10014.

No Maps on my Taps. 58 minutes, color, 1979. Film by George T. Nierenberg. With Chuck Green, Bunny Briggs, and Sandman Sims. Contact: Direct Cinema Ltd., P.O. Box 69799, Los Angeles, CA 90069.

Songs Unwritten: A Tap Dancer Remembered: 60 minutes, color, 1984. Tribute to the life and work of tap master Leon Collins. Contact: The Leon Collins Archive, P.O. Box 28128, Philadelphia, PA 19131.

Talking Feet. 90 minutes, color, 1986. Features traditions of step dance styles of the South, with background booklet, history, dance analysis, and step notation. Contact: Box 1592, Lexington, VA 24451.

Tap Dancin'. 58 minutes, color, 1980. Produced and directed by Christian Blackwood. Contact: Blackwood Films, 251 West 57th Street, New York, NY 10019.

That's Dancing! MGM compilation of dance. Available commercially for rental.

That's Entertainment!, Part I. MGM compilation, Available commercially for rental.

That's Entertainment!, Part II. MGM compilation, available commercially for rental.

Video Encyclopedia of Tap Technique. Compilation, color, 1990. Produced by Susan Goldbetter, directed by Skip Blumberg. Features Charles "Cookie" Cook, Brenda Bufalino, and Kevin Ramsey. Contact: Susan Goldbetter, 635 Carroll Street, Brooklyn, NY 11215.

ADDENDUM

Dance Crazy in Hollywood, 60 minutes, color, 1990. Directed by Robert Kuperberg. Documentary on legendary Hollywood choreographer, Hermes Pan. During the golden age of movies musicals he was Hollywood's premier choreographer, working with Fred Astaire, among others. Includes comments by Hermes Pan and clips from many of his movies. Contact: RM Arts, London, 46 Great Marlboro Street, London, WIV1DB.

Dance in America: Tap, 57 minutes, color, 1989. Director Don Mischer. Hosted by Gregory Hines, features current performances by Honi Coles, Tommy Tune, Hinton Battle, Gregg Burge, Savion Glover, Bunny Briggs, Buster Brown, Jimmy Slyde, Sandman Sims, Fred Strickler, Brenda Bufalino with the American Tap Dance Orchestra, LaVaughn Robinson and Germaine Ingram, Manhattan Tap, Jennifer Lane, Camden Richman, and Dianne Walker. Contact: PBS Video, 800/344-3337.

Dancing Man, A: Peg Leg Bates, 58 minutes, color, 1991. Directed by Dave Davidson. Documentary on the life of one of tap's most colorful performers, Peg Leg Bates. It chronicles the life and work of this one-legged performer, how he overcame his childhood accident, and became one of the most beloved American entertainers of live theatre and television. Footage of his performances is woven together with vintage photographs and interviews with friends, fans, and fellow performers. Contact: PBS Video, 800/344-3337. Distributor: Hudson West Productions, 819 Washington Street, Hoboken, NJ 07030. 201/798-5189.

Eddie Brown's Scientific Rhythm, color, 1990. Directed by Sharon Arslanian. Interviewed and accompanied by jazz pianist and composer Paul Arslanian (musical director of the JTE from '78-'84), Brown talks about his career and the development of his unique improvisational Rhythm tap style. He demonstrates his "scientific rhythm" to a variety of music. Also included are three improvised dances to live music. Contact: Images, 11 Massasoit Avenue, North Hampton, MA 01060.

Essentials of Tap Technique, The, 6 1/2 minutes, color, 1990. Produced by Susan Goldbetter, directed by Skip Blumberg. Features Charles "Cookie" Cook, Brenda Bufalino, and Kevin Ramsey. A highly graphic analysis of tap dance essentials. At once aurally and visually compelling, video art and dance art create a visual of flawless technique and style. Contact: Susan Goldbetter, 635 Carroll Street, Brooklyn, NY 11215.

History of American Tap: Louis DaPron, 45 minutes, color, 1978. Famed choreographer Louis DaPron is interviewed one-on-one by tap dancer/choreographer Danny Daniels. Includes tap demonstration in an informal studio setting. Contact (for viewing only): Dance Collection, New York Public Library for the Performing Arts, 40 Lincoln Center Plaza, NY 10023.

History of American Tap: Nanette Fabray, 63 minutes, color, 1978. Broadway and Hollywood dancer, Nanette Fabray is interviewed one-on-one by tap dancer/choreographer Danny Daniels. Includes tap demonstration in an informal studio setting. Contact (for viewing only): Dance Collection, New York Public Library for the Performing Arts, 40 Lincoln Center Plaza, NY 10023.

History of American Tap: Fred Kelly, 58 minutes color, 1978. Choreographer/teacher Fred Kelly (Gene Kelly's brother) is interviewed one-on-one

by tap dancer/choreographer Danny Daniels. Includes tap demonstration in an informal studio setting. Contact (for viewing only): Dance Collection, New York Public Library for the Performing Arts, 40 Lincoln Center Plaza, NY 10023.

History of American Tap: Hal Leroy, 45 minutes, color, 1978. Broadway and Hollywood legomania dancer Hal Leroy is interviewed one-on-one by tap dancer/choreographer Danny Daniels. Includes tap demonstration in an informal studio setting. Contact (for viewing only): Dance Collection, New York Public Library for the Performing Arts, 40 Lincoln Center Plaza, NY 10023.

History of American Tap: Fayard Nicholas, 42 minutes, color, 1978. Renowned dancer Fayard Nicholas (of legendary Nicholas Brothers) is interviewed one-on-one by tap dancer/choreographer Danny Daniels. Includes tap demonstration in an informal studio setting. Contact (for viewing only): Dance Collection, New York Public Library for the Performing Arts, 40 Lincoln Center Plaza, NY 10023.

History of American Tap: Jack Williams, 45 minutes, color, 1978. Broadway dancer Jack Williams is interviewed one-on-one by tap dancer/choreographer Danny Daniels. Includes tap demonstration in an informal studio setting. Contact (for viewing only): Dance Collection, New York Public Library for the Performing Arts, 40 Lincoln Center Plaza, NY 10023.

Honi Coles: The Class Act of Tap, 58 minutes, 1993. Produced by Stephan Chodorov. Directed by Jim Swenson. Charles "Honi" Coles's rhythmic and choreographic genius is studied by dancers the world over. This documentary features scenes of the vaudeville era, including clips with John Bubbles, Bill Robinson, and historical footage of early Honi Coles, interviews with Honi, his students and colleagues. Distributor: VPI/Videfilm Producers Int. Ltd., 250 West 57th Street, Suite 1701, New York, NY 10107, 212/581-0400.

Let's Tap, 52 minutes, 1994. Produced by Editing Productions, France. Choreography, André Halimi. Performed by Fred Astaire, Gregory Hines, Nicholas Brothers, etc.. Explores the history of tap dance, its origins and development. The film includes extracts from feature films and rare archive footage, which allow the viewer to discover the art of Fred Astaire, The Nicholas Brothers, Gregory Hines, etc. Distribution/TV Telmondis, 18, rue Troyon, F-75017 Paris, France, 33-1/45 74 22 00.

Masters of Tap, 60 minutes, color, 1983. Directed by Jolyon Wimhurst. Video taped at a master class in Riverside Studio in London. Includes dances performed for the students by Honi Coles, Chuck Green, and Will Gaines. Contact: Home Vision, 5547 North Ravenswood Avenue, Chicago 60640-1199, 1/800/826-3456.

Milt and Honi, 90 minutes, color, 1994 (still in production). Produced and directed by Louise Tiranoff. Narrated by Gregory Hines, documents a rehearsal from 1985 at Pace University in New York with Milton Hinton and Honi Coles. Also self-narrated story by Honi about his life and how he became a jazz tap dancer and by Milt on his life and how he became a jazz bass player, and how they met up while performing with Cab Calloway. Also featured: Brenda Bufalino and musicians Mickey Tucker and Bob Rosengarden. Contact: Louise Tiranoff, 488 14th Street, Brooklyn, NY 11215.

Mr Bojangles' Memory—Og, Son of Fire, 7 minutes 24 seconds, 1991. Producers: Centre Georges Pompidou/Arcanal. Director: Bob Wilson. Performed by: Charles "Honi" Coles. Robert Wilson takes the viewer on a journey in memory of Bill Bojangles at the New York Cotton Club during the twenties. Charles "Honi" Coles plays the role of Mr. Bojangles. The video was produced for an exhibition at the Centre Georges Pompidou in the framework of the 1991 Festival d' Automne. Distributor: Archanal, 92, Avenue Kleber, F-75116 Paris, France, 33 1 47 27 30 60.

Nicholas Brothers, The: We Sing and We Dance, 53 minutes, color, 1992. A film by Chris Bould, Rigmor Newman, and Bruce Goldstein. A documentary on the lives of the legendary Nicholas Brothers. Features interviews with Cab Calloway, Bobby Short, Hammer, Max Roach, Dorothy Nicholas Marrow, Maurice Hines, Gregory Hines, and Mikhail Baryshnikov. Contact: Picture Music International, Channel Four, 60 Charlotte Street, London, W1P 2AX.

Opening Shot—Savion Glover, 25 minutes, 1993. Produced by London Weekend Television/Bravo. Directed by Gerald Fox. A film about Savion Glover, the young tap dancer and tap choreographer. The film looks at the whole world of tap dancing through his eyes and features him dancing with greats like Gregory Hines, Jimmy Slyde, and Tarik Winston, dancing on the Broadway stage, giving master classes, and filming on the set of Sesame Street. Contact: London Weekend Television, London TV Centre, GB-London SE1 9LT, United Kingdom, 44 71 261 34 88.

Paul Draper On Tap, 30 minutes, black and white, 1979. Produced and directed by Roger Englander. The 71-year-old dancer Paul Draper talks about his childhood, his early career, his partnership with harmonica virtuoso Larry Adler, his marriage to Balanchine dancer Heidi Vosseler, and his blacklisting in the 1940s. Also featured are Lee Theodore and Bob Fosse and the American Dance Machine. Two solos of Paul Draper, dance class of American Dance Machine, and ADM performs Draper's three movement work "Tap in Three Movements." Contact: WGBH Boston, PBS Video, or (for viewing only) Dance Collection, New York Public Library for the Performing Arts, 40 Lincoln Center Plaza, NY 10023.

Percussive Step Dance, 38 minutes, color, 1992. Produced by Ira Bernstein. Compilation of performance excerpts of world percussive dance styles, including English clogging, Irish step dancing, French-Canadian step dancing, South African Boot dancing, Jazz tap, and Appalachian flatfoot clogging. Contact: Ira Bernstein, 85 Dogwood Avenue, Malverne, NY 11565.

Someone Stole the Baby, 25 minutes, color, 1992. Produced and directed by Susie Applebaum and Karmen Jelinvich. Documentary on Brenda Bufalino and the American Tap Dance Orchestra, featuring performances and interviews with Brenda Bufalino, Honi Coles, and Tony Waag. Contact: Woodpeckers, 170 Mercer Street, New York, NY 10012.

Tap Dog, The, 5 minutes, 1993. Produced by ABC Television, Australia. Directed by Stephen Burstow.

Performed by The Tap Dogs, choreography by Dein Perry. Set in an industrial landscape, this work opens the way to a new contemporary style of tap dancing. Distribution/TV and non-commercial—ABC Television/Australia, GPO Box 9994, Sydney 2001, Australia, 61-2/950-3424.

Ten Toe Percussion Ensemble, The, color, 1988. Directed by Ira Bernstein. Overview of percussive dance styles from around the world, including rhythm tap. Comprised of live performances of solo step dances of the various traditions. Contact: Ira Bernstein, 85 Dogwood Avenue, Malverne, NY 11565.

That's Entertainment!, Part III, feature film compilation film series of the great musical numbers from MGM studio releases, focuses primarily on the golden age of movie musicals; available commercially for rental and through theatrical releases.

Two Takes on Tap, 60 minutes, color, 1993. Directed by Sharon Arslanian. Presents video portrait of Brenda Bufalino (artistic director of the American Tap Dance Orchestra) and Lynn Dally (artistic director of the Jazz Tap Ensemble). The two discuss their careers, approaches to choreography, process, and visions for the future. The film also features performance footage of Bufalino, Dally, Honi Coles, Eddie Brown, ATDO and JTE. Contact: Images, 11 Massasoit Avenue, North Hampton, MA 01060.

*Special thanks to Ira Bernstein for helping to compile this material.

SPECIAL MATERIAL ACKNOWLEDGMENTS

The photographs, sheet music covers, records, and graphics listed below are not only from the collections of the dancers comprising this book, but from invaluable collectors throughout the United States. The items are acknowledged in order from left to right: left to right top, then left to right bottom.

7 Alma Hines Kilfoyl
8 Tri Star Pictures

10 Sue DaPron
12 Sue DaPron

24 Willie Covan
27 Willie Covan
Willie Covan
29 Willie Covan

31 Peter Mintun
33 Courtesy of the Bob Grimes Show Music Library, photographed by Maxine Cass
34 Rusty E. Frank
Rusty E. Frank
35 Rusty E. Frank

38 Leonard Reed
40 Leonard Reed
43 Leonard Reed
44 Leonard Reed
Leonard Reed

47 Peg Leg Bates
49 Photograph by Maurice of Chicago, courtesy of Peg Leg Bates
50 Peg Leg Bates
51 Peg Leg Bates
53 Rusty E. Frank
54 Photograph by Herbert Dallinger, courtesy of Rusty E. Frank
56 Photograph by Larence S. Bull, courtesy of George Murphy
57 Photograph by John Miehle, courtesy of George Murphy
Rusty E. Frank
58 Ernie Smith Collection
Rusty E. Frank
Courtesy of the Bob Grimes Show Music Library, photographed by Maxine Cass

65 Fayard Nicholas
67 Fayard Nicholas
69 Courtesy of the Bob Grimes Show Music Library, photographed by Maxine Cass
71 Fayard Nicholas
Courtesy of the Bob Grimes Show Music Library, photographed by Maxine Cass
72 Ernie Smith Collection
73 Harold Nicholas

76 Hermes Pan
77 Hermes Pan
78 Hermes Pan
80 Hermes Pan
Hermes Pan
81 Hermes Pan
Hermes Pan
82 Hermes Pan
83 Hermes Pan
84 Hermes Pan

86 Courtesy of the Bob Grimes Show Music Library, photographed by Maxine Cass
88 Rusty E. Frank
89 Rusty E. Frank
90 Courtesy of the Bob Grimes Show Music Library, photographed by Maxine Cass
91 Rusty E. Frank
Rusty E. Frank
92 Rusty E. Frank

95 Ralph Brown
96 Photograph by Bruno, courtesy of Ralph Brown
97 Ralph Brown
99 Ralph Brown

103 Dorothy Toy
104 Paul Wing
105 Rusty E. Frank
106 Dorothy Toy
108 Dorothy Toy
109 Dorothy Toy
110 Dorothy Toy

113 Photograph by James Kriegsmann, courtesy of Rusty E. Frank
114 George Nierenberg
115 Photograph by James Kriegsmann, courtesy the Ernie Smith Collection
116 Photograph by James Kriegsmann, courtesy the Ernie Smith Collection

119 Jeni LeGon
121 Jeni LeGon
123 Jeni LeGon
124 Jeni LeGon
125 Jeni LeGon
126 Jeni LeGon

130 LaVaughn Robinson
131 Ernie Smith Collection
132 Ernie Smith Collection

135 Vilma Ebsen
136 Courtesy of the Bob Grimes Show Music Library, photographed by Maxine Cass
137 Vilma Ebsen
138 Drawing reproduced by special arrangement with Hirschfeld's exclusive representative, The Margo Feiden Galleries, New York
139 Vilma Ebsen
140 Vilma Ebsen
142 Vilma Ebsen

145 Photograph by Murice Seymour, courtesy of Donald O'Connor
147 Photograph by Bloom of Chicago, courtesy of Donald O'Connor
148 Peggy Ryan
149 Courtesy of the Bob Grimes Show Music Library, photographed by Maxine Cass
150 Lynn Rabin
Tom Lehrer

154 Warren Berry
    Warren Berry
156 Warren Berry
158 Warren Berry
159 Ernie Smith Collection
161 Warren Berry

164 Rusty E. Frank
165 Jane Withers
166 Jane Withers
167 Jane Withers
    Jane Withers

170 Fred Kelly
171 Fred Kelly
172 Fred Kelly
173 Fred Kelly
174 Fred Kelly
175 Fred Kelly
180 Fred Kelly
181 Linda Sohl-Donnell, photo by Phillip Channing
182 Courtesy of the Bob Grimes Show Music
    Library, photographed by Maxine Cass
184 Linda Sohl-Donnell, photos by Phillip Channing

191 Gene Nelson
192 Gene Nelson
193 Courtesy of the Bob Grimes Show Music Library,
    photographed by Maxine Cass
194 Gene Nelson
195 Gene Nelson
196 Gene Nelson
    Gene Nelson
    Gene Nelson
197 Gene Nelson
199 Gene Nelson
200 Gene Nelson
    Gene Nelson

204 Peggy Ryan
205 Peggy Ryan
206 Peggy Ryan
207 Sue DaPron
208 Peggy Ryan
209 Peggy Ryan

212 Ernie Smith Collection
213 Photograph by Murray Korman, courtesy of Maceo
    Anderson
215 Maceo Anderson

218 Prince Spencer
220 Maceo Anderson
221 Maceo Anderson

224 Prince Spencer
225 Prince Spencer
226 Prince Spencer
228 Prince Spencer
229 Maceo Anderson

233 Photographs by Barret Gallaher, courtesy of Paul
    Draper
234 Rusty E. Frank
236 Courtesy of the Bob Grimes Show Music Library,
    photographed by Maxine Cass
237 Peter Mintun
238 Reproduced with permission from the Dance
    Collection, the New York Public Library at
    Lincoln Center, Astor, Lenox, and Tilden
    Foundations

242 Rusty E. Frank
244 Rusty E. Frank
    Rusty E. Frank
245 Courtesy of the Bob Grimes Show Music Library,
    photographed by Maxine Cass
246 Rusty E. Frank
247 Rusty E. Frank
248 Rusty E. Frank

251 Frances Nealy
253 Frances Nealy
254 Frances Nealy
    Frances Nealy
255 Frances Nealy
256 Frances Nealy

258 Rusty E. Frank
    Rusty E. Frank
    Rusty E. Frank
260 Rusty E. Frank

263 Cholly Atkins
264 Cholly Atkins
    Cholly Atkins
265 Peter Mintun, photographed by Maxine Cass
    Peter Mintun, photographed by Maxine Cass
266 Cholly Atkins
267 Cholly Atkins
268 Cholly Atkins
269 Cholly Atkins
270 Cholly Atkins

272 Brenda Bufalino
275 Brenda Bufalino
276 Brenda Bufalino

283 Rusty E. Frank
284 Ernie Smith Collection
285 George Nierenberg
287 Rusty E. Frank
288 Maceo Anderson
    Louis Simms Carpenter
289 Louis Simms Carpenter
290 Ernie Smith Collection
294 Paul Wing
293 Frances Neely

299 Alex and Sara Hassan, photographed by Maxine
    Cass
300 Alex and Sara Hassan, photographed by Maxine
    Cass
    Alex and Sara Hassan, photographed by Maxine
    Cass
303 Alex and Sara Hassan, photographed by Maxine
    Cass
    Peter Mintun, photographed by Maxine Cass
304 Courtesy of the Bob Grimes Show Music Library,
    photographed by Maxine Cass
309 Courtesy of the Bob Grimes Show Music Library,
    photographed by Maxine Cass
315 Courtesy of the Bob Grimes Show Music Library,
    photographed by Maxine Cass

Appendix C: All records photographed by Maxine
Cass

322 courtesy of Peter Mintun
323 courtesy of Eric Bernhoft, Peter Mintun
324 courtesy of Eric Bernhoft, Peter Mintun
325 courtesy of Peter Mintun, Peter Mintun, Eric
    Bernhoft
326 courtesy of Eric Bernhoft
327 courtesy of Peter Mintun, Eric Bernhoft

INDEX

Italicized numbers indicate illustrations.

Aaron, Charlie, 283
About Tap (documentary), 332
Accent on Girls (film), 304
Ace and Eddie, films of, 302
Ackerman, Jack, 296
Acrobatic (tap style), 47, 48, 72, 155, 156, 229, 230, 279
Acrobatic tappers, 119, 211, 216
Acts, tap, *See* Appendix A, 283-296
Adair, Yvonne, *200*
Adams, Burle, 220
Adelphi Theatre (London), 126
Adler Larry, 232, 237, 238, *238*, 239, 335
Ad Lib (tap style), 279
Adolphous, Joseph (choreographer), 110
Adrian, Iris, films of, 315
"Advanced Tap" (record), 324
"Advanced Tap Routine" (record), 324
Affairs of Geraldine (film), 316
After Seben (film), 299
"Ain't Misbehavin'" (record), 326
Ain't My Sugar Sweet (film), 312
Al and Lloyd, 297
Albee, E. F., 145
Albertson, Frank, films of, 300
Albertson, Jack, 234
Albright School of Dance, 191, 192
Aldine Theatre (Pittsburgh), 172
Alexander, Danny, 302
Alexander's Ragtime Band (film), 308
Algiers (film), 247
Al Gilbert's Hollywood Theatreical Dance Schoo, 296
Ali Baba Goes to Town (film) 306
All-American Co-Ed (film), 310
All Ashore (film), 320
All by Myself (film), 312
All-Colored Vaudeville Show (film), 65, 303
"All Dark People Is Light on Their Feet" (song), 70

Allen, Gracie, films of, 306, 309
Allyson, June, films of, 198, 317, 318
Alston and Johnsons, films of, 316
Alton, Bob, 151, 178, 193, 198, 241, 247, 283
"Always" (song), 54
Always a Bridesmaid (film), 312
Always Leave Them Laughing (film), 318
Amateur dance contests, 24, 48, 50, 96
Ambassador Hotel (Los Angeles), 149
American Dance Machine, 335
American Guild of Variety Artists, 7
American in Paris, An (film), 319
American Tap Dance Orchestra, 333, 335, 336
Ames, Jerry, 296, 328
Anchors Aweigh (film), 315
Anderson, Eddie "Rochester," films of, 305, 309, 321
Anderson, Gordon, 269
Anderson, Maceo, 10, 211-216, *213, 215, 220,* 228, *229,* 283; doing the Bottle Dance, *228;* films of (*See* Four Step Brothers, The)
Anderson, Williams and Walker, 214
Andrews, Patty, films of, 312, 313
Andrews Sisters, films of, 202, 309, 310, 315, 316
Animal Crackers (stage show), 78
Anything Goes (stage show), 53
Apollo Boys, 297
Apollo Girls, 297
Apollo Theatre (New York), 7, 8, 39, 74, 149, 183, 217-218, 220, 221, 235, 269, 297
Applebaum, Susie, 335
April in Paris (film), 319
April Showers (film), 318
Are You with It? (film), 318
Argentine Nights (film), 309
Arizona Wildcat (film), 309

Armstrong, Louis, 66, 251, *258*, 259, 267, 297
Army Chorus, film of, 314
Arnte, Diamond Tooth Billy, 296
Around the World (tap movement), 279
Around the World - with no hands (tap movement), 25, 28
Arrangers, musical, 274, 277
Arslanian, Paul, 334
Arslanian, Sharon, 334, 336
Art Deco, life-style of, 64, 111
Arthur, Jean, 245
Arthur Murray Dance Studios, 279
Artist and Models (film), 306
Astaire, Adele, 22, 56, 76, 85, 140, 141, 283, *283*
Astaire, Fred, 10, 22, 46, 53, 56, 59, 63, 66, 70, 73, 75, 76, 77, *78,* 79, *82,* 83, 84, 85, 86, 90, 105, 123, 134, 137, 140, 141, 147, 160, 175, 191, 199, 201, 209, 216, 219, 243, 246, 248, 249, 252, 333, 335; films of, 11, 301, 302, 304, 305, 306, 307, 308, 309, 311, 312, 314, 316, 317, 318, 319, 320; George Murphy and, *57;* Hermes Pan and, *83, 84;* Ginger Rogers and, 76, 79, 83, *84*, 87; recordings of, 322-324
Astaire and Rogers, 79, 87
Astaire-Rogers series, 76, 83
Astaires, The, 283
"Asturias" (song), 237
At Home Abroad (stage show), 125, 126
Atkins, Charles "Cholly," 10, 262-270, *263, 264, 266, 267, 270,* 283; films of, 320. *See also* Coles and Atkins
Atlantic City, 138
Atlantic City (film), 314
Auer, Misha, 245
Aunt Sally's Kiddie Club (radio show), 163
Austin, Vivian, 284; films of, 313, 316
Australian Jazz Quartet, 277
Avant-garde jazz, 21, 277

Babb, Dorothy, 151, 203, 284; films of, 309, 313, 317
Babes in Arms (film), 309
Babes in Arms (stage show), 70
Babes on Broadway (film), 311
Babes on Swing Street (film), 209, 314
Baby Burlesks (film series), 86
Baby Take a Bow (film), 87, 302
Bach, music by, 236, 239
Bailey, Bill, 49, 213, 259, 260, 284; films of, 305, 313, 320
Bailey, Pearl, 49, 126, 213
Baker, Josephine, 121, 125
Balaban and Katz theaters (Chicago), 120
Balanchine, George, 70, 236, 335
Ball, Lucille, 69, *80*
Ballet, 53, 72, 236
Ballet Dancers' Nightmare (film), 310
Ballrooms, 114
Bal Tabarin Club (San Francisco), 243, 252
Baltimore, 67, 68, 259, 260, 281
Bambalina (dance), 96, 279
Band Wagon, The (film), 320
Banjo on My Knee (film), 305
Bankhead, Tallulah, 68
Barber Shop Blues (film), 301
Barclift, Nelson, 194
Barkleys of Broadway, The (film), 77, 84, 318
Barnes, Mae, 284
Barnet, Charlie, 112, 133, 257, 259
Barrel turn (tap movement), 209
Barto and Mann, 284; films of, 301
Barton, James, 284; films of, 299, 301, 303, 319
Baryshnikov, Mikhail, 335
Basie, Count, 95, 112, 120, 133, 182, 265, 259, 260, 277, 297; chorus line of, 121; orchestra of *260*
Bates, Peg Leg, 10, 46-51, *47, 49, 50, 51,* 259, 260, 284, 333; in amateur shows, 48; in Australia,

50; in carnivals, 47, 49; in *Ed Sullivan Revue*, 47, 50; in *Hot Chocolate*, 49; in *Ken Murray's Black-outs*, 51; with *Lew Leslie's Blackbirds*, 47, 49; in minstrel shows, 47, 48; in nightclubs, 47, 50; and stealing steps, 47; in theaters, 50; on T.O.B.A. circuit, 47, 49; in vaudeville, 47, 47, 50, 50; Toy and Wing and, 109

Battle, Hinton, 333

Bayes, Nora, 24

Beachcomber (New York nightclub), 110

Beale St. Mama (film), 316

Beautiful but Broke (film), 314

Bebop, 21, 187, 252, 261, 271-272, 273, 277

"Beethoven's Fifth" (musical composition), 239

"Beginner's Tap" (record), 324

Behind the Eight Ball (film), 311

Belfer, Hal, 296

Bell, Gene, 10, 284

Bell, Hal, films of, 318

Belle of New York, The, (film), 319

Belliou, Chris, 10

Benefit shows, 72, 172, 180, 192, 203, 204

Berg, Eugene Leander. *See* Nelson, Gene

Berkeley, Busby, 32, 35, 75-76, 77, 79, 108, 241, 242, 246, 247

Berkeley Hotel (London), 106

Berle, Milton, 2, films of, 318

Berlin, Irving, 54, 82, 170, 178, 190, 194, 198, 242

Bernie, Ben, 225

Bernstein, Ira, 335, 336

Berry, Ananias, 74, 154, 155, 156, 156, 157, 158, 158, 159, 160, 161, 282; with Duke Ellington, 155; films of 305. *See also* Berry Brothers, The

Berry, James, 74, 154, 155, 156, 156, 157, 160-161, 161, 284; dancing at parties, 155; with Duke Ellington, 155; in *Our Gang Comedies*, 155. *See also* Berry Brothers, The

Berry, Warren, 10, 74, 155, 156-161, 156, 159, 161, 284. *See also* Berry Brothers, The

Berry, Brothers, The, 8, 38, 65, 74, 122, 153-161, 154, 156, 214, 215, 216, 266, 284; at Cotton Club, 156-157, 158, 159; films of, 155, 310, 312, 318, 319; in stage shows, 155

Bert Levy Circuit (vaude-ville), 106

Best Foot Forward (film), 312

Best Foot Forward (stage show), 207

"Between the Devil and the Deep Blue Sea" (song), 160

Big Apple (dance), 170

Big Bands, 107, 109, 129, 257, 260, 297

Big Broadcast of 1936, The (film), 65, 70, 303

Big Broadcast of 1937, The (film), 305

Big Timers (film), 315

Bill Robinson Revue, The, 182, 183, 185

Billy and Ann, films of, 314

Billy and Milly, 284

Billy and Milly with Sugar Nichols, 308

Billy Rose's Diamond Horse-shoe (film), 316

Birdland (New York night-club), 277

Black and Tan (film), 299

"Black and Tan Fantasy" (song), 232

Black Angel (film), 316

Black Bottom (dance), 41, 77, 146, 147, 279

Blackburn Twins, films of, 318

Blacklisting, McCarthy Era, 239-240

Black Narcissus (film), 299

Black Network (film), 305

Black-up, 279

Blackwood, Christian, 333

Blake, Atta, 284

Blake, Eubie, 28

Blue, Ben, 107, 245

"Blue Danube Waltz, The" (song), 236

Blue Rhythm (film), 301

Blue Skies (film), 316

Blum, Al, 284

Blum, Bea, 284

Blum, Gussie, 284

Boarding House Blues (film), 155, 318

Boeuf sur le Toit, Le (New York nightclub), 77

"Bojangles of Harlem" (re-cord), 323

"Bolero" (musical composi-tion), 274

Bolger, Ray, 73, 134, 284, 284; films of, 305, 307, 308, 310, 311, 314, 317, 318, 319, 320

Book of Tap, The (book), 296

Borne, Hal, 82

Born Happy (stage show), 256

Born to Dance (film), 204, 305

Born to Sing (film), 311

Bosko, cartoons of, 321

Bosko Bagdad (cartoon), 321

Boston, 259-260, 261, 272, 276

Bould, Chris, 335

Bow, Clara, 154

Bowery to Broadway (film), 146, 314

Bowes, Major, 225, 226

Boyfriend (film), 309

Boyle, Johnny, 55, 151, 307

Bradley, Bernard, 290; films of, 132. *See also* High Hatters, The

Bradley, Clarence "Buddy," 284

Bradley, Grace, 321

Bradshaw, Tiny, 259

Brahms, music by, 239

Brandow, Jerry, films of, 319

Brant, Peg E., 10, 284; films of, 316

Break (tap movement), 279

Breakfast in Rhythm (film), 313

Brice, Fanny, 32, 116, 117

Brigadoon (film), 320

Briggs, Bunny, 7, 8, 10, 111-117, 113, 114, 115, 116, 133, 259, 260, 272, 284, 333; Fanny Brice and, 116, 117; dance style of, 115-116; films of, 302, 319; and high society, 115, 116; Porkchops and, 114; Luckey Roberts and, 114-115; with swing bands, 112

Bright Eyes (film), 162, 163 164, 164, 165

Bring on the Girls (film), 314

Broadhurst Theatre (New York), 199, 200

Broadway, 22, 29, 31, 54, 70, 75, 76, 77, 138, 158, 170, 171, 178, 179, 187, 190, 197, 199, 207, 237, 242, 245, 270

Broadway (film), 311

Broadway Buckaroo, The (film), 309

Broadway Highlights No. 4 (film), 303

Broadway Melody (film), 299

Broadway Melody of 1936 (film), 136, 140, 142, 303; "Broadway Rhythm," sheet music for, 136; "Sing Before Breakfast," 140

Broadway Melody of 1938 (film), 56, 58, 58, 306

Broadway Melody of 1940 (film), 53, 56, 57, 85, 309

Broadway Rhythm (film), 314

Broadway Theatre (New York), 194

Broadway Thru a Keyhole (film), 301

Broadway to Hollywood (film), 301

Brown, James "Buster," 333

Brown, Clifford, 272, 276

Brown, Eddie, 10, 180, 182-183, 185, 284, 334, 336; Bill Robinson and, 183, 185; as street tapper, 182, 185; with swing bands, 182

Brown, Ernest, 284

Brown, Gibson and Reed, 182

Brown, Emelda "Jean-Jean," 13

Brown, Joe E., films of, 301

Brown, Joe, Jr., films of, 311

Brown, King Rastus, 224, 225, 284

Brown, Ralph, 10, 94-101, 95, 96, 97, 259, 284; in amateur contest, 96; Cab Calloway and, 100; at Cot-ton Club, 95, 98; as ec-centric dancer, 100; films of, 303, 317, 318; Hoof-ers Club and, 95, 96; Her-man Stark and, 98; and stealing steps, 97

Brown, Rocky, films of, 315

Brown, Stanley, 260, 272, 274, 276, 284-285; troupe of, 276

Brown Buddies, 284

Bryant, Marie, 118, 127, 285; films of, 314

Bryant, Willie, 39, 43, 43, 45, 66, 122, 281, 285; Leonard Reed and, 43

B. S. Chorus (dance), 97

Bubbles, John, 42, 73, 76, 94, 95, 96, 100, 126, 260, 263, 267, 280, 281, 285, 334, 293; films with, 313

Buchanan, Jack, films of, 307, 320; recordings of, 324

Buck and Bubbles, 7, 49, 66, 73, 216, 227, 285;

films of, 299, 300, 303, 306, 314, 317
Buck and Wing (tap style), 9, 26, 46, 47, 72, 76, 77, 147, 252, 279; dancers, 32, 223
Buck Benny Rides Again (film), 309
Buck dancers, 32, 34
Buck dancing, 32, 224
Buckner, Conrad "Little Buck," 285, 286
Buck Privates (film), 310
Buddy and Judy, 285
Buddy Rich and His Orchestra (film), 318
Bufalino, Brenda, 10, 271-278, *272, 275, 276,* 285, 333, 334, 335, 336; avant-garde jazz and, 277; Stanley Brown and, 272, 274, 276; in jazz clubs, 272; Max Roach and Clifford Brown Quintet and, 276; narrative of tap and, 278; power of rhythm and, 278; in Strickland Sisters, 273; in USO shows, 273
"Bugle Blues" (song), 160
"Bugle Call Blues" (song), 114
Bugle Woogie (Soundie), 321
Bundle of Blues (film), 301
Bunny, Bugs, cartoons of, 321
Buono, Angelo, *195*
Burch Mann Dancers, films of, 315
Burge, Gregg, 333
Burgess, Betty, films of, 303
Burlesque, 9, 22, 212, 224, 259, 260
Burns, George, 285; films of, 306
Burns, Sammy, 285
Burns and Allen, 285
Burt, Billy, films of, 310
Burstow, Stephen, 335
Busby Berkeley Girls, films of, 313
Businessmen of Rhythm, 285; films of, 320
Buskin', 133
Butler, David, 164
Butterfly (film), 321
By an Old Southern River (film), 310, 311
"Bye, Bye Blues" (song), 147, 233, 235
Bye, Bye, Bonnie (stage show), 31
By Request (film), 303, 305
By Word of Foot (documentary), 332

Cab Calloway Revue, The, 267
Cabin in the Sky (film), 313
Café de Paris (London), 55
Café Rendezvous (film), 308
Cafe Society (Hollywood nightclub), 252
Cagney, James, 32, 55, 87, 285, 307, 314, 319, 321; films of, 302
Cagney, Jean, films of, 314
Cain and Mabel (film), 306
Cake Walk (dance), 279
Cakewalk Strut (dance movement), 155
Call All Stars (film), 306
Calling All Kids (film), 313
Call Me Madam (film), 146, 320
Call Me Mister (film), 319
Calloway, Cab, 55, 65, 68, 69, 95, 98-100, 121, 125, 133, 156, 169, 174, 175, 177, 251, 257, 259, 264, 267, 276, 335; orchestra of, 157, 178, 258, 264, 266
Campus Confessions (film), 308
Cane Dancers, 154
Cane dancing, 74, 155, 159, 160
"Can't Help Lovin' Dat Man" (song), 238
Can This Be Dixie? (film), 305
Cantor, Eddie, 69, 138; films of, 301, 315, 318
Cantor, Mark, 14
Capezio, 175
Capitol Theatre (New York), 50, 73, *106,* 159
Captain January (film), 87, 88, 89, 305; "At the Codfish Ball," 88, *89*
Carefree (film), 308
Carlos, Ernest, 285
Carnegie Hall, 239
Carnivals, 9, 22, 40, 41, 49; black shows in, 41
Carnival Show (film), 308
Carolina Blues (film), 314
Carpenter, Louis Simms, 10, 285
Carroll, Mickey, 296
Carroll, Nancy, 299; films of, 301
Carson, Jack, films of, 318
Carter, Benny, *258,* 259
Castle, Nick, 88, 166, 167, 168, 241, 242, 243, 246, *247,* 285
Caught Plastered (film), 301
Cavalcade of Bands (film), 319

Cavallaro, Carmen, 109
Center Theatre (New York), 193
Central Avenue (Los Angeles), 108
Central Park Casino (New York), 54
Cha-Cha (dance), 170
Challenge, tap, 125, 132, 192, 211, 229, 230, 279
Champagne Supper Club (San Francisco), 256
Champion, Gower, 199; films of, 319, 320
Champion, Marge, 199; films of, 319, 320
Chaney, Isaiah "Lon," 285
Changing of the Guard (film), 305
Channing, Carol, 199
Chaplin, Charlie, 68
Charise, Cyd, 249
Charisse, Nico, 193
Charleston (dance), 30, 38, 40, 41, 42, 77, 113, 114, 279; contests, 40, 41. *See also* Tap Charleston
Chase, Charlie, films of, 305
Chasing Rainbows (film), 300
Chatter (film), 313
Check and Double Check (film), 300
Cherry Blossom Café (Los Angeles), 105
Chez Paree (Chicago nightclub), 107, 237
Chicago, 9, 25, 28, 41, 105, 108, 120, 122, 138, 143, 145, 147, 172, 207, 220, 226, 267
Chicago Theatre (Chicago), 106, 120, 264
Chicken Shuffle (dance) 250
Child dancers, 23-24; Bunny Briggs, 111-116; Willie Covan, 24-28; The Five Kellys, 172; Jeni Legon, 120; The Nicholas Brothers, 65-72, 130; Donald O'Connor, 146-149; Frankie Owens, 203-206; Peggy Ryan, 203-206; Shirley Temple, 59, 86-93; Jane Withers, 162-168
Chilton and Thomas, 233, 285; films of, 306
China Doll (New York nightclub), 102
Chinese nightclubs, 102, 103
Chip Off the Old Block (film), 314
"Chittlin' Circuit," 215, 279
Chiyo, Princess, films of, 308
Chocolateers, The, 7, 260, 285; films of, 311, 312

Chocolate Steppers, 285
Chodorov, Stephan, 334
Cholly and Dotty, 99, 118, *266, 267,* 285
Choo Choo Swing (film), 313
Chopin, music of, 239
"Chop Suey Circuit," 102
Choreographers, 82, 203, 205, 209, 242
Chuck and Chuckles, *285,* 286
Church circuit, 155
Clarence (film), 306
Clark, Bert, 192
Clark, Judy, 286; films of, 314, 315, 317
Clark, Mae, films of, 301
Clark Brothers, films of, 318
Class acts, 22, 27, 46, 262-263, 270, 279
Classical (tap style), 9, 46, 72, 279
Classical music, tap dancing to, 10, 231-240
Classical tappers, *34*
Clayton, Lou, 286
Clean Pastures (film), 306
Cleveland, 49, 101
Cliff and Radcliff, 286
Clifford, Ruth, 321
Cline, Edward, 207-208
Clog dancing, 280
Close rhythm (tap style), 22, 97, 129, 252, 280
Club Alabam (Los Angeles nightclub), 100, 227, 228, 251, 252
Club Eureka (Sacramento nightclub), 252
Club Trocadero (Hollywood nightclub), 9, 12
Club Zanzibar (New York nightclub), 50
Cochran, C. B., 125, 126, 232
Cocoanut Grove (Hollywood nightclub), 103, 237, 251
Cocteau, Jean, 233
Cohan, George M., 286; show of, 31, 33, 35
Colbert, Claudette, 87
Cole, Jack, 247
Coleman, Henry, 226
Coles, Charles "Honi," 10, 133, 212, *263,* 266, 267, *268, 269, 270,* 277, 286, 333, 334, 335, 336; films of, 320. *See also* Coles and Atkins
Coles and Atkins, 46, 113, 259, 262, 263, *268, 269, 270,* 286; films of, 320
Colfax, Lady, 232
Colleen (film), 32, *34* 232, *234,* 236, 305; "You Gotta Know How to Dance," 236

College Holiday (film), 305
College Queen (film), 321
College Rhythm (film), 321
College Swing (film), 308
Collier, Emelyne, recording of, 324
Collins, Charles, films of, 305, 308
Collins, Dean, 286; films of, 312, 315, 317
Collins, Leon, 286, 333
Collins, Raymond, films of, 307
Colony Club (Hollywood nightclub), 251
Columbia Concerts, 238
Columbia Studios, 243, 248
Colvard, Frank, 297
Comedic tappers, 134-136, 146, 160, 263, 269
Comedy (tap style), 46, 72, 73, 134, 146, 269, 280
Compton, Betty, 286; films of, 301
"Computer Tap," 297
"Concerto" (Gershwin), 235
"Concerto for Tap Dancer and Orchestra" (concerto), 296
Condos, Frank, 286. See also Condos Brothers, The
Condos, Lorraine, 2
Condos, Nick, 216, 282, 286. See also Condos Brothers, The
Condos, Steve, 2, 8, 10, 49, 130, 171, 286, 318, 319, 332; Toy and Wing and, 108. See also Condos Brothers, The
Condos and Brandow, films of, 320
Condos Brothers, The, 49, 128, 130, 213, 214, 243, 246, 259, 260, 286; films of, 307, 308, 309, 310, 315, 317;
Coney Island (film), 313
Conine, Tommy, 286, 296
Connie's Inn (Harlem nightclub), 47, 49, 50
Connolly, Bobby, 241, 286
Conrad, Betty, 173
Coogan, Jackie, films of, 308
Cook, Charles "Cookie," 10, 286, 333, 334
Cook, H. L., 40, 41
Cook and Brown, 266, 286; films of, 306, 311, 313
Cookie's Scrapbook (documentary), 332
Coonan, Dorothy, 321
Cooper, Betty Jane, films of, 306
Cooper, Gary, 87

Cooper, Jackie, films of, 305
Cooper, Ralph, 10
Copasetics, The, 286, 333
Corbet Brothers, films of, 301
Cordero, Thelma, films of, 317
Coronado (film), 303
Cortauld, Samuel, 232
Cosie Smith and Her Six Pickaninnies, 24, 25
Costello, Gracie, 286
Costello, Lou, films of, 313
Cotton Club (Harlem nightclub), 39, 47, 49, 50, 55, 64-65, 68-70, 73, 95, 98, 99, 100, 102, 103, 125, 139, 155, 156, 158, 159, 174, 177, 180, 213, 214, 215, 216, 253, 266, 267, 297
Cotton Club Boys, The, 264, 266, 286
Cotton Club Girls, films of, 302
Cotton Club musical revue, 175, 177
Courtney, Inez, films of, 301
Covan, Dewey, 25, 27, 286
Covan, Florence, 27, 286
Covan, Willie, 10, 23-29, 24, 27, 29, 66, 108, 242, 246, 247, 260, 286; films of, 25, 308; Four Covans and, 24, 27, 28; as MGM dance instructor, 25; in minstrel shows, 25 26; as "pick," 24; in stage shows, 24-25
Covan and Ruffin, 24, 29, 286
Cover Girl (film), 314
Coward, Noel, 232
Coy, Johnny, 198, 204, 209; films of, 209, 286, 314, 316, 317, 320
Coyne, Jeanne, films of, 320
Cramp Roll (tap movement), 100, 280
Crash of 1929, 55, 137
Crawford, Joan, 76, 87, 90, 248; films of, 300, 301
"Crazy Feet" (record), 322
Crazy House (film), 313
Criterion Theatre (New York), 159
Crosby, Bing, 87, 151
Cross, Jimmy, 286
Cross, Stumpy, 191, 196, 198; films of, 314
Croyden Hotel (Chicago), 108
Cunningham, Skip 10
Curly Top (film), 303
Curran Theatre (San Francisco), 256

Curtis, Tony, films of, 321
Cushman's Garden of Glorious Girls (stage show), 78
Cutaway, 75, 280
Cutout and Leonard, 41, 286

Daddy Long Legs (film), 320
Dailey, Dan, 159, 199, 286; films of, 159, 311, 312, 317, 318, 319, 320
Dale, Virginia, films of, 311
Dale and Lean, 286
Daley, Cass, films of, 311
Dally, Lynn, 336
Damerel, Donna, films of, 302
Dames (film), 32, 76, 302
Damsel in Distress, A (film), 76, 306
Dance Caravan, 297
Dance contests, amateur, 24, 48, 50, 96
Dance Crazy in Hollywood (documentary), 333
Dance directors, 75, 77, 79, 82, 178, 201, 204, 241-243, 246-247. See also names of individual dance directors
Dance halls, 23, 114
Dance Impressions (film), 314
Dance in America (documentary), 333
Dance instructors, 25, 79. See also Dance teachers
Dancemania (film), 313
Dance of Life, The (film), 314
Dancer, Earl, 122, 124
Dance Revue (film), 313
Dancers, tap. See Appendix A, 283-296
Dancers in the Dark (film), 301
Dance schools, 86, 169, 172, 203, 204, 267
Dance studios, 63, 88
Dance teachers, 172, 191, 204, 243
Dancing Co-Ed (film), 309
Dancing Colleens, The (film), 299
Dancing contests, tap, 183
Dancing Feet (film), 305
Dancing Fletchers, The, 296
Dancing Lady (film), 76, 301
Dancing Man (documentary), 333
Dancing on a Dime (film), 132, 309
Dancing Pirate (film), 305
"Dancing to Save Your Sole" (record), 324
Dandridge, Dorothy, films of, 311

Dandridge Sisters, The, 65, 157
Daniels, Danny, 296, 334
Daniels, Marion, films of, 308
DaPron, Louis, 5, 9, 10, 12, 12, 151, 203, 206, 334, 207, 209-210, 241, 242, 243, 246, 286; films of, 209, 305, 306, 309, 310, 311, 312, 313, 314, 315, 316, 317, 318
Darktown Follies (film), 300
Darrow, John, 198
Daughter of Rosie O'Grady, The (film), 199, 319
Davidson, Dave, 333
Davies, Jack, 237
Davies, Marion, 287; films of, 302, 306
Davis, Bobby, films of, 314, 319
Davis, Joan, films of, 308, 314, 315, 318
Davis, Sammy, Jr., 220, 287, 302; films of, 318, 321
Day, Doris, 201, 287; films of, 319
Day, Marilyn, films of, 313
Debussy, music of, 239
DeCamp, Rosemary, films of, 314
Deep in My Heart (film), 170, 177, 179, 320; "I Love to Go Swimmin' with Wimmen," 170, 179
de Mille, Agnes, 82, 242, 247, 269, 297
Dennet and Dae, films of, 310
DeParis, Sydney, 277
DeParis, Wilber, 272, 277
Depression, Great, 63, 86, 87, 134, 158, 162, 173, 174, 185, 251
de Sylva, Buddy, 90
Detroit Theatre (Detroit), 148
Deviled Ham (film), 306
Devil Is a Sissy, The (film), 305
de Wit, Jacqueline, films of, 316
Diamond, John, 287
Diane, Dolores, 287
Dietrich, Marlene, 248
Dimples (film), 305
Disabled dancers, 47-51, 254, 256
Dixiana (film), 66, 300
Dixieland Jamboree (film), 317
Dixon, Harlan, 55, 287; films of, 307

Dixon, Lee, 32, *34*, 35, 287, *287*; films of, 305, 307, 317

"Doin' the New Low-Down" (song), 182, 183, 185, 192; records of, 326, 327; sheet music for, *182*

Dolly Sisters, The (film), 316

Donahue, Jack, 22, 55, 137, 140, 287

Dong, Arthur, 14

Don Redman and His Orchestra (film), 302

Don't Gamble with Love (film), 303

Dorn, Lou, 105

Dorsey, Jimmy, 259

Dorsey, Tommy, 251, 259; band of, 251, 297

"Do the New York" (song), 30

Dotson, Clarence "Dancing," 287

Double Crossbones (film), 319

Double Rhythm (film), 317

Double wings (tap step), 192, 229, 230

Douglas Brothers, films of, 314

Dowling, Eddie, 287

Down Argentine Way (film), 65, 309

Down on the Barn (film), 308

Downs, Johnny, 287; films of, 303, 305, 306, 307, 308, 310, 311, 316

Down to Earth (film), 317

Doyle, Jimmy, 287

Doyle and Dixon, 287

Draper, Paul, 10, 32, *34*, 36, 141, 231-240, *233*, *234*, *236*, *237*, *238*, 287; Larry Adler and, 232, 237-239, 335; Jack Albertson and, 234; blacklisting of, 232, 239-240; classical music and, 231, 232, 236, 239; concert tours by, 232, 238-239; films of, 232, 234, 236, 305, 312, 318; Ruby Keeler and, *234*, *236*: learning ballet, 236-237; in London, 232-233; in nightclubs, 236, 237; in Paris, 233-234; in vaudeville, 233, 235, 236

Drayton, Thaddeus, 287

Du Barry Was a Lady (film), 313

Dubbing taps, 70

Duchess of Idaho (film), 319

Duchin, Eddie, 237

Dudley, Bessie, 287; films of, 301

Dudley, Sherman, 37

Duffy, Alice, 273-274

Duffy's Tavern (film), 198, 316

Duke is Tops (film), 308

Dunbar, Dixie, 118, 126, 243, 288; films of, 302, 305, 306, 308, 309

Duncan, Arthur, 288

Dunhills, The, 288, *288*, films of, 317, 319

Dunn, Billy, films of, 316

Dunn, James, 87; films of, 302, 303

Dunn, Johnny, films of, 302

Dunne, Irene, films of, 306

Dupree, Roland, 151, 203, 207, 288; films of, 309, 311, 315

Dvorak, Ann, films of, 304, 321

Eadie Was a Lady (film), 316

Eager Beaver (film), 316

Earl Carroll's Sketchbook (film), 317

Earle Theatre (Philadelphia), 133, 257, 281

Easter Parade (film), 178, 179, 243, 247, 249, 318; "Shaking the Blues Away," 247

Eaton, Mary, films of, 299

Ebsen, Buddy, *58*, 87, 88, *89*, 90, 93, 118, 134, *135*, *136*, 137, 138, *139*, 140, *140*, 141, *142*, 143, 288; in *Broadway Melody of 1938*, *58*; films of, 303, 305, 306, 310, 312; at the Palace, 139; in *Whoopee*, 138; in *Ziegfeld Follies*, 142. *See also* Ebsens, The

Ebsen, Norma, 137

Ebsen, Vilma, 10, 118, 134, *135*, 136, *137*, *139*, *140*, *142*; dance teacher of, 137; films of, 303; at the Palace, 139; in *Whoopee*, 138; in *Ziegfeld Follies*, 142. *See also* Ebsens, The

Ebsens, The, 46, 118, 134-143, *135*, *139*; caricature of, *138*; films of, 303; at the Palace, 139; shows in, 136, 138, 142; in *Ziegfeld Follies*, 142

Eccentric (tap style), 9, 22, 46, 72, 98, 134, 280

Eccentric tappers, 95, 100, 143, 149

Eckstine, Billy, 259

Eddie Brown's Schientific Rhythm (documentary), 334

Ed Sullivan Revue, 47

Ed Sullivan Show, The, 187, 226

Edwards, Gus, 203

Edward Sisters, The, 118, 126, 288

El Fey Club (New York speakeasy), 31, 33

Ellen, Vera, 288

Ellington, Duke, 55, 65, 95, 98, 121, 127, 133, 155, 182, 214, 215, 216, 232, 233, 251, 252, 257, 259, 260

Ellis, Robert, films of, 318

El Rancho Vegas (Las Vegas hotel), 221

Elswit, Freddie, 109

Emperor Jones, The (film), 302

Englander, Roger, 335

Erin's Famous Tap Dancers, films of, 299

Erving Plummer's (rehearsal hall), 52, 234

Essence (tap movement), 280

Essentials of Tap Technique, The (film), 334

Ethel Meglin Dance Studio, 86

Evans and Evans, 288

Eve Knew Her Apples (film), 316

Evergreen (film), 302

Everything I Have Is Yours (film), 319

Everything Is Rhythm (film), 305

Exile, The (film), 321

Fabray, Nanette, 334

Fagan, Barney, 288; films of, 301

Family tap acts: Berry Brothers, 155-161; The Ebsens, 135-143; The Five Kellys, 172; The Nicholas Brothers 65-74; The O'Connor Family, 146-148

Famous Meglin Kiddies, 86, 92

Fanchon and Marco, dancing school of, 192

Fanchon and Marco (vaudeville circuit), 50, 106, 145, 148, 280; "Ideas," 105; Bombay unit of, *145*

Fanchon and Marco Juvenile Revue, 192

Fanchonettes, The, 192

Fascinating Rhythms (book), 297

Faye, Alice, 87, 288; films of, 306, 307, 308, 316

Felix, Seymour, 69, 241

Fellows, Edith, 164

Feudin', Fussin' and A-Fighting (film), 318

Fitch, Bob, 13

Fields, Benny, films of, 315

52nd Street (film), 306

Films. *See* names of individual films and Appendix B, 299-321

Film Vodvil (film), 314

First a Girl (film), 304

First Baby, The (film), 305

Five Hot Shots, 288; films of, 299, 305

Five Kellys, The, 169, 170, *172*, 288

Five-tap wing (tap step), 230

Flash (tap style), 9, 22, 27, 46-47, 72, 119, 269, 280

Flash acts, 155, 211

Flash dancing, 269

Flash tappers, 74, 131, 134, 154, 223, 228, 263, 280

Fleet's In, The (film), 311

Fletcher, Beale, 296

Fletcher, Peggy, 296

Flirtation Walk (film), 32, 302

Florence Club, The, (Boston nightclub), 260

Flying Colors (stage show), 138

Flying Down to Rio (film), 76, 79, 191, 302; "Carioca, The," 79

Flying Feet (film), 313

Flynn, Errol, 59

Follow the Boys (film), 314

Follow the Fleet (film), 85, 305

Follow Through (film), 300

Foolin' Around (film), 313

Footlight Parade (film), 32, 76, 302

Footlight Serenade (film), 311

Forbidden City, (San Francisco nightclub), 102, 103

Ford, Eddie, 260

Ford, Max, 288

Fordyce, Lorna, 289

For Me and My Gal (film), 53, 311

42nd Street (film), 32, 33, 35, 36, 76, 174, 302

Fosse, Bob, 335; films of, 320

Foster, Susanna, 210

Four Blazers, The, 259, 289

Four Covans, The, 22, 24, *27*, 28, 29, 66, 242, 260,

289, 297; films of, 300, 321

Four Flash Devils, The, 259, 260, *288*, 289

Four Fords, The, 289

Four Hot Shots, films of, 307

Four Jacks and a Jill (film), 310

Four Jills in a Jeep (film), 314

Four Rockets, The, 289

Four Specs, films of, 307

Four Step Brothers, The, 8, 46, 65, 121, 122, 131, 211-212, *212, 213*, 215-216, *215*, 218, *220*, 221, *224, 226*, 228, 230, 259, 281, 289, 296; Bottle Dance by, *228;* films of, *212*, 300, 301, 312, 313, 314, 315, 317, 318, 320; in France, *221, 222, 229*

Fowl Play (film), 299

Fox, Bebe, 288; films of, 313

Fox, Gerald, 335

Fox Studios, 31, 86, 88, 89, 91, 122, 162, 163, 164, 165, 193, 198

Fox theaters (Detroit), 109, (St. Louis), 148, (Washington, D.C.), 220, 225, 226

Foy, Eddie, Jr., 289; films of, 302, 312

Francis the Mule (film series), 146

Fred and Ginger, 289, *289*

Fred and Sledge, 288

Freeze and melt (tap movement), 155, 280

Freshman Year (film), 308

Frisco, Joe, films of, 302

Fun in Fun (film), 307

Funny Face (film), 56

Furman, Jaakko, 296

Gable, Clark, 87, 90, 248

Gaiety Theatre (London), 70

Gaines, Will, 335

Gains, Bubba, 289

Gals, Incorporated (film), 313

Gangway (film), 306

Garden Party, The (film), 302

Gardner, Ava, 248

Garland, Judy, 56, 148, 164, 289; films of, 306, 309, 311, 313, 318, 319

Garrett, Betty, films of, 248, 318, 320

Garson, Greer, 248

Gay Divorcée, The (film), 302

Gay New Orleans (show), 297

Gaynor, Mitzi, films of, 320

Geary Theatre (San Francisco), 256

Geil, Joe "Corky," 203, 289

Gene Kelly Studio of Dance, 169, 173, 175

Gentlemen Prefer Blondes (stage show), 269, 270; "Mamie Is Mimi," 269

George White Show Girls, 245

George White's Scandals (revue), 245, 302, 304, 316

Gershwin, George, 53, 55, *82*, 234

Gershwin, Ira, *82*

Get Goin' Louisiana Hayride (stage show), 225

Get Hep to Love (film), 203, 311

Ghost Catchers (film), 315

Giants of Rhythm, The 270, 289

Gilbert, Al, 296, 297

Gilbert, Gloria, 149, 289

Gilbert, John, 321

Gilbert, Paul, films of, 321

Gillespie, Dizzy, 95, 182, 271

Ginger (film), 165, 166

Girl Crazy (film), 301, 313

Girl Crazy (stage show), 270; "The Man I Love," 270

Girl Next Door, The (film), 320

Girls' Town (film), 311

Give a Girl a Break (film), 320

Give My Regards to Broadway (film), 318

Give Out, Sisters (film), 203, 311

Globe, The, (Boston burlesque house),259

Glorifying the American Girl (film), 299

Glover, Savion, 333, 335

Goddard, Paulette, films of, 311

Going Hollywood (film), 302

Going Native (film), 305

Go into Your Dance (film), 32, 33, *35*, 304

Goldbetter, Susan, 333, 334

Gold Diggers of Broadway (film), 299

Gold Diggers of 1933 (film), 32, 76, 302

Gold Diggers of 1935 (film), 304

Gold Diggers of 1937 (film), 305

Golden Anchor (Boston nightclub), 260

Golden Gate Theatre (San Francisco), 104, 106

Golden Hoofs (film), 310

Goldstein, Bruce, 335

"Golliwog's Cake Walk" (son), 237

Good Companions (film), 302

Goodell, Danzi, films of, 308

Goodman, Benny, 100, 109, 251, 257, 259; band of, 251

Good News (film), 321

Good News (film), 317

Good News (stage show), 53, 55, 56

Gordon and Rogers, 289

"Got a Bran' New Suit" (record), 326

"Got to Dance My Way to Heaven" (record), 325

Gould, Dave, 76, 79, 204

Gould, Morton, 296

Go West, Young Lady (film), 310

Grable, Betty, 76, 77, *80*, 198, 199, 243, 289; films of, 304, 307, 308, 310, 311, 312, 313, 314, 316, 317, 318, 319

Granger, Micki, 13

Granger, Steve, 13, 191, 289

Granlund, Nils T., 33

Grapes of Wrath, The (film), 206

Grauman, Sid, 104

Grauman's Chinese Theatre (Hollywood), 104, 238

Grayson, Kathryn, 248

Great American Broadcast, The (film), 72, 310

Great Feats of Feet (documentary), 333

Great Gabbo, The (film), 299

Great Ziegfeld, The (film), 305

Green, Buddy, films of, 309

Green, Chuck, 49, 289, 332, 333, 335

Green, Claire, films of, 309

Green, Mitzi, films of, 301

Green, Walter, 296

Green, Willie, 289

Greenlee, Rufus, 289

Greenlee and Drayton, 38, 289

Greenwich Village (film), 211, *212*, 315

Greenwood, Charlotte, 87, 289; films of, 310

Grey, Virginia, films of, 311

Grofé, Ferde, 234

Gross, Etta, 289

Guinan, Texas, 31, 33, 35; speakeasy of, 31, 33, 35

Gumm Sisters, The, 148, 164

Gus Edwards' International Colortone Revue, Gus Edwards' Kiddie Revue (film), 321

Gus Sun Time (vaudeville circuit), 37, 144, 148

Hale, Teddy, 49, 74, 133, 187, 259, 261, 289; films of, 317

Haley, Jack, 87, 290; films of, 306

"Half of It Dearie, Blues, The" (record), 322

Hal Kemp and His Orchestra (film), 308

Hall, Adelaide, 66

Hallelujah! (film), 300

Hammer, (MC), 335

Hampton, Lionel, 109, 133, 251, 297

Hancock, Bill, 333

Handel minuets, 236, 237, 239

Handy, W. C., 156

Haney, Carol, films of, 320

Hansen, Ted, 192

Happiness Ahead (film), *105*, 107-108, 302

Happy (of The Four Step Brothers), *212, 213, 224*, 228

Happy Days (film), 300

Happy Landing (film), 308

Harbert, Carita, 10, 27, 296; Four Covans and, 297

Harlem, 38, 47, 49, 64, 65, 67, 68, 74, 94, 95, 96, 111, 113, 114, 115, 125, 136, 139, 149, 155, 212, 213, 216, 217, 218, 227, 263, 266, 269, 276

Harlem After Midnight (film), 303, 304

Harlem Hotcha (film), 313

Harlem Is Heaven (film), 301

Harlem Opera House, 44, 45, 98

Harlem Rhumba (film), 311

Harlem Variety Revue (film), 320

Harley-Sadler (traveling road show), 296

Harmonica music, 232, 238, 239

Harold Teen (film), 303

Harris, Sam, 56

Harris, Theresa, films of, 309

Harris and Hunt, films of, 313, 314

Harry and Fats, 297

Harry Day and Della, 313

Harvest Moon Ballroom (New York), 50

Harvey Girls, The (film), 317

Haver, June, 198, 199, *199;* films of, 318

Have You Got Any Castles? (film), 308

Hawaiian Nights (film), 309
Hawaiian tap acts, 273-274
Hawkins, Erskine, 259
Hayworth, Rita, 77, *81*, 248, 249, 290; films of, 311, 312, 314
Head over Heels (film), 306
Healy, Danny, 55, 68; films of, 299
Heart o' the Hills (film), 321
Heel and toe (tap style), 280
Heel drop, 280
Hefner, Hugh M., 13
Hello Baby (film), 300
Hello Everybody (film), 302
Henderson, Fletcher, 121
Henie, Sonja, 192, 193
Hepburn, Katharine, 245
Here Come the Co-Eds (film), 316
Here Come the Girls (film), 211, 320
Her Lucky Night (film), 316
Herman, Woody, films of, 202
He's My Guy (film), 313
Hey, Rookie (film), 315
Hi, Buddy! (film), 313
Hi, Good Lookin' (film), 315
Hideaway Girl (film), 305
Hi-De-Ho (film), 317
Higginbotham, J. C., 182-183
High Hatters, The, 290, 297; films of, *132*
Highlanders, The, 290
High School (film), 309
High School Hoofer (film), 321
High Toned (film), 300
"Hi-Tech Tap," 297
Hill, Florence, 290; films of, 301
Hill, Teddy, 160
Hilliard, Harriet, films of, 315
Hillman Brothers, The, 290
Hines, Earl, 112, 259
Hines, Gregory, *7, 8,* 7-8, 11, 332, 333, 335
Hines, Maurice, *7,* 335
Hines Kids, The, 7, *7*
Hinton, Milt, 335
Hippodrome, (Baltimore theater), 106
Hippodrome, The (New York theater), 29
Hips, Hips, Hooray! (film), 303
Hirschfeld, Al, *138*
History of American Tap: Louis DaPron (video), 334
History of American Tap: Nanette Fabray (video), 334
History of American Tap: Fred Kelly (video), 334

History of American Tap: Hal Leroy (video), 334
History of American Tap: Fayard Nicholas (video), 334
History of American Tap: Jack Williams (video), 334
History of Jazz Dancing (documentary), 333
Hit Parade of 1941, The (film), 309
Hit Parade of 1943 (film), 313
Hits and Bits of 1922 (revue), 41
Hit the Deck (film), 320
Hi Ya Chum (film), 311
Hiya Sailor (film), 313
Hoctor and Byrd, 297
Hoctor, Betty, 297
Hoctor, Danny, 297; films of, 321
"Hokuspokus" (record), 325
Holder, Roland, 290
Hold Everything (stage show), 55
Holdt, Edna, recordings of, 324
Hold That Co-Ed (film), 308
Holiday Inn (film), 311
Hollywood, 9, 11, 12, 25, 29, 45, 54, 55, 56, 69, 70, 75, 76, 77, 119, 146, 155, 163, 166, 169, 170, 178, 179, 190, 191, 192, 194, 195, 199, 203, 204, 205, 206, 207, 221, 222, 240, 242, 243, 245, 250, 251, 252, 255
Hollywood Canteen, 10, 251-251
Hollywood Ice Revue, 192
Hollywood Professional School, 204
Hollywood Revue of 1929 (film), 300
Hollywood Rhythm (film), 304
Holt, David, 203, 290; films of, 305
Holy Terror, The (film), 306
Honest Crooks (film), 300
Honey Bunch Company, The, 137
Honeymoon Ahead (film), 316
Honeymoon Lodge (film), 313
Honi Coles: The Class Act of Tap (documentary), 334
Honolulu (film), 309
Hoofers, 94, 95, 96, 99, 118, 126, 134, 143, 149, 151, 182, 191, 198, 211, 235, 242, 245, 280

Hoofers Club, 37, 38, 42, 43, 74, 94, 95, 96, 126, 136, 212, 213, 214
Hoofers, The, 296
"Hoofer's Suite," 296
Hooker, Dynamite, 157, 290
Hooray for Love (film), 119, 123, 124, 125, 304
Hope, Bob, *71*, 290; films of, 321
Hopkins, Claude, 95, 259
Hopkins, Linda, 256
Horn, Pat, 297
Horne, Joyce, 290; films of, 315
Horne, Lena, 65, 98, 215
Horne, Lois, films of, 305
Hot Chocolate (stage show), 49
Hotel Chase (St. Louis), 109
Hotel Pierre (New York), 236
Hot Mikado, The, (ice show), 263, 265, 266, 267, 297; Bill Robinson in, *265*; program for, *265*
Howard, Eugene, 245
Howard, Willie, 245
Howard Theatre (Washington, D. C.), 259, 281
"How'm I Doin' (Hey-Hey)" (record), 325
How's About It (film), 313
"How to Learn to Tap Dance" (record), 326
Hula tap, 272
Hulbert, Jack, films of, 305; recording of, 324
Humphreys, Dickie, 290; films of, 313, 318
Huston, Walter, films of, 314
Hutton, Betty, films of, 311, 319
Hutton, Ina Rae, 290; films of, 302, 304, 307
Hyde and Seek, 290
Hyte, Les, 95

"(I Ain't Hep to That Step but I'll) Dig It" (record), 324
"I Can't Be Bothered Now" (record), 323
I Can't Give You Anything but Love, Baby (film), 310
Ice Capades, The (ice show), 170
Ice shows, 193
Ice sating, 192
I Don't Care Girl, The (film), 320
I Dood It (film), 313
"I'd Rather Lead a Band" (record), 323
If I had My Way (film), 310
If You Knew Susie (film), 318

"I Got Rhythm" (song), 239
"I Like New York in June" (song), 274
"I'll Be Loving You, Always" (song), 117
"I'll Capture Your Heart" (record), 324
I Love Melvin (film), 320
"I Love to Go Swimmin with Wimmen" (song/dance), 170, 179
"I Love You Truly" (song), 268
"I'm Looking at the World Through Rose-Colored Glasses" (song), 42
Imperial Theatre (New York), 138
Improvisation (tap style), 72, 280
In and Out (film), 300
Ingram, Germaine, 333
Inky, 290
In Old Kentucky (film), 304
In Person (film), 304
International Rhythms (film), 308
In the Navy (film), 310
In the Spotlight (film), 321
In Tirol Steht ein Berg (record), 325
Invitation to the Dance (film), 319
Is Everybody Happy? (film), 300
It Ain't Hay (film), 211, 313
"It Ain't Necessarily So" (song), 237, 239
It Comes Up Love (film), 311
It Happens on Ice (ice show), 193
It's Always Fair Weather (film), 175, 320
It's Love Again (film), 305
It's Love Again (film-Great Britain), 305
It's Swing Ho - Come to the Fair! (film), 309
"It Was Just One of Those Things" (song), 237
"I've Been Working on the Railroad" (song), 239
"I've Got a Feelin' You're Foolin'" (record), 326
Ivory, Jean, films of, 316
I Wonder Who's Kissing Her Now (film), 199, 317

Jack of All Trades (film), 305
Jackson, Ellis, recording of, 325
Jackson, John "Jack," *27*
Jacobs, Bill, 199
Jamboree (radio show), 174
James, Frank, 252, *2254, 256*

James, Freddy, *212, 224,* 228, 290
James, Harry, 251; band of, 251, 297
James and Nealy, *254*
Jam Session (film), 315
Japanese Internment camps (WWII), 110
Jason, Sybil, 10, 290; films of, 304, 305
Jazz, 21, 64, 111, 231, 271, 272
Jazz Age, 21, 31, 65, 111, 232
Jazz bands, 250
Jazz Chorus, 268
Jazz clubs, 272, 276
Jazz dancers, 216, 271-273, 274, 276-278
Jazz dancing, 268
Jazz Etude (film), 310
Jazz Hoofer (documentary), 333
Jazz Singer, The (film), 32
Jazz tap, 22, 280
Jazz Tap Ensemble, The, 335
Jean, Gloria, 151, 210; films of, 311, 10
Jelinvich, Karmen, 335
Jenkins, Freddie, recording of, 325
Jerry Ames Tap Dance Company, The, 296
Jesse, James, and Carnell, 290, 297
Jessel, George, 199
Jig Top, 41, 280
Jilly's Black Magic Club (New York nightclub), 277
Jimmy Lunceford and His Dance Orchestra (film), 305, 306
Jimmy Ryan's (nightclub), 277
Jingle tap, 280
Jitterbug (dance), 127
Jitterbug tap, 211
Jiveroo (film), 313
Jivin' in Be-bop (film), 317
Jivin' Jacks and Jills, The, 146, 151, 202-203, 207, 210, 243, 290; films of, 311, 312, 313, 316
Jivin' Jam Session (film), 312
Johnny Doughboy (film), 312
Johnny Nit's (rehearsal hall), 52
"Johnny One Note" (song), 70
Johnson, Dariel, 290
Johnson, Eudell, 290; films of, *132.* See also High Hatters, The
Johnson, Foster, 297
Johnson, Jack, 68

Johnson, Juliet, 54, 55
Johnson, Van, 198; films of, 320
Johnson, Ziggy, 255
Johnson and Johnson, films of, 316
Johnson and Murphy, 53, 54
Johnsons, The, 290
Jolson, Al, 32, *33, 35,* 68, 124
Jones, July, films of, 316
Jones, "Lollypop," films of, 317
Joplin, Scott, 115
Jordan, Louis, 133, 220
Jump for Joy (stage show), 127
Jumpin' at the Jubilee (film), 315
Jumpin' Jack from Hackensack (film), 313
Jump rope tap, 175, 272, 280
Junction 88 (film), 318
Junior Prom (film), 317
"Just a Crazy Song" (record), 326
Just Around the Corner (film), 87, *92,* 308
Just Imagine (film), 300
"Just Like Taking Candy from a Baby" (record), 324

Kahn, Stanley, 10, 297
"Kanotation," (tap notation), 297
Kane, Helen, films of, 300
Kane, Kathryn "sugar," 308
Kane, Marjorie "Babe," films of, 299
Kansas City, 39, 40, 41
Karavaeff, films of, 309
Kathleen (film), 310
Kay, Marilyn, 290
Kaye, Danny, films of, 242, 316
Kaye, Sammy, 259
Kean, Betty, 290; films of, 312, 313, 315
Keeler, Ruby, 9, 10, 30-36, *31, 33, 34, 35* 118, 124, 174, *234,* 290, *243;* on Broadway, 31, 33; as Buck dancer, 32, as Buck and Wing dancer, 32, *34,* 36; with Eddie Cantor, *31;* as classical dancer, *34;* with Lee Dixon, *34,* 35; with Paul Draper, *34, 35, 236;* films of, 32, 34, 35, 234, 299, 302, 304, 307, 311, 312; Al Jolson and 32, *35;* in nightclubs, 33, 35
Keene, Richard, films of, 300

"Keep a Song in Your Soul" (record), 326
"Keep a Twinkle in Your Eye" (record), 326
Keep Smiling (film), 308
Keith, B. F., 145
Keith (vaudeville circuit), 24, 37, 47, 50, 144, 226
Keith-Orpheum (vaudeville circuit), 215
Keith theaters (Boston), 259
Kelly, Fred, 10, 168, 170, *170,* 171-179, *171, 172, 173, 174, 175,* 178, 191, 290, 334; awards received by, 170; as dance instructor, 169, 170; as director and choreographer, 170; films of, 179, 314, 320; in "This Is the Army" unit, 178
Kelly, Gene, 8, 10, 53, 56, 88, 146, *150,* 151, 169, 170, *170,* 171, *172,* 174, 175, 177, 178, 179, 198, 216, 248, 281, 290; on Broadway, 170, 178; as dance instructor, 169; films of, 170, 179, 311, 313, 314, 315, 317, 318, 319, 320
Kelly, James, 169, *170,* 171, *172*
Kelly, Joan, 169, 171, *172*
Kelly, Louise, 169, 170, 171, *172,* 173; as dance instructor, 170
Kelly, Margaret, films of, 318
Kelly, Patsy, films of, 304
Kelly Brothers, The, 170, *176,* 177, 178, 179, 290; Cab Calloway and, 177-178
Kenny and Lloyd, 297
Kern, Jerome, 82
Kidd, Michael, films of, 320
Kid from Brooklyn (film), 317
Kid Millions (film), 56, 65, 69, 303
Killer Diller (film), 318
King, Evelyn, 297
King, Jimmy, 297
King, King, and King, 216, 290, 297
King Cole Trio with Benny Carter and His Orchestra (film), 319
King for a Day (film), 303
King of Burlesque (film), 305
King of Jazz (film), 301
King's Tropical Inn (Culver City, Calif., nightclub), 251
Kirstein, Lincoln, 236
Kissing Bandit, The (film), 318

Kiss Me Kate (film), 243, 248, 320
Kiss Me Kate (stage show), 270; "Too Darn Hot," 270
Kiss the Boys Goodbye (film), 321
Kit Kat Club (Culver City, Calif., nightclub), 251
Kit Kat Club (London nightclub), 55
Knight, June, 136
Knight Is Young, the (film), 308
Kreuger, Lorraine, films of, 313
Kunneke, Evelyn, recordings of, 325
Kuperberg, Robert, 333

Ladies' Man (film, 317
Lady Be Good (film), 155, 160, 310
"Lady Is A Tramp, The" (song), 70
Lafayette Hall (New York), 259
Lafayette Theatre (Harlem), 42, 43, 49, 67, 96, 114, 126, 212, 213, 257, 281
Lahr, Bert, films of, 318
Lamarr, Hedy, 247
Lambs Club (New York actors' club), 55
Lamont, Sonny, films of, 304, 309
Landry, Clarence "Frenchy," 290, 297; films of, *132*
Lane, Jennifer, 333
Lane, William Henry, 291
Lang, Harold, 291
Langdon, Harry, 321
La Redd, Cora, 118, 215, 291; films of, 302, 303
Las Palmas Theatre (Hollywood), 199
Last Frontier Hotel (Las Vegas), 221
Last Word (Los Angeles nightclub), 252
Las Vegas, 210, 221, 230, 270
Lathrop Brothers, films of, 306
Latin Casino (Philadelphia), 263
Laughing Sinners (film), 301
Laurel and Hardy, films of, 307
Lawrence, Baby, 8, 49, 133, 187, 259, 260, 261, 267, 272, 291, 233
Lawrence, Rosina, films of, 305
Lazar, Irving "Swifty," 194
"Lazy River" (song), 235

Leave It to Me (stage show), 170, 178
Le Boeuf sur le Toit (Paris nightclub), 233
Ledgin, Cy, 297
Lee, Billy, 291
Lee, Dixie, films of, 300, 304
Lee, Dorothy, films of, 301
Lee, Mable, 297
Lee, Sammy, 241
Legacy, The (film), 301
Legomania (tap style), 9, 22, 46, 47, 48, 49, 72, 74, 134, 136, 149, 280, 281
LeGon, Jeni, 10, 118-127, *119, 121, 123, 124, 126,* 243, 259, 260, 291; with Count Basie, 120-121; films of, 304, 306, 310; Four Step Brothers and, 121-122; Hoofers Club and, 126; in London, 125; in Los Angeles, 123; in nightclubs, 122; in pants, 119; Bill Robinson and, 119, 123, 124; as soubrette, 120; Fats Waller and, 124; with The Whitman Sisters, 119, 122
Lehrer, Tom, 13
Leigh, Janet, films of, 319, 320
Lend an Ear (show), 199, 200; "Who Hit Me" dance from, *200*
Leonard, Eddie, 291; films of, 310
Leonard and Crackaloo, 41
Leonard and Willie, 41
Leo Reisman Orchestra, 109, *109*
Leroy, Hal, 74, 134, 136, *290*, 291, 334; films of, 302, 303, 304, 305, 306, 307, 308, 310, 321
LeRoy, Mervyn, 108
Leslie, Joan, 291; films of, 314, 316
Leslie, Lew, 49, 71
LeTang, Henry, 8, 291
Let's Dance (film), 319
Let's Go Native (film), 301
"Let's Say Goodnight Till the Morning" (record), 324
"Let's Say It with Firecrackers" (record), 324
Let's Schuffle (film), 312
Let's Shuffle (film), 310
Let's Tap (documentary), 334
"Let Yourself Go" (record), 323
Levine, Susan "Tag-a-long," films of, 312
Levy, Burt, 148
Lewis, Sammy, films of, 301

Lew Leslie's Blackbirds (revue), 47, 49, 50, 70, *71,* 125, 126, 155
Lido Club (Paris), 222
Life of the Party, The (film), 306
Lillie, Bea, 125
Lincoln Theatre (Harlem), 112, 114
Lincoln Theatre (Kansas city), 40, 41
Lincoln Theatre (Los Angeles), 253
Lincoln Theatre (Philadelphia), 66, 67
Liszt, music of, 239
Little Big Shot (film), 304
Little Colonel, The (film), 87, *91,* 92, 304
Little Eva (Hollywood nightclub), 252
Littlefield, Catherine, 193
Little Miss Broadway (film), 53, 57, 59, 87, 308
Little Miss Nobody (film), 305
Little Nellie Kelly (film), 310
Little Princess,The (film), 87
Littlest Rebel,The (film), 87, 304
Living in a Big Way (film), 317
Lloyd, Harold, 68
Loews (vaudeville circuit), 47, 50, 144, 148, 235
Loews Penn Theatre (Pittsburgh), 177
Loews Warfield (theater), 106
Logan, Ella, 107, 245; films of, 307
Logan, Josh, 194
London, 53, 55, 56, 59, 71, 106, 107, 109, 125, 126, 155, 178, 195, 232, 236
London Palladium (theater), 106, 107, 109
Long, Baron, 250, 251
Long, Nick, Jr., *136;* films of, 303, 305, 307
Long, Walter, 291, 314
Look for the Silver Lining (film), 318
Los Angeles, 10, 25, 29, 31, 51, 100, 104-105, 107-108, 123, 145, 148, 151, 156, 158, 161, 168, 192, 195, 201, 206, 216, 250, 252, 253, 255, 256
Los Angeles Philharmonic, 239
Louis, Joe, 68, *196*
Love, Bessie, films of, 299, 300
Love, Dickie, films of, 313
Love and Hisses (film), 306

Love in Syncopation (film), 317
Lovely to Look At (film), 320
Loy, Myrna, 87
Luckey Roberts and His Society Entertainers, 112, 114
Lucky Starlets (film), 305
Lullaby of Broadway (film), 191, 319
Lunceford, Jimmie, 65, 95, 182, 259
"Lush Life" (song), 277
Lydon, Jimmy, films of, 316
Lying Lips (film), 317
Lyman, Abe, 109
Lyons, Carnell, 297
Lyons, Cleophus, films of, 317

Margo Feiden Galleries, 138
McAllister, Blue, 291
McCabe, Betty, 291; films of, 313
McCracken, Joan, films of, 317
McDaniel, Hattie, films of, 306
McDonald, Flash, 10, 212, *215,* 217-222, *218, 220, 221, 228, 229,* 291; at the Apollo, 220-221; doing Bottle Dance, *228;* films of, *See* Four Step Brothers, The; in The Four Step Brothers, 218; in France, 221, 222; Louis Jordan and, 220; in Las Vegas, 221; in New York, 221-222; Frank Schiffman and, 220-221
McDonald, Grace, 118, 203, 291; films of, 309, 310, 311, 312, 313, 314, 316
McDonald, Ray, 291; films of, 311, 317, 318, 319, 320
McGee, Jack, 203, 291
Machine Age, the, 21
Mack, Lavinia, 291
Mack, Ted, 226
Malone, Ray, 296
McKay, Barry, films of, 302
McKinney, Nina Mae, films of, 300, 301
McNab, Jane, 203, 291
McNab, Jean, 203, 291
MacRae, Gordon, 199
MaCree, Maxie, 291
Madden, Owney, 99, 214
Madison, Johnny, 291
Madison Square Garden, 72
Magna Studios, 200
Mahjongs, The, 291; films of, 302

Mahony, Will, 22, 291; films of, 303
Main Street Follies (film), 304
Maisie Gets Her Man (film), 312
Majestic Theatre (Houston), 243
Major Bowes' Amateur Hour (radio show), 225
Major Bowes' Amateurs in Variety Revue (film), 304
Major Bowes' Dixie Jubilee (show), 225
Major Bowes' Second Anniversary Dixie Jubilee (show), 226
Major Bowes' World's Fair Revue, 226
"Malagueña" (musical composition), 237
Mal Hallet and His Orchestra (film), 309
Malone, Chisey, 137, 138
Malone, Ray, films of, 313, 315
Maltin, Leonard, 13
Mambo (dance), 170
Mammy (film), 301
Manhattan (film), 310
Manhattan Merry-Go-Round (film), 306
"Manhattan Serenade" (song), 235
Manhattan Tap, 333
Manning, Jack, 291
Mannix, Eddie, 59
Mansfield Theatre (New York), 207
March of Time, The (film), 301
Mario Braggioti's Orchestra, 236
Markham, "Pigmeat," 318
Markin' Time (film), 300
Marrow, Dorothy Nicholas, 335. *See also* Nichols, Dorothy
Marsh, Joan, films of, 305
Marshall, Vera, films of, 306
Martin, Mary, 178
Martin, Tony, films of, 319
Marx Brothers, The, 68, 78, 245
Marx, Chico (orchestra of), 109
Masters of Tap (documentary), 335
Matthews, Jessie, films of, 301, 302, 304, 305, 306, 308; recordings of, 325-326
Mattison, Ethlyn, 291
Mattison, Johnny, 291
Maxie Ford (tap step), 280
Maxies, 147

Max Roach and Clifford Brown Quintet, 276
Mayfair, Mitzi, 243, 291; films of, 301, 302, 314
Mayfair Hotel (London), 55
Mayo, Virginia, 201, 291; films of, 319, 320
Mayor of 44th Street, The (film), 312
McNulty, Dorothy, 321. See also Singleton, Penny
"Me and the Ghost Upstairs" (record), 324
Medbury, Theresa, 13
Medrano Stadium (France), 221, 229
Meet Me After the Show (film), 319
Meet Me at the Fair (film), 320
Meet the Bride (film), 306
Meet the People (stage show), 207
Meglin Kiddies, 304
Melody for Two (film), 307
Melody Lane (film), 310
Melody Ranch (film), 310
Merman, Ethel, 69, 198
Merry Mannequins (cartoon), 321
Merry Monahans, The (film), 208, 210, 315
Mess Around, the (dance), 114, 280
Metro Movietone Revue #2 (film), 321
Metropolitan Theatre (Boston), 259
MGM Studios, 25, 29, 76, 77, 84, 125, 142, 170, 175, 198, 204, 206, 241, 242, 247, 248, 336
Michael's (rehearsal hall), 52, 55
Mickey McGuire Comedies (film series), 164
Mickey's gala Premier (cartoon), 321
Midnight Menace (film), 317
Midnight Steppers, The, 43, 291
Midshipmaid, The (film), 301
Milkman, The (film), 146, 319
Miller, Ann, 9, 10, 25, 46, 49, 118, 122, 126, 241-249, 242, 243, 244, 246, 247, 248, 291, 297; Fred Astaire and, 249; Busby Berkeley and, 242, 247; Nick Castle and, 247; choreographers and, 246-247; Jack Cole and, 247; Willie Covan and, 242, 247; dance style of, 243, 244, 246; films of, 243,

245, 306, 307, 308, 310, 311, 312, 314, 315, 316, 317, 318, 319, 320; Hermes Pan and, 247-248; Eleanor Powell and, 245-246; in revues, 245; as world's fastest tap dancer, 243
Miller, Curly, 291
Miller, Glenn, 142, 251; band of, 251
Miller, Junie, 114, 116
Miller, Marilyn, 55, 118, 140, 291; films of, 300, 301
Miller, Susan, films of, 321
Miller, Sydney, 164
Miller, Taps, 291; films of, 314
Miller and Lyles, 24
Miller Brothers, The, 291
Miller Brothers and Lois, 118, 214, 259, 260, 291; films of, 317
Millions in the Air (film), 304
Mills, Florence, 126
Mills, Shirley, 291
Mills Blue Rhythm Band (film), 302
Mills Brothers, The, 95, 101, 266, 267
Milt and Honi (documentary), 335
"Minnie the Moocher" (song), 68, 98, 105
Minstrel Man (film), 315
Minstrel shows, 22, 24, 25, 26, 47, 48, 49, 223
Mintun, Peter, 13
Miramar Hotel, 191
Miranda, Carmen, 81
Mischner, Doug, 333
Mitchell, Dolores, 203, 291
Mitchell, Jimmy "Sir Slyde," 259, 260
Mitchell, Julian, 33
Mocambo, The (Hollywood nightclub), 251
Moke and Poke, 291
Montgomery, Jack, 292
Montgomery, Sammy, 292
Montmartre (New York nightclub), 54
"Mood Indigo" (song), 232
"Moonlight Cocktail" (song), 115
Moonlight in Hawaii (film), 310
Moonlight in Vermont (film), 313
Moonlight Masquerade (film), 312
Moon over Miami (film), 76, 310; publicity shot from, 76

Moore, Constance, films of, 315
Moran, Gai, films of, 321
Mordecai, Jimmy, films of, 300
"Morton Gould's Concerto for Tap Dancer and Orchestra" (concerto), 296
"Morton Gould's Hoofer's Suite," 296
Mosby, Esvan, films of, 300
Moten, Benny, 297
Mother Wore Tights (film), 199, 317
Motion pictures, See names of individual motion pictures and Appendix B, 299-321
Moulin Rouge (Staten Island nightclub), 117
Mouse, Mickey, cartoons of, 301, 321
Mouse, Minnie, cartoon of, 301
Movie industry, 251
Movies, See names of individual movies and Appendix B, 299-321
Mozart, music of, 239
Mr. Big (film), 146, 313
Mr. Bojangles' Memory - Og, Son of Fire (documentary), 335
Mr. Broadway (film), 302
Muellett, Jimmy, 204
Mule kicks (dance step), 230, 280
Munshin, Jules, 248; films of, 318
Murder at the Vanities (film), 303
Murder in Swingtime (film), 307
Murder with Music (film), 316
Murphy, George, 10, 52-59, 53, 54, 56, 57, 58, 69, 87, 88, 90, 93, 190, 195, 204, 206, 292; Fred Astaire and, 57; in Broadway Melody of 1938, 56; at cotton Club, 55; films of, 53, 56, 306, 307, 308, 309, 310, 311, 312, 314, 315; Juliet Johnson and, 54, 55; in Little Miss Broadway, 57; in London, 53, 55, 59; musical shows in, 53, 56; in nightclubs, 54; Eleanor Powell and, 56; in rehearsal halls, 55; screen partners of, 53, 56; Shirley Temple and, 57, 59
Murray, Arthur, 137, 232, 279

Musical Beautyshop (film), 301
Musical Memories (film), 304
Musicals, movie, 75-77, 166; filming innovation, 79. See also names of individual movies and Appendix B, 299-321
Music Box (Hollywood nightclub), 227
Music Box Theatre (New York), 56
Music Goes 'Round, The (film), 305
Music Is Magic (film), 304
"Music Makes Me" (record), 322
"My Best Gal" (film), 313, 315
My Blue Heaven (film), 319
"My Funny Valentine," (song), 70
My Gal Sal (film), 81, 312; "On the Gay White Way," 81
"My Heart Belongs to Daddy" (song), 178
My Maryland (vaudeville show), 77, 78
"My One and Only" (record), 322
"My Reverie" (song), 109
Myrt and Marge (film), 302
My Sister Eileen (film), 320
My Son Is Guilty (film), 309
My Wild Irish Rose (film), 317

"Nagasaki" (song), 226
National Endowment for the Arts, 2
National Tap Dance Day, 278
Naughty Nineties, The (film), 310, 316
Nazarro, Cliff, recordings of, 326
Neagle, Anna, films of, 311
Nealy, Frances, 10, 250-256, 251, 253, 254, 255, 256, 292; Count Basie and, 256; Frank James and, 254, 256; in Los Angeles, 253, 255; as nightclub performer, 251, 252, 254, 255; Ike Parrish and, 255, 256; as a Reedette, 253; Bill Robinson and, 256
Nearly Eighteen (film), 313
Neill, Noel, films of, 321
Nelson, Gene, 8, 10, 166, 190-201, 192, 193, 194, 195, 197, 199, 200, 292, 297; Army days of, 193-198; films of, 191, 199, 200, 201, 317, 319, 320,

321; Ted Hansen and, 192; June Haver and, 199; ice skating and, 192-193; in revues, 192, 199; style of, 191; training of, 192
Nelson, Miriam Franklin, 193, 198, 297, 316
Never a Dull Moment (film), 313
New England Conservatory, 260
New Faces of 1937 (film), 243, 307
"New Low-Down" (song), 100
Newman, Rigmor, 335
New Orleans, 9, 122
New Orleans jazz, 277
New York City, 9, 28, 31, 32, 35, 38, 42, 43, 45, 49, 65, 67, 68, 70, 72, 87, 94, 95, 96, 101, 102, 106, 107, 109, 110, 111, 114, 116, 125, 126, 137, 138, 142, 145, 149, 155, 156, 170, 175, 177, 178, 183, 191, 193, 194, 199, 200, 207, 212, 220, 221, 222, 226, 232, 234, 236, 245, 253, 255, 256, 257, 259, 260, 263, 266, 267, 269, 272, 276, 281
"Nice Work If You Can Get It" (record), 323
Nicholas, Dorothy, 67, 335
Nicholas, Fayard, 8, 10, 65, 66, *71, 72, 78,* 157, 292, 334; films of, *See* Nicholas Brothers, The recordings of, 326
Nicholas, Harold, 8, 10, 65, 67, 69, *71, 72, 72, 73,* 130, 157, 292; films of, 302, 314, 315. *See also* Nicholas Brothers, The
Nicholas Brothers, The, 7, 8, 46, 64-74, *65, 67, 69, 71, 72, 73,* 98, 107, 109, 122, 123, 125, 130, 156, 166, 174, 177, 214, 215, 243, 246, 292, 334, 335; Fred Astaire and, 70; John Bubbles and, 73; Eddie Cantor and, 69; at the Cotton Club, *65,* 68-69, 80; dancing style of, 72; films of, 65, *72,* 301, 303, 305, 306, 309, 310, 312, 313, 314, 315, 317, 318; Bob Hope and, *71;* in London, 70; in Philadelphia, 66, 67; in Ziegfeld Follies, 70, *71*

Nicholas Brothers, The: We Sing and We Dance (documentary), 335
Nicholas' Collegians, 66
Nicholas Kids, The, 67, 68
Nierenberg, George T., 333
Night Club Girl (film), 316
Night in a Niteclub (film), 30
Nightlife, The (Hollywood nightclub), 251, 252, 255
Night Parade (film), 300
"Night Time" (record), 324
Night World (film), 301
Nilsson Twins, films of, 317
Nip, Tommy, 232
Nit, Johnny, 292; films of, 305
Nitwits, The (film), 304
Nixon Theatre (Pittsburgh), 170, 172
Nolan, O'Neill, 292
No Maps on my Taps (documentary), 333
No No Nanette (stage show), 175
Nora Bayes and Her Picks, 24
Nordstrom, Clarence, films of, 302
North Star (film), 313
"No Strings" (record), 322
Novelty (tap style), 46, 47, 49, 51, 98, 280
Nugent, Eddie, films of, 302, 305, 321
Nugent, Pete, 277, 292

Oakie, Jack, 87, *149,* 209, 292; films of, 300, 301, 310, 314, 315, 316
O'Connell, Pattie, 13
O'Connor, Bill, *145,* 151
O'Connor, Donald, 9, 10, 144-152, *145, 147, 148,* 149, *150,* 151, 166 203, 204, *206,* 207, *207, 208,* 209, 210, 216, 243, 246, 292, 297; films of, 146, 150, 202, *206, 208,* 307, 309, 311, 312, 313, 314, 315, 316, 317, 318, 319, 320: Gene Kelly and, *150,* 151; musical shows of, 146; Bill Robinson and, 149; in vaudeville, *145,* 146, 147-148
O'Connor, Effie, *145*
O'Connor, Jack, *145,* 147, 148
O'Connor, Millie, *145*
O'Connor, Patsy, *145,* 147, 292; films of, 313
O'Connor Family, *145,* 146, 292

O'Dea, Sunnie, films of, 310, 311
Of Thee I Sing (stage show), 53, 55, 56
Oh, Evaline (film), 321
"Oh, How I Hate to Get Up in the Morning" (song), 178
O'Hanlon, George, films of, 318
Oklahoma! (film), 82, 191, 200, 242, 297, 320; "Everything's Up to date in Kansas city," *200*
Old Kentucky (minstrel show), 26
Old Man Rhythm (film), 304
O'Neal, Zelma, films of, 300
One for the Money (stage show), 170
125 Club (Harlem nightclub), 276
One man dance, 280
One Mile from Heaven (film), 307
On Stage Everybody (film), *209,* 316
On the Town (film), 243, 248, 318
On the Wrong Trek (film), 305
On with the Show (film), 66, 300
On Your Toes (film), 309
Opening Shot - Savion Glover (documentary), 335
Orchestra Wives (film), 312
"Oriental" revues, 102
Oriental Theatre (Chicago), 106
Orpheum (vaudeville circuit), 24, 37, 144, 145, 182
Orpheum theaters: (Boston), 259; (Kansas city), 40; (Los Angeles), 105, 106, 256, (Portland), 106, (San Diego), 106, (San Francisco), 104, 185, (Seattle), 106
Our Gang Comedies (film series), 155, 160
Over the Top (tap step), 224, 227, 229, 230, 280
Owens, Frankie, 45

Pack Up Your Troubles (film), 309
Paddle and roll, 280
Paddy O'Day (film), 304
Page, Anita, films of, 299, 300
Paige, Robert, films of, 309
Painting the Clouds with Sunshine (film), 319

Palace Theatre (New York), 24, 28, 29, 38, 39, 43, 139, 159, 281
Pal Joey (stage show), 170, 207
Palladium (London), 178, 191, 195
Palmer, Aaron, 119, 292
Palmer, "Pops," 119
Pan, Hermes, 10, 75-85, *76, 77, 78, 80, 81, 82, 83, 84,* 199, *199,* 241, 242, 243, 246, 247, *247, 248,* 292, 333; Fred Astaire and, 76-77, 78, 79, 82, 83, 84, 85; Lucille Ball and, *80;* Hal Borne and, 82; on Broadway, 77; films of, 310, 311, 312, 313, 314; George Gershwin and, 82; Dave Gould and, 76, 79; Betty Grable and, 80; Rita Hayworth and, 81; as innovator, 79; Marx Brothers and, 78; Carmen Miranda and, *81;* Ginger Rogers and, *84;* in Tab shows, 78-79; in vaudeville, 77
Panama Hattie (film), 155, 193, 312
Pantages (vaudeville circuit), 144
Pantages Theatre (San Francisco), 104
"Papa De Da Da" (song), 160
Parachute Battalion (film), 310
Paradise Club (Atlantic City nightclub), 267
Paramount on Parade (film), 301
Paramount Studios, 9, 12, 83, 151, 198, 201, 246
Paramount theaters, 235; (Los Angeles), 100, 105, 192; (New York), 50, 68, 106, 107, 159, 221, 229, 230
Pardon Me, But You Look Just Like Margie (film), 314
Pardon My Gun (film), 321
Pardon My Sarong (film), 312
Paree, Paree (film), 303
Paris, 47, 50, 73, 229, 233
Parker, Charlie, 95, 187, 271, 277
Parrish, Ike, 252, *255,* 256
Parrish and Nealy, *255,* 256
Pass, 281
"Passing" (song), 38
Pastor, Tony, 109, 144
Paterson, Pat, films of, 306

Patrick the Great (film), 148, 206, 208, 210, 316; "When You Bump into Someone You Know and Love," 206

Patricola, Tom 292; films of, 300, 316

Patterson and Jackson, 292; films of, 318

Paul Draper and Company, 234

Paul Draper On Tap (documentary), 335

Paul Whiteman's Orchestra, 55

Payne, Jimmy, 292, 297

Peach-O-Reno (film), 301

Pearl Theatre (Philadelphia), 67, 259, 281

Peckin' (film), 312

Pen and Ink, 41, 292

Pennington, Ann, 118, 292; films of, 299, 300

Penthouse Rhythm (film), 315

Pepper, Buddy, 206

Percussive Step Dance (documentary), 335

Perrone, Johnny, films of, 300

Perry, Dein, 335

Pete, Peaches, and Duke, 270, 292

Pete and Peaches, 292

Peterson, Pete, 10, 292

Peters Sisters, films of, 306

Phelan, Pat, films of, 321

Philadelphia, 40, 66, 67, 68, 128, 129, 130, 133, 171, 175, 226, 252, 256, 257, 260, 281

Phil Waiman's (rehearsal hall), 52, 232

"Piano," 292

Pick, 23, 24. *See also* Pickaninny

Pickaninny, 23, 24, 25, 280

Pickford, Mary, 155, 321

"Pick Yourself Up" (record), 323

Picture dancing, 262

Picture Palace (film), 303

Pie, Pie Blackbird (film), 65, 301

Pied Pipers, The, 229

Pigskin Parade (film), 305

Pin-Up Girl (film), 80, 315; "Once Two Often," 80

Pirate, The (film), 65, 318

Pit bands, 130, 257

Pitch a Boogie Woogie (film), 317

Pitts, Juanita, 118, 252, 292

Pitts and Pitts, 252

Pittsburgh, 169, 171, 172, 177, 179

Plantation (Los Angeles nightclub), 252

Platt, Marc, films of, 316, 317

Plaza Hotel, Persian Room of, (New York nightclub), 236, 237; ad for, *237*

Polar Palace (Hollywood), 192

Poor Little Rich Girl, The (film), 87, 306

Poppin' the Cork (film), 314

Pops and Louis, 7, 119, 122, 260, 292; films of, 313

"Porkchops," 114

Porkchops, Navy, Rice, and Beans, 114

Porkchops and Gillespie, 292

Porter, Bill, *264*

Porter, Cole, 82, 178

Potluck (film), 307

Powell, Dick, 87

Powell, Eleanor, 29, 32, 49, 53, 56, *56,* 58, 63, 85, 86, 118, 122, 125, 126, 134, *136,* 140, 163, 204, 242, 243, 245-246, 292, 296; films of, *58,* 59, 303, 304, 306, 307, 309, 310, 312, 313, 314, 315, 316, 319; recordings of, 326

Powell, Jane, 248; films of, 319

Powell, William, 87

Precision tap, 262, 269

Presentation, 257, 258, 259, 260, 281

Primitive dances, 274

Primrose, George, 293

Prinz, Leroy, 105, 201, 241

Priorities on Parade (film), 312

Prisoner of Swing, The (film), 308

Prival, Bert, 193

Private Buckaroo (film), 203, 312

Private Lessons, 303

Production houses, 172

"Professional [tap]" (record), 324

Professor O'Brien's Normal School of Dancing, 273, 274

Prohibition, 31, 65, 77, 251

Prologue, 281

Promotional shows, 192

Proser, Monte, 110

Public Jitterbug No. 1 (film), 309

Publix (vaudeville circuit), 106

Pullbacks (tap step), 233, 281

Pulling the Trenches (tap step), 10, 22, 42, 227, 230, 281

Puttin' on the Ritz (film), 301

"Puttin' on the Ritz" (record), 322

Quine, Richard, films of, 311

Radcliff, Frank, 293

Radio, 21, 22, 65, 146, 165, 174, 175

Radio City Music Hall, 155, 159, 192, 205, 228, 229, 230, 238

Radio City Revels (film), 308

Radio City Rockettes, 293, 297

Radio Hook-up (film), 308

Radio stars, 187

Raft, George, 68

Ragtime, 21, 231

Rain (film), 104

Rainbow Room (New York nightclub), 237

Rall, Tommy, 248, 293; films of, 320

Ramsey, Kevin, 333, 334

Randolph, Elsie, films of, 307

Randolph, Roy, 191

Ransdell Dance School (Los Angeles), 107

Rascals (film), *167,* 308

Ratliff's Dancing Academy, 203

Ravel, music of, 239, 274

Ray, Peter, 293

Ray Anthony and His Orchestra (film), 319

Raye, Martha, 109; films of, 303

Ready, Willing and Able (film), 32, 34, *34,* 307

Reagan, Ronald, 190, 195

Rebecca of Sunnybrook Farm (film), 87, 91, 308; "Toy Trumpet," *91*

Reb Spike's Band (film), 299

Reckless Age (film), 315

Rector, Eddie, 38, 49, 96, 267, 279, 293

Red, *213*

Red and Curly, 133, 293

Red and Struggles, 293; films of, 302

Redheads on Parade (film), 304

Redman, Don, 259

Redman, Eddie, 255

Red Nichols and His World-Famous Pennies (film), 306

Reed, Leonard, 13, 10, 37-45, *38, 40, 43, 44,* 66, 96, 122, 212, 253, 281, 293; blacklisting of, 44; Willie Bryant and, 39, *43,* 44, 45; carnival work and, 40-41; Charleston and, 40, 42; Hoofers Club and, 38-39, *42;* as innovator, 38; "passing," 38; as producer, 39, 45; shows in, 41; in vaudeville, *44;* Whitman Sisters and, 43

Reed and Bryant, 43, 44, 66, 293

Reedettes, The, *253*

Regal Theatre (Chicago), 120, 121

Regent Theatre (Los Angeles), 105

Rehearsal halls, 52-53, 55, 85, 92, 121, 142, 168, *199,* 226, 232, 233, 234; large, 52-53; snake pits, 53

Reisman, Leo, 140

Renaissance Casino (New York dance hall), 114

Reveille with Beverly (film), 314

Reyburn, Stuart, 193

Reynolds, Al, films of, 304

Reynolds, Debbie, 201, 248; films of, 320

Reynolds, Marjorie, films of, 311

"Rhapsody" (song), 235

Rhapsody in Blue (film), 316

"Rhapsody in Blue" (song), 55

Rhythm, 7, 8, 9, 25, 26, 32, 47, 48, 72, 73, 74, 187, 278

Rhythm, Western, 131

Rhythmania (film), 314

Rhythm Bound (revue), 39, *44*

Rhythm dances, 100, 268

Rhythm dancing, 131

Rhythmitis (film), 306

Rhythm of the Islands (film), 211, 314

Rhythm on the Roof (film), 303

Rhythm Pals, The, 263, 264, 294; ad for, *264;* films with, 306

Rhythm tap, 22, 34, 47, 216, 263, 281

Rhythm tappers, 47, 77, 130-131, 134, 136, 211, 216, 222, 230, 263, 267

Rice, Thomas Dartmouth, 293

Rich, Buddy, films of, 318

Rich Brothers, The, 214

Richman, Camden, 333

Richman, Harry, 293; films of, 301

Richmond, June, 65

Rico, Pat, 296, 297

Ride 'Em Cowboy (film), 312
Riff (tap movement), 281
Right, Teddy, 42
Rio de Janiero, 109
Rio, Rita, films of, 313
Rise and Shine (film), 311
Rise of Rosie O'Reilly, The (stage show), 31, 33
Ritz Brothers, 293; films of, 309, 311, 313
Rivoli Theatre (Toledo), 225
RKO (vaudeville circuit), 106
RKO Boston (Theater), 259
RKO Palace (Cleveland), 106
RKO Studios, 70, 76, 78, 79, 80, 82, 84, 119, 123, 175, 243, 245, 248
RKO Theatre (Cincinnati), 106
Roach, Max, 272, 276, 335
Road Demon (film), 308
Roadhouses, 250-251
Road to Utopia (film), 317
Roberta (film), 78, 80, *80*, 304
Roberta (stage show), 53
Roberti, Lyda, films of, 301
Roberts, Dorothy, films of, 310
Roberts, Luckey, 111, 112, 114, 115, 116
Robeson, Paul, 125
Robinson, Bill, 7, 22, 28, 36, 38, 42, 46, 63, 65, 66, 68, 72, 74, 86, 87, 88, 90, *91*, *92*, 93, 94, 95, 96, 97, 98, 112, 113, 119, *119*, 123, 124, *124*, 134, 149, 156, 163, 166, 175, 180-185, *181*, *184*, 192, 209, 213, 219, 224, 225, 226, 227, 243, 252, 256, 260, 263, *265*, 266, 278, 293, 297, 334, 335; cartoons of, 306, 308, 321; films of, 300, 301, 303, 304, 307, 308, 309, 310, 312, 314; recordings of, 326-327
Robinson, Fannie, 90
Robinson, LaVaughn, 10, 128-133, *130*, 293, 333; buskin' clubs, 133; as street tap dancer, 128-129, 131, 133, Germaine Ingram and, 333
Rocco and Saulter, films of, 306
Rockettes, The, 192, 205, 229, 273
Rock 'n Roll Revue (film), 320
Rodgers and Hart, 70
Rodgers, Ginger, 32, 63, 70, 77, 78, 79, *82*, 83, 84, 90, 123, 166, 219, 243, 245, 249, 293; films of, 302,

304, 306, 307, 308, 312, 318
Rogers, Harry, 237
Rogers, Will, 122, 163, 165
Roller skate tap, 175, 273
Romberg, Sigmund, 179
Ronnell and Edna, films of, 317
Rookies on Parade (film), 311
Room Service (film), 245
Rooney, Anne, 293
Rooney, Mickey, 25, 87, 164, 293; films of, 301, 309, 311, 313
Rooney, Pat, 224, 227
Rooney, Pat, Jr., films of, 304, 306, 307
Rooney, Pat, Sr., 293; films of, 304, 309
Rooney, Pat, III, films of, 313
Rooney family with Pat Rooney, Sr., films with, 300
Roosevelt, Eleanor, 166, 195
Roosevelt, Franklin Delano, 165, 195, 227
Rosalie (film), 307
Roseland Ballroom, 170
Rosengarden, Bob, 335
'Round the World (vaudeville circuit), 257, 260, 281
Routine, 281
Roxie Hart (film), 312
Roxy Theatre (New York), 50, 106, 109, 159, 170, 230
Roy, Harry, films of, 305
Royal Theatre (Baltimore), 257, 281
Royal Wedding (film), 319
Rubber legs (tap movement), 281
Ruby Keeler (film), 299
Ruffin, Leonard, 24, 28
Rufus Jones for President (film), 302
Russian (tap style), 281
Russian kick-out (tap step), 227, 230
Ruth, Roy Del, 59
Rutherford, Ann, films of, 309
Rutledge and Taylor, 293
Ryan, Peggy, 10, 118, 126, *149*, 151, 202-210, *204*, *205, 206, 207, 208, 209,* 243, 246, 294; on Broadway, 206-207; Johnny Coy and, *204;* dance teachers of, 204; Louis DaPron and, 209-210; in dramatic roles, 206; films of, 203, 204, 206, 207, 208, 209, 300, 307, 311, 312, 313, 314, 315, 316,

318, 319, 320; in The Jivin' Jacks and Jills, 203, 207; Donald O'Connor and, *206,* 207, *208,* 209; Gene Snyder and, *205*

Sadie Montgomery and Leonard, 41, 294
Sailing Along (film), 308
"Saint James Infirmary" (song), 98
Saint Louis Blues (film) 300
"Saint Louis Blues" (song), 157
Sally (film), 300
Sally Irene & Mary (film), 308
Saloons, 23, 25
Salt and Pepper, 294
Sammy, Sunshine, 157, *212*, 294
Samovar Serenade (film), 309
Samuel Brothers and Edith Fleming, films of, 308
San Antonio Rose (film), 311
San Carlo Opera House (Naples), 195
Sandford, Sandy, 274, 276, 277
Sandin' Joe (film), 316
Sandrich, Mark, *82*
San Francisco, 9, 25, 148, 185, 207, 252, 256
San Francisco Opera House, 239
Sarah Venable and Her Picks, 24
Sardi's (Hollywood nightclub), 251
Saulters, Dotty, *266,* 267, *267,* 294; films of, 307
Savoy Ballroom (New York), 99, 100
Sawyer, Geneva, 88
Scandal (film), 302
Scarlatti sonata, 239
Scheerer, Bobby, 14, 151, 203, 294, *294;* films of, 313, 315, 319
Scheerer, Robert. *See* Scheerer, Bobby
Schiffman, Frank, 218, 220-221
School of American Ballet, 236
Scott, Raymond, 297
Scriabin, 239
Seasoned Greetings (film), 321
Sebastian, Frank, 251
Sebastian's Cotton Club (Los Angeles nightclub), 266
Second Chorus (film), 83, 311; "Me and the Ghost Upstairs," *83*

Seeing Red (film), 309
Seeley, Blossom, 24
See My Lawyer (film), 316
Selva, Jimmy, 175
Sensations of 1945 (film), 315, 316
Sensations of 1932 (stage show), 233
Seven Days Ashore (film), 315
Seven Little Foys, The, 169, 172
Seven Little Foys, The (film), 321
Shaw, Artie, 109
Swanee Inn, The (Hollywood nightclub), 253
Shadows in Swing (film), 311
"Shadrack" (song), 206
Shall We Dance (film), 82, 175, 307
"Shall We Dance?" (record), 323
Shamrock Hill (film), 318
Shangri-la, The (Philadelphia nightclub), 256
Shea's Theatre (Buffalo), 106
Shearing, George, 182
Sheehan, Winfield, 122
Shep's Playhouse (Hollywood nightclub), 252, 253
She Loves Me Not (film), 321
"She's a Latin from Manhattan" (song), 33; sheet music for, *33*
She's Back on Broadway (film), 320
She's for Me (film), 314
She's My Lilly, I'm Her Willie (film), 303
She's Working Her Way Through College (film), 191, 320
Shilkret, Nathaniel, *82*
Shimmy (dance), 41, 113
Shim Sham Shimmy (dance routine), 10, 22, 38, 43, 97, 253, 281
Shine on Harvest Moon (film), 315
Ship Ahoy (film), 312
Shipley, Glenn, 10, 294
Shipmates Forever (film), 86, 304
Shirley Club (Massachussetts nightclub), 258
Shooting High (film), 310
Shoot the Works (stage show), 55
Short, Bobby, 335
Showboat (film), 306
Show Business (film), 315
Show of Shows (film), 300
Shuffle (tap step), 25

Shuffle Along (stage show), 25

Shultz, Dutch, 214

Shurr, Louis, 55, 56

Sidewalks of New York, The (stage show), 31

Sidney, Robert, 194

Silvers, Phil, films of, 314

Silver Slipper (New York speakeasy), 31, 35

Sims, Howard "Sandman," 8, 294, 333

Sinatra, Frank, 229, 248, 94; films of, 315, 318

Sing, Baby, Sing (film), 306

Sing, Dance, Plenty Hot (film), 310

Sing a Jingle (film), 315

Sing Another Chorus (film), 311

Singing Marine, The (film), 307

Singing Sheriff, The (film), 315

Singin' in the Rain (film), 146, 150, 151, 320; "Make 'Em Laugh," 146, 150; "Fit as a Fiddle," *150*

Singleton, Penny, 3221

Sing Your Way Home (film), 316

Sing Your Worries Away (film), 312

Sing You Sinners (film), 151

Sinnett, Rose Marie, 321

Six Birds of Rhythm, The, 55

Six Cotton Club Boys, The, 156

Six Hits and a Miss (film), 312

Skelly, Hall, films of, 299

Skyline Revue (film), 308

Sky's the Limit, The (film), 201, 314

Slapsy Maxie's (Los Angeles nightclub), 251, 252, 255

"Slap That Bass" (record), 323

Slate Brothers, The, 294; films of, 300, 308, 310

Slick Hare (cartoon), 321

Slide (tap step), 281

Slightly Scandalous (film), 317

Slightly Terrific (film), 315

Slim and Sweets, films of, 314

Slow Poke (film), 302

Slyde, Jimmy, 10, 257-261, *258,* 272, 274, 294, 332, 333, 335; with big bands, 259, 260-261; dancing style of, 259; Eddie Ford and, 260; as nightclub performer, 260; as violinist, 259

Slyde Brothers, The, 259, 260

Small and Mayes, 294

Smalltown Deb (film), 311

Small Town Girl (film), 242, 243, 246, 320; "I've Gotta Hear That Beat," *242,* 246

Smash Your Baggage (film), 302

Smiles (stage show), 140

Smith, Alma, 294

Smith, Cosie, 24, 25

Smith, Jimmy, 294

Smith, Kate, films of, 302

Snake Hips (dance movement), 122, 281

Sneak Inn (Culver City, Calif., nightclub), 251

Sneaks & Emil, 294

Sneed, Ray, films of, 317

Snow, Valaida, 155, 156, 158

Snyder, Gene, 205

Sobol, Louise, 70

Society Sound, 111, 112

Soft Shoe (dance style), 22, 43, 45, 46, 47, 72, 73, 117, 141, 174, 206, 263, 264, 268, 270, 281

Soft Shoe, Slow, 263, 268

Soft Show tap, 269

Soft Shoe dancers, 28, 134, 234

Soft Shoe dancing, acrobatic, 159-160; exotic, 159

"Soft Shoe Routine" (record), 324

Solid Senders (film), 317

Someone Stole the Baby (documentary), 335

Something in the Wind (film), 317

Something to Sing About (film), 307

Sonata for a Tap Dancer, A (dance), 239

Song and Dance Man, A (film), 314

Song Is Born, A (film), 317

Song of the Open Road (film), 315

Songs Unwritten (documentary), 333

Sothern, Ann, 56, 59, 69; films of, 318

So This Is Africa (film), 321

So This Is Paris (film), 191, 321

Soubrettes, 42, 118, 120, 127

Source Unknown (film), 302

Sparks, Martha Lee, films of, 300

Special Services, 106

Speakeasies, 22, 31, 77

Spencer, Prince, 10, 212, *215, 218, 220,* 223, 224-230, *224, 225, 226, 229,* 230, 294; doing Bottle Dance, *228;* films of, *See* Four Step Brothers, The; Major Bowes and, 225-226; in The Four Step Brothers, 228-230; impersonations by, 227; in Los Angeles, 227-228; Ted Mack and, 226; radio performances by, 226; in shows, 225; in vaudeville, 226

Spiner, Brent, 13

Sport Parade, The (film), 301

Springtime in the Rockies (film), 312

Stage Door (film), 243, 245, 307

Stage Door Canteen (film), 314

Stamper, George, 294

Standard Restaurant (Philadelphia), 130

Standard Theatre (Philadelphia), 40, 66, 67, 130, 257, 281

Stand Up and Cheer (film), 87, 88, 303

Stanley Brown Dance Studio, 260, 272

Stanley Theatre (Pittsburgh), 177

Stanton, Ronnie, 294; films of, 316

"Stardust" (song), 178

Stark, Herman, 98, 99, 157

Starlift (film), 319

Starling, Pat, films of, 315, 316

Star Maker, The (film), 309

Starr, Patsy, films of, 308

Star Reporter Series, The (film), 306

Start Cheering (film), 307

State and Lake Theatre (Chicago), 106

Stealing steps, 8, 38, 42, 47, 94-95, 97, 113

Step Lively (film), 315

Steppin' Along (film), 300

Stepping Fast (film), 315

Stepping Tones (record company), 296

Stewart, Nick, 297

Stewart, Jimmy, 245

Stewart, Richard, 294

Stone, Ezra, 194

Stone, Paula, films of, 303

Stoopnocracy (film), 302

"Stop time," 28, 281

Storey, Lloyd, 297

Stork Club (Hollywood nightclub), 251

Storm, Gale, films of, 313

Stormy Weather (film), 56, 314

"Stormy Weather" (song), 238

Story of Vernon and Irene Castle, The (film), 84, 309

Stowaway (film), 306

Strand Theatre (New York), 50, 109, 159, 267

Strand Theatre (York, Pennsylvania), 109

Strayhorn, Billy, 277

Street tap dancers, 128-133, 182

Strickland Sisters, The, 272, 273

Strickler, Fred, 333

Strictly in the Groove (film), 312

Strike Me Pink (film), 306

Strong Man, The (film), 321

Strut, the (dance), 74, 155, 158, 160-161, 281

Stump and Stumpy, 198, 260, 294; films of, 312, 318

Styles and Smiles (film), 308

Stylists, 25, 49, 98, 138

Styne, Jule, 270

Sublett, John "Bubbles," 294. *See also* Bubbles, John

Suitcase tap, 175, 272

Sullivan, Ed, 50, 70, 110; television show of, 47

Sultans, The, 297

Summer Stock (film), 319

Sundown Revue (stage show), 42-43

Sunny (film), 301, 311

Sunny, Eddie, and Eddie, 294

Sunny and Eddie, 294

Sunshine Sammy and His Brothers, films of, 300

Sun Valley Serenade (film), 65, 311

"Surrey with the Fringe on Top" (song), 239

Sutton, Jimmy, 297

Swanson, Gloria, 68

Swapping steps, 55

"Sweet Adeline" (song), 26

Sweet and Low (film), 318

"Sweet Georgia Brown" (song), 28, 29

Sweetheart of the Campus (film), 311

Sweethearts (film), 308

Sweetie (film), 300

Sweeties (film), 307

Sweet Jam (film), 314

Sweet Music (film) 304

Sweet Rosie O'Grady (film), 314

Sweet Shoe (film), 307

Swenson, Jim, 334

Swing (film), 307, 308

Swing, Sister, Swing (film), 308

Swing Age, 271, *See also* Swing Era

Swing bands, 63, 182

Swing Era, 187, 202, 203, 258, 259

Swing for Sale (film), 307

Swing Frolic (film), 312

Swing Hutton Swing (film), 307

Swing Maniacs, The, films of, 315

Swing music, 112, 229, 251, 266, 271, 272

Swing Orchestra, 257

Swing Out Sister (film), 316

"Swing Tap" (sheet music), 299

Swing Time (film), 57, 89, 306

Swingtime Johnny (film), 315

Symphony Hall (Chicago), 239

Symphony in Black (film), 304

Syncopated City (film), 303

Syncopation, 73, 74, 282

Tabloid Show, 78, 282

Takahashi, Dorothy, 105, 107. *See also* Toy, Dorothy

Takahashi, Helen, 105, 107. *See also* Toy, Helen

Take It or Leave It (film), 315

Take Me Out to the Ball Game (film), 315

"Taking a Chance on Love" (song), 268

Talking Feet (documentary), 333

Tall, Tan and Terrific (film), 317

Tango Twist (dance step), 67

Tanguay, Eva, 24

Tap Charleston, 38, 40, 269, 282

Tap coaches, 242. *See also* Dance Instructors

Tap Dancin' (documentary), 333

Tap Dog, The (documentary), 335

Tap Dogs, The, 336

Tap Happy (film), 146

"Tap in Three Movements," 335

Tapps, Georgie, 294; films of, 306, 307

Tap shoes, manufacturers of, 175; types of, 175

Tap teachers, 88. *See also* Dance instructors, Dance Teachers, *and* Tap coaches

TAP! The Tempo of America (documentary), 2

"Tap Your Tootsies" (record), 324

Tarnished Angel (film), 245, 308; "It's the Doctor's Orders," sheet music for, 245

Tars and Spars (film), 317

Taylor, Johnny, films of, 305

Taylor, Robert, 87

Taylor, Winston, and Howard, 294

Taylor, Yuval, 13

Tchaikovsky, 239

Tea for Two (film), 191, 319

Television, tap acts on, 187

Temple, Shirley, 10, 25, 53, 56, *57*, 59, 63, 86-93, *87*, *88*, *89*, *90*, *91*, *92*, 118, 119, 162, 163, *164*, 165, 166, 175, 294; in *Baby Burlesks*, 86; as box-office star, 87, 90; costars of, 87, 88, 89-93; films of, 11, 86-87, 302, 303, 304, 305, 306, 308, 310; as Meglin Kiddie, 86; George Murphy and, 57; Bill Robinson and, 90-93; tap teachers of, 88

Ten Minutes to Live (film), 301

Ten Toe Percussion Ensemble, The (documentary), 336

Terpers, 252

Texas Carnival (film), 319

Thanks a Million (film), 304

That Night in Rio (film), 81, *81*

That's Dancing! (film), 333

That's Entertainment!, Part I (film), 333

That's Entertainment!, Part II (film), 333

That's Entertainment!, Part III (film), 336

That's My Gal (film), 211, 318

"That's Not Cricket" (record), 326

That's the Spirit (film), 204, 302, 316

Theater Owners Booking Association. *See* T.O.B.A.

Theaters, 21, 118, 129, 130, 141, 169, 172, 211, 220, 238, 257, 259

Theodore, Lee

There's a Girl in My Heart (film), 319

There's No Business Like Show Business (film), 146, 320

They Learned About Women (film), 301

"They Say He Ought to Dance" (record), 326

This Is the Army (film), 170, *194*, 195, 314; "What the Well-Dressed Man in Harlem Will Wear," *196*, 198

This Is the Army unit, 178, 190-191, 194-198; black contingent of, 198; in Great Britain, 195; in Hollywood, 195; in Italy, 195; in Los Angeles, 195; in Marianas, *196;* in Middle East, 195; in New Guinea, 197; in New York, 194; in the Philippines, *195;* South Pacific tour of duty, 196, *197;* tour programs for, *191;* in Washington, D.C., 195

This Is the Life (film), 165, 166, 304, 315

This'll Make you Whistle (film), 307

This Way Please (film), 307

Thompson, Clyde "Slim," 317

Thompson, Tommy, films of, 313

Thompson, Ulysses S. "Slow Kid," 24, 295

Thousands Cheer (film), 314

"Three Blind Mice" (song), 239

Three Brown Jacks, The, films of, 305, 306

Three Browns, The, 285

Three Cheers for Love (film), 306

Three Chefs, films of, 285, 313, 314

Three Chocolateers, films of, 312

Three De Loveliers, films of, 308

Three Dukes, films of, 287, 302

Three Eddies, The, 288

Three Fish Brothers, The, 177

Three Gobs, films of, 289, 307

Three Little Girls in Blue (film), 317

Three Little Words, 43, 270, 295

Three Little Words (film), 319

Three Mahjongs, The, 105, *105*, 107-108; films of 302. *See also* Toy and Wing

Three Ra Ra girls, The, 147

Three Rhythm Boys, films of, 307

Three Sailors and a Girl (film), 320

Three Sparks of Rhythm, 295

Three Stooges, 245

Thrill of a Lifetime (film), 309

Thrill of Brazil, The (film), 317

Thrills of Music: Buddy Rich and His Orchestra (film), 318

Thunderbird Hotel (Las Vegas), 221

Thunderbolt (film), 300

Tiffany Twins, The, 297

Till the Clouds Roll By (film), 317

Timberg, Herman, Jr., films of, 306, 307

Time, the Place, and the Girl, The (film), 317

Time of Your Life, The (film), 232, 318

Time of Your Life, The (stage show), 170, 171

Time Out for Rhythm (film), 248, 311

Time Step, 26, 42, 70, 127, 129, 138, 147, 232, 282

Tin Pan Alley (film), 65, 310

Tip Tap Toe (film), 321

Tip, Tap and Toe, 65, 229, 295; films of, 303, 305, 307, 312, 313, 315

Tiranoff, Louise, 335

Tivoli (vaudeville circuit), 50

Tivoli Theatre (Chicago), 120

T.O.B.A. (black vaudeville circuit), 24, 28, 37-38, 41, 43, 47, 49, 119, 144, 214, 282

Todd, Michael, 266

Tom and Jerry, cartoons of, 315

Tommy Conine Trio, The, 295

Tommy Ryan's Diner (Culver City, Calif.), 251

Tonight and Every Night (film), 316

Tony Pastor and His Orchestra, 107

Tony Pastor's New Fourteenth Street Theatre, 144

"Tony's in Town" (record), 325

Too Many Girls (film), 310

Too Much Harmony (film), 321

Toot That Trumpet (film), 311

Top Banana (film), 320

Top Hat (film), 70, 304
"Top Hat, White Tie and Tails" (record), 323
Top Hatters, The, 295
Top Man (film), 314
Top of the Town (film), 203, 204, 205, 307
Tops and Wilder, films of, 317
Tops and Wilder, films of, 313
Top Speed (film), 301
Top Speed (stage show), 77, *77*, 78
Tower Theatre (Kansas), 106
Toy, Dorothy, 2, 102–110, *103, 105, 106, 108, 109, 110 294*, 295; films of, 302, 306; in The Three Mahjongs, 105, *105*, 107–108; in vaudeville, 105, 106, 107, 108–110; in nightclubs, 107, 110; ramifications of WWII, 106, 110; dancing with big bands, 109; in Chicago, 105, 108; in London, 106, 109; rehearsing, 105, 108; Busby Berkeley and, 108; Willie Covan and, 108; Steve Condos and, 108; Peg Leg Bates and, 109. *See also* Toy and Wing
Toy, Helen, *105*, 107–108, 110. *See also* Three Mahjongs, The
Toy and Wing, 2, 102–110, *103, 105, 106, 109, 110 294*, 295; films of, 302, 306; in vaudeville, 105, 106, 107, 108–110; in The Three Mahjongs, 105, *105*, 107–108; in nightclubs, 107, 110; ramifications of WWII, 106, 110; dancing with big bands, 109; in Chicago, 105, 108; in London, 106, 109; in Rio de Janiero, 109; rehearsing, 105, 108; Busby Berkeley and, 108; Willie Covan and, 108; Steve Condos and, 108; Peg Leg Bates and, 109; Mervyn LeRoy and, 108
Toy Sisters, The, 106, 110
Tracy, Spencer, 87
Trading eights, 10, 282
Tramp bands, 129
Treacher, Arthur, 87; films of, 316
Tricks, 278
Triplet (tap step), 100, 282
Triple Wing (tap step), 147

Trocadero (Hollywood nightclub), 251
True to the Army (film), 312
Trumpet Serenade (film), 312
Tucker, Mickey, 335
Tucker, "Snake Hips," 122; films of, 304
Tucker, Sophie, 24
Tucker, Travis, 41, 42
Tune, Tommy, 333
Turnbull, Glenn, 297
Turner, Lana, 248; films of, 309
Turn Off the Moon (film), 307
Tweed Me (film), 312
Twenties, Roaring, 30
20th Century-Fox Studios, 65, 72, 76, 80, 81, 91, 92, 159, 167, 199, 212
Twice Blessed (film), 316
Two Black Dots, The, 214
"Two colored" rule, 38
Two Girls on Broadway (film), 310
Two Takes on Tap (video), 336
Two Tickets to Broadway (film), 319
Tyler Twins, The, 295; films of, 307

Uncle Tom's Cabin (film), 299
Underdog, The (film), 301
Underworld (film), 307
Units, 145, 148, 257, 259
Universal Studios, 146, 148, 151, 202, 203, 204, 205, 206, 207, 208, 209, 210
Up in Lights (film), 309
Ups and Downs (film), 307
Up the River (film), 309
Uptown Theatre (Philadelphia), 257, 281
Uptown Theatre (Chicago), 120, 121
Use Your Imagination (film), 302
U.S.S. Texas (film), 301

Valentino, Rudolph, 250
Van, Bobby, films of, 320
Varsity Drag (dance), 55
Varsity Show (film), 307
Varsity Vanities (film), 310
Vaudeville, 9, 22, 24, 28, 29, 37, 39, 43, 44, 50, 55, 63, 65, 66, 77, 119, 134, 135, 144–148, 149, 151, 169, 180, 182, 192, 207, 233, 257, 258, 259, 260, 266, 272, 273; for black dancers, 37, 38, 41, 43, 47, 49, 119. *See also* T.O.B.A.

Vaudeville circuits, 24, 43, 144, 146, 148, 153, 156, 224, 235
Vaudeville Reel No. 4 (film), 304
Vaudeville stars, 187
Vaudeville theaters, 38, 47, 144–145, 148, 156, 158–159, 172, 234, 235, 236
Vecchio, Jimmy, 295; films of, 319
Venable, Sarah, 24
Vera-Ellen, 118, 248; films of, 316, 317, 318, 319, 320
Verbes, Erno, films of, 312
Vernon, Wally, films of, 308
Vernon Country Club (Vernon, Calif.), 251
Video Encyclopedia of Tap Technique (documentary), 333
Violin Concerto (Beethoven), 236
Virginia Lee and Lathrop Brothers, 295
Vitaphone Shorts, 203
Vivaldi sonata, 239
Voice of Vaudeville, "Cliff Nazarro's Modern Minstrels" (film), 321
Voice of Vaudeville, "The Four Covans" (film), 321
Vosseler, Heidi, 335

Waag, Tony, 335
Wabash Avenue (film), 319
Wake Up and Live (film), 307
Waldorf, The, 238; Empire Room of (New York nightclub), 237
Walker, Danton, 110
Walker, Dianne, 333
Walker, Jimmy, films of, 317
Walking Down Broadway (film), 309
Walking My Baby Back Home (film), 320
Waller, Fats, 124, 259
Walters, Chuck, 140, 198, 241
Walter Wanger's Vogues of 1938 (film), 307
Waltz Clog, 174, 224, 227, 282
"Waltz Clog" (record), 324
"Waltz in Swing Time" (record), 323
"Waltz in Swing Time" (song), 82
Warner Bros. Studios, 32, 33, 34, 35, 178, 193, 194, 196, 199, 201, 234, 236
Warner Brothers Theatre (Philadelphia), 67

Washington, D.C., 67, 195, 225, 226, 259, 260, 281
Washington, Ford Lee "buck," 285
Washington Melodrama (film), 311
Wash Your Step (film), 306
Waters, Ethel, 65, 66, 68, 98, 122, 124, 125, 268
Wayburn, Ned, 295
Way of All Freshman, The (film), 302
Way Out West (film), 307
Weaver, Marjorie, films of, 308
Weber, Love Jean, 295
Wedding of Jack and Jill (film), 204, 300
Weidler, Virginia, 206
Weinglass, Dewey, 295
Wells, Cyril, 305
Wells, Mordecai, and Taylor, 295
"We Should Be Together" (song), 57, 59
West, Buster, 295, 308
West, Mae, 25
West Point Story, The (film), 191, 192, 319
"What a Wonderful World" (record), 326
What's Buzzin' Cousin? (film), 314
What's Cookin? (film), 151, 202, 203, 207, 208, 312
Wheeler, Bert, films of, 301, 303, 304, 321
"When Day Is Done" (song), 239
When Johnny Comes Marching Home (film), 312
When Love is Young (film), 307
When My Baby Smiles at Me (film), 318
"When You Gotta Sing, You Gotta Sing" (record), 326
"Where or When" (song), 70
Where's Charley (film), 320
Whimhurst, Jolyon, 335
White, Al, 201
White, George, 295
White, Marjorie, films of, 300
White, Paul, 114, 127
White, Sammy, films of, 306
White Christmas (film), 242
Whiteman, Bob, 107
Whiting, Jack, 295; films of, 308
Whiting, Margaret, 270
Whitman, Alberta, 119, 122, 295
Whitman, Alice, 118, 119, 122, 126, 295
Whitman, Essie, 119

Whitman, Mabel, 119
Whitman, Pops, 43, 122, 295, 297
Whitman, Sister May, 122
Whitman Sisters, The, 43, 295
Whitman Sisters' New Orleans Troubadours, 119, 121, 122
Whitney, Eleanore, 118, 243, 246, 295; films of, 304, 305, 306, 307, 308, 309
Whole Show, The (film), 303
Whoopee (stage show), 31, 136, 138, 301
Whoopee Party, The (cartoon), 321
Wiggans, Jack, 67, 295
Wild and Woolly (film), 307
Wild Bird (hoofer), 235
Wild Boys of the Road (film), 321
Wilde, Lee, films of, 316
Wild West, Dancing in the, 23, 25-26
William Morris Agency, 50, 108, 177
Williams, Al, *212, 213, 215, 220, 224,* 228, *229*
Williams, Bert, 38
William, Cootie, 95
Williams, Esther, *247,* 248
Williams, Frances, 295; films of, 301
Williams, Jack, 295, 297, 334; films of, 313
Williams, Les, 333
Williams, Louis, 119
Williams, "Rubber Legs," films of, 302
Williams, S.B., 41
Williams and Walker, 28, 154, 155, 214

"Willie Covan's Dance Studio Annual Revue," 29
Will Mastin Trio, The, 226, 227, 295; films of, 318
Wills, Beverly, films of, 316
Wills, Lou, Jr., 2, 297
Wilshire Ebell Theatre, 123
Wilshire Theatre (Santa Monica, Calif), 191
Wilson, Robert "Bob", 335
Wilson, Derby, 49, 96, 156, 260, 295
Wilson, Iron Jaw, 295
Winchell, Walter, 70, 139
Winfield, Raymond, 229, 295
Wing, Paul, 2, 10, 102-110, *103, 104, 105, 106, 109, 110* 294, 295; films of, 302, 306; in Charleston contests, 104; in Los Angeles, 104-105; Sid Grauman and, in The Three Mahjongs, 105, *105,* 107-108; 104; in vaudeville, 105, 106, 107, 108-110; in nightclubs, 107, 110; in the army during WWII, 106, 110; dancing with big bands, 109; in Chicago, 105, 108; in London, 106, 109; rehearsing, 105, 108; Busby Berkeley and, 108; Willie Covan and, 108; Steve Condos and, 108; Peg Leg Bates and, 109. *See also* Toy and Wing
Wing, Tony, 10, 296
Wing (tap step), 43, 125, 127, 147, 224, 269, 282
Wing Brothers, The, 295
Wing dancers, 131
Winston, Tarik, 335

With a Twist of the Wrist (film), 311
Withers, Jane, 10, 162-168, *164, 165, 166, 167,* 206, 296; Nick Castle and, 166, 167, 168; films of, 162, 163, 164-165, 166, 304, 305, 306, 307, 308, 309, 310, 311, 312, 313, 315, 316; in radio, 163, 164; Bill Robinson and, 166; Will Rogers and, 163, 165; Franklin D. Roosevelt and, 165; Shirley Temple and, 163, *164*
Wizard of Oz, The (film), 135; 296, "If I Only Had a Brain," 136
Wonder Bar (film), 303
Wonder Man (film), 316
Wonder, Tommy, 297
Woods, Tommy, 299
Woolsey, Robert, , 301, 321
Words and Music (film), 318
World War I, 21, 35, 38, 48
World War II, 10, 146, 178, 187, 190-198, 208. 209, 263, 267; entertainment units during, 190-191, 193-198. *See also This Is the Army* unit
Worthey and Thompson, 296
"Wrap Your Cares in Rhythm and Dance" (record), 326
"Wrap Your Troubles in Dreams" (song), 226

"Yam, The" (record), 323
"Yam Step Explained, The" (record), 323
"Yankee Doodle" (song), 239

Yankee Doodle Dandy (film), 314
"Yankee Rose" (song), 98, 100
Yates, Billy, 191, 196, 198, 296
"Yes, Mr. Brown" (record), 324
Yes Sir, That's My Baby (film), 318
Yolanda and the Thief (film), 316
"You Are My Lucky Star" (record), 326
You Can't Have Everything (film), 307
You Can't Take It with You (film), 245
"You Gotta Know How to Dance" (song), *34*
You'll Never Get Rich (film), 311
Young People (film), 87, 310
You're a Sweetheart (film), 307
You're My Everything (film), 155, 159, 319; "Chattanooga Choo-Choo," 159
Youth on Parade (show), 226
Youth Will Be Served (film), 310
You Were Meant for Me (film), 318
Yo Yo and Raye Pearl, 296

Zerby, Jon, 297
Ziegfeld Follies (film), 317
Ziegfeld Follies, The (stage show), 55, 70, *71,* 136, 137, 142
Zig Me with a Gentle Zag (Soundie), 321
Zis-Boom-Bah (film), 311

Rusty E. Frank, M.N.A. is a tap dancer, producer, and tap dance preservationist. She began tap dancing at age six, studying with many of the great tap masters, including her mentor, Louis DaPron, as well as Brenda Bufalino, Steve Condos, Gene Nelson, Miriam Nelson, LaVaughn Robinson, Bob Scheerer, Lou Wills, Jr., and Jon Zerby. In 1989, 1990, and 1991, she produced, directed, and appeared in the sellout all-star tap revue **Jazz Tap!** featuring The Nicholas Brothers, Jeni LeGon, Arthur Duncan, Brenda Bufalino, and Savion Glover. She has danced professionally over the years with The San Francisco Tap Troupe, Six Feet, Pedal Extremities, Tapology, The Rhythm Rascals, and Mulligan and Whitmore, "Tops in Taps."

Rusty's current work, the documentary **TAP! The Tempo of America**, is the recipient of a National Endowment for the Arts grant. She is also the producer of **Leonard Reed's SHIM SHAM SHIMMY**, an instructional tap video featuring the originator of that historic dance. Rusty owns and operates "On Tap!," through which she promotes tap dance productions and markets tap dance supplies. Her writing credits include ten years of public relations work in San Francisco and Washington D.C., and for international organizations in Canada, Ethiopia, and Japan. Rusty lectures and teaches master classes throughout the United States at universities, dance programs, and tap festivals.

Rusty E. Frank received the National Association of Dance's 1992 annual Soul of Shipley Award, and Dance in Action's 1991 award for Contribution to Dance. She graduated summa cum laude from the University of California in Santa Cruz and received her Masters from the University of San Francisco. She currently lives in Los Angeles, California.